Lifewise

Home Economics
for Junior Certificate

Maria Randles · Maria Kennelly

Edco

The Educational Company of Ireland

First published 2011
The Educational Company of Ireland
Ballymount Road
Walkinstown
Dublin 12
www.edco.ie

A member of the Smurfit Kappa Group plc

ISBN 978–1–84536–395–6

Editor: Jane Rogers

Proofreader: Jennifer Armstrong

Design and layout: Identikit

Indexer: Jane Rogers

Cover photography: Getty, Imagefile

Illustrations: Steph Dix, Maria Murray

Photographs: Alamy, Bank of Ireland, Bord Bia, Peter Costello, Crafts Council of Ireland,
Getty, Joanne Hynes, Imagefile, iStockphoto, Rex Features, Science Photo Library,
Shutterstock, Sustainable Energy Authority of Ireland

Printed by W&G Baird

12D17

Foreword

Lifewise provides the student with a functional and comprehensive text for Junior Certificate Home Economics. The book incorporates the following features:

- Colour-coded sections and chapters for ease of reference.
- Vibrant, full-colour images and user-friendly text to appeal to students.
- New recipe section (recipes from the previous text may be accessed via edcoDigital).
- A worked sample of the Practical Cookery Exam design brief.
- Up-to-date information on food, consumer and environmental issues, reflecting current trends and legislation.
- Higher level material is clearly indicated.
- Content reflects all available exam questions.
- A revision section at the end of each chapter includes questions from past Higher Level exam papers.
- Widespread use of Weblinks to highlight relevant websites.
- Integration of associated topics in the text through the use of Link icons.
- Key exam concepts are highlighted throughout the text.
- A summary of the main points is given at the end of each chapter.
- High-quality, full-colour photographs and diagrams enhance the text and assist learning. All illustrations are modelled on the style used in the Junior Certificate examination.

The workbook to accompany the text offers:

- A fresh new approach to learning and revision of course content.
- Widespread use of graphic organisers to facilitate different learning styles, with an emphasis on independent student-led learning.
- Full-colour photographs.
- Templates that reflect the requirements of the Junior Certificate examination marking scheme.

Teachers may access the *Lifewise* e-book and further teacher resources by registering on www.edcodigital.ie.

The authors wish to thank their husbands and children for their important contribution and support throughout the development of *Lifewise*.

Contents

Section one Food studies

Chapter 1   **Food and nutrition**   2
Chapter 2   **The digestive system**   18
Chapter 3   **A balanced diet**   22
Chapter 4   **Special diets**   32
Chapter 5   **Food safety and storage**   40
Chapter 6   **Meal planning and food presentation**   48
Chapter 7   **Starting to cook**   57
Chapter 8   **Foods**   77
Chapter 9   **Food processing**   135
Chapter 10   **Recipes**   154
Chapter 11   **The practical cookery exam**   207

Section two Consumer studies

Chapter 12   **Consumers**   214
Chapter 13   **Shopping**   217
Chapter 14   **Consumers' rights and responsibilities**   229
Chapter 15   **Consumer protection**   232
Chapter 16   **Money management**   240
Chapter 17   **Quality**   247
Chapter 18   **Advertising**   251

Section three Social and health studies

Chapter 19   **Family, roles and relationships**   258
Chapter 20   **New life**   264
Chapter 21   **The body**   272
Chapter 22   **Health**   286
Chapter 23   **Health hazards**   290

Section four   Resource management and home studies

Chapter 24	**Management**	298
Chapter 25	**Home and community**	302
Chapter 26	**Design**	305
Chapter 27	**Room planning**	310
Chapter 28	**Safety and first aid**	314
Chapter 29	**Technology in the home**	321
Chapter 30	**Services to the home**	333
Chapter 31	**Home hygiene**	344
Chapter 32	**The environment**	348

Section five   Textile studies

Chapter 33	**Textiles in use**	356
Chapter 34	**Clothes**	362
Chapter 35	**Fabric care**	370
Chapter 36	**Fibres and fabrics**	377
Chapter 37	**Needlework skills**	393

Option one   Child care

Chapter 38	**Child development**	408
Chapter 39	**Food and nutrition**	413
Chapter 40	**Hygiene and safety**	417
Chapter 41	**Clothing**	421
Chapter 42	**Health and child care facilities**	423
Chapter 43	**Children with special needs**	427
Chapter 44	**The family and the law**	429
Chapter 45	**Child care project**	431

Option two   Textile skills

Chapter 46	**Textile skills**	434

Option three   Design and craftwork

Chapter 47	**Design and craftwork**	446
	Index	451

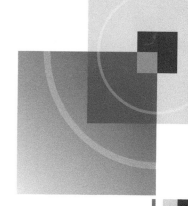

Section one
Food studies

Chapter 1
Food and nutrition

We need food to keep us alive. There is a great variety of food available in Ireland. We choose foods for various reasons. It is important to make wise food choices to promote health and to avoid disease.

Functions of food

- Food helps the body to **grow**.
- Food provides the body with **energy** and **warmth**.
- Food **protects** the body against disease.

Factors affecting food choice

- **Lifestyle.** Some people spend more time than others preparing and cooking food. Convenience foods and snacks have become popular in many busy households.
- **Nutritional value.** Many people choose foods which are considered healthy, for example foods that are low in sugar, salt or fat.
- **Cost.** People will not buy foods that are too expensive.
- **Culture.** Certain foods are linked to particular countries, for example rice and China. Special occasions such as Christmas are celebrated with certain dishes.
- **Religion.** Some religions have rules regarding foods, for example pork is not allowed in the traditional Jewish diet.
- **Availability.** Potatoes are plentiful in Ireland and pasta is common in Italy. **Staple foods are those that are plentiful and most commonly eaten in a country.**
- **Foods in season.** Some foods are available only at certain times of the year. Raspberries and strawberries are in season (at their best) in summer.

Preparing food

Foods in season

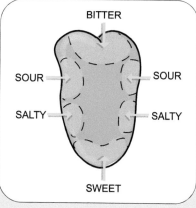

Personal likes and dislikes

Advertising

- **Advertising.** Advertising encourages people to buy certain foods. Many foods which are heavily advertised are high in sugar and fat.
- **Personal likes** and **dislikes.** We may like or dislike the appearance, smell and taste of certain foods. The illustration shows the four different kinds of taste that can be sensed by the taste buds on the tongue.

Link...

Chapter 18 Advertising

Nutrition

Certain words or terms are used when referring to nutrition. The most important ones are:

- **Nutrient** – a chemical in food that nourishes the body, e.g. protein.
- **Composition** – what the nutrient is made of.
- **Source** – a food that contains the nutrient.
- **Function** – what the nutrient does in the body.
- **Recommended dietary allowance (RDA)** – the amount of the nutrient we should eat each day.
- **Deficiency disease** – ill effects that are caused by lack of the nutrient.

Nutrients

A **nutrient** is a chemical in food that nourishes the body. There are six types of nutrient:

- proteins
- vitamins
- fats
- minerals
- carbohydrates
- water.

Note: Although water is not regarded as a nutrient, it is essential for life.

Nutrition

Typical values	100g contains	Each pack (550g) contains	%GDA*	GDA* for a typical adult
Energy	665kJ 160kcal	3645kJ 870kcal	44%	2000kcal
Protein	7.3g	40.2g		
Carbohydrate	16.6g	91.2g		
of which sugars	3.6g	19.6g	22%	90g
Fat	6.9g	38.1g	54%	70g
of which saturates	2.4g	13.4g	67%	20g
mono-unsaturates	3.0g	16.5g		
polyunsaturates	1.1g	5.9g		
Fibre	0.6g	3.3g		
Sodium	0.3g	1.4g		
Salt equivalent	0.6g	3.5g	58%	6g

*Guideline daily amounts

Nutrients

Macronutrients and micronutrients

Proteins, fats and carbohydrates are needed in large amounts. They are called **macronutrients**. Vitamins and minerals are needed in smaller amounts. These are called **micronutrients**.

Macronutrients	Micronutrients
● Proteins	● Vitamins
● Fats	● Minerals
● Carbohydrates	

Proteins

Composition of proteins

- Proteins are made up of **amino acids**.
- Amino acids are small units that are attached together, like beads on a necklace.
- Amino acids are made up of the elements carbon, oxygen, hydrogen and nitrogen. Nitrogen is needed for growth.

> During digestion the amino acids are separated. They are then used to build new cells and repair damaged cells in the body.

Link...

Chapter 2 The Digestive System

Classification of proteins

Higher Level

Proteins are made up of amino acids. Some amino acids are called **essential amino acids** because they are so important in the diet.

Foods which contain all the essential amino acids are said to have **high biological value** protein. These foods usually come from animal sources, such as meat. An exception to this is the protein found in soya beans. This is a high biological value protein from a plant source.

Low biological value protein usually comes from plant sources, such as peas, beans and lentils (pulse vegetables).

Higher Level

Foods that contain high biological value protein	Foods that contain low biological value protein
● Meat ● Fish ● Eggs ● Milk and dairy produce (e.g. cheese, yoghurt) ● Soya beans ● Quorn	● Peas ● Beans ● Lentils ● Nuts ● Whole cereals ● Muesli

High biological value protein

Low biological value protein

Functions of protein

● It helps the body cells to **grow**.
● It helps the body to **repair** damaged cells, e.g. healing wounds.
● It forms **hormones** and **enzymes** for the body to work properly.
● Protein is used for **heat** and **energy** when there are not enough energy foods in the diet.

Higher Level

Recommended dietary allowance

The recommended dietary allowance (RDA) is the amount of a nutrient which you need to eat every day. The RDA of protein depends on your weight. **Adults need one gram of protein for every kilogram that they weigh.** Therefore, if a person weighs 60kg, he/she needs 60g of protein each day.

Activity

Examine the nutrition information on a variety of food labels to find out the protein content per 100g. Which food has the highest protein content?

Fats

Composition of fats

- Fats are made from **fatty acids** and **glycerol**.
- Each molecule of glycerol is attached to three fatty acids.
- Glycerol and fatty acids contain the elements carbon, hydrogen and oxygen.

> During digestion, the fatty acids are separated from the glycerol and they are used to produce energy in the body.

glycerol — fatty acid

glycerol — fatty acid

glycerol — fatty acid

Link...

Chapter 2 The Digestive System

Classification of fats

Fats are divided into two groups.

- **Saturated fats** come mainly from animal sources.
- **Unsaturated fats** come from plant and marine (fish) sources.

Sources of fats	
Saturated fats	**Unsaturated fats**
• Butter • Meat • Milk and cream • Cheese • Eggs • Suet	• Sunflower oil • Olive oil • Nuts • Seeds • Polyunsaturated margarine, e.g. Flora • Fish oils, e.g. cod liver oil • Oily fish, e.g. mackerel, salmon

Food containing saturated fats

Food containing unsaturated fats

Functions of fats

- Fats provide heat and energy.
- Fats contain the vitamins A, D, E and K because these vitamins dissolve in fat.
- A layer of fat under the skin insulates the body and prevents heat loss.
- Fats protect delicate organs such as kidneys and nerves.
- Fats give a feeling of fullness and delay the feeling of hunger.

Link...

Balanced diet for adolescents, page 25
Low-fat diet, page 35
Obesity, page 34
Coronary heart disease, page 35

Activity

Compare a selection of food labels to find out:

- which has the highest fat content
- which products contain the highest saturated content.

Carbohydrates

Composition of carbohydrates

- Carbohydrates are made up of **simple sugars**, for example **glucose**.
- Simple sugars are joined together to form **starch**.
- Carbohydrates contain the elements carbon, hydrogen and oxygen.

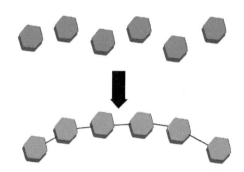

Link...

During digestion, the simple sugars are separated and they are used to produce energy, see page 18

Classification of carbohydrates

Carbohydrates are divided into three groups:

- sugars
- starches
- dietary fibre.

Sources of carbohydrate		
Sugars	**Starches**	**Dietary fibre**
Fruit (fresh and dried), milk, cakes, biscuits, soft drinks, jam, ice cream, honey, sugar	Cereals, potatoes, root vegetables, pulse vegetables	Vegetables, fruit, brown rice, brown bread

Sources of sugar   Sources of starch   Sources of dietary fibre

Activity

Examine a selection of food labels to check for 'hidden' sugar.
Look out for words such as sucrose, glucose and fructose.

Functions of carbohydrates

- Sugars and starchy foods provide heat and energy.
- Fibre helps the movement of food through the body.
- Fibre gives a feeling of fullness.

Link...

Low-sugar diet, page 32

Link...

High-fibre diet, page 33

Fibre

Fibre is very important in the diet. It absorbs water and becomes bulky in the intestine. This prevents constipation and other bowel diseases. When cereals are **refined** or processed, the fibre is removed. White flour is an example of a **refined cereal**. **Whole cereals** (unrefined) are better for the body because they contain fibre.

Recommended dietary allowance

The RDA for fibre is 30g for an average person. In Ireland we do not eat enough fibre, so we need to increase our fibre intake by eating more fruit, vegetables and whole cereals.

Activity

Measure one tablespoon of All-Bran into a bowl. Pour 150ml hot water over the All-Bran. Leave to soak for 10 minutes. Observe what happens to the volume of the All-Bran. This activity shows that water is important in the diet for fibre to work properly.

Vitamins

Vitamins are needed in very small amounts in the body. They are divided into two groups.

- **Water-soluble** (dissolve in water) – vitamin B group and vitamin C.
- **Fat-soluble** (dissolve in fat) – vitamins A, D, E and K.

Water-soluble vitamins			
Vitamin	**Functions**	**Sources**	**Deficiency diseases**
B group	• Release of energy from food • Healthy nerves • Growth • Helps prevent neural tube defects (spina bifida) in the unborn child	• Red meat, fish, milk, cheese, eggs, brown bread, nuts, peas, beans, yeast, fortified breakfast cereal	• Increased risk of neural tube defects in babies • Beri-beri (a nerve disease) • Pellagra: tongue and skin become sore
C (ascorbic acid)	• General health • Healthy skin and gums • Helps the body absorb iron • Helps to heal wounds	• Fruit: blackcurrants, kiwi fruit, oranges, cranberries, strawberries • Vegetables: peppers, tomatoes, new potatoes, cabbage, broccoli	• Scurvy • Slow healing of wounds • Increased risk of infection

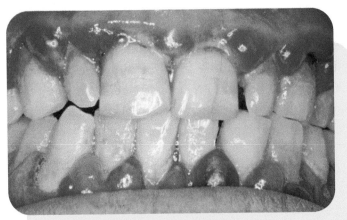

Lack of vitamin C causes a disease called scurvy. The skin and gums become sore.

Recommended dietary allowance
Water-soluble vitamins are not stored in the body and therefore need to be consumed regularly. The RDA for vitamin C is 50–60mg per day.

Link...

Guidelines on retaining vitamins when preparing and cooking food, page 119

Fat-soluble vitamins

Vitamin	Functions	Sources	Deficiency diseases
A (carotene is changed to vitamin A in the body)	Growth Healthy eyes Healthy skin Healthy linings of nose and throat	Fish liver oils, oily fish, offal, butter, margarine, eggs	Slow growth Night blindness Rough, dry skin
D	Healthy bones and teeth	Sunshine, fish liver oils, oily fish, liver, eggs, margarine, fortified milk	Rickets in children Osteomalacia in adults Osteoporosis in adults Unhealthy teeth
E	An antioxidant Healthy red blood cells	Nuts, seeds, eggs, cereals	Anaemia in newborn babies
K	Helps blood to clot	Made in the intestine; green vegetables, cereals	Blood clotting problems

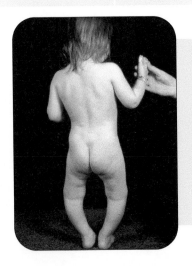

Lack of vitamin D causes rickets. Vitamin D is needed to absorb calcium so that strong bones can grow. Children with rickets have soft bones that bend easily.

Hypervitaminosis

Fat-soluble vitamins are stored in the body and therefore it is possible to consume too much of them. **Hypervitaminosis** is an excess of vitamin A or vitamin D in the diet, which is harmful to the body. It is usually caused by taking too many vitamin supplements.

Minerals

Minerals are essential for a healthy body. Some minerals are needed in relatively large amounts, e.g. calcium. Other minerals are needed in very small amounts and they are called **trace** minerals.

Some important minerals are:

- calcium
- iron
- sodium
- phosphorus
- fluorine
- iodine.

Calcium

The National Teens' Food Survey found that 42 per cent of teenage girls and 23 per cent of teenage boys are not getting enough calcium in their diet.

Source: Irish Universities Nutrition Alliance (IUNA) *National Teens' Food Survey 2008*.

Functions

Calcium is needed for strong bones and teeth.

Vitamin D is needed for calcium to be used in building bones. Regular exercise like walking and running is very important for building strong bones.

Deficiency diseases

If there is not enough calcium in the body, the bones become soft. This is called rickets in children and osteomalacia in adults. Osteoporosis (brittle bones) and tooth decay can also occur.

Sources

Calcium is found in milk, cheese, yoghurt, tinned fish (salmon and sardines), bread, green vegetables, sesame seeds and water.

Recommended dietary allowance

Calcium: 1200mg.

Iron

Functions

Iron helps to make healthy red blood cells. Iron is needed to make **haemoglobin**, which is a substance in red blood cells. Haemoglobin helps to carry oxygen around the body to give us energy.

The National Teens' Food Survey found that 74 per cent of teenage girls and 19 per cent of teenage boys are not getting enough iron in their diet.

Source: IUNA *National Teens' Food Survey 2008*.

Deficiency diseases

When we do not consume enough iron, we feel tired, weak and 'run down'. Eventually, this leads to a disease called **anaemia**.

Sources

Red meat, liver, fortified breakfast cereals, whole cereals, brown bread and green vegetables.

Fortified breakfast cereal

Absorption of iron

Although iron is found in many foods, it is not easily absorbed from some foods. It is important to consume **vitamin C** with foods containing iron to help absorption. Drinking orange juice (which contains vitamin C) with breakfast cereal (which contains iron) is an example of this.

Recommended dietary allowance

Iron: 14mg.

Fluorine, phosphorous and sodium

Vitamin	Functions	Sources	Deficiency diseases
Fluorine	● Healthy teeth	● Drinking water, fish	● Tooth decay
Phosphorous	● Combines with calcium for strong bones and teeth	● Meat, fish, poultry, eggs, milk, cheese, pulse vegetables, whole cereals	● Rare because it is found in so many foods
Sodium (salt)	● Controls water balance in the body	● Table salt, bacon, processed meats, snack foods, butter, cheese	● Muscle cramps

Recommended dietary allowance

Salt: 6g.

> To calculate the amount of salt in a food, multiply the amount of sodium by 2.5.

Each pack contains				
Sugar	Fat	Saturates	Salt	Keep refri
19.6g	38.1g	13.4g	3.5g	30
22%	54%	67%	58%	
your guideline daily amount				Use b

A high salt intake causes coronary heart disease, high blood pressure, stroke and kidney damage.

Activity

Examine the food labels on a variety of foods to find out the salt content.

Link...

Low-salt diet, page 32

Water

It is recommended that we drink at least 2–2.5 litres (8 glasses) of water per day. Lack of water in the diet causes **dehydration** and this is linked to many health problems.

Sources of water

Tap or bottled water; drinks such as milk, tea and coffee. Most foods, especially fruit and vegetables, contain water.

Functions of water

- Satisfies thirst.
- Helps digestion.
- Helps remove waste from the body, for example in urine.
- A source of minerals such as fluoride and calcium.
- Part of all body fluids.

Activities

1 Dried foods do not contain water. List as many dried foods as you can.

2 Do a class survey to find out the amount of water consumed daily by class members.

Energy

In the body's cells food is burned and energy is produced. Oxygen is needed for this process, which is called **oxidation**.

Measuring energy

Energy in food is measured in **kilocalories** (kcal) or **kilojoules** (kJ).
1 kcal = 4.2 kJ.

Here are some common activities and the amount of kilocalories used per hour.

Activity	Kilocalories used per hour
Sleeping	70
Watching TV	80
Sitting, standing, writing	90
Dressing, walking	180
Strenuous housework	300
Cycling	450
Dancing	500
Swimming, squash	700
Football, running	900

Factors that influence energy requirements

Some people need more energy than others. The amount of energy you require depends on the following factors.

- **Size:** big people need more energy than small people.
- **Age:** adults need more energy than young children.
- **Activity:** active people need more energy than inactive people.
- **Climate:** people in cold climates need more energy than people in warm climates.
- **Gender:** males usually need more energy than females.
- **Pregnancy:** pregnant and breastfeeding women need extra energy.

Active people need more energy

Average RDA for energy		
	Age range (years)	Energy (kcal)
Children	1–3	1300
	4–6	1700
	7–10	2000
Adolescents		
Male	11–18	2600
Female	11–18	2100
Men		
Sedentary		2500
Very active		3500
Women		
Sedentary		2100
Very active		2500
During pregnancy		2400
During lactation		2700

Energy balance

Energy balance means that energy input should be equal to energy output. If we take in extra energy, it will be stored in the body in the form of fat. Excess fat stored in the body leads to the person becoming overweight. A diet lacking in energy can lead to being underweight.

Empty kilocalories

Some foods provide energy but do not contain any other nutrients. They provide empty kilocalories. Fizzy drinks and table sugar contain empty kilocalories.

Empty kilocalories

Summary

- The **functions of food** are growth, energy, warmth and protection against disease.
- **Factors affecting food choice** include cost, availability, lifestyle, culture, nutritional value and the senses.
- The four **tastes** sensed by the taste buds are sweet, sour, bitter and salty.
- **Staple** foods are those which are plentiful and most commonly eaten in a country.
- A **nutrient** is a chemical in food that nourishes the body.
- **Macronutrients** are nutrients needed in large amounts, e.g. proteins, fats and carbohydrates.
- **Micronutrients** are nutrients needed in small amounts, e.g. vitamins and minerals.
- **Proteins** are needed for growth, repair, heat and energy. Proteins are made up of **amino acids**. Proteins are classified into high biological value protein and low biological value protein.
- **Fats** are made from **fatty acids** and **glycerol**. Fats are classified into saturated fats and unsaturated fats.
- **Carbohydrates** are made up of simple sugars called **glucose**. Carbohydrates are divided into three groups: sugars, starches and fibre.
- **Fibre** helps the movement of food through the body.
- When cereals are **refined** or processed, the **fibre is removed**.
- Vitamins are divided into two groups: **water soluble** (vitamin C and B group vitamins) and **fat soluble** (vitamins A, D, E and K).
- **Hypervitaminosis** is caused by an excess of vitamin A or D in the diet.
- Nutrients needed in very **small** amounts are called **trace minerals**.
- **Calcium** is necessary for healthy bones and teeth.
- **Iron** is necessary to form haemoglobin in red blood cells.
- **Oxidation** occurs when oxygen burns up food in the body's cells, releasing the energy.
- **Energy balance** means that energy input must be equal to energy output in order to have the correct body weight.
- Foods that contain **empty kilocalories** provide energy but do not contain any other nutrients.

Revision Questions

1 List four tastes that can be sensed by the taste buds on the tongue.

2 What do the letters RDA stand for?

3 Name two macronutrients and two micronutrients.

4 Name four foods that are good sources of: (a) high biological value protein; (b) low biological value protein.

5 Explain each of the following: (a) amino acid; (b) high biological value.

6 Explain the terms: (a) glycerol; (b) glucose; (c) refined cereal.

7 Give **two** examples of **each** of the following: (a) saturated fats; (b) unsaturated fats.

8 Name four foods with a high sugar content.

9 Give two sources of dietary fibre.

10 Give one important function of each of the following vitamins: (a) vitamin A; (b) vitamin B group.

11 Explain the term 'hypervitaminosis'.

12 Name one vitamin required to prevent each of the following deficiency diseases: (a) scurvy; (b) night blindness; (c) beri-beri; (d) rickets.

13 Name the vitamins that help with the absorption of each of the following minerals: (a) calcium; (b) iron.

14 Explain 'trace' in relation to the content of nutrients.

15 List four foods that have a high iron content.

16 List four foods that have a high calcium content.

17 List one important function for each of the following: (a) calcium; (b) iron.

18 List two foods with a high sodium content.

19 State the recommended daily salt intake of an adult.

20 List four factors that influence a person's energy requirements.

21 Explain the terms 'energy balance' and 'empty kilocalories'.

Chapter 2
The digestive system

Food must be broken down before it can be used by the body. This happens in the digestive system.

Function of the digestive system

- Food is broken down into tiny particles.
- Nutrients are passed into the blood so that they can be used by the body.
- Waste matter is excreted.

Food undergoes many changes before nutrients pass into the blood. Two types of change occur:

- **physical** change or breakdown
- **chemical** change or breakdown.

Physical change

- The teeth **cut** and **grind** the food into smaller particles in the mouth.
- The stomach **churns** the food into a smooth mixture called **chyme**.

Chemical change

Digestive enzymes

Digestive enzymes are chemicals present in the digestive juices. They help to break down food into smaller particles for absorption into the blood. Each enzyme works on one nutrient.

1. **Proteins** are changed into **amino acids.**
2. **Fats** are changed into **fatty acids** and **glycerol.**
3. **Carbohydrates** are changed into simple sugars, e.g. **glucose.**

Higher Level

1 Protein

2 Fat

glycerol — fatty acid
glycerol — fatty acid
glycerol — fatty acid

3 Carbohydrate

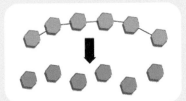

Carbohydrates are broken into shorter chains by one enzyme and then into simple sugars by another enzyme.

Parts of the digestive system

Food enters at the mouth and travels through various organs. The waste is removed through the anus. The parts of the digestive system are shown in the diagram.

1 Mouth

The teeth cut and grind the food into smaller particles. The food is mixed with saliva.

Saliva contains an enzyme called **salivary amylase**. Salivary amylase changes carbohydrate (starch) into shorter chains (maltose).

2 Oesophagus

This tube joins the mouth to the stomach. The food is pushed along this tube into the stomach by a muscular movement called **peristalsis**.

3 Stomach

The stomach is a muscular bag. It stores the food and **churns** it into a smooth liquid called **chyme**. An enzyme called pepsin is produced in the stomach. Pepsin changes protein to peptide chains. Acid is produced in the stomach, which helps pepsin to work.

The chyme goes gradually out of the stomach into the small intestine.

6 Small intestine

The small intestine is a long tube (about 6m) that joins the stomach to the large intestine. Bile, pancreatic juice and intestinal juice are added to food in the small intestine.

Enzymes in the small intestine cause **chemical changes**:

- proteins and peptide chains are changed into amino acids
- sugars (carbohydrates) are changed into simple sugars such as glucose
- fats are changed into fatty acids and glycerol.

The digested food is **absorbed** into the blood.

5 Pancreas

The pancreas produces enzymes.

4 Liver

The gall bladder in the liver produces bile, which helps to break down fats.

Absorption

Absorption is the movement of digested food from the small intestine into the blood. The inner layer of the small intestine is covered with tiny hair-like fingers called **villi**. Digested food goes from the small intestine into the blood through the villi.

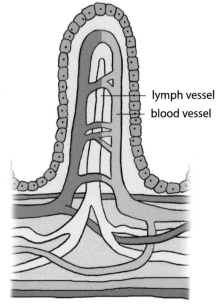

lymph vessel
blood vessel

Villus

- Glucose and amino acids go directly into the blood.
- Fatty acids and glycerol go into the lymph system first and then into the blood.
- The blood transports the digested food around the body, where it is used in the cells for growth and energy.

The large intestine

The large intestine is attached to the small intestine. Vitamin K and B group vitamins are made in the large intestine. Waste called **faeces** is pushed along the large intestine by muscular movement called **peristalsis**. Muscles at the end of the large intestine (rectum) force the faeces out of the body through the anus. **Fibre** in the diet makes the waste bulky, which helps the movement of waste along the intestine.

Link...

High-fibre diet, page 33

Guidelines for a healthy digestive system

- Eat a diet high in fibre.
- Drink lots of water.
- Reduce alcohol consumption.
- Visit the doctor for digestive problems.
- Eat or drink probiotic foods such as probiotic yoghurt.

Drink lots of water

Summary

- **Digestion** means breaking down food into tiny particles so that it can be used by the body.
- **Physical change** occurs when the teeth **cut** and **grind** the food and when the stomach **churns** the food.
- **Chemical change** occurs when **enzymes** break down proteins, fats and carbohydrates into smaller molecules.
- **Digestive enzymes** are chemicals which help to break down food into smaller particles for absorption into the blood.
- During digestion, **proteins** are changed into **amino acids**. **Fats** are changed into **fatty acids** and **glycerol**. **Carbohydrates** are changed into simple sugars, e.g. **glucose**.

Revision Questions

1. Outline the function of the digestive system.
2. Differentiate between the physical and chemical breakdown of food.
3. Describe two physical changes that occur during digestion.
4. What are digestive enzymes?
5. Name the enzyme present in saliva.
6. State the products each of the following nutrients is converted to during digestion: (a) protein; (b) fat; (c) carbohydrate.
7. (a) Name five parts of the digestive system.
   (b) Select any two parts you have named and outline their role in digestion.
8. Explain what is meant by: (a) peristalsis; (b) chyme; (c) villi; (d) faeces.
9. What is the role of fibre in digestion?
10. Suggest some guidelines that should be followed to promote a healthy digestive system.

Chapter 3
A balanced diet

A balanced diet provides all the body's requirements for growth and development. It contains all the nutrients the body needs in the correct amounts (50 per cent of our energy needs from carbohydrate, 33 per cent from fat, 16 per cent from protein, as well as minerals, vitamins and water).

A good way of getting a balanced diet is by eating a certain number of portions each day from each of the four food groups on the left:

Cereal and potato group: provides energy, fibre and B vitamins.

Fruit and vegetable group: provides minerals, vitamins, energy and fibre.

Food and drinks high in fat and/or sugar: eat a very small amount of these foods.

Milk group: provides protein, fat, calcium and vitamins.

Meat group: provides protein, fat, iron and vitamin B.

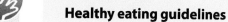

There are no good or bad foods, only good or bad diets.

Healthy eating guidelines

- Reduce intake of saturated fat, sugar and salt.
- Increase intake of fruit, vegetables, fibre, water, iron and calcium.

Eating a well-balanced diet and following the healthy eating guidelines helps prevent a number of health problems such as heart disease, some forms of cancer, high blood pressure, osteoporosis, obesity, tooth decay, constipation and diabetes.

The food pyramid is another way of representing the food groups. It indicates the recommended number of portions per day from each food group:

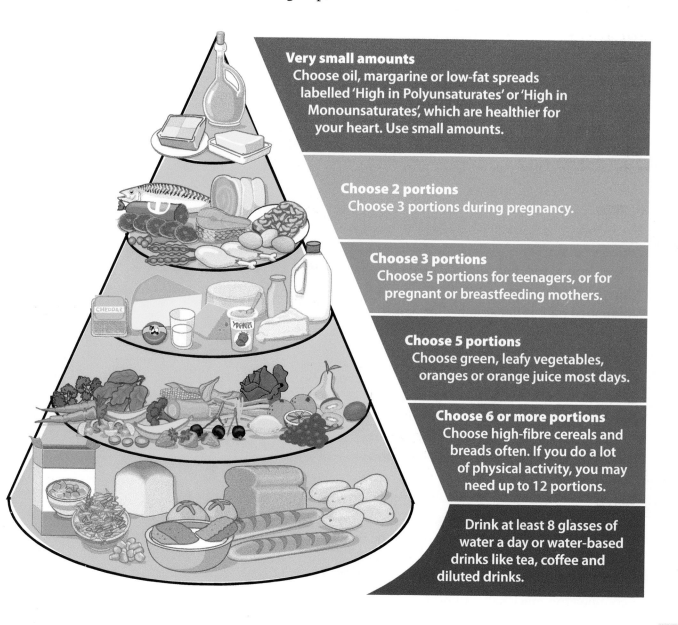

Very small amounts
Choose oil, margarine or low-fat spreads labelled 'High in Polyunsaturates' or 'High in Monounsaturates', which are healthier for your heart. Use small amounts.

Choose 2 portions
Choose 3 portions during pregnancy.

Choose 3 portions
Choose 5 portions for teenagers, or for pregnant or breastfeeding mothers.

Choose 5 portions
Choose green, leafy vegetables, oranges or orange juice most days.

Choose 6 or more portions
Choose high-fibre cereals and breads often. If you do a lot of physical activity, you may need up to 12 portions.

Drink at least 8 glasses of water a day or water-based drinks like tea, coffee and diluted drinks.

What is a portion?

Meat group	Fruit and vegetable group	Cereal and potato group (preferably wholegrain)	Milk group (preferably low-fat)
• 60g (2oz) cooked meat or poultry • 90g (3oz) fish • 2 eggs • 60g (2oz) Cheddar-type cheese • 2 large tablespoons boiled peas/beans • 90g (3oz) nuts	• Average serving of cooked fruit • Large serving of cooked vegetables or salad • Medium-sized fresh fruit • Small glass of fruit juice	• 1 slice bread • Bowl of cereal • 1 large tablespoon boiled rice or pasta • 1 medium potato	• Glass of milk • Carton of yoghurt • Average bowl of milk pudding (e.g. rice pudding) • 30g (1oz) Cheddar-type cheese

Balanced eating for different age groups

Our food needs change as we grow from childhood to adulthood.

Link...

Option 1 Child Care

Babies

- Newborn babies rely on milk for the first four to six months of life as their digestive systems cannot cope with solid foods. Breastfeeding is recommended, as it provides all the nutrients in proportion to the baby's needs. It passes immunity from the mother to baby and it creates a strong bond between mother and baby.
- Dried cow's milk formula is available as an alternative to breast milk.
- Skimmed milk is not suitable for babies as it lacks fat and fat-soluble vitamins A and D.
- Babies are weaned (introduced to solid foods) at four to six months. Foods should be smooth and easy to swallow and they should provide protein, iron and vitamin C.
- Never add salt or sugar to a baby's foods. Avoid honey and highly spiced, fatty and fried foods.
- Babies under six months should never be given wheat-based foods, nuts or seeds.
- From eight months on, a baby should be eating a varied diet, with foods from all the food groups.
- Cow's milk is not suitable until the baby is one year old as it contains too much salt and protein.

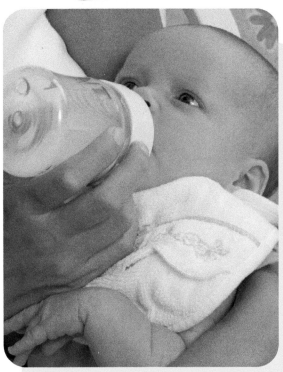

Newborn babies rely on milk

Young children

- Healthy eating habits should be developed from an early age so that they will continue in later life.
- Young children grow very rapidly, so they need plenty of protein, calcium, iron and energy.

Young children need protein for growth

- Children have small stomachs and should be offered regular meals and snacks, rather than being allowed to 'pick' through the day.
- They should eat plenty of fruit and vegetables for vitamin C, iron and fibre.
- They should avoid high-fat, salty or sugary snacks between meals.
- Parents should eat at the same time as their child and discourage any food 'fads' that may develop.
- Meals should be calm and relaxed, without the television on, as children are easily distracted.
- Children can be highly influenced by food advertising on television. Parents need to stand firm against this.

Adolescents

- Between the ages of 10 and 15 years, boys and girls go through a rapid growth spurt. This calls for a diet high in protein, calcium, iron and vitamins A and D.
- Foods from the bread, cereals and potato group will

Active teenagers need plenty of energy foods

provide energy, and should be included in every meal.
- Include healthy snacks like fresh fruit, yoghurt, nuts, dried fruits, rice cakes or seeds.
- Milk and dairy foods are particularly important at this stage to provide calcium for the development of strong bones and teeth and to prevent osteoporosis later in life.

- Girls should eat plenty of iron-rich foods to prevent anaemia.
- Teenagers should eat a good variety of foods and balance the food eaten with exercise. This is needed to build strong bones, for good concentration, and to keep a healthy weight. It is also important for healthy skin and muscles.
- Teenagers sometimes experiment with vegetarianism and other diets. A doctor should be consulted before starting any type of diet. Many weight loss diets are low in essential nutrients and this can affect concentration, particularly at exam time.
- Teenagers should avoid skipping meals during the day. Skipping meals can lead to overeating later in the day or at night.

Irish teenagers are consuming a higher energy and fat intake from biscuits, confectionery and snacks than from milk, cheese or yoghurt.

Source: IUNA *National Teens' Food Survey 2008.*

Adults

- For adults, good nutrition is important for repair and maintenance of the body, and to help prevent disease.
- Adults should eat a good variety of foods to ensure that they get their daily requirements from all the food groups.
- Protein is required to repair and replace cells.
- An adult's energy needs vary depending on gender and level of activity. Males require more energy than females because of their larger size. Also, a **manual** worker requires more energy than a **sedentary** worker because physical activity burns up more energy.
- Adults should avoid too much saturated fat and sugar to reduce the risk of weight problems and coronary heart disease.
- Oily fish such as mackerel and salmon should be eaten twice a week as they contain omega 3 fats, which help to prevent heart attacks and strokes, and improve memory and concentration.
- Salt intake should be controlled to reduce the risk of high blood pressure and stroke.

A manual worker requires more energy

- Plenty of fibre will prevent bowel disorders and control appetite.
- Women should ensure a high intake of calcium to reduce the risk of osteoporosis and enough iron to prevent anaemia.
- Alcohol intake should be kept to a minimum (not more than 14 units a week for women and 21 units for men).

Link...

Alcohol, page 292

Physical activity burns up more energy

Manual occupations are those that require physical strength and activity, e.g. farmer, builder, aerobics instructor. **Sedentary** occupations require little physical effort, e.g. teacher, secretary, computer programmer.

During pregnancy, a woman needs foods that provide concentrated sources of nutrients

Pregnant and breastfeeding women

- Before becoming pregnant, a woman should ensure that she is eating a balanced diet and is reasonably fit.
- During pregnancy, a woman must make sure her diet provides all the essential nutrients for her own health and her baby's growth and development. She must eat foods that provide concentrated sources of nutrients.
- Protein, calcium, phosphorus and vitamins A and D are all needed for growth of the foetus and development of bones and teeth.
- Iron and vitamin C are needed to prevent anaemia and fight infections. Vegans or vegetarians need to be particularly careful to get enough iron.
- Folic acid should be taken before and during pregnancy to prevent spina bifida and other neural tube defects (NTDs) in the baby.

- Fibre-rich foods and plenty of fluids are required to prevent constipation, which can be quite common during pregnancy.
- Energy intake should be increased slightly, but the woman must avoid gaining too much weight as it puts her at risk of needing a Caesarean section, or developing blood pressure problems or diabetes.
- Pregnant women are advised to avoid pâtés, undercooked meat, unpasteurised milks or cheese made from unpasteurised milk, raw or undercooked eggs because of the risk of listeria.
- Large quantities of liver should be avoided as it contains high levels of vitamin A, which can be harmful to the baby.
- Alcohol and cigarettes, spicy or rich foods, strong tea and coffee should be avoided.
- Breastfeeding mothers must eat a well-balanced diet to make good-quality breast milk. They should avoid nicotine and alcohol and drink coffee in moderation.

Link...

Option 1 Child Care

Elderly people

- A healthy diet and regular exercise can help elderly people live a full life and keep their independence into old age.
- Appetite may be reduced by depression, which is common among elderly people. The sense of thirst decreases with age, so it is important for an older person to make an effort to drink even when not thirsty.
- Easily digested protein foods, such as chicken and white fish, are needed for repair and growth of new cells.
- Fruit and vegetables are good sources of vitamin A and C, fibre and folic acid, and important in preventing constipation. Iron is needed to prevent anaemia.
- Calcium and vitamin D are important in maintaining healthy bones and preventing osteoporosis. Fortified, low-fat dairy products are recommended, especially for older people who are unable to leave their house.
- Vitamin B is needed for healthy nerves and release of energy.
- Saturated fats and salt should be cut down to reduce the risk of heart disease and stroke. Unsaturated fats and omega 3 fats from oily fish can help people with arthritis.
- Elderly people living alone should be aware of the importance of food and continue to eat well when cooking for one.

Regular exercise can help elderly people

Convalescents/invalids

- When someone is sick or recovering from illness, they need a diet to help recovery. This will depend on what the person has been suffering from.
- A person recovering from an accident will need a diet rich in protein for repair of damaged cells.
- Zinc, which is found in meat, yoghurt and some fruit and vegetables, and vitamin C are needed for healing and to fight infection.
- Convalescents should follow their doctor's advice on suitable foods. All meals should be prepared and served hygienically.
- Meals should be attractive, nourishing and served in small portions, as the appetite may be small.
- Energy foods should be cut down as the convalescent may be have to stay in bed.
- Foods should be light and easy to digest. Avoid spicy or fatty foods or reheated foods.
- Stewing, steaming, boiling and baking are suitable methods of cooking.
- Ensure plenty of fluids are taken, especially if the patient has a fever. Avoid tea or coffee as they may cause fluid loss.

Activities

1. Keep a food diary (a list of all the foods you eat) for one day. Tick the number of items you have eaten from each of the food groups. Are you eating the recommended number of items from each group? Are there any changes you could make? You can download a food diary from www.nhfireland.ie. Click on Eat Smart and choose 'food diary' in the text.

2. What dietary and lifestyle advice would you give a 25-year-old man who would like to lose weight? For some hints, go to www.nhfireland.ie, click on Eat Smart and then on 'Swap and Save tips'.

3. Anne and Fiona are both 23 and share an apartment. They take turns to cook the evening meal. Anne is a secretary and Fiona is a nurse. What factors should these young women consider when planning their meals? Suggest a menu for an evening meal for Anne and Fiona.

4. Plan a day's menu for a pregnant woman who is recovering from a bout of flu.

5. Find out which foods contain folic acid. (Tip: use food labels and food tables.) Design a dinner menu which includes folic acid for a pregnant woman.

Summary

- A **balanced diet** contains all the nutrients the body needs in the correct proportions.

- The four **food groups** are cereals and potatoes; fruit and vegetables; milk products; and meat.

- **Babies:** Breastfeeding is recommended; weaning begins at four to six months; avoid adding salt or sugar to foods; from eight months the baby should be eating a good, varied diet.

- **Young children:** Require adequate protein, calcium and energy; healthy eating habits should be developed and food fads discouraged; frequent meals and snacks are needed; avoid sugary, high-fat snacks; beware of food adverts on TV.

- **Adolescents:** Energy requirements are high due to growth spurts; adequate amounts of calcium and iron are essential; a good variety of foods should be eaten and balanced with physical activity; excessive amounts of high-fat, salty and sugary foods should be avoided.

- **Adults:** Requirements depend on gender and level of activity (sedentary or manual); a good variety of foods should be eaten; intake of saturated fat, salt and sugar should be controlled; adequate fibre should be consumed; women should ensure high intakes of calcium and iron; alcohol should be kept to a minimum.

- **Pregnant and breastfeeding women:** Foods that provide concentrated sources of nutrients should be eaten; protein, calcium, phosphorus, vitamins A and D and folic acid are needed for the healthy growth and development of the foetus; unpasteurised cheeses, pâté, liver, alcohol, cigarettes, spicy and rich foods should be avoided; breastfeeding mothers should avoid certain foods that may upset the baby's stomach.

- **Elderly people:** Less energy is required as activity decreases; easily digested foods, fruit and vegetables are required; iron and calcium are important to prevent anaemia and strengthen bones; saturated fats and salt should be cut down.

- **Convalescents:** Follow the doctor's advice; ensure hygienic preparation and serving of food; include foods that are light and easy to digest; ensure plenty of fluids are taken.

Revision Questions

1 What is meant by a balanced diet?

2 Insert **each** of the following foods in the correct position on the food pyramid:

   chicken, apples, bread, cheese, crisps.

3 Indicate on the diagram of the food pyramid which of the food groups should be: (a) eaten most; (b) eaten least; (c) eaten in moderation.

4 State the proportions (percentage) of (a) protein and (b) fat which should be included in a well-balanced diet.

5 List four healthy eating guidelines.

6 The introduction of solid foods into a baby's diet is called weaning. True or false?

7 Why is skimmed milk unsuitable for babies and young children?

8 What are the nutritional needs of adolescents?

9 What is a sedentary occupation?

10 Adults who are not active should reduce their calorie intake. True or false?

11 Give two dietary guidelines which should be followed during pregnancy.

12 What are the nutritional needs of elderly people?

13 What is meant by a 'convalescent'?

Chapter 4
Special diets

Low-sugar diet

When you eat sugar you get a quick energy boost but it does not last long. A habit of continuously craving sweet foods can easily develop. It is better to get energy from foods such as wholemeal bread, porridge, rice and pasta because they provide a longer-lasting supply of energy.

Health problems associated with a high-sugar diet

- Overweight and obesity.
- Tooth decay.

Guidelines for reducing sugar intake

- Drink water instead of drinks sweetened with sugar.
- Choose low-sugar breakfast cereals, biscuits, cakes.
- Limit sweets, honey, chocolate and syrup in the diet.
- Use sugar substitutes instead of sugar to sweeten foods.
- Replace high-sugar snacks with fresh fruit, vegetables, seeds and unsalted nuts.

Replace high-sugar snacks with fresh fruit and unsalted nuts

A low-sugar food contains 5g or less of sugar per 100g of food. A high-sugar food has more than 10g of sugar per 100g of food.

Low-salt diet

The recommended daily salt intake for an adult is 6g. A high salt intake causes coronary heart disease, high blood pressure, stroke and kidney damage. Salt is labelled on foods as salt or sodium.

Effects of high salt intake

- High blood pressure.
- Stroke.
- Coronary heart disease.
- Kidney damage.

Guidelines for reducing salt intake

- Reduce the amount of salt you add at the table and during cooking.
- Use herbs, spices and pepper to flavour food instead of salt.
- Avoid foods with a high salt content such as packet soups and sauces, stock cubes, ketchup and savoury snacks such as potato crisps, popcorn, salted nuts.
- Choose fresh meat instead of processed meat.
- Read food labels to check for salt or sodium. Monosodium glutamate (MSG) is also a type of salt.

Weblink

Irish Heart Foundation:
www.irishheart.ie

A low-salt food has 0.1g or less of sodium per 100g of food. A high-salt food has 1.5g or more of sodium per 100g of food.

High-fibre diet

Fibre is found only in plant foods. When plant foods are processed, the fibre is removed. These **refined** (processed) foods, such as white flour, contain very little fibre. Therefore, unprocessed or whole foods should be included in the diet to provide fibre.

Benefits of a high-fibre diet

Fibre soaks up water, which makes the food bulky inside the body. This causes muscular movement in the intestine, which pushes the food quickly along. Therefore, fibre prevents constipation and other bowel disorders. Fibre does not contain calories but it gives a feeling of fullness, so it is useful for losing weight.

Link...

Fibre, page 9
Cereals and baking, page 122

Effects of low fibre intake

- Constipation occurs when faeces (waste) become stuck in the bowel.
- Bowel disease is caused when hard faeces (waste) become stuck in the bowel wall. This can lead to bowel cancer.
- Piles (swollen blood vessels) occur in the anus as a result of hard waste passing through.

A high-fibre food contains 6g or more of fibre per 100g of food.
A low-fibre food has less than 0.5g of fibre per 100g of food.

Guidelines for increasing fibre intake

- Choose whole cereals such as brown bread, brown rice and whole pasta instead of refined cereals.
- Eat high-fibre breakfast cereals.
- Leave the skins on fruit and vegetables where possible.
- Choose whole fruits instead of fruit juices.
- Include peas, beans and lentils in the diet.
- Include nuts and seeds in the diet.

Link...

Fibre, page 9
Cereals, page 122

Obesity

Obesity means being 20 per cent or more over the recommended weight for height and build. Obesity has become a major health problem in Ireland.

Causes of obesity

- **Overeating.**
- **Lack of exercise:** Physical exercise is needed to balance energy input with energy output.
- Eating large portions of high-energy food can cause an **energy imbalance**.
- **Poor nutritional knowledge.**

Obesity in a child

Health problems associated with obesity

Obese people are at risk of developing the following health problems:

- heart disease
- diabetes
- stroke
- high blood pressure
- poor self-image.

Guidelines for reducing the risk of obesity

- Take regular physical exercise.
- Do not eat between meals.
- Avoid crash diets – gradual weight loss is more likely to last.
- Avoid sauces and desserts which are high in sugar and fat.
- Drink water instead of drinks sweetened with sugar.
- Remove visible fat from meat.
- Grill, steam or boil food instead of frying.
- Choose low-fat dairy products such as low-fat milk, cheese and yoghurt.
- Choose high-fibre foods such as fresh fruit and vegetables instead of snacks containing fat and sugar.
- Do not add sugar to tea or coffee.

A low-fat food has 3g or less of fat per 100g of food. A high-fat food has more than 20g of fat per 100g of food.

Link...

Fats, page 6

Low-fat/low-cholesterol diet

There are both healthy and unhealthy sources of fat. We need to be aware of the **amount** of fat we eat as well as the **type** of fat we eat.

Health problems associated with a high-fat diet

- Obesity.
- Coronary heart disease.
- Other diseases, such as diabetes, are made worse.

Foods with a high fat content

- Butter
- Meat fat
- Margarine
- Cakes
- Biscuits
- Lard
- Cream
- Savoury snacks
- Chocolate
- Cheese

Foods with a high fat content

Coronary heart disease

Coronary heart disease occurs when the arteries of the heart become blocked with a substance called cholesterol. **Cholesterol** is a fatty substance that clings to the walls of the arteries. Heart disease is a major cause of death in Ireland.

Causes of heart disease

- A history of heart disease in a person's family.
- Being overweight.
- A diet containing a lot of **saturated** fat.
- Lack of exercise.
- Smoking.
- Too much alcohol.
- Stress.

Healthy artery

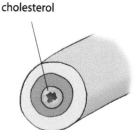

cholesterol

Artery with cholesterol

Guidelines for reducing the risk of coronary heart disease

Reduce fat intake

- Use low-fat spread instead of butter.
- Choose low-fat dairy products such as low-fat milk, cheese and yoghurt.
- Grill, steam, bake or microwave instead of frying food.
- Choose lean meat, fish or poultry without the skin instead of fatty meat.
- Increase the intake of fruit and vegetables in the diet.
- Cut out fatty foods such as cakes and chocolate.
- Avoid high-fat sauces such as cream or cheese sauces.

Link...

Fats, page 6

Vegetarian diets

A vegetarian does not eat meat. There are various types of vegetarian diet.

- A **vegan** lives on plant and cereal foods. He/she does not eat meat, meat products, poultry, fish, dairy products or eggs.
- **A lactovegetarian** does not eat meat, meat products, fish or poultry. He/she does eat dairy products and eggs.

Higher Level

Reasons for choosing a vegetarian diet

- Some vegetarians believe it is wrong to kill animals.
- Religious reasons, for example Hinduism.
- It can be a healthy option.
- It is cheaper.
- Fashion.
- Peer pressure.

Guidelines for planning a vegetarian diet

- Use only vegetable stock and vegetable fats.
- Eat a wide variety of foods.
- Choose whole cereals.
- Include textured vegetable protein (TVP) and Quorn (see page 90).
- Use fortified soya milk to provide calcium.
- Include pulses and nuts to provide protein.
- Avoid convenience foods containing animal products.
- Ensure that menus are balanced.

Link...

Meat substitutes, page 90

Weblink

www.indi.ie (vegetarian fact sheet)
www.vegetarian.ie (nutrition page)

Savoury main course dishes:

- vegetarian burgers
- vegetarian curry
- vegetable risotto
- vegetarian pasta dishes, e.g. vegetarian lasagne
- vegetable stir-fry
- quiche
- pizza
- ratatouille
- nut roast
- omelette.

Sweet dishes:

- fruit crumbles
- carrot cake
- fruit cakes
- fruit salads.

Vegetarian pizza

Coeliac disease

A person who has **coeliac disease** cannot digest gluten. Gluten is a **protein** found in **wheat**. When people with coeliac disease eat gluten, it damages the gut and this causes weight loss and symptoms such as cramps, diarrhoea and anaemia.

Foods to avoid

- All products made from **wheat, barley, oats** and **rye**. Wheat products include bread, cakes, tarts, biscuits, pasta and breakfast cereals.
- Products containing breadcrumbs such as sausages and breaded fish.
- Many convenience foods.
- Packet soups and sauces.

Foods allowed

A number of manufacturers make gluten-free food, for example:

- Barkat: pizza bases, rice and corn pasta, e.g. lasagne and spaghetti
- Free From (Tesco): bread, rolls, scones, muffins
- Kelkin: gluten-free cereals
- Doves Farm: self-raising and plain flour.

Gluten-free symbol

Weblink

www.coeliac.ie
www.indi.ie – click on Factsheets, then Clinical Conditions and look for 'Coeliac disease and a gluten-free diet'

Diabetes

When a person has diabetes, the body cannot produce insulin or it cannot use insulin to control the level of sugar in the blood. This can cause the person to feel unwell. If diabetes is not treated, it can lead to serious health problems.

Type 1 diabetes (insulin-dependent diabetes) occurs when insulin is not produced at all in the body. Sugar collects in the blood and goes into the urine without producing any energy. A person with Type 1 diabetes must take insulin. Injections and other methods are used to give insulin.

Type 2 diabetes (non-insulin-dependent) occurs when the body cannot use the insulin it produces. This happens mainly in adults and it is linked to being overweight. It is controlled by weight loss and a strict diet.

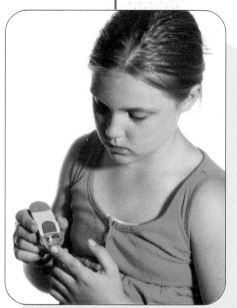

Modern method of checking blood sugar level

Guidelines for controlling diabetes

- Reach the correct body weight.
- Exercise regularly to balance blood sugar levels.
- Eat regularly and never miss a meal or snack.
- Eat high-fibre carbohydrate foods.
- Avoid foods high in sugar. Some artificial sweeteners may be used instead of sugar.

Summary

- A **high-sugar diet** causes overweight, obesity and tooth decay.
- A **high-salt diet** causes high blood pressure, coronary heart disease, stroke and kidney damage.
- A **low-fibre diet** causes constipation, bowel disease and piles.
- **Obesity means being 20 per cent or more over the recommended weight for height and build. Problems** include diabetes, heart disease, high blood pressure, stroke and poor self-image.
- **High-fat diet: problems** – overweight and obesity, coronary heart disease, diabetes made worse.
- **Coronary heart disease** occurs when the arteries of the heart become blocked with a substance called cholesterol.
- **Vegans** live on plant and cereal foods.

Summary

- **Lactovegetarians** eat dairy produce but do not eat meat, fish or poultry.
- **Coeliac disease** is an intolerance of a **protein** substance called **gluten**. Avoid wheat, rye, oats and barley.
- **Diabetes: Type 1 diabetes** occurs when insulin is not produced in the body. **Type 2 diabetes** occurs when the body cannot use the insulin it produces.

Revision Questions

1 List four foods that have a high sugar content.

2 Suggest four ways of reducing the intake of sugar in the diet.

3 What effects can a high salt intake have on the body?

4 Name four foods that have a high salt content.

5 State the recommended daily salt intake of an adult.

6 Explain why it is important to include dietary fibre in the diet.

7 Suggest four ways to increase fibre in the diet.

8 Obesity has become a major health problem.

   (a) Outline the causes of obesity.

   (b) List four health problems associated with obesity.

   (c) Suggest four healthy eating guidelines which should be followed to reduce the risk of obesity.

9 (a) Explain what you understand by coronary heart disease.

   (b) List three main causes of heart disease.

   (c) What precautions should be taken to reduce the risk of heart disease?

10 Suggest four ways of reducing the intake of fat in the diet.

11 Give three reasons why people might choose a vegetarian diet.

12 Explain each of the following types of vegetarian diet: (a) vegan diet; (b) lactovegetarian diet.

13 What guidelines should be followed when planning meals for a vegetarian?

14 Coeliac disease is an intolerance to which protein substance?

15 List four foods that must be avoided by those on a coeliac diet.

16 Sketch the symbol found on gluten-free flour and products.

17 Define the term 'diabetes'.

18 List four dietary rules which must be followed by diabetics.

Chapter 5
Food safety and storage

Causes of food spoilage

The main causes of food spoilage are **enzymes** and **micro-organisms** such as **moulds, yeasts** and **bacteria**.

1 **Enzymes** are chemicals that are found naturally in foods such as fruit and vegetables. They cause them to ripen and eventually decay or rot. When fruit is damaged, enzymes are released and cause bruising. This makes it rot faster.

2 **Micro-organisms** are tiny plants or animals. They cause the food to break down, rot or go sour. It then discolours, smells bad or becomes sticky or slimy.

   a) **Moulds** look like soft cotton wool on food, and spoil its appearance and taste. They need warmth, moisture and air to grow, but are killed by sunlight. They are used to make antibiotics, e.g. penicillin, and certain types of cheese such as Cashel Blue and Camembert.

   b) **Yeasts** grow on foods containing moisture and sugar, such as fruit, fruit juices and syrups. They affect the taste and texture of foods. They are killed by heat. Yeasts are used in bread-making, brewing (beer) and wine-making, and to produce vitamin supplements.

Enzymes

Moulds

Yeasts

c) **Bacteria** (germs) are invisible to the naked eye. They are found everywhere – on our skin, in our bodies, in the air, in sinks, on worktops and on our clothes. In the food industry, they are used to make cheese, yoghurt and vinegar. In small amounts most bacteria are harmless. This is known as '**an acceptable level of contamination**'. However, bacteria can cause food spoilage, food poisoning and other diseases.

> **Bacteria** is the plural of **bacterium**.

The growth of micro-organisms

The five conditions necessary for the growth of micro-organisms are:

1 Food

Bacteria like moist high-protein foods such as meat, poultry, eggs and dairy products.

Food

2 Warmth

The ideal temperature for most bacteria is 30–45°C. Boiling kills most bacteria and cold temperatures slow down their growth. However, freezing food does not kill bacteria.

3 Moisture

Bacteria like damp conditions and moist foods.

4 Oxygen

Many micro-organisms need oxygen to survive, but some can survive without it, for example in canned and vacuum-packed food.

Moisture

5 Time

When all the conditions for growth are present, bacteria can double every 10 to 20 minutes, so that in about six hours 1 million could be produced from just one bacterium!

Congratulations!

How does food become infected by bacteria?

Humans

People carry bacteria in the intestine, nose, mouth and on the hands, particularly if they do not wash after using the toilet or handling pets.

Food handlers must be very careful about personal hygiene. They should not work with food if suffering from an infectious disease.

Unwashed hands are a common cause of food poisoning

Cross-contamination

Cross-contamination occurs when bacteria from one food 'cross' onto another food and contaminate it, e.g. raw and cooked meat on the same board.

Separate colour-coded chopping boards should be used to avoid cross-contamination

Colour-coded chopping boards for different types of food

Insects

Insects carry dirt and bacteria on their legs. When they land on food, they vomit and excrete on it as they eat.

Pets and vermin

Pets, rats and mice also carry bacteria and should be kept out of the kitchen and away from food.

Dirty kitchen utensils and kitchen cloths

These may contain bits of food and allow bacteria to multiply, particularly if used cloths are left in a warm kitchen.

Insects carry bacteria

Food poisoning

Food poisoning is an illness caused by eating or drinking food or drink which contains large numbers of **pathogenic** (disease-causing) bacteria. The symptoms are stomach pains, nausea (feeling sick), diarrhoea and vomiting. Here are some of the most common food-poisoning bacteria.

Salmonella

This is found in the intestines of animals and humans. It is spread by flies and vermin and by poor standards of personal hygiene. Hands **must** be washed after using the lavatory in order to avoid salmonella. It can be found in meat, poultry, eggs and shellfish.

Staphylococcus

This is found in the nose, throat, skin and in cuts and boils. It is essential that food handlers cover any cuts and do not cough or sneeze over food to avoid the spread of staphylococcus. Unpasteurised milk and cold meats may be affected.

Listeria

This may grow and multiply in chilled foods, as it prefers lower temperatures. It may affect poultry, pâté, soft cheeses, coleslaw, pre-cooked chilled meals and chilled pre-packed salads. Pregnant women should avoid these foods, as listeria may cause miscarriage.

E. coli

This is found in the intestines of animals and humans. It may be spread by poor hygiene. Foods must be cooked thoroughly to prevent E. coli poisoning. It may be found in undercooked minced beef and beef burgers, salami, unpasteurised milk, cheese and yoghurt.

Food hygiene guidelines

Food

- Keep all foods cool, clean and covered.
- Store perishables in a cool place.
- Check expiry dates on perishables.
- Keep raw and cooked meats separate to avoid cross-contamination.
- Use separate chopping boards for raw and cooked foods.
- Cook eggs, meat, fish and poultry thoroughly to kill bacteria.
- Thaw frozen meat and poultry thoroughly before cooking.
- Cool and cover leftovers, and refrigerate.
- Reheat leftovers until piping hot to ensure that all bacteria are destroyed.

> Perishable foods are foods that have a short shelf life. They are usually stored in the refrigerator.

Food handlers

- Keep up a high standard of personal hygiene.
- Wash hands before handling food.
- Cover or tie back hair and wear a clean apron.
- Handle food as little as possible.
- Avoid touching face or hair while preparing food.
- Keep fingernails clean and short. Do not wear nail varnish.
- Do not cough or sneeze over food.
- Avoid wearing rings, earrings or watches when preparing food.
- Do not lick fingers.
- Cover any cuts or burns with a waterproof dressing.

The kitchen

- The kitchen should be well designed, with good lighting and ventilation.
- Ensure that plenty of hot water and cleaning materials are available.
- Wash and disinfect all work surfaces and equipment regularly.
- Change kitchen cloths daily and disinfect often.
- Keep kitchen bin covered. Empty daily and disinfect once a week.
- Disinfect sink and draining board regularly.
- Keep pets out of the kitchen at all times.
- Sweep kitchen floor daily and wash and disinfect regularly.

Food storage

Food must be stored properly to ensure that it stays at its best for as long as possible.

Proper storage:

- protects food from flies and dust
- prolongs its shelf life
- makes finding the food easier in the kitchen
- ensures that the kitchen is clean and well organised
- reduces waste.

> The shelf life of a food is the length of time a food remains safe and fit to be eaten.

Guidelines for food storage

1 Store foods correctly according to their type.

- **Non-perishables**, e.g. dry, bottled and tinned foods: Store in a cupboard in their own or airtight containers.
- **Semi-perishables**, e.g. bread, cakes, fresh fruit and vegetables: Store breads and cakes in a bread bin or tin. Fruit and vegetables may be stored in a rack or basket. Some semi-perishables, e.g. salad vegetables, can be stored in the refrigerator.
- **Perishables**, e.g. eggs, milk, cream, fresh meat, frozen or fresh 'ready to cook' meals, etc.: These have the shortest shelf life and must be used within three or four days. Store in the refrigerator at 4°C.
- **Frozen:** Store in the freezer at −18°C. Star markings on frozen foods and freezers:

*	Keeps for one week at −6°C
* *	Keeps for one month at −12°C
* * *	Keeps for three months at −18°C
* * * *	Keeps for up to one year at −18°C.

> The 'best before' date is a guide to the **quality** of the food. It is used on foods with a long shelf life (3 to 18 months), e.g. biscuits. It states the date by which food should be eaten.
>
> The 'use by' date is a guide to the **safety** of the food. It is used on foods with a short shelf life (up to 6 weeks), e.g. eggs. It states the date by which food should be eaten.

2 Note the 'best before' and 'use by' dates on perishables.

3 Use up older foods before opening new ones.

4 Store foods away from cleaning agents.

5 Keep cupboards and storage containers clean to prevent contamination by bacteria.

6 Once packages are opened, store dry foods (e.g. rice and pasta) in airtight containers to prevent them becoming stale or infested by insects.

7 Never refreeze thawed frozen food.

'Use by' date

Packaging materials

There are many packaging materials available for storing and preparing foods.

Disposable materials, such as **greaseproof paper, aluminium foil, kitchen paper** and **cling film**, should only be used once, as they cannot be cleaned thoroughly after use.

Plastic, china, glass and **tin** containers may be **reusable**. Some have sealable lids to prevent food drying out.

Packaging materials

Summary

- Causes of food spoilage are **enzymes** and micro-organisms such as **moulds, yeasts** and **bacteria**.

- Although moulds, yeasts and bacteria cause food spoilage, they also have many uses in **food production**.

- Micro-organisms need **food, warmth, moisture, oxygen** and **time** in order to grow and multiply.

- Food may be contaminated with bacteria by **humans, insects, animals, cloths, kitchen utensils** and other foods (cross-contamination).

- **Cross-contamination** is when bacteria from one food 'cross' onto another food and contaminate it.

- **Food poisoning** is caused by eating or drinking anything which contains large numbers of **pathogenic bacteria** such as **salmonella, staphylococcus, listeria** and **E. coli**.

- Note hygiene guidelines for food, food handlers and the kitchen.

- The **shelf life** of a food is the length of time it remains safe and fit to be eaten. **Perishables** must be eaten within three to four days, **semi-perishables** last up to a week and **non-perishables** may have a shelf life of up to a year if unopened.

- Note **star markings** on frozen foods and freezers.

- The **'best before'** date is a guide to the **quality** of the food.

- The **'use by'** date is a guide to the **safety** of the food.

- **Packaging materials** may be disposable or reusable.

Revision Questions

1 List the main causes of food spoilage and explain the conditions that favour the growth of food spoilage micro-organisms.

2 Name two bacteria that cause food poisoning. Give two sources of each.

3 Name one food poisoning bacterium that is associated with poultry.

4 Describe two symptoms of food poisoning.

5 Explain the term 'cross-contamination'.

6 List four rules that should be followed when storing food.

7 Explain each of the following terms displayed on food packaging: (a) best before date; (b) use by date.

8 Explain what is meant by: (a) perishable food; (b) shelf life.

9 Classify the following foods into (a) non-perishables; (b) semi-perishables; (c) perishables:

   jam, lettuce, cream, sugar, sausages, potatoes, dried pasta, tinned rice, mayonnaise, fresh pasta, ice cream, biscuits, fresh carrots, frozen broccoli.

10 Giving reasons, state how leftover chicken casserole should be stored.

11 Under the headings given, state where you would store each of the following foods:

   apples, butter, fish fingers, flour, sausages, cooking oil, bananas, lettuce, cooked rice, ice cream, milk.

Refrigerator	Food cupboard	Vegetable rack	Freezer

12 What precautions should be taken when (a) buying, (b) storing and (c) cooking 'ready-to-cook' meals to avoid the risk of food poisoning?

Chapter 6
Meal planning and food presentation

When planning family meals, consider the following guidelines:

1 **The occasion:** Consider the type of meal (lunch or dinner), the number of courses and whether it is a formal or informal meal.

2 **Cost:** It should be within your budget.

3 **Time of year and seasonal availability:** Hot foods are often welcome in cold weather, while cold foods may be more enjoyable on warm days. Certain foods are 'in season' at different times of the year. This means that they taste better, are cheap and are widely available.

4 **Time:** Choose dishes that can be prepared and cooked in the time available.

5 **Personal preferences and dietary restrictions:** Consider the likes and dislikes of the diners and any special dietary needs they may have, e.g. coeliac disease.

6 **Nutrition:** The meal should be nutritious and well balanced.

7 **Skill:** Consider the skill and experience of the cook. Beginner cooks should stick to simple recipes.

Informal meal

Buffet meal

Formal dining

8 **Equipment available:** Check that the necessary equipment is available before starting to prepare a dish.

9 **Variety:** Vary the cooking methods, colour, flavour and textures of the foods being served.

Meals of the day

Traditionally, daily meals consist of one main meal and two light ones.

- Breakfast is the first meal of the day.
- Lunch (luncheon) may be a light or large meal served in the middle of the day.
- Dinner is usually the main meal of the day, served in the evening.
- If the main meal of the day is eaten at lunchtime, the evening meal is called tea or supper.
- Snacks are often eaten between meals, e.g. 'elevenses' or mid-afternoon.
- Meals may contain a *starter* or *appetiser*. This stimulates the appetite for the remaining courses.

Recent trends show an increasing number of people eating 'on the move' and eating more snacks.

Menus

A menu is a list of all the dishes served at a meal. There are two types of menu commonly found in restaurants.

1 **Table d'hôte:** a set menu, with two to five courses. There is a limited choice within each course. It is usually less expensive than à la carte.

2 **À la carte:** this menu has a long list of dishes, each priced separately. There is more variety than the table d'hôte, but it is more expensive. Single dishes can be ordered separately.

À la carte menu

Appetisers
Greek Salad	€4.00
Anchovy and Olive Bruschetta	€3.50
French Onion Soup	€4.00
Chicken Liver Pâté	€4.50
Crab Claws	€5.00

Main Courses
Salmon in Puff Pastry	€16.00
Crispy Roast Duck	€17.00
Roast Stuffed Pork Steak	€15.00
Honey-glazed Gammon	€13.50
Lamb Cutlets with Herbs and Mustard	€16.50
Chargrilled Fillet Steak	€19.50
Chicken Korma	€14.00
Chilli Con Carne	€12.50

Side Dishes
Selection of Seasonal Vegetables	€4.00
French Fries	€4.00
Baked Potato	€3.00
Seasonal Side Salad	€4.00

Desserts
Strawberry Mousse	€4.00
Lemon Meringue Pie	€4.00
Profiteroles	€4.00
Summer Fruit Pavlova	€4.00
Sachertorte	€5.00
Pistachio Ice Cream	€5.50
Crème Brûlée	€5.00
Rhubarb Crumble	€4.00
Selection of Irish Farmhouse Cheeses	€5.00

Table d'hôte menu

Cream of Vegetable Soup
Seafood Cocktail
Caesar Salad
Deep-fried Garlic Mushrooms

Pasta alla Carbonara
Thai Green Chicken Curry
Vegetarian Lasagne
Baked Trout with Almonds
Roast Rib of Beef

Selection of Seasonal Vegetables
Creamed and Roast Potatoes

Chocolate Pudding
Homemade Apple Pie
Strawberry Cheesecake
Selection of Homemade Ice Creams

Tea or Coffee

€30.00

Writing your own menus

You can design your own menu card to suit any meal you plan. When writing menus for family meals or cookery assignments, there is no need to offer a choice within courses. Use a blank card or a folded sheet of stiff paper. Follow these guidelines:

- Write dishes in the centre of the card.
- List courses in the order in which they will be eaten – starter, main course, dessert – but *do not* write 'starter', 'main course' and 'dessert'.
- Be very specific about the type, cut and cooking method of meat used, e.g. *grilled* lamb *cutlets*.
- Mention accompaniments, e.g. sauces.
- Avoid using words like 'and' or 'served with'.

Sample menus

Breakfast menus

* Plan a breakfast menu for a school-going child, to include an egg dish.

* Keeping the healthy eating guidelines in mind, plan a three-course breakfast menu for a teenager.

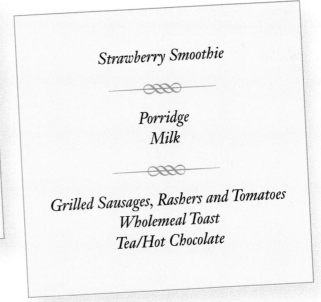

Orange Juice

————✣————

Scrambled Eggs on Toast

————✣————

Wholemeal Bread, Jam
Hot Chocolate

Strawberry Smoothie

————✣————

Porridge
Milk

————✣————

Grilled Sausages, Rashers and Tomatoes
Wholemeal Toast
Tea/Hot Chocolate

* Taken from Junior Cert exam questions.

Light lunch or supper menus

* Plan a two-course lunch menu for a teenager, to include a homemade beefburger.

* Plan a packed lunch menu, including cheese, for a teenager.

Homemade Beefburger
Baked Potato Wedges
Carrot and Orange Salad

Poached Pears
Chocolate Sauce

Wholemeal Cheese and Ham Salad Roll
Blueberry Muffin

Orange and Banana Milkshake

Water

Lunch or dinner menus

* Design a three-course dinner menu, suitable for a family meal, to include frozen mixed vegetables.

* Design a balanced three-course dinner menu suitable for a lactovegetarian.

Vegetable Soup

Roast Chicken
Gravy
Roast Potatoes
Steamed Mixed Vegetables

Bakewell Flan
Ice Cream

Caesar Salad

Veggie Bake
Baked Potatoes

Nutty Fruit Crumble
Custard

* *Taken from Junior Cert exam questions.*

Food presentation

1 All serving dishes and tableware should be spotlessly clean, and any splashes should be wiped from plates before serving the food.

2 All hot dishes should be served piping hot on hot plates. Cold dishes should be served on cold plates.

3 Ensure that the table is properly set before the meal is served.

4 A **garnish** or **decoration** will improve the appearance of the dish if properly chosen and tastefully used.

When food is presented and served attractively, it stimulates the appetite and encourages us to eat

Lemon is used to add colour and flavour to fish dishes

Remember:
- A **garnish** is used to improve the appearance of savoury foods.
- A **decoration** is used to improve the appearance of sweet foods.

Garnishes

Here are some suggestions for garnishing savoury dishes/foods:

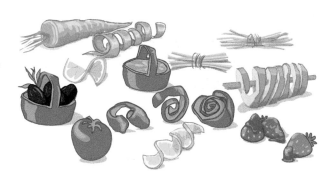

Dish/Food	Garnish
Soup	● Chopped parsley, cream, croûtons
Fish dishes	● Lemon wedges or twists, sprigs of chopped parsley, tomato basket or rose, sauce (on the side or in a sauce boat), cucumber fans, carrot curls
Meat, omelettes and salad dishes	● Sprigs of fresh herbs, chopped herbs, julienne vegetables, tomato rose, sliced cucumber or tomato, cucumber fans or twists, edible flowers, e.g. chive or nasturtium, radish roses, spring onion tassels

Decorations

Here are some suggestions for decorating sweet foods:

Dish/Food	Decoration
Pastry dishes	● Pastry leaves or other shapes, sieved icing sugar, caster sugar
Cakes and desserts	● Piped cream decorations, fruit decorations, e.g. glacé cherries or strawberry fans, chocolate-coated strawberries, feathered glacé icing, chopped nuts, chocolate (grated, curls or leaves), 'sprinkles', orange zest, mint leaves

Pastry

Small cakes

Table setting

Here are some guidelines.

- All cutlery should be clean and polished and glassware should be sparkling.
- Cutlery is placed in order of use, i.e. cutlery used first is placed on the outside, and diners work from the outside inwards.
- Tablemats or tablecloths should be spotless.
- Ensure condiment containers (for salt, pepper, mustard, etc.) are clean and filled.
- Napkins should be rolled or folded and placed on side plates.

Table settings may vary according to the occasion, the type of meal being served and the needs of the diners

- Choose a low centrepiece so that the diners can see one another across the table.
- Place iced water on the table just before the guests are seated.
- When serving a guest, serve from the left and take away from the right.

Link...

Setting a breakfast tray, page 79

Activity

Choose an attractively presented dish from an illustrated cookery book. Follow the recipe for preparing and cooking the dish. Present the dish as in the cookery book.
Evaluate your results.

Summary

- When **planning meals**, consider nutrition, cost, time, skill, equipment, personal preferences and dietary restrictions, time of year and seasonal availability, variety, the occasion.

- A **table d'hôte menu** is a set menu with limited choice. It is less expensive than an à la carte menu.

- An **à la carte menu** has wide variety and individual prices, but is more expensive than a table d'hôte menu.

- A **garnish** improves the appearance of **savoury** dishes.

- A **decoration** improves the appearance of **sweet** dishes.

- Guidelines for **table setting**: all cutlery clean and placed in order of use; cloths and napkins spotless; condiment containers filled; napkins on side plates; low centrepiece; iced water served at the last minute; serve from left and remove from right.

Revision Questions

1 Explain each of the following terms: (a) table d'hôte; (b) à la carte.

2 What is the purpose of serving a starter at the beginning of a meal?

3 Plan a three-course menu to include a ready-to-cook frozen fish dish in the main course. Suggest two suitable garnishes for the main dish.

4 Plan and set out a menu for a two-course main meal for yourself and three friends that can be prepared and served in one hour. Evaluate the nutritive value of the meal.

5 Set out a menu to include baked beans for a main meal for a strict vegetarian.

6 Plan a set of menus for one day for an adult who is obese.

7 Set out a menu, to include pizza, suitable for a teenager's main meal.

8 Plan and set out a three-course dinner menu to include vegetable soup.

9 (a) Plan and set out a suitable menu for a picnic lunch for you and your friends.

   (b) Give two reasons for your choice of food and drink items.

   (c) Make a list of the equipment you would pack.

   (d) State how you would keep the food cool on a warm day.

10 Plan a packed lunch menu which includes fish and is suitable for a teenager.

11 Design a three-course dinner menu, suitable for a family meal, to include frozen mixed vegetables.

12 Plan a two-course dinner menu that includes minced meat.

13 Design a balanced breakfast menu, to include porridge, suitable for a school-going teenager.

14 Name a different garnish suitable for each of the following foods: (a) soup; (b) fish cakes; (c) cheese omelette; (d) mushroom soup.

15 Name a different garnish suitable for each of the following foods: (a) grilled fish; (b) shepherd's pie.

16 What kind of dish is a garnish used for?

17 Name a different food for which each of the following garnishes/decorations would be suitable: (a) a wedge of lemon; (b) chopped parsley; (c) glacé cherries; (d) a sprinkle of icing sugar.

18 Why is lemon used to garnish fish dishes?

Chapter 7
Starting to cook

Before you start to cook, ensure that you, your work area and your equipment are **clean!**

Link...

Food hygiene guidelines, page 44

Before

1 Wear clean protective clothing.
2 Tie back or cover hair.
3 Wash hands before touching food and after contact with any of the following: toilet, rubbish bin, animals, handkerchief, soil, raw meat.
4 Cover any cuts.
5 Ensure all equipment, work surfaces, sinks and floor are clean.
6 Having selected a recipe, collect all ingredients.
7 Collect all the equipment required.
8 Weigh and measure ingredients and arrange on plates or bowls on the table.
9 Preheat oven if necessary.
10 Prepare tins/dishes.

During

1 Follow your recipe step by step. Clear away peelings, skins or eggshells as you go along.

2 Keep the table clean and free of clutter. Wipe up spills immediately.

3 Wash up as you go along, if possible.

4 Keep perishables in the fridge until required.

5 Do not lick your fingers when preparing food.

6 Avoid touching your hair or face.

7 Do not replace the tasting spoon in food after use.

8 Avoid wasting food.

9 Use oven gloves when handling hot utensils.

10 Take care when using sharp knives.

11 Turn saucepan handles in, away from the edge of the cooker.

After

1 Clean up properly after you have finished.

2 Stack dirty utensils to one side of the sink. Wash and stack washed utensils on the draining board.

3 Ensure all equipment is dried properly and replaced correctly.

Recipes

A recipe is a set of instructions for making something from a given list of ingredients.

● Name of dish.

→ *Peanut Butter Cookies*

Serves 2

● Types and amounts of food needed.

Ingredients

100g butter
100g brown sugar
100g crunchy peanut butter
1 egg, beaten
200g plain flour

● Some recipes include this. It helps to save time when you are getting started.

Equipment

2 large baking trays (18 × 28 cm), mixing bowls, wooden spoon, sieve, whisk, wire tray, palette knife.

Method

● The instructions set out in order.

1 **Preheat** oven to 180°C/gas mark 4.
2 **Cream** butter, sugar and peanut butter together until well mixed.
3 **Beat** in egg.
4 **Stir in** flour gradually and mix well.
5 **Roll** mixture into small balls and place on baking tray, leaving about 4cm between them. **Flatten** slightly.
6 **Bake** for 12–15 minutes, until golden.
7 **Cool** on a wire tray.

Weighing and measuring

In order to get good results when cooking, you must know how to weigh and measure ingredients accurately. Dry, solid foods are weighed in grams (g) and kilograms (kg) and liquid foods are measured in millilitres (ml) and litres (l).

A measuring jug is used to measure liquids such as milk, water and stock.

A weighing scale is used to weigh dry foods such as flour and sugar.

Measuring jug

Remember!
1kg = 1,000g
1l = 1,000ml

Weighing scale

Spoons are also used to measure dry or liquid ingredients.

1 teaspoon (**1 tsp**) = 5ml or 5g
1 dessertspoon (**1 dessertsp**) = 10ml or 10g
1 tablespoon (**1 tbsp**) = 15ml or 15g
(all level spoonfuls)

Some foods, e.g. margarine or butter, do not need to be weighed. The weight can be calculated using the guide on the foil wrapping or by dividing the food into sections. A 225g block of margarine can be divided into 9 × 25 g sections.

Measuring spoons

You might come across imperial measurements in old cookery books.
For easy reference, remember that 25g = 1oz.

Oven management

When a dish is to be cooked in the oven, it is important that the oven is set to the correct temperature and that the shelves are in the correct position before the oven is switched on. The oven must be **preheated** so that it has reached the correct temperature by the time the dish is ready to cook. Allow 10–15 minutes to preheat.

Link...
Cookers, page 325

In a **conventional oven,** the top shelf is the hottest, because hot air rises. The cooking temperature refers to the temperature in the centre of the oven (middle shelf). The lower shelf is slightly cooler. Never place dishes on the bottom of the oven, as they will not cook properly.

Conventional oven

In a **fan oven,** the temperature is the same on all shelves, as the fan circulates the hot air around the oven. If a recipe gives the temperature for a conventional oven only, reduce the fan oven temperature by 20°C, or foods may burn.

Modern electric cookers measure temperature in degrees Celsius/Centigrade (°C). Older cookers use degrees Fahrenheit (°F). Gas cookers use numbers (1–9).

Fan oven

Modern electric cooker

Oven temperatures			
Description	**Electric (°C)**	**Electric (°F)**	**Gas Mark**
Very cool	140°C	275°F	1
Cool	150°C	300°F	2
Warm	170°C	325°F	3
Moderate	180°C	350°F	4
Fairly hot	190°C	375°F	5
Fairly hot	200°C	400°F	6
Hot	220°C	425°F	7
Very hot	230°C	450°F	8
Very hot	240°C	475°F	9

Recipe costing

In order to calculate the cost of making a dish, you need to know:

- the amount of an ingredient used (g, kg, ml or l)
- the quantity in a full packet or container, e.g. a litre, 2kg, 225g, etc.
- the cost of a full packet or container.

Here is a worked example:
To work out the cost of 100ml milk @ €1.10 per litre:

$$\frac{\text{Amount of milk used} \times \text{cost of full carton}}{\text{Quantity in a full carton}} = \frac{100 \times 110}{1,000} = \frac{11}{1} = 11 \text{ cents}$$

Smaller ingredients like herbs, spices, seasoning and baking powder can be grouped together to total 10–20 cents.

Don't forget to allow fuel costs (usually 10–15 cents).

Activities

1 Find out the cost of these basic ingredients: (a) 1 litre milk; (b) half a dozen eggs; (c) 225g block of margarine; (d) 2kg white flour; (e) 1 litre cooking oil; (f) 500g caster sugar; (g) 500g rice; (h) 500g pasta; (i) 2kg wholemeal flour; (j) 1 litre buttermilk; (k) 500g minced beef; (l) an onion; (m) a red pepper.

2 Calculate the cost of making a loaf of wholemeal bread.

Ingredients	Cost
150g white flour	
150g wholemeal flour	
25g bran	
25g wheat germ	
50g margarine	
1 tsp bread soda	
2 tsp caster sugar	
1 egg, beaten	
350ml buttermilk	
fuel	

Recipe modification

Recipes may be **modified** or changed for the following reasons:

- to make the dishes more healthy (using the healthy eating guidelines)
- to change the size of the dish
- to introduce variety
- to substitute for missing ingredients
- to suit special diets, e.g. a coeliac diet.

It is important to remember that certain cake recipes, e.g. sponge, Madeira, are based on **exact** proportions of ingredients and should not be changed if the end product is to be successful.

However, substituting or adding extra ingredients to dishes such as soups, pasta dishes or stews is quite easy.

Here are some suggestions for modifying recipes to suit healthy eating guidelines.

To reduce sugar:

- Use artificial sweeteners, where possible.
- Use dried fruit such as dates, sultanas or raisins in fruit pies and crumbles to replace sugar and add fibre.
- Remove sugar from scones and breads.
- Toss fruit salad in unsweetened fruit juice.

Sugar

To reduce fat:

- Remove visible fat on meat.
- Use meat in smaller amounts. Combine with larger amounts of vegetables, especially pulses, brown rice, wholemeal pasta and wholemeal flour.
- Grill, bake or boil foods.
- Serve low-fat plain yoghurt instead of cream.
- Use whisking methods for cakes.
- Dry-fry meat (minced meat, rashers) in a non-stick pan and pour off excess fat.
- Use skimmed or low-fat milk when making sauces.
- Cut bread and chips thicker so that there is less surface area for fat.

Whipped cream

To reduce salt:

- Reduce or remove salt from recipes.
- Use low-sodium salt.
- Avoid using commercial stock cubes.
- Flavour foods with pepper, herbs and spices instead of salt.

To increase fibre:

- Use porridge oats for sweet and savoury crumbles.
- Substitute wholemeal pasta and rice for white.
- Use dried fruits for desserts.
- Use seeds for toppings for breads, buns and scones.
- Serve raw fruit and vegetables when possible.
- Add pulse vegetables to savoury dishes, e.g. casseroles, chilli.
- Leave skins on fruit, if possible, when used in fruit salads or other recipes.
- Use nuts in salads, desserts and baked foods.

Salt

Fibre

Activities

1 Adapt a traditional recipe for apple crumble to suit the dietary guidelines for reducing sugar and fat and increasing fibre.

2 Research casserole recipes in cookery books. Discuss how a beef or chicken casserole could be modified to suit the needs of a vegan.

3 Compile a list of your favourite pasta dishes. Look up the recipes and suggest ways of reducing the salt and fat content, and increasing the fibre content.

Food preparation equipment

Equipment for food preparation can be divided into three main groups:

1 Small equipment (utensils).
2 Small appliances.
3 Large appliances.

Small equipment

This includes bowls, saucepans, frying pans, casserole dishes, baking tins, chopping boards, rolling pins, knives, forks, spoons, vegetable peelers, mashers, balloon whisks, flour dredgers, pastry brushes, palette knives, spatulas and graters. These are called **utensils**.

Kitchen utensils are made from a variety of different materials and should be cared for according to type.

Material	Care and Cleaning	Utensils
Plastic	● Wash in hot soapy water. Rinse and dry. Keep away from direct heat.	● Fish slice, spatula, flour dredger, masher, chopping board, mixing bowl, measuring jug.
Silicone	● Soak in warm soapy water. Rinse and wipe clean. Do not use sharp utensils on silicone.	● Bakeware, whisk, spatula, pastry brush, measuring spoons, oven mitts, funnel, drainer, rolling pin.
Wood	● Wash in warm soapy water, scrubbing with the grain. Rinse and dry thoroughly. Keep away from direct heat to prevent warping.	● Rolling pin, wooden spoons and spatulas, chopping board, pastry brush.
Metals – aluminium, tin, stainless steel	● Wash in hot soapy water. Rinse and dry very well to prevent rusting. Never use abrasives or sharp utensils on non-stick pans. Store saucepans without lids to allow air to circulate.	● Saucepans, frying pans, woks, baking tins, grater, balloon whisk, sieve.
Glass and delft	● Wash in hot soapy water. Rinse and dry. Never place on a cold surface when hot or they may crack.	● Plates, mixing bowls, measuring jug, Pyrex plates and dishes.

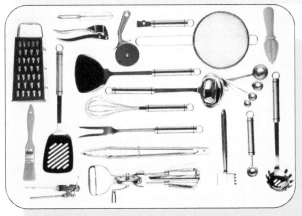

Cooking equipment – range of materials

Small appliances

These are small, portable electrical items which save time and energy when preparing food, e.g. food mixer, food processor, juice extractor, hand blender, smoothie maker, ice-cream maker, liquidiser.

When using small appliances:

● Always follow the manufacturer's instructions.
● When cleaning, never immerse the motor in water. Wipe over with a damp cloth.
● To clean liquidisers and food processors, half fill with hot soapy water and switch on. Take apart, rinse and dry well.
● Store with lids off to allow air circulation.

A small appliance

Large appliances

These are large pieces of equipment which are not usually moved, e.g. cooker, refrigerator, dishwasher, microwave oven.

Link...

Chapter 29 Technology in the Home

Large appliances

Activities

1 Fill in the table below. The first one has been done for you.

Utensil	Use
Spatula	Scraping food from bowls, pans, etc.
Balloon whisk	
Flour dredger	
Pastry brush	
Palette knife	
Grater	
Masher	
Vegetable peeler	
Funnel	
Rolling pin	

2 Fill in the table below. The first one has been done for you.

Appliance	Use
Food mixer	To cream, whisk or beat ingredients.
Food processor	
Juice extractor	
Liquidiser	
Hand blender	
Smoothie maker	
Ice-cream maker	

Summary

- Before starting to cook, prepare **yourself**, your **work area** and your **equipment.**

- A **recipe** is a set of instructions for making something from a given list of ingredients.

- When using an **oven**, arrange shelves and **preheat** beforehand.

- Recipes may be **modified** to follow healthy eating guidelines, to change the size of the dish, to introduce variety or to substitute for missing ingredients.

- **Small equipment** (utensils) should be cared for according to the material it is made from.

Revision Questions

1 Name each of the utensils shown below and suggest a use for each.

(a)

(b)

2 State a use for each of the pieces of equipment shown below.

(a)

(b)

3 Explain what is meant by modifying a recipe.

Food preparation skills

Once you have mastered the basic skills outlined below you can prepare a very wide variety of dishes.

Peelers are available to suit both left-handed and right-handed cooks.

Knives should be very sharp and should fit the hand comfortably. They should be suited to the task, for example slicing or chopping.

- **Peeling:** Use a peeler to remove the skin from vegetables and fruits such as apples, pears, potatoes, parsnips, carrots (thin peeling). Use a sharp knife to remove the skin from citrus fruits and squashes (thick peeling).
- **Chopping:** Cut into even-sized pieces. For example, to chop an onion:

    1 Cut the onion in half. Lay each half on the chopping board with the cut side down. Make cuts across it.

    2 Turn the onion and make cuts across the first cuts, as shown in the photograph.

- **Slicing:** Keep the knife blade facing the board. Use smooth strokes to cut the food into even slices.
- **Grating:** Use a grater or food processor to cut food into small, thin strips.
- **Dicing:** Use a sharp knife to cut food into small cubes.
- **Shredding:** Use a sharp knife or food processor to cut food into very fine strips.
- **Whisking/whipping:** Use a whisk to move the food around and around quickly in a bowl, e.g. whisking eggs or whipping cream.
- **Folding in:** Use a whisk or large metal spoon to mix two ingredients together. Cut into the mixture and gently turn it over and over until it is mixed evenly.
- **Blending:** Mixing smoothly. This usually means mixing a powder with cold liquid, e.g. cornflour with a liquid such as water or milk.
- **Coring:** Use a corer to remove the middle containing the seeds (core), e.g. when preparing an apple.

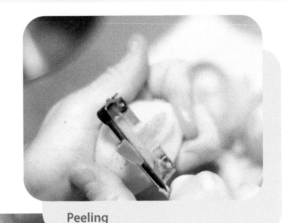

Peeling

Chopping

Shredding

Whisking/whipping

Cooking

Reasons for cooking food

- Food is safer to eat because harmful bacteria are killed.
- Flavours are developed, e.g. sautéed onions.
- Cooking makes food look more attractive, e.g. toasted sandwiches.
- Cooked food is easier to digest, e.g. rice, pasta, potatoes and fruit.
- Cooking preserves food so that it lasts longer, e.g. jam.

Effects of cooking on food

- Fat melts, e.g. butter.
- Colour changes, e.g. cake goes brown.
- Flavours develop.
- Protein becomes solid (coagulated), e.g. fried egg.
- Food softens and absorbs water, e.g. pasta, rice.
- Food loses water and shrinks, e.g. fish, meat.
- Nutrients are lost in the cooking liquid.

Colour changes

Flavours develop

Protein becomes solid

Food softens

Food loses water

Nutrients are lost

Effects of overcooking on food

- Foods becomes indigestible, e.g. overcooked cheese.
- Vitamins and minerals are lost.
- Colour, flavour and texture are damaged.

Methods of heat transfer in cooking

Heat travels to food in the following ways:

- conduction
- convection
- radiation.

Conduction

Heat travels through something **solid**, e.g. a metal.
    This occurs when the heat travels from a hot **saucepan** or **frying pan** into the food.

Cooking by conduction

Convection

Heat travels in **air or liquid that is moving.**
    This happens in a **fan oven** where the air is moving around the food. It also occurs when food is being boiled because the liquid is moving around the food.

Cooking by convection

Radiation

Heat travels to food in **rays** in the same way that it travels to Earth from the sun. Radiation occurs when food is **grilled.** The food does not touch the grill, but the heat reaches the food.

Cooking by radiation

Cooking methods

There are four main cooking methods:

1. **Moist methods** such as boiling, poaching, stewing, casseroling, steaming, pressure cooking.
2. **Dry methods** such as baking and grilling.
3. **Using fat** such as roasting and frying.
4. **Microwave cooking.**

Moist methods of cooking

Boiling

What it means: Cooking food in rapidly bubbling water in a saucepan.

Suitable foods: Rice, pasta, meat, vegetables.

Guidelines for boiling:
- Use a suitable sized pan so that very little water will cover the food.
- Use a tightly fitting lid.
- Once the liquid starts to bubble rapidly, reduce the temperature so that the liquid is barely bubbling. This is called **simmering**.

Boiling

Advantages:
- Low-fat method of cooking.
- Tougher cuts of meat can be boiled or stewed.
- Economical.

Disadvantages: Vitamins and minerals dissolve into the cooking liquid.

Poaching

What it means: Cooking food in water that is barely bubbling.

Suitable foods: Fish, eggs, fruit.

Guidelines for poaching:
- The cooking liquid should be barely bubbling before the food is put into it.
- Use the cooking liquid for a sauce if possible, for example with poached plums.

Poaching

Advantages:
- Low-fat method of cooking.
- Suitable for foods that need gentle handling.
- Foods absorb flavours from the liquid, for example plums or pears poached in flavoured syrup.

Disadvantage: Foods may break up.

Stewing

What it means: Cooking food slowly in a little liquid in a covered container. A heavy saucepan on the hob is used for stewing and a dish in the oven is used for casseroling. The cooking liquid is eaten with the dish.

Suitable foods: Meat, fish, vegetables.

Guidelines for stewing/casseroling:

- Use a heavy-based saucepan.
- Cover the container tightly to prevent evaporation.
- Meat and vegetables can be fried first to improve texture and flavour.

Advantages:

- Tough pieces of meat can be cooked.
- Low-fat method of cooking.
- A whole meal can be cooked in one pot.
- Nutrients which dissolve into the cooking liquid are served with the dish.

Disadvantage: Slow method of cooking.

Stewing

Higher Level

Steaming

What it means: Cooking food in steam rising from boiling water.

Suitable foods: Fish, vegetables.

Guidelines for steaming:

- Use herbs and seasoning to flavour food – steamed food can lack flavour.
- More than one dish can be steamed at the same time using a modern steamer.

Advantages:

- Vegetables are not immersed in water and therefore there is less loss of water-soluble vitamins and minerals compared to boiling.
- Healthy because no fat is added during cooking.
- Easy to control and little chance of overcooking.
- Various foods can be cooked at the same time.

Disadvantage: Flavour may be bland.

Steaming

Higher Level

Pressure cooking

Higher Level

What it means: Cooking food under pressure in a heavy saucepan with a special lid.

Suitable foods: Meat, vegetables, puddings.

Guidelines for pressure cooking:
- Add herbs or spices to the food to ensure a good flavour.
- Control the cooking time carefully to avoid overcooking.

Advantages: Quick method of cooking and therefore saves energy.

Disadvantages:
- Food can easily be overcooked.
- Skill is needed as it can be dangerous.

Dry methods of cooking

Baking

Higher Level

What it means: Cooking food in dry hot air in an oven.

Suitable foods: Breads, cakes, fish, vegetables, meat.

Guidelines for baking:
- Preheat the oven when required in the recipe.
- Use shelf position recommended in the recipe.
- Avoid opening the oven door during cooking.
- Batch-bake, or cook, as many dishes as possible at the same time.

Advantages:
- The crisp brown appearance of baked food looks attractive.
- Little loss of nutrients.

Disadvantage: Can waste energy if oven is used for only one dish.

Grilling

Higher Level

What it means: Cooking food by rays of heat in a hot grill.

Suitable foods: Tender pieces of meat, fish, vegetables.

Guidelines for grilling:
- Use only tender cuts of meat.
- Preheat the grill.
- Brush food with oil to prevent it drying out.
- Do not pierce food – this causes loss of nutrients.

Advantages:
- Low-fat method of cooking.
- Crispy texture.
- Quick.

Disadvantages:
- Grilling is not suitable for tough cuts of meat.
- Food may become dry.

Using fat

Roasting

What it means: Cooking food in an oven using hot fat or oil.

Suitable foods: Vegetables, poultry, meat.

Guidelines for roasting:
- The food should be coated in hot fat to prevent it drying out. This is called **basting**.
- Food should be uncovered before the end of cooking to improve the colour and flavour.

Advantages: Excellent flavour and texture.

Disadvantages:
- High in fat.
- Food dries out if it is not basted.

Higher Level

Roasting

Frying

What it means: Cooking food in hot fat in a frying pan (shallow frying), in a deep fat frier (deep frying) or by stir-frying in a wok.

Higher Level

Suitable foods: Tender cuts of meat, fish, eggs, vegetables, chips.

Guidelines for frying:
- Use only tender cuts of meat.
- **Shallow frying:** Use oil instead of saturated fats.
- **Deep frying:** Ensure that the oil is the correct temperature before adding food.
- **Stir-frying:** Cut foods into equal-sized pieces.
- Do not leave the pan unattended.

Advantages:
- Excellent flavour and texture.
- Quick.

Stir-frying

Disadvantages:
- High in fat.
- Fried food must be served immediately.
- Can be dangerous.

To sauté means to toss food lightly in hot oil, for example sautéed onion.

Reasons for coating food before cooking:
- To protect it from the hot fat during frying.
- To improve the texture, e.g. to make it crisp.
- To improve the flavour.
- To prevent food breaking up, e.g. fish coated in batter.

Microwave cooking

What it means: Microwaves cause the particles of food to vibrate. This causes heat to build up inside the food. The heat then travels through the food by conduction.

Suitable foods: Most foods can be cooked, thawed or reheated.

Guidelines for microwave cooking:

- Follow the manufacturer's instructions.
- Prick any food which has a skin, such as potatoes or sausages, to prevent them bursting.
- Cover food to avoid soiling the oven.
- Allow **standing time**. This is the part of the cooking process where the food continues to cook outside the oven. Follow instructions on food labels for standing time.

Link...

Microwave ovens, page 330

Accompaniments

An **accompaniment** is a food that is served with a dish. A sauce is an example of an accompaniment.

Dips, sauces and salsas are examples of accompaniments

Reasons for serving accompaniments:

- to improve appearance
- to improve flavour
- to provide a variety of textures
- to reduce richness, e.g. apple sauce reduces the richness of roast pork
- some accompaniments are traditional, e.g. stuffing and gravy with roast turkey.

Summary

- **Reasons for cooking food:** Safer to eat; flavour and appearance are improved; easier to digest; preserves food.
- **Effects of cooking:** Fat melts, colour changes, flavours develop, protein becomes solid, starchy food absorbs water, meat loses water and shrinks.
- **Heat transfer:**
  - **conduction** – heat travels through something solid
  - **convection** – heat travels in **air or liquid that is moving**
  - **radiation** – heat travels to food in **rays**.
- **Cooking methods:**
  - **moist methods** – boiling, poaching, stewing, casseroling, steaming, pressure cooking
  - **dry methods** – baking and grilling
  - **microwave cooking**
  - **using fat** – roasting and frying.
- **Microwave cooking:** Particles of food vibrate, causing a build-up of heat. Food continues to cook by conduction.
- An **accompaniment** is a food that is served with a dish.

Revision Questions

1. Give two reasons why some foods are cooked before eating.
2. What effect does overcooking have on food?
3. List five different methods of cooking and name a different food to which *each* method is suited.
4. Give three advantages of steaming.
5. Give one advantage and one disadvantage of grilling as a method of cooking.
6. State how potatoes or sausages are prevented from bursting while being cooked in a microwave oven.
7. Explain the term 'sauté'.
8. Explain the term 'baste'.
9. Give three reasons for serving accompaniments.
10. Explain each of the following cookery terms: (a) roux; (b) seasoning; (c) to glaze. (See Glossary, page 148.)
11. Explain each of the following cookery terms: (a) au gratin; (b) baking blind; (c) al dente. (See Glossary, page 148.)

Chapter 8
Foods

Breakfast is the most important meal of the day

Breakfast

Breakfast is the first and most important meal of the day. It fuels the body to help provide energy, better concentration and problem-solving ability throughout the day.

People who don't eat breakfast often consume more calories throughout the day and are more likely to be overweight. This is because someone who skips breakfast is likely to get hungry before lunchtime and snack on high-calorie foods, or to overeat at lunch.

Skipping breakfast can make a person drowsy and sluggish and have a slower reaction time.

For a healthy breakfast, try to include a variety of foods from all the food groups, if possible. Below are some suggestions.

Cereal and potato group

- **Cereals:** Porridge, muesli, cornflakes, Fruit & Fibre, All Bran, granola, Weetabix, Shredded Wheat.
- **Breads:** Wholemeal and white, toast, muffins, croissants, scones (white or brown), pancakes, bagels, crêpes, blinis, French toast, waffles.

Breakfast cereal

Fruit and vegetable group

- Fruit juices, e.g. orange, apple, grapefruit.
- Fruit smoothies.
- Whole or half fruits, e.g. orange, grapefruit, banana.
- Fruit segments or salads, e.g. orange, pineapple, mandarin.
- Stewed dried fruits, e.g. prunes, apricots.
- Grilled tomatoes and/or mushrooms.

Grilled tomatoes on toast

Milk group

- Hot or cold milk with cereals.
- Glass of milk, hot chocolate or latte.
- Cheeses.
- Yoghurts, yoghurt drinks or yoghurt smoothies.

Meat/protein group

- Eggs (boiled, poached, fried, scrambled, omelettes).
- Grilled rashers, sausages, black and white pudding.
- Kedgeree.
- Cold cooked meats.
- Grilled kippers.
- Peanut butter on toast.

Link...

Breakfast menus, page 51

Milk in hot drinks

Here are some **guidelines** for planning breakfast menus:

1 Include foods from all the food groups.
2 Consider the time of year (weather) and the likes and dislikes of the diners.
3 Consider any special dietary requirements, e.g. coeliac disease.
4 Choose grilled rather than fried foods.
5 Use low-fat spreads on bread.
6 Choose high-fibre breakfast cereals and avoid those with a high sugar content.
7 Allow enough time to sit down and enjoy your breakfast.

Setting a breakfast tray

● Collect all the necessary equipment for a single place setting.
● Ensure that all glassware and cutlery are sparkling.
● Use small dishes and jugs for butter, marmalade, sugar and milk.
● Include a mini floral arrangement to make it look attractive.
● Set tray as shown in the diagram.

Activities

1 Cereal bars are popular among teenagers. Conduct research on cereal bars to find out:
(a) the types available; (b) nutritive values; (c) cost.

2 Carry out a survey of your classmates to find out how many of them do not eat breakfast. List their reasons. How could teenagers be encouraged to eat breakfast on weekday mornings?

3 Plan breakfast menus for the following: (a) an active vegetarian adult; (b) an elderly woman with heart disease; (c) a coeliac.

Packed meals

Packed meals are commonly used by school-going children, teenagers, workers and people on the move. They are usually seen as a stop gap between breakfast and the main meal of the day. Because there may be a long break between these two meals, the packed lunch must provide enough food, energy and nutrients to keep an individual going for four to five hours.

A balanced packed lunch should include foods from the four food groups.

Here are some suggestions:

Cereal and potato group

● White or wholemeal bread, pitta bread, rolls, baps, crackers, herb breads, bread sticks, scones, croissants, panini, tortilla wraps.
● Barm brack.
● Spanish tortilla.
● Muffins.
● Potato salad.
● Popcorn.
● Cold pasta or rice salads.

Cold pasta salad

Fruit and vegetable group

- Fresh fruit, e.g. apples, oranges, bananas, kiwis.
- Fruit or vegetable salads.
- Vegetable soups.
- Dried fruit.
- Raw vegetable sticks, e.g. carrot and celery.
- Fruit juices and smoothies.
- Olives.

Fruit group

Milk group

- Milk, milkshakes, yoghurt, yoghurt drinks, smoothies, fromage frais.
- Hot chocolate, latte.
- Cheese and cheese spreads.

Meat group

- Cold sliced meats.
- Tinned fish, e.g. tuna salad.
- Chicken portions.
- Quiche.
- Sausage rolls.
- Hummus.
- Nuts.
- Hard-boiled eggs.

Milk group

Here are some **guidelines** for planning packed meals:

1 The meal should be tasty and include foods from all the food groups.

2 Include enough food to suit the needs and appetite of the individual.

3 Consider the likes and dislikes of the individual.

4 Do not include too many sugary or fatty foods.

5 Choose foods that travel well, i.e. do not dry out, squash or break up easily.

6 Vary the menus as much as possible. A packed lunch does not always have to include sandwiches!

7 Choose suitable packaging materials for the meal, e.g. plastic boxes and bottles, thermos flasks, foil, cling film.

8 Wrap different types of food separately and put the heaviest foods at the bottom of the container.

Meat group

Use cookie cutters when cutting sandwiches for children.

Types of sandwich:

- **Open:** One layer of bread covered with different toppings, e.g. lettuce, shrimp and cucumber with mayonnaise.
- **Party triangles:** Brown or white crustless bread with filling. May be cut into triangles, rounds or fingers.
- **Double decker:** Three slices of bread with various fillings in between.
- **Club:** Three slices of bread with two layers of filling.
- **Toasted** (sometimes called panini): Sandwich is made up and toasted under a grill or in a sandwich toaster. Use ingredients that heat or melt well.
- **Farmhouse:** Thick crusty bread with a thick layer of fillings.
- **Pinwheel:** Thinly sliced crustless bread spread with soft filling (e.g. pâté), rolled up, chilled and cut into slices like a Swiss roll.
- **Wrap:** Flour tortilla wrapped around a selection of ingredients, e.g. lettuce, chicken tikka.
- **BLT:** Bacon, lettuce and tomato, with mayonnaise. May or may not be toasted.
- **Rolled:** Thinly sliced crustless bread rolled up around a filling, e.g. cocktail sausages.
- **Pitta pockets:** Toasted pitta bread split and filled with a selection of hot or cold ingredients.

Different types of sandwich

Link...

Packed lunch menu, page 52

With a little imagination, different sandwiches can be made to suit every taste and every occasion. Try some of the following:

- tuna, chopped tomato, sweet corn and mayonnaise
- egg, spring onion, lettuce and mayonnaise
- cream cheese, chopped celery and chopped red pepper
- roasted red peppers, goat's cheese and pesto
- ham, cheese, chutney and lettuce
- crabmeat, avocado, tomato, mayonnaise and lettuce
- mozzarella, sundried tomatoes and ham.

Activities

1 Design a sandwich you would like to see available in your school canteen.

2 Plan a menu for a packed lunch for: (a) a pre-school child; (b) a builder; (c) a hill walker; (d) a teenager on a school trip.

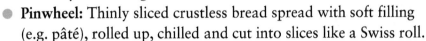

Soups

Soups can form a complete meal, depending on the ingredients. Soups containing meat, fish or vegetables can be very nutritious.

Types of soup

Thin soups

- **Clear soup:** A thin clear soup made with well-flavoured stock, eg. consommé.
- **Broth:** A thin soup containing finely chopped meat or vegetables and an ingredient containing starch, such as pearl barley or pasta.

Thick soups

- **Purée:** A soup that is thickened by liquidising it after it has been cooked, e.g. vegetable soup.
- **Thickened soups:** A soup to which a thickening agent has been added. Examples of thickening agents are potato, flour and cornflour.

Characteristics of a good soup

A good soup:

- is appetising
- is well flavoured
- has the right consistency, i.e. it is neither too thick nor too thin and does not have any lumps
- is not greasy
- is served very hot (unless it is a soup which is meant to be served cold).

Garnishes for soup

Garnishes for soup

Garnishes for soup include:

- herbs, e.g. chopped parsley, chives or leaves of various herbs
- croûtons (bread that has been diced and fried)
- cream.

Stock

Stock is water in which food has been cooked. It is used to make soups. Stock made from fresh ingredients:

- produces a fresh, wholesome flavour
- is much lower in salt than commercial stock cubes
- does not contain the additives commonly used in commercial stock cubes, such as flavour enhancers (see p. 142).

Commercial stock products can be used instead of fresh stock.

Stock

Convenience soups

A wide variety of convenience soups is available, such as:

● dried soups
● cartons
● canned soups
● chilled soups in containers.

Convenience soups

Advantages:

● Convenient to prepare.
● Can be cheaper than the fresh variety, e.g. asparagus soup.
● Adds variety to the diet.
● Useful in emergencies.
● Can be used as a base for other dishes, e.g. chicken soup used as a base for chicken and broccoli bake.

Disadvantages:

● Can contain flavour enhancers such as monosodium glutamate.
● Can contain excess salt.
● Inferior flavour, texture and food value when compared to freshly prepared soup.
● Chilled soups can be expensive.

Summary

● **Types of soup:**
   ◆ **thin soups:** consommé, broth
   ◆ **thick soups:** purée, thickened soups.
● **Stock** is water in which meat, fish or vegetables have been cooked.
● Examples of **thickening agents** used in soups are potato, flour and cornflour.

Revision Questions

1 Name two types of soup and give one example of each type.
2 Give two benefits of using stock when making soup.
3 Explain the term 'purée'.
4 (a) What is a thickening agent?
   (b) Name one thickening agent used to make soup.
5 List two characteristics of good soup.
6 Give two advantages and two disadvantages of using convenience soups.

Sauces

Sauces can be part of a dish or they can be served as an accompaniment. They may be sweet or savoury, hot or cold.

Advantages of using sauces

Sauces:

- add **flavour** to food
- provide contrast to the **texture** of food
- increase the **food value** of food (depending on the ingredients)
- **moisten** foods
- **offset the richness** in food, such as apple sauce with roast pork.

Types of sauce

- **Roux-based** sauces, e.g. white, cheese.
- **Egg-based** sauces, e.g. custard.
- **Fruit** sauces, e.g. apple, cranberry, orange.
- **Cold** sauces, e.g. mint.
- **Other sauces** include butterscotch and chocolate.

Cranberry sauce

Roux-based sauces

A **roux** is a mixture of fat and flour which, when cooked, is used to thicken soups and sauces. The consistency of roux-based sauces depends on the amount of liquid added. Milk is used in white sauce and stock is used in dark sauces.

Types of roux-based sauce			
Binding	**Coating**	**Stewing**	**Pouring**
• 25g fat	• 25g fat	• 25g fat	• 25g fat
• 25g flour	• 25g flour	• 25g flour	• 25g flour
• 125ml liquid	• 250ml liquid	• 375ml liquid	• 500ml liquid

To make a roux sauce:

1 Melt the fat in a saucepan.
2 Add the flour and cook over a low heat for one minute.
3 Remove from the heat and slowly add the liquid, stirring all the time.
4 Return to the heat and bring to the boil, stirring all the time.
5 Simmer for five minutes and serve.

Variations on white sauce:

- **Mushroom sauce:** Add 50g sautéed mushrooms.
- **Cheese sauce:** Add 50g grated cheese and ½ tsp made mustard.
- **Parsley sauce:** Add 2 tbsp finely chopped parsley.

Traditional sauces

Certain sauces are traditionally served with roast meats, such as:

- bread sauce and cranberry sauce with roast turkey
- mint sauce with roast lamb
- horseradish sauce with roast beef
- apple sauce with roast pork or goose.

Mint sauce is traditionally served with lamb

Convenience sauces

Convenience sauces

Convenience sauces are available in various forms, for example bottled, dried, frozen, canned and in cartons. They have the advantages that they reduce the preparation time of certain dishes and they are useful for people with poor cooking skills. However, convenience sauces can have a high sugar and salt content and they may contain various amounts of additives.

Summary

- **Sauces** are used to improve appearance and flavour, increase food value, moisten foods and offset richness.
- A **roux** is a mixture of equal quantities of fat and flour which are cooked together until smooth.
- Sauces often increase the kilocalorie content of dishes.
- **Convenience sauces** may contain sugar, salt and additives.

Revision Questions

1. Give four reasons why sauces may be used to accompany food.
2. Suggest a sauce that is traditionally served with each of the following roast meats: (a) turkey; (b) lamb; (c) pork.
3. Explain the cookery term 'roux'.
4. Give two advantages and two disadvantages of using convenience sauces.

Meat

Meat is the flesh of animals and birds. It includes:

Cooked ham

- carcass meat
  - ◆ sheep, e.g. lamb and mutton
  - ◆ cattle, e.g. veal, beef
  - ◆ pig, e.g. pork, ham, bacon
- poultry, e.g. chicken, turkey
- game, e.g. wild animals and birds such as pheasant
- **offal**, which is the edible internal organs of animals, e.g. liver and kidney.

Nutritive value

- **Protein:** Excellent source of high biological value protein. Useful for growth.
- **Fat:** Meat is high in saturated fat. Fat can be visible or invisible. Fat provides energy.
- Meat does not contain **carbohydrate**, therefore it is often served with foods containing carbohydrate such as potatoes, pasta and bread.
- **Vitamins:** Meat contains B group vitamins, which release energy from food.
- **Minerals:** Meat is an excellent source of iron for healthy red blood cells. It also contains calcium and phosphorus for healthy bones.
- **Water:** Meat contains about 60 per cent water.

Higher Level

Composition of red meat					
Protein	**Fat**	**Carbohydrate**	**Vitamins**	**Minerals**	**Water**
20–25%	20%	0%	B group	Iron, calcium, phosphorous	60%

Structure of meat

Meat is made up of long fibres. These fibres are held together in bundles by connective tissue. Fat is distributed between the fibres.

- **Tough meat** contains longer, thicker fibres and more connective tissue. Tough meat is found in older animals and in parts of an animal that is very active, such as the leg and neck.
- **Tender meat** comes from young animals and inactive parts of the animal, such as the back.

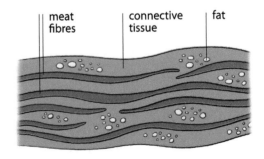

meat fibres   connective tissue   fat

Structure of meat

Causes of toughness in meat

- **Age:** Older animals have tougher meat.
- **Activity:** Meat from active parts of the animal, such as the leg or neck, is tough.
- **Incorrect hanging:** Meat must be left to hang in certain conditions after slaughter to make it tender.
- **Incorrect cooking:** Tough cuts of meat become tougher if they are cooked incorrectly.

Tenderising meat

1 **Hang** meat to allow enzymes to tenderise it.
2 **Pound** the meat with a steak hammer to break up the fibres.
3 **Mince** or cut the meat into small pieces.
4 Use **moist methods** of cooking, such as stewing.
5 **Marinate** the meat before cooking, i.e. soak it in a **marinade** – a mixture of oil, vinegar, herbs and other flavouring ingredients.
6 Use **chemical tenderisers**, such as papain.

Cuts of meat (beef)

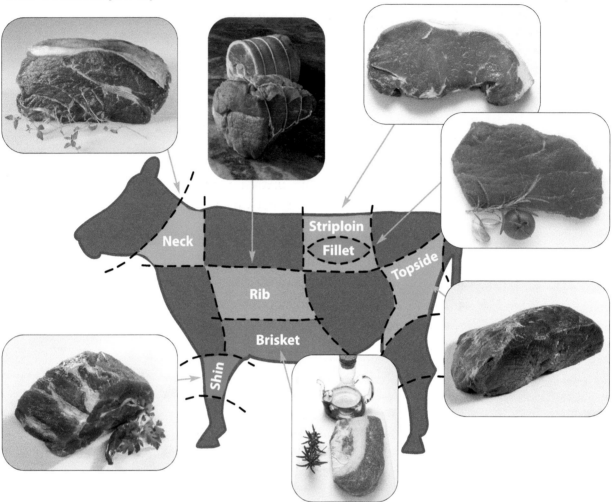

Cooking methods for meat	
Tender cuts	**Tough cuts**
● Grilling	● Stewing
● Frying	● Casseroling
● Roasting	● Boiling
● Stir-frying	● Pressure cooking
	● Braising

Buying meat

● Buy meat in a reliable, hygienic shop.
● It should be of good quality and have low fat content.
● Meat should appear slightly moist and have a good colour.
● It should not smell.
● Check the expiry date on pre-packed meat, such as minced meat.
● Choose a suitable cut of meat for the dish you intend to cook.

Reasons for cooking meat

- Bacteria are destroyed, which makes meat safer to eat.
- Cooking improves the flavour.
- Cooking improves the appearance of meat.

Preparing meat for cooking

- Defrost frozen meat thoroughly before cooking.
- Do not prepare meat beside ready-to-eat foods.
- Trim away visible fat.
- Choose a suitable cooking method for the cut of meat.
- Weigh meat to calculate the cooking time.

Effects of cooking on meat

- Bacteria are destroyed.
- Protein coagulates on the surface, which seals in the juices.
- Fat melts.
- Colour changes. Red meat turns brown.
- Meat shrinks.
- Flavours develop.

Meat products

Meat products are made from meat and other ingredients such as breadcrumbs or oatmeal that create bulk in the product. Many also contain salt and other additives. Meat products include:

- sausages
- nuggets and goujons
- black and white pudding
- burgers
- pâté
- cooked meats, such as corned beef.

Link...

Food labelling, page 143

Meat content labelling legislation means that the consumer can see how much meat is in a meat product and also how much fat is present. This allows the consumer to make more informed choices about the meat products they buy.

Meat products

Meat substitutes

Meat substitutes are foods that are used instead of meat. They are used in the diet of vegetarians as a meat substitute, or they can be added to meat during cooking to make the meat go further. Examples are:

- **Tofu:** A soya protein product.
- **Textured vegetable protein (TVP):** This is made from soya beans. It is available in cubes, minced or in convenience foods.
- **Quorn:** Made from fungi. It has a better texture than TVP and is used to make substitute meat products such as stews and pies.

Products made from meat substitutes

Advantages of meat substitutes:

- they do not contain saturated fat
- they contain fibre
- they are cheaper than meat
- they are suitable for vegetarians
- they have a longer shelf life than meat.

Link...

Vegetarian diets, page 36

Poultry

Poultry is the flesh of specially reared domestic birds, e.g. chicken, turkey, duck or goose. **Free-range poultry** is poultry that is allowed to wander freely in a natural environment.

Nutritive value

- Poultry contains around the same amount of **protein** as red meat.
- It contains **less fat** than red meat.
- It contains **less iron** than red meat.
- As there is **no carbohydrate** in poultry, it is often served with foods containing starch, such as pasta, potatoes or bread.

Buying poultry

Fresh poultry

- Buy poultry in a clean shop.
- Check the expiry date.
- It should not be discoloured.
- It should not have an unpleasant smell.
- Flesh should be firm and plump.

Frozen poultry

- Poultry should be frozen solid.
- Packaging should be sealed.
- Poultry should be below the load line in open freezers.
- It should not be discoloured.

Roast chicken is a popular poultry dish

Storing poultry

Fresh poultry

- Fresh poultry should be covered and stored in a refrigerator.
- Keep raw poultry away from ready-to-eat foods in order to avoid cross-contamination.

Frozen poultry

- Put frozen poultry into a freezer as soon as possible after buying it.
- Once thawed, do not refreeze.

Preparing and cooking poultry

Salmonella is a food-poisoning bacteria that is associated with poultry. In order to avoid food poisoning, follow these guidelines.

- Thaw frozen poultry thoroughly before cooking. A full chicken should be placed in a refrigerator for 24 hours to defrost.
- Do not prepare poultry beside ready-to-eat foods.
- Cook thoroughly. The juices should run clear (not pink) when the thickest part of the flesh is pierced or cut.

Summary

Meat

- **Food value:** Protein, fat, B group vitamins, iron, calcium and phosphorus. Meat does not contain carbohydrate.
- **Toughness:** Caused by age and activity.
- **Tenderising:** Hanging, pounding with a steak hammer, mincing, moist methods of cooking, marinating, chemical tenderisers.
- **Buying meat:** Clean shop, low fat content, good colour, odourless, check expiry date, suitable for dish.
- **Storing meat:** Separate raw meat from ready-to-eat foods, remove wrapping, refrigerate or freeze, use before expiry date.
- **Separate raw meat from ready-to-eat foods to prevent cross-contamination**.
- **Cooking methods:** Tender cuts – grilling, frying, roasting and stir-frying. Tough cuts – stewing, boiling, braising and pressure cooking.
- **Effects of cooking:** Micro-organisms are destroyed, protein coagulates, fat melts, meat shrinks, flavours develop, colour changes.
- **Meat substitutes:** Tofu, TVP and Quorn.

Poultry

- **Food value:** Protein, less fat than meat, no carbohydrate.
- **Free-range** poultry is allowed to wander freely in a natural environment.
- **Salmonella** is a type of food-poisoning bacteria that is associated with poultry.

Revision Questions

1. Explain the term 'edible offal' and give one example.
2. Give the nutritional composition of red meat. (Refer to six nutrients.)
3. Outline the importance of including red meat in the diet of teenagers.
4. (a) Outline the causes of toughness in meat.
   (b) List and explain three methods of tenderising red meat.
5. What guidelines should be followed when (a) buying, (b) storing and (c) cooking minced meat?
6. Name three meat products.
7. What is TVP?
8. Suggest two dishes in which TVP can be used.
9. Give three guidelines for: (a) buying poultry; (b) preparing poultry.
10. What are the advantages of using meat substitutes?
11. Name one food-poisoning bacteria that is associated with poultry.

Fish

Fish is a delicious, healthy food. It is low in fat and easy to cook.

Classification of fish

Fish is classified into three groups according to its food value:

- **white fish**, e.g. sole, haddock, whiting, cod, plaice
- **oily fish**, e.g. trout, sardines, salmon, mackerel, herring
- **shellfish**, e.g. lobster, mussels, prawns, crab.

White fish

Oily fish

Shellfish

Nutritive value

Fish is important in the diet because it contain the following nutrients.

- **Protein:** Fish contains almost the same amount of high biological value protein as meat. Protein is useful for growth.
- **Fat:** Unsaturated fat is found in oily fish. White fish does not contain fat. Fat provides energy. Fat in fish helps brain development.
- **Vitamins:** Fish provides vitamin B, which helps release energy from food. Oily fish provides vitamin A for healthy eyes and vitamin D for healthy bones.
- **Minerals:** Calcium is found in shellfish and in tinned fish with soft bones, e.g. tinned salmon. Calcium is needed for healthy bones. Iron is found in oily fish and shellfish. Iron is needed for healthy blood. Iodine is in all types of fish. Iodine is needed for controlling the release of energy from food.
- **Water:** Oily fish contains less water than white fish or shellfish.

Fish does not contain carbohydrate, so it is often served with foods that do contain carbohydrate.

Composition of fish						
Type	Protein	Fats	Carbohydrates	Vitamins	Minerals	Water
White fish	17–20%	0%	0	B group	Iodine	70–80%
Oily fish	17–20%	13%	0	A, D, B group	Iodine	65%
Shellfish	17–20%	2.5%	0	B group	Iodine, calcium	72%

Buying fresh fish

- Buy from a reliable source.
- The eyes should be bright and bulging.
- Gills should be bright red.
- Markings should be bright and clear.
- Skin should be moist and unbroken.
- Scales should not come off easily.
- Fish should not have an unpleasant smell.

Fish can be bought in the following forms:

- whole ungutted fish
- gutted fish
- fillets
- steaks and cutlets.

Storing fresh fish

- Place it on crushed ice and keep it in the fridge.
- Cover to prevent the flavour from entering other foods.
- Separate from ready-to-eat foods.
- Wash before use.
- Use within 24 hours.

Preparing fresh fish

1 If the skin is being left on, remove scales by scraping with a knife from tail to head and rinse.
2 Cut off the head.
3 Slit the underside of the fish and remove the gut. For flat fish, slit below the gill and remove the gut.
4 Remove the fins and tail using scissors.
5 Remove any black membrane with salt.
6 Rinse and dry using kitchen paper.

Whole ungutted fish

A fish fillet

Fish cutlets

Filleting fish

Round fish:

1 Cut along the centre of the backbone using a sharp knife.
2 Working from head to tail, remove the flesh from the bones, pressing the knife against the bones and working in short, sharp strokes.
3 Remove the other fillet in the same way.

Flat fish:

Four fillets are taken from flat fish, two from each side.

1 Use a sharp, pointed knife to cut down the backbone from head to tail.
2 Insert the knife close to the bone and remove the flesh from the bone.
3 Repeat to remove the second fillet.
4 Repeat on the underside of the fish.

Skinning fillets of fish

1 Lay the fillet on a board, skin side down.
2 Hold the tail end firmly.
3 Using a sawing movement from side to side, remove the flesh from the skin, pressing the blade close to the skin.

Cooking fish

Fish is cooked in a variety of ways.

- **Poaching:** Simmer gently in stock, milk or water. Suitable for all types of fish.
- **Steaming:** Use a steamer or steam between two plates over boiling water. Suitable for fillets or small whole fish.
- **Grilling:** Use fillets, cutlets or whole fish, such as mackerel.
- **Baking:** Fish can be stuffed or baked in a sauce.
- **Frying:** Fish can be coated to protect it from the high temperature of the oil. Batter, egg and breadcrumbs or oatmeal are used to coat it.
- **Stir-frying:** Suitable for fish with firm flesh such as monkfish.
- **Microwave cooking:** Suits all types of fish.
- **Stewing:** Fish can be stewed gently in a sauce, e.g. curry sauce.

Effects of cooking on fish

- Micro-organisms are killed.
- Protein coagulates (sets).
- Connective tissue dissolves and fish breaks apart easily.
- Vitamin B is lost.
- Fish becomes opaque.

Fish in breadcrumbs

Processed fish

Fish is processed in various ways. Smoking, canning and freezing are common methods of processing.

Buying frozen fish

- Package should be frozen solid.
- Package should be sealed.
- Should be below the load line in open freezers.
- Check the expiry date.

Storing frozen fish

- Store as soon as possible in a freezer.
- Use by the expiry date.
- Follow the manufacturer's instructions for thawing and cooking.
- White fish should be used within six months of freezing.
- Oily fish should be used within three months of freezing.

Canned fish

Summary

- **Food value:** White fish contains protein, vitamin B and iodine. Oily fish also contains these nutrients as well as polyunsaturated fat, vitamins A and D and iron. Calcium is in shellfish and the bones of tinned fish. Fish does not contain carbohydrate.
- **Fresh fish** has bright and bulging eyes, bright red gills, clear markings and does not smell.
- **Frozen fish** should be frozen solid and used by the expiry date.
- Methods of **processing fish** include smoking, canning and freezing.
- Methods of **cooking fish** include baking, grilling, stewing, poaching, frying and steaming.
- **Effects of cooking:** Micro-organisms are killed, protein coagulates (sets), connective tissue dissolves and fish breaks apart easily, vitamin B is lost, fish becomes opaque.

Revision Questions

1 Classify fish and give two examples of each class.

2 Give the nutritional composition of fish and outline its value in the diet.

3 Explain why fish should be used in the diet of teenagers.

4 List three effects of cooking on fish.

5 What guidelines should be followed when (a) buying and (b) storing fresh fish?

6 Suggest three methods of cooking fish.

7 What are the effects of cooking on fish?

8 Name three fish products.

Eggs

Eggs are one of the most nutritious foods in the diet. They are great value, easy to cook and a very useful ingredient for both savoury and sweet dishes. They can provide meals in minutes, either on their own or when added to other ingredients.

Nutritive value

- **Protein** (high biological value): For growth. Found in the white and the yolk.
- **Fat:** Saturated fat is found in the yolk. For heat, energy and insulation.
- **Carbohydrates** are not present in eggs. Eggs are usually served with starchy foods to make up for this, e.g. scrambled egg on toast.
- **Calcium, iron, sulphur and phosphorus:** For bones, teeth and healthy blood. These minerals are in the yolk.
- **Vitamin A:** For growth, healthy skin and eyes.
- **Vitamin B:** For healthy nerves and release of energy.
- Eggs lack vitamin C.
- **Vitamin D:** For healthy bones.
- **Water** makes up 74 per cent of an egg.

> A standard portion of eggs (two eggs) provides one-third of the daily protein required by an average woman and almost one-quarter of an average man's requirement of protein.

Structure of an egg

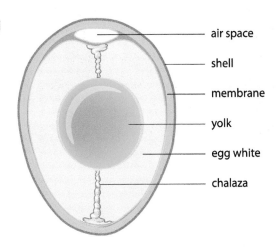

- air space
- shell
- membrane
- yolk
- egg white
- chalaza

Higher Level

Composition of an egg					
Protein	**Fat**	**Carbohydrate**	**Vitamins**	**Minerals**	**Water**
13%	12%	0%	A, B, D	Iron, calcium (1%)	74%

Uses of eggs

- **Eating on their own:** Scrambled, boiled, fried or poached.
- **Savoury dishes:** Quiche, omelette, pancakes.
- **Holding air:** Eggs trap and hold air when whisked, e.g. sponges.
- **Glazing:** Beaten egg may be brushed on pastry, bread and scones to give an attractive finish.
- **Coating:** Foods may be coated in egg and breadcrumbs before frying, e.g. fish.
- **Garnishing:** Hard boiled, sliced or sieved.
- **Thickening:** Eggs are used to thicken mixtures, e.g. custards.
- **Binding:** Eggs are used to bind foods together, e.g. fish cakes.
- **To enrich:** Eggs can add extra protein and flavour to dishes such as mashed potato or breads.
- **Emulsions:** Eggs help to hold oil and vinegar together, e.g. in mayonnaise.

Scrambled eggs

Quiche

Glazing

Garnishing

Mayonnaise

Buying eggs

The Bord Bia Egg Quality Assurance Scheme covers the production and packing of eggs.

Every **egg** is individually stamped with a code, which makes it fully traceable back to the farm where it was produced.

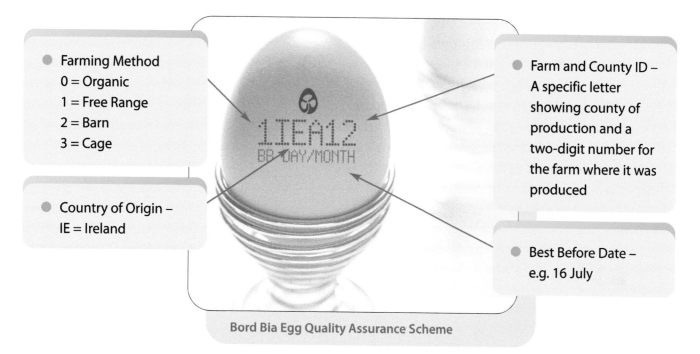

Farming Method
0 = Organic
1 = Free Range
2 = Barn
3 = Cage

Country of Origin –
IE = Ireland

Farm and County ID –
A specific letter showing county of production and a two-digit number for the farm where it was produced

Best Before Date –
e.g. 16 July

Bord Bia Egg Quality Assurance Scheme

Eggs that are produced and packed according to the quality assurance scheme will carry the Quality Assured logo on packs.

How to check whether an egg is fresh

If a fresh egg is placed in salted water, it will sink to the bottom. A stale egg will float on or near the surface. The reason for this is that as an egg ages, water evaporates through the porous shell; the amount of air inside the shell increases, making the stale egg lighter.

Look for the following information on an **egg box**.

- Number of eggs.
- EU size: Small, medium or large.
- EU egg class: Class is an indication of quality. Class A is the best quality.
- Registration number of the packing station.
- Name of the producer and/or packer.
- 'Free range' will be printed on the box if the hens have had the freedom to roam in a natural environment.

Storing eggs

- Store in a clean, cool, dry place, such as a refrigerator.
- Do not wash eggs, as this removes the natural protective layer.
- Store away from strong-smelling foods such as onions, as the smell will be absorbed through the porous shell.
- Store with the pointed end down so that they will keep fresh for longer.
- Don't use eggs after the 'best before' date.
- Don't use eggs that are damaged or dirty.
- If storing separated eggs, place the yolks in a bowl and cover with water. Store whites in an airtight container. Store both in the fridge.

Avoid cross-contamination

- Wash your hands before and after handling raw eggs.
- Throw away broken eggshells immediately – do not keep in the same tray as unbroken eggs.
- Handle raw eggs carefully, taking care not to splash onto food preparation surfaces, dishes, cloths, etc.
- Clean and disinfect surfaces after working with raw eggs.

Effects of cooking/heat on eggs

1 Bacteria are killed.

2 Protein coagulates (sets).

3 Egg white becomes cloudy and then white.

4 Eggs curdle if cooked at too high a temperature or for too long.

5 Overcooked eggs become hard and rubbery and are difficult to digest.

6 Lightly cooked eggs are more digestible.

Some tips on using eggs

- If you are going to whisk eggs, bring them to room temperature – they will whisk better than cold eggs.
- When making sauces, add hot liquids slowly to egg mixtures to prevent curdling.
- When separating egg whites from yolks, ensure that no trace of yolk gets into the white or the bowl, or the white will not whisk well.
- Also, ensure that the bowl and beater are spotlessly clean and free from any trace of fat (yolk). This ensures greater volume.
- Because of the risk of salmonella, it is recommended that the elderly, children and pregnant women avoid eating undercooked or raw eggs, e.g. in homemade cheesecakes, mousse, tiramisu, icings, ice cream or mayonnaise.

Activities

1 List four examples of egg dishes that are served with starchy foods.

2 List three foods rich in vitamin C which could be served with egg dishes.

Summary

- **Nutritive value:** Protein, fat, vitamins A, B and D, calcium, iron, sulphur, phosphorus, water.
- **Uses:** Eat on their own, savoury dishes, thickening, holding air, binding, glazing, enriching, garnishing, coating, emulsions.
- The **Bord Bia Egg Quality Assurance Scheme** covers the production and packing of eggs.
- **Effects of heat:** Bacteria are destroyed, protein coagulates, curdle if temperature is too high, overcooking makes eggs indigestible.
- **Storing:** Store in the fridge, pointed side down and away from strong-smelling foods. Do not wash. Do not use eggs that are damaged or dirty. Do not use after the 'best before' date.

Revision Questions

1 Outline the reasons why eggs should be included in the diet.

2 Name two important nutrients that are not found in eggs.

3 (a) Plan a balanced breakfast menu for a school-going child to include an egg dish.

(b) Name the food items in the menu you have planned that come from each of the following food groups: meat group, fruit/vegetable group, milk group, cereal/potato group.

4 Name the parts of the egg labelled 1, 2, 3, 4 and 5 in the diagram.

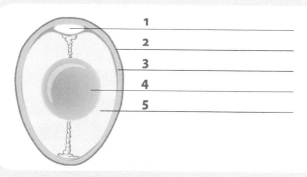

5 Name one sweet dish and one savoury dish in which eggs are used.

6 List five culinary uses of eggs and name a different dish to illustrate each use.

7 What guidelines should be followed when (a) buying and (b) storing eggs?

8 List four items of information you would expect to see on an egg box.

9 What is meant by 'free-range' eggs?

10 Name two groups of people who should avoid eating raw eggs and state why.

Milk and dairy foods

Milk is the most complete natural ready-made food there is. It provides all the essential nutrients needed by baby mammals. Milk and milk products such as cheese and butter have been part of the Irish diet for centuries. Today, cows produce most of the milk for commercial milk production, but buffaloes, sheep, goats and camels are also sources of milk.

Nutritive value

Milk contains the following nutrients.

- **Protein** (high biological value): For growth.
- **Fat:** Saturated fat is present in the cream. For heat, energy and insulation.
- **Carbohydrate** in the form of sugar: For energy.
- **Calcium and phosphorus:** For bones and teeth.
- **Vitamins A and D:** For growth, healthy skin, eyes and bones.
- **Vitamin B:** For healthy nerves and release of energy.
- **Water:** 87 per cent of milk is water.

> Milk contains important requirements for growth, such as protein, calcium and energy.
> Milk is one of the best sources of calcium.

Why is milk important in the diet?

- Dentists say that milk is one of the few drinks that is safe to drink between meals.
- Drinking milk may help to control body fat and control the risk of obesity. (Research has shown that young children who consume lots of milk and dairy produce tend to be leaner than those with lower intakes.)
- Milk is the original fast food. A glass of milk is a quick and nutritious snack for children and teenagers.
- A small carton of milk contains less fat than snacks such as a packet of crisps or a chocolate bar.

Higher Level

Average composition of milk per 100ml			
	Whole milk	**Skimmed milk**	**Fortified milk**
Energy (kcals)	64	33	47
Protein (%)	3.4	3.3	3.4
Fat (%)	3.5	0.1	1.5
Carbohydrate (%)	4.9	5.0	4.9
Vitamins	A, B, D	B	A, B, D, E
Calcium (mg)	118	120	163
Water (%)	87	90	89

Types of milk

- **Whole milk** or standard milk contains 3.5 per cent fat and is the most popular milk in Ireland.
- **Low-fat milk** (semi-skimmed) milk contains 1.5 to 1.8 per cent fat. It is also called light milk.
- **Skimmed milk** contains 0.1 to 0.3 per cent fat. It is not suitable for babies and young children, as it lacks fat-soluble vitamins.
- **Fortified milk** is low-fat or skimmed milk with extra vitamins (A and D), folic acid and calcium added. Omega 3 fatty acids may also be added.
- **Buttermilk** is the liquid remaining after butter is made. Cultured buttermilk has bacteria added to make it acid and sharp tasting. It is used for baking.
- **Evaporated milk** has some water removed before it is canned.
- **Condensed milk** is similar to evaporated milk, with added sugar. Condensed and evaporated milks are used in sweet-making and in desserts.
- **Dried milk** has all the water removed by evaporation.

Types of milk

- **Ultra heat treated (UHT) milk** is heated to 132°C for one second, then cooled and packed. It will keep for months without refrigeration. It is often called long-life milk.
- **Soya milk** is made from soya beans and is used as a dairy milk substitute.

Have a look at the chilled cabinet in your local supermarket to see the huge variety of milk products available.

Milk is pasteurised to kill harmful bacteria. The milk is heated to 72°C for 25 seconds, then cooled quickly. Whole milk is also homogenised to spread the cream evenly through the milk.

Activity

Suggest a suitable type of milk for each of the following people:
(a) a toddler; (b) an active teenager; (c) a man with high cholesterol; (d) an overweight woman; (e) an Arctic explorer.

Uses of milk in food preparation

Milk is a multi-purpose food. It has many different uses.

- As a drink on its own or added to others, e.g. tea, coffee, milkshakes, hot chocolate, latte.
- In breakfast cereals (hot and cold).
- In soups, e.g. mushroom soup.
- In desserts and puddings, e.g. bread and butter pudding, rice pudding.
- In sauces, e.g. white, parsley, cheese.
- In baked foods, e.g. bread, scones.
- In savoury dishes, e.g. quiche, pancakes.
- As milk products, e.g. yoghurt, cheese.

Milk in breakfast cereals

Effects of heat on milk

- Bacteria are killed.
- Protein coagulates (sets) and forms a skin on the milk.
- Flavour is changed.
- Loss of vitamins B and C.

Milk products

Cream

Cream is separated mechanically in the dairy. Because of its high fat content, cream has a very high energy value. It contains the fat-soluble vitamins A and D.

Milk in custard

Types of cream:

- **Standard cream:** Fat content – approximately 40 per cent. Suitable for pouring and whipping.
- **Double cream:** Fat content – 48 per cent. It is thicker than standard cream.
- **Reduced fat cream:** Fat content – 30 per cent.
- **Ultra heat treated cream (UHT):** Long-life cream which has been heat treated. It has a fat content of 18 per cent.
- **Cream from aerosols:** High air content; a long shelf life.
- **Soured cream:** Sharp flavour, thicker than standard cream. It has a culture of bacteria added and a fat content of 18 per cent.

If milk is left to stand, the fat in the milk will rise to the top. This is the cream.

A culture is a collection of bacteria or other micro-organisms which have been grown on a suitable medium.

● **Crème fraîche:** A cultured soured cream with a fat content of 30 per cent. It is thick, with a slightly sharp taste.

Types of cream

Activity

Compile a list of ways in which cream can be used in both sweet and savoury dishes.

Butter

Butter is made from cream that is churned until the fat globules come together to form a solid mass. The liquid that is left is called buttermilk. Butter is one of the few foods that can be described as completely natural.

Link...

Fats, page 6

Types of butter:

● **Sweet cream butter:** Made from fresh cream with some salt added for flavour. It contains 82 per cent fat and is the most commonly available butter in Ireland.
● **Unsalted butter:** No salt is added. Used mainly for sweet dishes.
● **Low-fat butter:** Contains about 40 per cent fat.
● **Dairy spreads:** Contain 50 per cent butter and 50 per cent vegetable oil, e.g. soya or olive.

Note: Margarine is made from vegetable oils. Both butter and margarine contain the same amount of fat and the same amount of energy, but they contain different types of fat.

Types of butter

Activity

Make a list of all the different types of butter, dairy spread and margarine that are available in your local supermarket. Compare them under the following headings: cost, ingredients, nutritive value.

Yoghurt

Yoghurt is made from milk to which a culture of bacteria is added. This thickens the milk and gives it a pleasant sharp taste. Yoghurt may be made from whole, low-fat or fully skimmed milk to which about 5 per cent skimmed milk powder is added. It is a convenient and nourishing food as it contains all the goodness of milk.

Yoghurt originated centuries ago among nomadic tribes in Turkey and south-eastern Europe.

Types of yoghurt:

- **Natural yoghurt:** Has no added flavouring.
- **Fruit yoghurt:** Has added fruit pieces or purée and sugar.
- **Set yoghurt:** Has a thicker consistency than fruit yoghurt.
- **Low-fat yoghurt:** Has no more than 1.5 per cent fat.
- **Greek yoghurt:** Similar to natural yoghurt, but has a thick, creamy texture.
- **Frozen yoghurt:** A frozen dessert containing yoghurt. It is lower in fat and more sharp-tasting than ice cream.
- **Yoghurt drink:** Has added milk and fruit flavouring.

Bio-yoghurt contains bifidobacteria and acidophilus bacteria, which are thought to help the digestive system.

Types of yoghurt

Uses of yoghurt:

- Straight from the carton as a **snack** or in **smoothies**.
- Natural yoghurt may be used in **dips, sauces, salad dressings, savoury dishes, marinades, cakes** and **desserts**.
- Other types may also be used as a **topping** for cereals and fruit.

Activity

Carry out a survey to find out the most popular flavour of yoghurt among your classmates. Present your results as a bar chart.

Cheese

Cheese-making is a natural and ancient method of preserving milk. It is believed that cheese-making originated in the Middle East 7,000 years ago. Cheese was known as a 'summer food' under Brehon Law in ancient Ireland. Today, cheese is available in a large variety of flavours, textures and shapes. The process of cheese-making, and the quality and type of milk used, all influence the flavour of the end product.

Nutritive value:

- **Protein** (high biological value): For growth. It is an excellent substitute for other animal foods such as meat, fish or poultry.
- **Fat** (saturated): For heat, energy and insulation. As it contains a high proportion of **saturated fat**, it should be eaten in moderation by those on low-fat diets or those with high cholesterol.
- There is no **carbohydrate** in cheese, so it should be served with starchy foods such as bread, crackers, pasta or potatoes.
- **Calcium and phosphorus:** For bones and teeth.
- **Vitamins A and D:** For growth, healthy skin, eyes and bones.
- **Vitamin B:** For healthy nerves and release of energy.
- Low **water** content.

Higher Level

Composition of cheese (%)						
	Fat	**Protein**	**Carbohydrate**	**Vitamins**	**Minerals**	**Water**
Cheddar	34.5	25.5	0	1.0	4.0	35.0
Cottage	4.0	13.6	1.4	1.2	1.0	78.8

Cheese production:

Rennet is an extract from the stomach lining of young animals which contains the enzyme rennin. Modern cheese-making techniques use rennet to separate the milk into curds and whey.

Fresh milk is **pasteurised** to destroy harmful bacteria.

▼

Bacteria are added to sour the milk.

▼

Rennet is added to clot the milk.

▼

The milk now consists of **curd**, a solid part, and **whey**, a watery substance.

▼

The whey is removed and the curd is cut into pieces and **salted**.

▼

The cheese is **pressed** into moulds – lightly for soft cheeses and firmly for hard cheeses.

▼

Blocks of cheese are stored and allowed to **ripen** for between three and 12 months.

Types of cheese:

- **Hard:** Cheddar, Emmenthal, Parmesan.
- **Semi-soft:** Edam, Port Salut, Blarney.
- **Soft:** Brie, mozzarella, cottage.
- **Processed:** Cheese slices, e.g. Easi-singles, cheese spread, cheese strings.
- **Blue-veined:** Irish blue, Stilton, Gorgonzola. Cheeses are injected with a harmless blue mould.
- **Farmhouse:** Gubbeen, Killorglin, Coolea. Locally produced cheeses, often made from unpasteurised milk.

Types of cheese

Uses of cheese:

Cheese is an extremely useful and versatile food. It is delicious when eaten in its natural state or when included in recipes, for example:

- savoury dishes, e.g. pizza, quiche, lasagne, macaroni cheese, baked potatoes
- biscuits, bread and scones
- desserts, e.g. cheesecake, tiramisu
- as a garnish (sprinkled over pasta)

'Au gratin' describes food covered with grated cheese or breadcrumbs and browned in the oven or under the grill.

- in au gratin dishes
- in sauces, e.g. cheese sauce
- as a snack, with crackers or bread, in sandwiches
- salads and dressings, e.g. blue cheese dressing
- savoury dips and fondues
- cheeseboards as an alternative to dessert.

Cheese in pasta salad

Cheese as a topping for baked potato

Effects of heat/cooking on cheese:

- Protein coagulates (becomes solid) and shrinks.
- Fat melts.
- Overcooking causes cheese to become stringy and indigestible. (Adding mustard helps to make cheese more digestible.)

Storage of dairy products

- Check the use by and best before dates before buying any dairy products.
- Store **covered** in a **cool, clean** place, such as a refrigerator.
- Keep milk out of sunlight, which destroys vitamin B and sours it.
- Pour milk into a clean jug when required.
- Wrap cheese in greaseproof paper and cover with tinfoil.
- Remove cheese from the fridge about one hour before serving, as the flavour of cheese is better when served at room temperature.

Activity

Look up some recipe books and suggest a suitable cheese for each of these dishes: (a) lemon cheesecake; (b) Greek salad; (c) cheese omelette; (d) tiramisu; (e) pizza; (f) cheese pastry; (g) cheese soufflé; (h) topping for pasta carbonara.

Summary

Milk:

- **Nutritive value:** Protein, fat, carbohydrate, calcium, phosphorus, vitamins A, B and D, water.
- **Types:** Whole, low fat, skimmed, fortified, buttermilk, evaporated, condensed, dried, UHT, soya.
- **Uses:** Drinking, baking, cereals, sauces, desserts, savoury dishes, soups, milk products.
- **Effects of heat:** Bacteria killed, protein coagulates, flavour changes, loss of vitamins B and C.

Cream:

- **Types:** Standard, double, UHT, aerosols, soured, crème fraîche.

Butter:

- **Types:** Sweet cream, unsalted, low fat, dairy spreads.

Yoghurt:

- **Types:** Natural, fruit, set, low fat, Greek, drinking.
- **Uses:** Snack, dips, sauces, salad dressings, savoury dishes, marinades, cakes, desserts, toppings.

Cheese:

- **Nutritive value:** Protein, fat, vitamins A, B and D, calcium, phosphorus.
- **Types:** Hard, semi-soft, soft, processed, blue-veined, farmhouse.
- **Uses:** savoury dishes, biscuits, desserts, garnish, sauces, snack, salads and dressings, dips, fondue, cheeseboard.
- **Effects of heat:** Fat melts, protein coagulates, overcooking causes indigestibility.
- **Manufacture:** Milk pasteurised, bacteria added, rennet added, whey removed and curd salted, pressed and ripened.

- **Storage of dairy products:** Check expiry dates; keep cool, clean and covered; keep milk out of the sun; wrap cheese in greaseproof paper; serve at room temperature.

Revision Questions

1 Milk is rich in calcium and is an important food that should be included in a person's daily diet. Give two reasons why calcium is important in the diet.

2 Name two other nutrients that can be found in milk and give the functions of each.

3 Suggest two ways of encouraging a friend who dislikes the taste of milk to include it in his/her diet.

4 Give two reasons why milk is generally heat treated.

5 Name one nutrient that is *not* present in milk.

6 Give two effects of heat on milk.

7 Name one type of milk that matches each of the following descriptions:

Description	Type of milk
Contains 0.1 to 0.3% fat	
Has all water removed	
Extra vitamins and minerals added	
A dairy milk substitute	

8 The following information is displayed on the label of a carton of fortified milk.

Nutritional information Typical values per 100ml	Fortified milk	Whole milk
Energy	205kJ/49kcal	269kJ/64kcal
Protein	3.4g	3.3g
Fat	1.5g	3.5g
Carbohydrate	5.2g	4.9g
Calcium	166mg	118mg
Vitamin A	120µg	52µg
Vitamin B	0.24mg	0.17mg
Folic Acid	70µg	6µg
Vitamin D	1µg	0.03µg
Vitamin E	1.5mg	0.09mg

Pasteurised and Homogenised

(a) Using the information given in the table above, evaluate the nutritive value of fortified milk.

(b) State which type of milk would be most suitable for (i) an energetic child and (ii) a pregnant woman. Give one reason for your choice in each case.

(c) Suggest three ways to include more dairy products in the diet.

(d) Explain the terms 'fortified' and 'homogenised'.

Revision Questions

9 Name four types of milk available in supermarkets and give a different use for each type.

10 Name four milk products.

11 How should milk be stored?

12 Give three reasons for including cheese in the diet of an energetic child.

13 Name the main nutrient that is not present in cheese.

14 List two foods you could serve with cheese in order to present a balanced meal.

15 Suggest a way of making Cheddar cheese more digestible.

16 Give three guidelines for storing cheese.

17

Cheese	Protein	Fat	Carbohydrate	Minerals	Vitamins	Water
Cheddar	27%	33%	0%	4% calcium	A + B	34%
Cottage	15%	4%	4%	1% calcium	A + B	77%

(a) Using the nutritional information in the table, state which type of cheese would be most suitable for: (i) an adult on a low-cholesterol diet; (ii) an energetic teenager. Give two reasons for your choice in each case.

(b) Using one of the cheeses named in the table, design a balanced snack suitable for a packed lunch.

(c) Suggest three other ways of encouraging teenagers to eat more cheese.

18 (a) Classify cheese and give one example for each class.

(b) Outline the stages involved in the manufacture of cheese.

(c) Give four uses of cheese in food preparation.

(d) Give two guidelines that should be followed when storing cheese.

(e) Explain the term 'au gratin'.

Fruit and vegetables should be eaten every day

Fruit and vegetables

Fruit and vegetables provide minerals, vitamins, energy and fibre. They should be eaten every day. They are at their best when in season.

Classification of fruits

Citrus Fruits	Berries/ Soft Fruit	Stone Fruits	Hard Fruits	Dried Fruits	Other
Oranges	Raspberries	Plums	Apples	Raisins	Grapes
Lemons	Blackberries	Apricots	Pears	Sultanas	Pineapples
Grapefruit	Strawberries	Peaches		Currants	Bananas
Limes	Gooseberries	Nectarines		Prunes	Melons
Satsumas	Blackcurrants	Cherries		Dates	Kiwis
Tangerines	Redcurrants	Avocados			Star fruit
	Olives				

Citrus fruits

Berries/soft fruits

Stone fruits

Hard fruit

Dried fruits

Pineapple

Nutritive value

- **Protein:** Very few fruits contain protein.
- **Fat:** Fruit does not contain fat. Exceptions are olives and avocados.
- **Carbohydrate:** Fruit contains **sugar** for energy. **Fibre** is found in fruit, particularly in the skin. Fibre prevents constipation.
- **Vitamins: Vitamin C** for healthy skin is found in fresh fruit, particularly in oranges and blackcurrants. Orange, red, yellow and green fruits are good sources of **vitamin A** for healthy eyes.
- **Minerals:** Some fruit, especially dried fruit, contains **calcium** for healthy bones and **iron** for healthy blood.
- **Water:** Fruit contains up to 95 per cent water.

Seasonal fruit and vegetables

At various times during the year, certain fruit and vegetables are at their best, i.e. they are **in season**. Fruits that are in season are the best quality and are plentiful and cheap.

Uses of fruit in the diet

1 **Fresh** as a snack.
2 **Drinks:** In juices and smoothies.
3 **Breakfast:** Fresh or cooked.
4 **Packed lunches:** Drinks, yoghurts, fresh, dried.
5 **Starters:** Crudités.
6 **Sauces:** Raspberry, apricot, apple.
7 **Salads and dressings:** Lemon, orange.
8 **Hot desserts:** Crumbles, tarts, stewed, baked and poached fruits.
9 **Cold desserts:** Fresh fruit flans, fruit salads.
10 **Baking:** Scones, muffins.
11 **Preserves:** Chutneys, jams, etc.

Preparing fruit

Wash in cold water to remove chemicals. Avoid peeling if possible to retain the fibre content. Prepare as close as possible to cooking or serving to avoid loss of nutrients.

● **Citrus fruits:** Wash and scrub to remove chemicals and wax if the rind is to be grated. Peel thickly to remove pith. Separate segments or slice.
● **Berry fruits:** Remove damaged fruit. Top and tail if necessary. Wash gently if necessary.
● **Stone fruits:** Peel if necessary. Remove stones.
● **Hard fruits:** Peel if necessary. Remove core. Cut to suit the chosen dish. Toss in lemon juice to avoid browning.

Effects of processing/cooking on fruit

● It becomes soft.
● Vitamin C is reduced (up to 25%).
● Micro-organisms are destroyed.
● The fibre becomes soft, which makes fruit more digestible.
● Vitamin C and minerals dissolve into the cooking or canning liquid.

Comparison of fresh and processed fruit

Fruit	Protein	Fat	Carbohydrate	Minerals	Vitamins	Water
Fresh	Trace	0%	5–20%	Calcium, iron	A, C	80–90%
Tinned	Trace	0%	20–30%	Calcium, iron reduced	A, C	70–80%
Dried	Trace	0%	50–60%	Calcium, iron increased	A	15–25%

Fresh

Tinned

Dried

Classification of vegetables

Greens	Roots	Pulses	Fruits
• Broccoli	• Carrot	• Peas	• Tomato
• Spinach	• Parsnip	• Beans	• Cucumber
• Cabbage	• Potato	• Lentils	• Pepper
• Cauliflower	• Onion		• Courgette
• Brussels sprouts	• Turnip		• Aubergine
	• Beetroot		• Pumpkin

Greens

Roots

Pulses

Fruits

Composition of vegetables						
Category	**Protein**	**Fat**	**Carbohydrate**	**Vitamins**	**Minerals**	**Water**
Greens	Trace	0%	2%	A, C	Calcium, iron	90–95%
Roots	Trace	0%	5–20%	A, C	Calcium, iron	75–90%
Pulses	2–7%	Trace	4–10%	A, C	Calcium, iron	75–90%
Fruits	Trace	0%	5–20%	A, C	Calcium, iron	80–90%

Nutritive value

- **Protein** (low biological value) is found in peas, beans and lentils, i.e. pulse vegetables. These vegetables are very important in the diet of a vegan (strict vegetarian) because protein is useful for growth.
- Vegetables do not contain fat, although pulses contain a small amount.
- **Carbohydrate: Sugar** is found in beetroot, carrots, parsnips and onions. **Starch** is in pulses and root vegetables, especially potatoes. Sugar and starch provide energy.
- **Fibre** is in all vegetables, especially in the skin. Fibre prevents constipation.
- **Minerals: Calcium** is found in green leafy vegetables and some root and pulse vegetables. Calcium is needed for healthy bones. **Iron** is found in greens and root vegetables. Iron is needed for healthy blood. **Trace** elements are found in pulse vegetables.
- **Vitamins: Vitamin C,** for healthy skin, is found in fresh young vegetables, especially peppers. **Vitamin A** (carotene), for healthy eyes, is found in carrots and green leafy vegetables. **Vitamin B group** is found in pulses. The B group vitamins release energy from food.
- **Water:** Vegetables contain a lot of water (75–95%).

Uses of vegetables in the diet

It is important that you eat **five** portions of fruit and/or vegetables every day.

- Include in breakfast dishes.
- Lunch and main meal.
- Juices.
- Salads and soups.
- Sandwiches.
- Snacks, e.g. carrot sticks.
- Pasta dishes.
- Stews and casseroles.
- Pizza toppings.
- Vegetable-based main courses, e.g. 'veggie' burgers.

Vegetable juice

Buying fresh fruit and vegetables

- Buy fruit and vegetables in season when they are cheap and of the best quality.
- Look for medium-sized fruit and vegetables because large ones lack flavour.
- Choose fresh, brightly coloured fruit and vegetables.
- Avoid bruised fruit and vegetables.
- Buy fruit and vegetables in usable quantities, as they do not keep for long.
- Avoid buying pre-packed fruit and vegetables, as packaging hides bruising and mould.

Organic produce

Organically grown fruit and vegetables are grown without the use of artificial fertilisers or chemicals. Food produced organically tends to be more expensive.

EU regulations and grading

EU regulations state that vegetables and fruit sold must be:

- clean, sound and free from chemicals
- graded with products of similar size
- marked clearly with country of origin, variety and class.

Classes

Class extra: Best quality.
Class I: Good quality.
Class II: Marketable quality, but may have some defects.
Class III: Marketable but inferior.

Storing fruit and vegetables

- Remove from packaging.
- Store root vegetables on a rack in a cool, dark, dry, well-ventilated place.
- Greens and fruits (except bananas) can be stored in the fridge. Use fresh vegetables as soon as possible after purchase.
- Dried pulses should be stored in airtight jars.

Preparing vegetables

In order to retain nutrients when preparing fruits and vegetables:

- prepare just before cooking
- eat vegetables raw and unpeeled if possible
- peel thinly to retain the fibre content
- use a sharp knife to avoid damage to the vegetables
- do not steep vegetables.

Category	Preparation
Greens	<ul><li>Remove wilted leaves</li><li>Separate the leaves and wash each leaf under cold running water</li><li>Chop if necessary using a sharp knife</li><li>Do not steep</li></ul>
Roots	<ul><li>Scrub</li><li>Remove ends. Peel if necessary</li><li>Use whole, cut into wedges, sliced or diced</li><li>Do not steep</li></ul>
Pulses	<ul><li>*Fresh*: Remove from pods. Wash in cold water</li><li>*Dried*: Soak overnight</li></ul>
Fruits	<ul><li>Wash in cold water</li><li>Peel only if necessary</li><li>Chop or slice</li></ul>

Cooking vegetables

Cooking method	Suitable vegetables
Boiling	Cabbage, Brussels sprouts, pulse vegetables
Steaming	All types
Microwave cooking	All types
Grilling	Tomatoes, peppers
Roasting	Root vegetables, peppers
Cooking in stews and casseroles	Root vegetables
Stir-frying	Courgettes, broccoli, onions, sweetcorn, peppers, carrots
Frying	Onions, tomatoes
Baking	Potatoes, peppers, tomatoes, parsnips
Stewing	Potatoes, carrots, parsnips, turnips, peppers

Steaming

Roasting

Cooking in stews

Stir-frying

Guidelines on cooking vegetables

- Cook for the shortest possible time. The texture should be **al dente**. This means that they should be slightly firm.
- Use cooking liquids in sauces to retain the vitamin and mineral content.
- Cover with a lid and use the minimum amount of water to prevent loss of vitamins and minerals.
- Do not reheat, as vitamins are destroyed.
- Never use bread soda when cooking vegetables.

Effects of cooking on vegetables

- Vitamins and minerals dissolve into the cooking liquid.
- Vitamin C is destroyed.
- Fibre becomes soft.
- Starch becomes more digestible, e.g. potatoes.
- Some colour, flavour and texture is lost.

Processed fruit and vegetables

Frozen fruit and vegetables keep their nutritive value

Link...
Chapter 9 Food Processing

Salads

Salads are refreshing and can be very nutritious depending on the ingredients. Foods from all of the food groups can be used to create a great variety of salads.

A nutritious salad

Guidelines for preparing salads:

- Handle salad leaves very gently because they bruise when roughly handled.
- Use a knife to slice open a head of lettuce from its base. (Twisting lettuce from the stem causes bruising.)
- Dry salad leaves thoroughly in a salad spinner or between clean tea towels. (Otherwise the dressing is watered down and loses flavour.)
- Include chopped herbs to add great flavour.
- Rinse off the liquid from canned pulse vegetables.
- Add toasted nuts and seeds for flavour and to increase nutritional value. (To toast, toss in a hot frying pan without oil.)
- Avoid overhandling the ingredients.
- Avoid a very wide mixture of ingredients. A few main ingredients are usually enough.
- Add salad dressing at the last minute, as it makes leaves go limp.

Summary

- **Classification of fruits:** Citrus, berries/soft, stone, hard, dried and others.
- **Nutritional value:** Carbohydrate in the form of sugar and fibre, vitamin C, vitamin A, calcium, iron, water.
- **In season:** Plentiful and excellent flavour.
- **Uses of fruit:** Snack, juices and smoothies, breakfast, packed lunches, starters, sauces, salads, desserts, baking, preserves.
- **Effects of processing:** Soft, vitamin C reduced, vitamins and minerals dissolve into the cooking liquid, micro-organisms destroyed, fibre becomes soft.
- **Classification of vegetables:** Greens, roots, pulses and fruits.
- **Nutritional value:** Protein in pulse vegetables, carbohydrate in the form of starch and fibre, calcium and iron, vitamins C, B and A (carotene), water.
- **Buying:** Buy in season, buy medium-sized, choose fresh produce, avoid bruised produce, buy in usable quantities, avoid pre-packed produce.
- **Organic:** Grown without the use of artificial fertilisers or chemicals.
- **Storing:** Remove packaging, store root vegetables on a rack, greens and fruits in a refrigerator and dried pulses in airtight jars.

Summary

- **Cooking vegetables:** Cook for the shortest possible time. They should have an **al dente** texture. Use cooking liquids in sauces; cover the saucepan and use the minimum amount of water; do not reheat; do not use bread soda.

- **Cooking methods:** Boiling, baking, steaming, microwaving, grilling, roasting, stir-frying, frying and stewing.

- **To retain nutrients in fruit and vegetables:** Prepare just before cooking, eat raw, peel thinly, use a sharp knife, do not steep.

- **Effects of cooking:** Vitamins and minerals dissolve into the cooking liquid, vitamin C is destroyed, fibre becomes soft, some colour, flavour and texture are lost.

- **Effects of processing:** Frozen: nutritive value retained. Canning in syrup: higher sugar content. Canning in oil: higher fat content. Dried: vitamins (B group and C) are lost.

Revision Questions

Fruit

1 Give two examples of fruit under each of the following headings: (a) citrus fruit; (b) hard fruit; (c) berries; (d) stone fruit.

2 Describe one advantage of buying fruit in season.

3 List two advantages of using fruit in the diet.

4 Suggest two ways of reducing the loss of nutrients when preparing fruit.

5 List three effects of processing on fruit.

6 Suggest two different uses for each of the following: (a) fresh fruit; (b) tinned fruit; (c) dried fruit.

Vegetables

1 Classify vegetables and name two vegetables from each class.

2 Which class of vegetable is most useful in a vegan diet? Explain why.

3 Give five reasons why vegetables should be included in the daily diet.

4 How can teenagers include more vegetables in their daily diet?

5 What steps should be taken when storing vegetables in order to retain the maximum food value?

6 Suggest a different vegetable for each of the following methods of cooking: (a) baking; (b) roasting; (c) stir-frying; (d) boiling.

7 Explain the term 'al dente'.

8 List two effects of cooking on vegetables. Suggest two ways of reducing the loss of nutrients when preparing vegetables.

9 Explain the term 'organically grown' vegetables.

Cereals and baking

Cereals are the seeds or grains of edible grass plants. They include **wheat, rice, rye, oats, barley** and **maize (corn)**. Cereals are **staple foods** in many parts of the world, as they are easily grown and widely eaten. They are also cheap and easy to cook.

Nutritive value

- **Protein** (low biological value): For growth.
- **Fat:** A small amount of unsaturated fat is present. For heat, energy and insulation.
- **Carbohydrate** is the main nutrient found in cereals. It is present in the form of **starch** and **fibre** (in unprocessed cereals). For heat, energy and digestion.
- **Vitamin B group** is present in unprocessed cereals. For healthy nerves and release of energy.
- **Iron, calcium** and **phosphorus** are present. For healthy blood, bones and teeth.
- **Water** content is low.

Range of cereal products

Higher Level

Average composition of cereals					
Protein	Fat	Carbohydrate	Vitamins	Minerals	Water
7–15%	2–7%	70–77%	B group (0.5%)	Calcium and iron (1%)	12%

Structure of a cereal grain

Here is what a grain of wheat looks like if it is cut in half and examined under a microscope.

The **bran** layer is the outer layer and provides fibre, iron and vitamin B. It is usually removed during the processing of cereals.

The **endosperm** (larger inner part) is mainly composed of starch and a protein called gluten. People with coeliac disease cannot absorb gluten.

The **germ** (small part in the centre) contains protein, fat and vitamin B and is the most nutritious part of the grain.

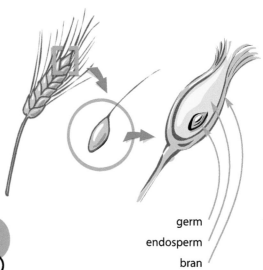

germ
endosperm
bran

Link...

Coeliac disease, page 37

Wholegrain cereal products

A refined cereal product

Cereals are usually processed in some way before we eat them. This makes them easier to chew and digest. The cereal grain is split up or parts of the grain (usually the bran and the germ) are removed, leaving only the endosperm.

Wholegrain cereal products contain all or most of the cereal grain. Examples are wholemeal flour, wholemeal bread, brown rice, rolled oats.

Refined cereal products are mainly composed of endosperm, e.g. white flour, white bread, cornflour, white rice.

Fortified cereal products have some of the vitamins and minerals that were removed during processing added back into the product, **or** they may have extra nutrients added, e.g. white flour and breakfast cereals.

Wheat cereal

Cereal products

Cereals are an extremely important source of food and can be used to make many different products.

Wheat

White and wholemeal flour, bread, pasta, biscuits, cakes, noodles, semolina, Weetabix and other breakfast cereals, couscous.

Rice

Brown and white rice, rice flour, Rice Krispies, ground rice, rice paper.

Wheat

Rice

Rice cakes

Maize

Popcorn, sweetcorn, cornflakes and other breakfast cereals, tortilla chips, tacos, corn on the cob, corn oil.

Barley

Beer, whiskey, pearl barley.

Rye

Rye flour, rye bread, rye whiskey, crispbread, e.g. Ryvita.

Oats

Porridge, muesli, rolled oats, oatmeal, Ready Brek and other breakfast cereals.

Pasta

Pasta is made from durum wheat that is finely ground down into semolina and then mixed with water to form a dough. Different colours are achieved by adding egg, spinach or tomatoes or by using wholemeal semolina. The dough is kneaded, pressed through a mould, cut and dried.

There are hundreds of pasta shapes, each of which allows sauce to cling in different ways. Thin and long pasta suits oily, more liquid sauces, while wider pasta and more complicated shapes (twisted, hollow or curved) are better for thicker, chunkier sauces.

Fresh, dried and tinned pasta, e.g. spaghetti in tomato sauce, are available.

Corn on the cob

Popcorn

Soup with pearl barley

Rye breads

Oats

Rolled oats

Different types of pasta

Rice

Rice was first discovered in the Far East and has been grown for nearly 5,000 years. As a cereal grain, it is the most important staple food for a large part of the world's population, especially in Asia, the Middle East, Latin America and the West Indies. It is also widely grown in Italy and the USA.

The main types of rice are:

- **Long-grain rice:** Used in savoury dishes and as an accompaniment to stews and curries. Also known as Patna or Carolina rice. Basmati (Indian) and jasmine (Thai) are types of long-grain rice.
- **Medium-grain or risotto rice:** Used in risottos and dishes where the rice grains are moulded together, e.g. arborio and carnaroli (Italian).
- **Short-grain rice:** Used for rice puddings and other sweet rice dishes.
- **Brown rice:** A long-grain rice which contains some of the bran layer. Has a nutty flavour and a chewy texture. Takes longer to cook than white rice.
- **Pre-cooked rice:** Has been cooked fully and then dehydrated. It cooks quickly, e.g. boil-in-the-bag rice and instant rice. Frozen and microwaveable rice are also available.

Food Safety Alert!

If storing cooked rice, cool rapidly and store at below 4°C. If reheating, ensure rice is piping hot, to reduce the risk of food poisoning.

Effects of cooking on cereals

- Starch becomes more digestible.
- Starch grains swell and burst, e.g. popcorn.
- The grains absorb liquid, e.g. rice absorbs water.

Link...

Methods of cooking rice, page 160

Flour

Flour is made by grinding up cereals such as wheat, rice, oats, rye and maize. In Ireland, most flour is made from wheat.

Gluten is a protein found in wheat. When the flour is moistened, the gluten becomes elastic and allows the dough to become very stretchy so that it rises well.

Types of flour

Type	Description	Uses
Wholemeal flour	● Contains the whole wheat grain, with nothing added or taken away	● Wholemeal bread, scones, rolls and pastry
Brown flour	● Some of the bran and germ are removed during milling	● Brown bread and rolls, and pastry
White flour	● All of the bran and germ are removed. It is made up of starchy endosperm only	● White bread and rolls, cakes, pastry, biscuits and for thickening soups and sauces
Self-raising flour	● Brown or white flour with a raising agent, e.g. baking powder, added	● Uses as for white flour, with the exception of pastry and thickening
Strong flour	● Flour that is milled from spring wheat, which has a high gluten content	● Making yeast bread and some pastries
Gluten-free flour	● The gluten is removed	● Used to make bread, biscuits, etc. for coeliacs

Types of flour

Can you name some of these breads and their countries of origin?

Bread

Bread is one of the world's oldest staple foods. It has been eaten for thousands of years, since people learned to grind grains between two stones to make flour. Nowadays there is huge variety in the types of bread available.

Baking

Home baking guidelines

1 Before starting to mix any ingredients, prepare tins (see page 131), arrange oven shelves and preheat oven to the correct temperature at least 15 minutes before you start.
2 Ensure all ingredients are fresh (check expiry dates).
3 Weigh and measure ingredients accurately according to the recipe.
4 Follow the recipe carefully, step by step.
5 Take care when adding liquid to dry ingredients to ensure the correct texture or consistency.
6 Knead lightly and avoid overhandling pastry, bread and scone dough.
7 Time carefully and avoid opening the oven door unnecessarily.
8 Check to see if cake is cooked using the appropriate method (see page 128).
9 Cool on a wire tray.

Common faults in cake making

Fault	Cause
Cake sinks	Too much raising agent
	Too much sugar
	Undercooked
	Disturbed during cooking
Close, heavy texture	Too much liquid in the mixture
	Too little raising agent
	Mixture over-beaten
Peaked, cracked top	Oven too hot
	Tin too small
	Mixture too stiff or too wet
	Mixture over-beaten
Cake very dry	Overcooked
	Too little liquid
	Too much raising agent

How to test whether a cake is cooked

1 Bread and scones: Sound hollow when tapped underneath.

2 Cakes (Madeira, all-in-one and fruit cakes): Warmed metal skewer comes out clean from cake, with no uncooked mixture clinging to it.

3 Sponges (whisked): Shrinks in from the sides of the tin and springs back when pressed lightly with the fingers.

Raising agents

A **raising agent** is a substance used to make a gas in a dough or batter. This causes the dough to rise and become light.

Sponge cake

When the gas (O_2 or CO_2) has been produced in the dough, it is then put into the oven.	The heat of the oven causes the gas bubbles to get bigger.	The bubbles push upwards and make the dough rise.	The heat of the oven forms a crust on top, which prevents any more rising.

There are four types of raising agent:

1 **Air**
2 **Baking powder**
3 Bread soda
4 Yeast.

1 **Air** is a natural raising agent. It is used in sponges, meringues, pastry and batters. Air may be brought into the mixture by:

a) sieving the flour
b) raising your hands high over the bowl when rubbing in fat
c) whisking ingredients
d) creaming ingredients.

2 **Baking powder** and 3 **bread soda** are **chemical raising agents.** They depend on a chemical reaction to make the gas.

A tin of **baking powder** contains a mixture of an acid and an alkali. These become active when liquids such as milk, water or eggs are added.

acid + alkali + liquid = CO_2
baking powder + milk/water/eggs = CO_2

Baking powder is used in all types of cakes, buns and biscuits.

Bread soda is an alkali. It must be mixed with an acid and a liquid to make CO_2. Buttermilk is both acid and liquid.

Vinegar or lemon juice can be added to fresh milk if buttermilk is not available. Cream of tartar (a white powder) is another acid which may be used.

alkali + acid + liquid = CO_2
bread soda + buttermilk = CO_2

Bread soda is used in soda bread and scones, gingerbread and some cakes.

Baking powder

Buttermilk and bread soda

4 **Yeast** is a **biological** raising agent that makes CO_2 in dough. Yeast is used in commercially baked bread and homemade yeast breads, buns and some pastries, e.g. Danish pastries.

Ensure you use the correct amount of raising agent. Too little will produce a heavy, flat product, while using too much raising agent will cause the mixture to rise so fast that it can't support itself, and it will then collapse.

Make sure you set the oven to the correct oven temperature for the recipe, as this can affect how the raising agent works.

Link...
Yeast, page 40

Methods of making bread and cakes

- **The rubbing-in method:** The fat is rubbed into the flour. The other dry ingredients are then added, followed by the liquid. **Uses:** Plain cakes and scones, pastry.
- **The creaming method:** The fat and sugar are creamed together, the eggs are beaten in and the flour is then folded into the mixture. **Uses:** Queen cakes, Madeira cakes and rich fruit cakes.
- **The whisking method:** The eggs and sugar are whisked together until thick and creamy. The flour is then folded in very lightly. **Uses:** Sponge cakes, flans, Swiss rolls.
- **The all-in-one method:** All the ingredients are placed in a bowl and beaten together. Soft tub margarine or block margarine/butter at room temperature should be used. **Uses:** All-in-one Madeira, chocolate or coffee cakes.
- **The melting method:** The ingredients that melt, e.g. fat, sugar, treacle, syrup, are heated and melted before being added to the dry ingredients. **Uses:** Gingerbread and boiled fruit cakes.

Scones

Madeira cake

Swiss roll

Chocolate cake

Gingerbread

Commercial cake mixes

Cake mixes consist of a mixture of flour, raising agent, fat, sugar and other additives. Dried milk or egg may also be included. They are made up by adding liquid ingredients such as milk, water or eggs. Follow the instructions on the packet.

Cake mixes

Advantages:

- Labour saving.
- Quick and easy.
- Useful in emergencies.
- Give confidence to beginners.

Disadvantages:

- High in sugar and salt, low in fibre.
- Photos on package may be misleading.
- Expensive.
- May contain additives.

Preparing cake tins

- **Bread and scone tins:** Sprinkle lightly with flour.
- **Sponge tins:** Grease with melted fat or oil, then sprinkle lightly with equal amounts of flour and caster sugar.
- **Swiss roll tins:** Cut a piece of greaseproof paper about 5cm larger than the tin all around. Place the tin on it and outline the shape. At each corner, make a cut from the angle of the paper as far as the corner of the tin. Grease both the paper and the tin. Fit paper into the tin, overlapping at the corners.

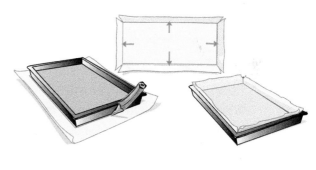

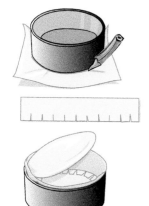

- **Large cakes:** Grease the tin and line the bottom and sides with a layer of greaseproof paper. Grease the paper to prevent cracking.
- **Silicone bakeware:** Oil lightly. Does not need to be paper lined.

Silicone bakeware

Pastry

Pastry is a mixture of flour, fat and water which is made into a dough, then kneaded, shaped and baked. It may be made richer by adding other ingredients, such as sugar, eggs or extra fat. Pastry may be used in sweet and savoury dishes.

Sweet pastries

Types of pastry	
Type	**Uses**
Shortcrust	● Sweet and savoury tarts, pies, flans, sausage rolls
Rich shortcrust	● Sweet tarts, flans, pies
Cheese pastry	● Cheese straws, biscuits, quiches, savoury flans
Wholemeal pastry	● Savoury flans, quiches, pies, tarts
Flaky pastry, rough puff pastry, puff pastry	● Pies, tarts, sausage rolls, mille feuille, vol-au-vents, mince pies
Choux pastry	● Profiteroles, éclairs
Filo pastry	● Spring rolls, savoury baskets, baklava (a Greek dessert)

When a recipe asks for 200g shortcrust pastry, this means pastry made with 200g flour and 100g margarine, etc.

To 'bake blind' means to bake a pastry case without any filling.

Guidelines for making pastry

1 Weigh ingredients accurately and use the correct proportions.
2 Keep the ingredients and utensils as cool as possible.
3 Add the water carefully. Do not allow pastry to become sticky.
4 Mix with a knife and knead lightly on a floured board.
5 Avoid overhandling.
6 Roll pastry lightly and as little as possible.
7 Avoid stretching pastry, as it will shrink during baking.
8 Allow pastry to relax in a refrigerator before baking.
9 Bake in a hot oven so that the starch grains in the flour burst and absorb the fat.

Activities

1 Find out what types of bread are associated with different countries.

2 Find recipes in a cookery book for each of the methods of cake-making listed on page 130.

3 Collect some pasta recipes from cookery books. List the different ways in which pasta can be used.

Summary

- **Types of cereal:** Wheat, barley, rice, oats, maize, rye.
- **Nutritive value of cereals:** Low biological value protein, a little fat, starch and fibre, vitamin B, iron, calcium and phosphorus, low water content.
- **Cereals** may be wholegrain, refined or fortified.
- **Pasta** is made from durum wheat, which is ground down to semolina, then made into a paste, cut into shapes and dried.
- **Types of rice:** Long grain, medium grain, short grain, brown, basmati, pre-cooked.
- **Effects of cooking:** Starch swells, liquid is absorbed, starch becomes digestible.
- **Guidelines for home baking:** Prepare tins, oven shelves and preheat oven; weigh fresh ingredients accurately; follow recipe; ensure correct consistency of mixture; avoid overhandling dough; time accurately; check if cooked; cool on a wire tray.
- **Types of flour:** Wholemeal, brown, white, self-raising, strong, gluten-free.
- A **raising agent** is used to produce a gas in a batter or dough. The gas bubbles get bigger in the heat of the oven, which raises the dough. A crust is formed, which stops any further rising.
- **Types of raising agent:** Air, bread soda, baking powder, yeast.
- **Methods of making bread and cakes:** Rubbing in, creaming, whisking, all-in-one, melting method.
- **Types of pastry:** Shortcrust, rich shortcrust, cheese, wholemeal, flaky, rough puff, puff, choux, filo.
- **Guidelines for making pastry:** Use correct proportions of ingredients; keep ingredients and utensils cool; mix with a knife and avoid overhandling; knead and roll lightly; do not stretch; chill before baking; bake in a hot oven.

Revision Questions

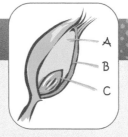

1 Name the parts of the cereal grain labelled A, B and C.
2 Name one different type of flour that matches each of the following descriptions:

Description	Type of flour
Contains the outer husk and bran	
Contains extra gluten	
Suitable for coeliacs	
Raising agent has been added	

Revision Questions

3 Match each of the following foods with the cereal they are made from:

spaghetti   cooking oil   porridge   popcorn   Weetabix

Corn	**Oats**	**Wheat**

4 Cereals are a staple food in many countries.

(a) Explain why cereals are important in the diet.

(b) List three different products made from each of the following cereals:

(i) wheat; (ii) rice.

(c) What is the difference between a wholegrain cereal product and a refined cereal product?

(d) Explain why some cereal products such as breakfast cereals are fortified.

5 Rice is an excellent source of carbohydrate. This nutrient should provide 50–55 per cent of the total energy intake in order to provide a well-balanced diet.

(a) State the proportions (%) of (i) protein and (ii) fat that should be included in a well-balanced diet.

(b) List two types of rice available to the consumer and suggest a different dish in which each type you have listed can be used.

(c) Name three rice products.

(d) Explain why rice products are frequently fortified with minerals and vitamins.

6 List three items of nutrition information you would expect to find on a packet containing a rice product. State the advantages of including nutrition information on food packaging.

7 Give two effects of cooking on cereals.

8 (a) Explain the function of gluten in bread-making.

(b) Sketch the symbol found on gluten-free flour and products.

(c) What rules should be followed when home baking?

(d) List four types of flour used in home baking and suggest a different use for each one.

9 (a) Name three methods of making bread or cakes and describe each method.

(b) Suggest a different use for each method you have named.

(c) Why are raising agents used in making cakes and bread?

(d) Name four raising agents used in home baking and explain how any one of them works.

(e) Give two advantages and two disadvantages of using commercial/convenience bread or cake mixes.

10 List three rules that should be followed when making pastry.

11 Suggest three uses for shortcrust pastry.

Chapter 9
Food processing

Any change to the natural state of a food is called **food processing**. Food is changed or processed in various ways, either to make it more attractive or to make it last longer without spoiling. Any method of treating food to make it last longer is called **food preservation**.

Reasons why food is processed:

- Micro-organisms are killed.
- It prevents waste.
- It prevents enzyme activity.
- It adds variety to the diet.
- Nutritive value is retained.
- Seasonal food is available all year.
- Food is easier to transport and store.

Food preservation

Micro-organisms need certain conditions in order to grow. If any of these conditions are removed, the food will last longer. The **conditions** required for the growth of micro-organisms are:

- food
- warmth
- moisture
- oxygen
- pH (acid or alkaline).

Warmth is removed by freezing

Freeze drying

Smoking

Canning

Pasteurisation

Methods of food preservation

- **Freezing:** Very low temperatures are used. Water changes to ice.
- **Freeze drying:** Food is frozen. Then moisture is removed.
- **Drying:** Moisture is removed.
- **Pasteurisation:** Milk is heated and cooled rapidly to kill harmful bacteria.
- **Canning:** High temperatures are used. Cans are airtight.
- **Jam making:** Fruit is boiled. There is a high sugar content. Jars are airtight.
- **Bottling:** Very high temperatures are used. Glass jars are sterilised and airtight.
- **Preservatives:** Chemicals such as sugar, salt, vinegar and smoke prevent the growth of micro-organisms. Micro-organisms cannot live in a high concentration of these substances.
- **Irradiation:** Energy waves are passed through the food to kill micro-organisms.

Link...

The growth of micro-organisms, p. 41

Freezing

Freezing preserves food because it:

- reduces the temperature of food so that micro-organisms are inactivated and cannot grow (−18°C to −30°C)
- changes the water in food to ice, and micro-organisms cannot grow without moisture in the form of water.

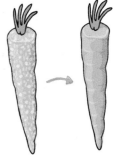

Quick freezing

Quick freezing forms very small ice crystals in food, which help to keep the food firm when it thaws.

    Slow freezing forms large ice crystals in food. When food is thawed, the food becomes soft and nutrients are lost.

    Blast freezing is carried out commercially at a temperature of −30°C. This is the best method of freezing because cell walls are not damaged.

Slow freezing

Important!

Freezing protects food from micro-organisms until it begins to thaw. Once it thaws, the micro-organisms can multiply again. This can cause food poisoning. Therefore thawed food should not be refrozen.

Guidelines for freezing

- Choose good-quality fresh food.
- Chill food before freezing.
- Use the fast freeze section of the freezer.
- Open-freeze foods that are likely to stick together.
- Freeze food in usable quantities.
- Allow air circulation between the packages in the freezer.
- Label all packages clearly.

Strawberries being open-frozen

Foods unsuitable for freezing:

- **Vegetables with a high water content,** such as cucumber.
- **Bananas and avocados:** They blacken.
- **Milk, cream and mayonnaise:** Fat and water separate.
- **Whole eggs:** They crack (but whites and yolks can be frozen separately).

Packaging foods for freezing

Guidelines:

- Packaging should be moisture-proof and vapour-proof.
- Seal bags with wire ties or freezer tape.
- Remove as much air as possible.
- Allow headspace to allow liquids to expand.
- Wrap sharp edges with foil to prevent tearing the packaging.
- Label packages clearly.

Seal bags with wire ties

Types of freezer packaging:

- Good freezer packaging is needed to prevent **freezer burn,** which damages the food.
- **Bags:** Strong polythene freezer bags.
- **Rigid containers:** Waxed cartons, plastic boxes and aluminium containers.

Freezer packaging

Freezing vegetables

- Prepare vegetables as for cooking.
- **Blanch** vegetables (see below) for the recommended time in boiling water.
- Chill the vegetables in iced water.
- Open-freeze vegetables that stick together, such as peas.
- Package in freezer bags and remove air.
- Seal and label.

Blanching times for vegetables:

- 1 minute – peas.
- 3 minutes – cauliflower florets, celery, parsnips, turnips, French beans, broad beans, broccoli.
- 4 minutes – onions, sprouts, carrots.

Blanching means putting food in boiling water for a short time to kill enzymes.

Freezing fruit

- Freeze as soon as possible after picking.
- Prepare fruit as for cooking.
- Open-freeze berry fruits. When frozen, pack in freezer bags or boxes. Seal and label.
- Hard fruits can be frozen in syrup. When packaging, allow headspace for expansion.
- Label all fruit clearly.

Freezing breads, cakes and pastries

- Freeze either raw or cooked.
- Pack in freezer bags. Seal and label clearly.
- Pack decorated cakes upright in polythene boxes.
- Use breads and scones within one month of freezing.

Freezing meat

- Trim away visible fat.
- Separate burgers, chops and steaks using waxed paper.
- Remove as much air as possible before sealing.
- Label clearly.

Freezing stews and casseroles

- Make in the usual way except that the sauce should be a little thinner.
- Shorten cooking time by 20 minutes to allow for reheating.
- When packaging, allow headspace for expansion.
- Label clearly.

Buying frozen food

- The temperature of shop freezers should be −18°C.
- Buy frozen food from a reliable source.
- Food should be frozen solid.
- Check the expiry date.
- Packaging should be properly sealed and not damaged.
- Food should be stored below the load line in open freezers.

Thawing frozen food

- Follow instructions for thawing on the label.
- Thaw food overnight in a refrigerator. Thaw food thoroughly, especially meat and poultry.
- Only defrost food in a microwave if you intend to cook the food immediately after it is thawed.
- **Do not refreeze thawed food unless it is cooked thoroughly first.**

Symbol indicating food is suitable for home freezing

Freezing home-grown produce

Advantages of using a freezer

- Food can be bought in bulk and stored, which saves money.
- Food is available out of season.
- Freezing retains colour, flavour and texture of food.
- Leftovers can be frozen and used later, which saves money.
- Freezing home-grown produce saves money.

Canning

In the canning process, heat destroys micro-organisms and the food is kept in airtight cans to prevent any further contamination by micro-organisms.

Buying canned food

- Avoid bulging, dented or rusting cans because the contents may cause food poisoning.
- Read the label to check the contents. Fruit may be canned in syrup or fruit juice. Fish may be canned in oil, brine (salty water) or sauce. Fruit may be canned in syrup or fruit juice.
- Check the expiry date.

Drying

In the drying process, heat removes the water from food. This prevents micro-organisms from growing because they cannot live without moisture.

Dried foods

Buying dried food

- Packaging should be intact.
- Check the expiry date.

Irradiation

During irradiation, energy waves are passed through the food. Micro-organisms are killed. Food keeps for a long time.

Irradiated and unprocessed strawberries

Frozen, canned and dried food – some comparisons

	Frozen foods	**Canned foods**	**Dried foods**
Food value	Do not lose their vitamin and mineral content	Vitamins are destroyed	Vitamins are destroyed
Appearance	Do not lose their colour, especially if blanched before freezing	Colour is lost	Some colour is lost Drying also changes the shape and size of some foods, e.g. vegetables and fruits
Flavour	Flavour is retained	Some flavour is lost	Some flavour is lost
Texture	Do not become too soft	Fruit and vegetables become soft	Texture changes

Higher Level

Additives

Food **additives** are substances added to food by manufacturers in order to **improve** the food in some way.

Functions of additives:

- Improve the appearance and flavour of food.
- Make food last longer.
- Reduce the risk of food poisoning.
- Improve the texture of food.
- Improve the food value of foods, i.e. nutritive additives.

E numbers

An E number means that the additive has been tested by experts and has been accepted as safe in the EU. Under EU law, food additives must be listed on food labels.

Fortified foods

Extra nutrients are sometimes added during processing to increase the nutritive value of the food. Sometimes substances are added which may help to control certain diseases such as coronary heart disease.

Fortified foods

Advantages of additives:

- They make food last longer and reduce waste.
- They allow a wider choice of foods.
- They preserve food and so reduce the risk of food poisoning.
- Good-quality food can be consistently provided.

Disadvantages of additives:

- Additives may deceive the consumer.
- May cause side effects such as hyperactivity or skin rash.
- A mixture of additives may be harmful to the body over time.
- Some people overuse foods containing additives such as MSG and they do not enjoy the taste of fresh foods.

Warning labels

Food and drink containing certain colours such as Sunset Yellow must display the name or E number of the colour and must state, 'may have adverse effect on activity and attention in children'.

Additive	Function	Examples
Colours (E100–E199)	● Add colour to foods to make them look more appealing	● Beta-carotene ● Sunset Yellow (E110) ● Allura Red (E129)
Flavourings (these do not have E numbers)	● Improve the flavour of food	● Sugar ● Salt (sodium) ● Spices ● Saccharine and aspartame are artificial sweeteners
Flavour enhancers (E620–E640)	● Make the flavour seem stronger	● Monosodium glutamate (MSG) (E621)
Preservatives (E200–E299)	● Keep food from going bad	● Salt ● Vinegar ● Sorbic acid
Antioxidants (E300–E399)	● Prevent foods that contain fat going rancid (bad)	● Vitamin C ● Vitamin E
Emulsifiers and stabilisers	● Emulsifiers force oil and water to mix. Stabilisers prevent water and oil separating	● Emulsifier: lecithin (E422) ● Stabiliser: guar gum (E412)
Nutritive additives	● Improve the nutritional value of food and replace nutrients lost during processing	● Vitamins and minerals added to breakfast cereals

ADDITIONAL INFORMATION
- Suitable for Vegetarians.
- Contains Dairy (Lactose), Wheat (Gluten) and Soya Ingredients.

INGREDIENTS
Potatoes, Sunflower Oil, Cheese & Onion Flavouring [Onion Powder, Autolysed Yeast Powder, Salt, Whey Protein Concentrate, Dextrose, Flavour Enhancers (E621, E635), Parsley, Paprika Powder, Cheese Powder, Colour (Turmeric Extract), Flavourings].

Product containing flavour enhancers

Activity

Collect labels from your favourite packaged foods. List two additives in each product and write the function of each additive in your list.

Food labelling

The purpose of food labelling is to **inform** consumers about foods. Labelling must not mislead the consumer.

Information on labels of packaged foods

- **Name of the product.**
- **List of ingredients in descending order of weight.**
- **Net quantity.**
- **Date mark:** The product should be used by this date.
- **Storage instructions.**
- **Name and address of manufacturer.**
- **Place of origin.**
- **Instructions for use:** Preparation or cooking instructions.
- **Nutrition information** is compulsory only if a nutritional claim is made on a product, e.g. 'low in fat'.

Link...

Product labelling, page 224

Advantages of nutrition information:

- Helps consumers to follow a healthy diet.
- People on special diets can choose or avoid certain foods.
- People with food allergies can avoid certain foods.

Date marking

There are two types of date marking.

- **Best before date:** This is used on foods with a long shelf life (three to 18 months). It states the date by which the food should be eaten. Examples include flour, cereals and biscuits.
- **Use by date:** This is used on foods with a short shelf life (up to six weeks). It states the date by which the food should be eaten. Examples include eggs, milk, yoghurt.

Unit pricing

This is the price per kilogram or per litre. It is required on foods sold loose, such as fruit, and pre-packaged foods sold in varying quantities, such as cheese.

The cheese in the photo costs €17.69 per kg

Activity

Design a label for a homemade product of your choice. Include all relevant items of information on the label.

Convenience foods

A **convenience food** is a pre-packed food which can be prepared quickly and easily.

Eating 'on the go', 'deskfast' and 'dashboard dining' are common today

Convenience foods have become popular because:

- Many people cannot or choose not to spend time preparing food.
- Some people do not have adequate cooking skills.
- Advertising encourages people to use convenience foods.
- There is very little waste.
- There is a wide variety available.
- Some children pester parents to buy fast food.
- Convenience foods are convenient!

Types of convenience food

- Canned and bottled foods, e.g. sauces such as curry sauces, soups, vegetables and stews.
- Frozen foods, e.g. vegetables, ready meals and pastries.
- Dried foods, e.g. packet soups and sauces.
- Ready-to-cook foods (the food is prepared but needs to be cooked), e.g. chicken Kiev.
- Cook-chill foods, which are already cooked and chilled and just have to be reheated, e.g. lasagne.

Cook-chill food

Reheating cook-chill foods:

- Cook-chill foods must be stored continuously at a temperature below 4°C in a shop or at home, otherwise food poisoning bacteria such as listeria can multiply to dangerous levels.
- Cook-chill foods must always be **thoroughly cooked or reheated** to destroy bacteria. Foods reheated in a microwave should be stirred to ensure that the food is thoroughly heated throughout.

Link...

Guidelines for diet during pregnancy, page 27

Advantages of using convenience foods

- Saves time and energy.
- Very little skill is required, so they are useful for those with poor cooking skills.
- They add interest to meals by including exotic ingredients.
- They can be fortified with vitamins and minerals.
- They are useful in emergencies.
- Avoids waste.

Disadvantages of using convenience foods

- Often inferior in food value, colour and flavour when compared to fresh produce.
- Often contain excess salt, fat and sugar.
- Expensive.
- May contain lots of additives.
- Overpackaging is wasteful and damaging to the environment.

Summary

- **Food processing:** Any change to the natural state of a food.
- **Food preservation:** Any method of treating food to make it last longer.
- **Reasons for processing:** Micro-organisms are killed, prevents waste, prevents enzyme activity, adds variety, retains nutritive value, availability of seasonal food, easier to transport.
- **Methods of preservation:** Freezing, freeze drying, drying, pasteurisation, canning, jam making, bottling, preservatives, irradiation.
- **Freezing:** Temperature reduced, micro-organisms are inactivated, water changed to ice, micro-organisms cannot grow without moisture.
- **Freezer packaging:** Moisture-proof, vapour-proof and fully intact.
- **Blanching:** Kills enzymes.
- **Buying frozen food:** Frozen solid, within the expiry date, packaging intact, temperature of shop freezers should be –18°C.
- **Canning:** Heat destroys micro-organisms. Food is kept in airtight cans.
- **Drying:** Heat removes the water from food, inactivates micro-organisms.
- **Irradiation:** Energy waves are passed through the food. Micro-organisms are killed.
- **E numbers:** Have been accepted as safe in the European Union.
- **Food additives:** Colours, flavourings, flavour enhancers, preservatives, antioxidants, emulsifiers and stabilisers, nutritive additives.
- **Food labels must include** the name of the product, list of ingredients, net quantity, date mark, storage instructions, name and address of manufacturer, place of origin, instructions for use.
- **Best before date** on non-perishable food products.
- **Use by date** on perishable food products.
- **Unit pricing:** Price per unit/kilogram.
- **Cook-chill foods:** Cooked and chilled, must be **thoroughly reheated**.

Revision Questions

1 List three methods of preservation and explain how one of the methods you have listed is carried out.

2 Name two methods of preserving food at home and suggest a different food suitable for each method.

3 Explain how freezing preserves food.

4 Give three advantages of using a freezer.

5 Select one food and describe in detail how you can preserve and store it in the home.

6 List the guidelines to be followed when (a) buying and (b) thawing frozen food.

7 Why should you *not* refreeze thawed food?

8 Compare frozen and canned vegetables under each of the following headings: (a) food value; (b) colour; (c) flavour; (d) texture.

9 Explain the term 'brine'.

10 What information does this symbol give the consumer?

11 (a) Identify three types of additive used in food processing.

(b) Give one function of each additive listed.

12 Explain the term 'fortified food'.

13 List five items of information you would expect to find on the label of packaged food.

14 What does an E number on the list of ingredients on a food label mean?

15 List two advantages of nutrition information being printed on packaged food labels.

16 Explain each of the following terms displayed on food packaging: (a) best before date; (b) use by date.

17 Give two advantages and two disadvantages of using convenience foods.

Glossary of cooking terms

accompaniment A food that is traditionally served with another food.

aerate To introduce air into a mixture, e.g. by sieving flour.

à la carte According to a menu that prices each item separately.

al dente An Italian expression meaning cooked, but firm when bitten.

anchovy Any of numerous small fishes, used in starters and as a garnish.

angelica The candied stalks of angelica (a genus of plants of the carrot family), often used as a decoration on cakes and desserts.

aperitif A drink taken before a meal to stimulate the appetite.

au gratin Describes food cooked in sauce with sprinkled cheese or breadcrumbs and browned in the oven or under a hot grill.

au lait Made or served with or containing milk.

bagel A hard, glazed, ring-shaped bread roll.

baguette A long, thin, crusty French loaf.

bain-marie A large container filled with simmering water in which other containers of food are kept warm.

bake Cook in an oven.

baking blind A method of cooking a tart without a filling.

bap A soft, thin-crusted bread roll.

barbecue 1. To roast or grill on a rack over hot coals. 2. To cook in a highly seasoned, spicy sauce.

baste To moisten with melted fat at intervals during cooking.

batter A mixture consisting of flour, egg and milk or water that is thin enough to pour or drop from a spoon.

bean curd A soft, cheese-like food which is prepared from soy bean milk.

beating Introducing air into a mixture by mixing vigorously.

bind To cause a dry mixture to hold together with a minimum of liquid.

blanch To put food briefly into boiling water to remove skin or to whiten it.

blend To mix ingredients smoothly, usually blending a starchy powder and a cold liquid.

boil To cook food in water at 100°C, shown by rapid bubbling.

bouillon A stock.

bouillon cube A cube of evaporated, seasoned meat extract.

bouquet garni A small bunch of herbs tied in muslin, used to add flavour to soups and stews.

braise To cook meat or fish on a bed of vegetables.

brine Salt water.

broil To grill.

buffet Food placed on a table for people to serve themselves.

canapé A starter consisting of a piece of bread, toast or a biscuit topped with a savoury snack.

casserole To cook food slowly in a heatproof dish in an oven.

chill To refrigerate.

chowder A thick soup or stew of seafood.

coat To cover food with a protective layer.

condiments Something used to enhance the flavour of food.

consistency The texture of a mixture.

consommé A thin, clear, meat soup made from a well-seasoned stock.

court bouillon Vegetable stock used to poach foods.

cream To beat fat and sugar together until the mixture looks like whipped cream.

croissant A flaky, rich, crescent-shaped roll of bread or pastry.

croûtons Diced pieces of fried bread served with soup or salads.

crudités Small pieces of raw vegetable cut into slices or sticks and served as a starter.

dough A thick mixture of flour and water used in bread making.

dredge To coat food by sprinkling with sugar, etc.

essence Liquid flavouring added to food.

flan A shallow sponge with a sweet or savoury filling.

fold To add a dry ingredient to a creamed mixture, using a metal spoon, to keep the lightness of the mixture.

forcemeat Stuffing for meat or other foods.

fricassee A white stew of chicken or other food.

garnish To decorate a dish.

glaze To give a glossy coating to baked dishes by brushing with egg or milk.

grill To cook under a hot grill.

herbs Leaves and stems of plants which give a particular flavour to foods.

infuse To give flavour to a liquid by heating flavourings in it at a low temperature.

liaison A thickening or binding agent.

marinade A mixture of wine, oil, vinegar and seasonings, used to tenderise and flavour meat.

menu A list of dishes available for a meal.

mix To combine ingredients together.

panard A thick sauce used to bind ingredients, e.g. croquettes.

parboil To half-cook food by boiling before finishing by another method.

pasta Dough made from flour and water and enriched with oil or egg which is shaped and used fresh or dried, e.g. spaghetti.

peel To remove the skin of a food.

poach To cook in gently simmering, seasoned liquid.

pulses Dried peas, beans and lentils, also called legumes.

purée A sieved mixture of fruit or vegetables.

quiche A savoury, custard-filled tart.

raising agent An ingredient which makes baked dishes rise.

rechauffé A French term for a reheated dish.

rind Hard or tough outer layer of a foodstuff, e.g. fruit or bacon.

roast To cook in fat in the oven.

roux A mixture of flour and fat used as the basis for sauces.

rub in To crumble fat into flour to achieve a short texture for pastry.

sauté To fry food quickly in a small amount of hot fat.

seasoning Using herbs, salt, pepper or spices to add flavour.

shortening Any fat used in baking to give a brittle texture.

simmering To cook in liquid which is just under boiling point.

skimming Removing froth, scum or fat from a liquid.

spices Seeds, berries and leaves of plants that have distinct flavours and are used whole or ground to give flavour to food.

sprig A small branch of a leafy plant, e.g. parsley.

steam 1. To cook over a boiling water bath so that steam rises up through the food to cook it. 2. To cook food in a steamer.

stew To cook food slowly in a little liquid in a tightly covered heavy saucepan over low heat.

stir-fry To fry food for a few minutes in very little oil, stirring with a large spoon or spatula, as in Chinese cooking.

syrup A concentrated sugar and water solution.

whisk To introduce air into a mixture by beating with a whisk.

Food tables

		Portion weight g	Energy kcal	Energy kJ	Protein g	Fat g	Carbohydrate g	Fibre g	Minerals Calcium mg	Iron mg	Vitamin A mg	Vitamin C mg
Beverages – non-alcoholic												
Cocoa, powder	1 level tsp	3	9	39	0.6	0.7	0.3	N	4	0.3	0	0
Coffee, instant, powder/granules	1 heaped tsp	2	2	8	0.3	0	0.2	0.1	3	0.1	0	0
Drinking chocolate, powder	3 heaped tsp	15	55	233	0.8	0.9	11.6	N	5	0.4	N	0
Tea, infused	1 cup or mug	195	Tr	Tr	0.2	Tr	Tr	0	Tr	Tr	0	0
Biscuits – plain												
Crackers, cream	3 crackers	21	92	390	2.0	3.4	14.3	1.3	23	0.4	0	0
Crispbread, rye	3 crispbreads	24	77	328	2.3	0.5	16.9	2.8	11	0.8	0	0
Biscuits – sweet												
Chocolate biscuits, e.g. Club, Penguin	1 biscuit	25	131	549	1.4	6.9	16.9	0.7	28	0.4	Tr	0
Digestive biscuits, chocolate	2 biscuits	30	148	621	2.0	7.2	20.0	0.9	25	0.6	Tr	0
plain	2 biscuits	30	141	593	1.9	6.3	20.6	1.4	28	1.0	0	0
Semi-sweet biscuits, e.g. Marie, Rich Tea	2 biscuits	15	69	289	1.0	2.5	11.2	0.3	18	0.3	0	0
Shortbread	2 fingers	35	174	730	2.1	9.1	22.4	0.8	32	0.5	95	0
Bread and bread rolls – plain												
Bread, brown, from large loaf, medium sliced	2 slices	70	153	649	6.0	1.4	31.0	4.1	70	1.5	0	0
white, from large loaf, medium sliced	2 slices	75	176	752	6.3	1.4	37.0	2.9	83	1.2	0	0
wholemeal, from large loaf, medium sliced	2 slices	70	151	640	6.4	1.8	29.1	5.2	38	1.9	0	0
Breakfast cereals												
All Bran	1 serving	45	113	482	6.8	1.5	19.4	13.5	31	5.4	0	0
Porridge, made with milk	1 serving	160	186	781	7.7	8.2	21.9	1.3	192	1.0	90	2
made with water	1 serving	160	78	334	2.4	1.8	14.4	1.3	11	0.8	0	0
Rice Krispies	1 serving	35	129	550	2.1	0.3	31.4	0.4	7	2.3	0	0
Shredded Wheat	2 pieces	45	146	623	4.8	1.4	30.7	4.5	17	1.9	0	0
Special K	1 serving	35	133	566	5.4	0.4	28.9	0.9	25	4.7	0	0
Sultana Bran	1 serving	35	106	450	3.0	0.6	23.7	5.4	18	10.5	Tr	N
Weetabix	2 Weetabix	40	142	604	4.3	0.8	31.3	3.4	14	2.4	0	0
Cakes and pastries												
Flapjack	1 flapjack	30	145	608	1.4	8.0	18.1	0.8	11	0.6	69	0
Fruit cake, made with white flour	1 slice	60	212	894	3.1	7.7	34.7	1.5	36	1.0	N	0
made with wholemeal flour	1 slice	60	218	915	3.6	9.4	31.7	1.8	51	1.1	96	0
Gingerbread	1 slice	65	246	1038	3.7	8.2	42.1	0.9	53	1.0	85	0
Jam tarts, made with white flour pastry	1 jam tart	35	129	543	1.2	4.6	22.2	0.9	25	0.6	N	Tr
made with wholemeal flour pastry	1 jam tart	35	129	544	1.5	5.3	20.1	1.2	8	0.7	22	1
Muffins, bran	1 muffin	70	190	804	5.5	5.4	31.9	6.0	84	2.3	57	Tr
plain	1 muffin	70	198	839	7.1	4.4	34.7	1.9	98	1.3	47	Tr
Cheeses												
Brie	1 slice	40	128	529	7.7	10.8	Tr	0	216	0.3	128	Tr
Cheddar	1 slice	40	165	683	10.2	13.8	0	0	288	0.1	145	Tr
Cottage cheese	1 serving	45	44	186	6.2	1.8	0.9	0	33	0	21	Tr
Cream cheese	1 serving	30	132	542	0.9	14.2	Tr	0	29	0	127	Tr
Edam	1 slice	40	133	553	10.4	10.2	Tr	0	308	0.2	80	Tr

Food tables

		Portion weight g	Energy kcal	Energy kJ	Protein g	Fat g	Carbohydrate g	Fibre g	Minerals Calcium mg	Iron mg	Vitamin A mg	Vitamin C mg
Cheeses (continued)												
Fromage frais	1 serving	45	51	211	3.1	3.2	2.6	0	40	0	45	Tr
Parmesan	2 heaped tsp	9	41	169	3.5	2.9	Tr	0	108	0.1	34	Tr
Roquefort	1 slice	40	150	621	7.9	13.2	Tr	0	212	0.2	119	Tr
Stilton, blue	1 slice	40	164	680	9.1	14.2	0	0	128	0.1	154	Tr
Cream – in drinks and soups												
Double cream	1 serving	25	112	462	0.4	12.0	0.7	0	13	0.1	164	0
Single cream	1 serving	25	50	204	0.7	4.8	1.0	0	23	0	84	0
Eggs												
Boiled egg	1 size 2	60	88	367	7.5	6.5	Tr	0	34	1.1	114	0
Fried egg	1 size 2	60	107	447	8.2	8.3	Tr	0	39	1.3	129	0
Scrambled egg	2 eggs	140	346	1435	15.0	31.6	0.8	0	88	2.2	430	Tr
Fat – on bread												
Average on 1 slice bread/large loaf and both sides bread roll												
Butter	Medium layer	8	59	242	0	6.5	Tr	0	1	0	71	Tr
Low-fat spread	Medium layer	8	31	128	0.5	3.2	0	0	3	Tr	87	0
Fish												
Cod steaks, grilled	2 steaks	130	124	523	27.0	1.7	0	0	13	0.5	0	0
Herring fillets in oatmeal, fried	2 fillets	110	257	1073	25.4	16.6	1.7	43	2.1	54	0	0
Kipper fillets, baked	2 fillets	130	267	1112	33.2	14.8	0	0	85	1.8	64	0
Mackerel fillets, fried	2 fillets	110	207	862	23.7	12.4	0	0	31	1.3	57	0
Plaice fillets, steamed	2 small fillets	120	112	470	22.7	2.3	0	0	46	0.7	0	0
Salmon cutlet, steamed	1 cutlet	125	216	899	22.0	14.2	0	0	31	0.8	0	0
Sardines canned in oil, drained	1 serving	70	152	634	16.6	9.5	0	0	385	2.0	Tr	Tr
Tuna canned in oil, drained	1 serving	95	275	1142	21.7	20.9	0	0	7	1.0	N	0
Fish fingers, fried	4 fish fingers	100	233	975	13.5	12.7	17.2	0.6	45	0.7	0	0
Fruit												
Apple	1 apple	120	42	181	0.2	0	11.0	1.7	4	0.2	5	2
Apricots	3 apricots	110	28	119	0.6	0	6.8	1.9	18	0.3	253	7
Banana	1 banana	135	63	273	0.9	0.3	15.4	2.4	5	0.3	27	8
Gooseberries	11 gooseberries	70	26	110	0.4	0	6.4	2.2	13	0.4	28	42
Grapefruit	½ grapefruit	140	15	63	0.4	0	3.5	0.4	11	0.1	0	27
Lemon	1 wedge	25	4	16	0.2	0	0.8	1.2	28	0.1	0	20
Melon, cantaloupe	½ melon	360	54	227	2.2	0	11.9	1.8	43	1.8	709	54
Orange	1 orange	245	64	277	1.5	0	15.7	3.4	76	0.7	15	93
Peach	1 peach	125	40	171	0.8	0	9.9	1.4	5	0.4	91	9
Pear		150	44	188	0.3	0	11.4	2.3	9	0.2	2	3
Plums		105	38	161	0.5	0	9.5	1.9	11	0.3	37	3
Strawberries		100	26	109	0.6	0	6.2	2.0	22	0.7	5	60

A trace value for a nutrient is represented by Tr. Where a nutrient is present in significant quantities, but there is no reliable information on the amount, the value is represented by N.

Food tables

		Portion weight g	Energy kcal	Energy kJ	Protein g	Fat g	Carbohydrate g	Fibre g	Minerals Calcium mg	Iron mg	Vitamin A mg	Vitamin C mg
Fruit – canned in syrup												
Fruit salad	1 serving	130	124	527	0.4	0	32.5	1.3	10	1.3	65	4
Mandarin oranges	16 segments	115	64	273	0.7	Tr	16.3	0.3	21	0.5	9	16
Peaches	6 slices	110	96	410	0.4	0	25.2	1.0	4	0.4	46	4
Pears	3 quarters	135	104	441	0.5	0	27.0	2.0	7	0.4	3	1
Raspberries	15 raspberries	90	78	333	0.5	0	20.3	4.1	13	1.5	12	6
Strawberries	10 strawberries	85	69	292	0.3	0	17.9	0.8	12	0.8	0	18
Fruit – dried												
Apricots	8 apricots	50	91	388	2.4	0	21.7	10.8	46	2.1	300	0
Currants	2 handfuls	35	85	364	0.6	0	22.1	2.1	33	0.6	2	0
Prunes	8 prunes	40	54	228	0.8	0	13.4	4.8	12	1.0	55	0
Raisins	2 handfuls	35	86	367	0.4	0	22.5	2.1	21	0.6	2	0
Sultanas	2 handfuls	35	88	373	0.6	0	22.6	2.2	18	0.6	2	0
Fruit juices												
Orange juice, canned, sweetened	1 glass	200	102	434	1.4	0	25.6	0	18	0.6	16	62
freshly squeezed	1 small glass	70	27	113	0.4	0	6.6	0	8	0.2	6	35
Orange squash, concentrated, to make up approx ⅓ pt	1 glass	45	48	205	0	0	12.8	0	4	0	N	0
Meat												
Bacon joints, collar, boiled, lean	1 serving	85	162	681	22.1	8.2	0	0	13	1.6	0	0
Bacon rashers, back, grilled	4 rashers, fat trimmed	45	131	548	13.7	8.5	0	0	6	0.7	0	0
Beef joints, topside, roast, lean	1 serving	85	133	560	24.8	3.7	0	0	5	2.4	0	0
Lamb chops, loin, grilled, lean	2 chops	160	195	819	24.5	10.9	0	0	8	1.9	0	0
Pork chops, loin, grilled, lean	1 chop	135	180	753	25.8	8.5	0	0	7	0.9	0	0
Milk as a drink												
Cows' milk, semi-skimmed	Approx ⅓ pt	195	90	380	6.4	3.1	9.8	0	234	0.1	45	2
skimmed	Approx ⅓ pt	195	64	273	6.4	0.2	9.8	0	234	0.1	2	2
whole	Approx ⅓ pt	195	129	536	6.2	7.6	9.4	0	224	0.1	109	2
Milk on puddings												
Condensed milk, whole, sweetened	Over pudding	45	150	633	3.8	4.5	25.0	0	131	0.1	55	2
Evaporated milk, whole	Over pudding	30	45	189	2.5	2.8	2.6	0	87	0.1	37	0
Nuts and seeds												
Cashew nuts	20 kernels	40	224	939	6.9	18.3	11.2	N	15	1.5	4	Tr
Hazelnuts	30 kernels	25	95	393	1.9	9.0	1.7	1.4	11	0.3	0	0
Peanuts	32 kernels	30	171	709	7.3	14.7	2.6	2.2	18	0.6	0	Tr
Walnuts	9 halves	25	131	542	2.7	12.9	1.3	1.2	15	0.6	0	0
Offal												
Kidney, lambs', fried	1 serving	75	116	488	18.5	4.7	0	0	10	9.0	120	7
Liver, lambs', fried	1 serving	90	209	873	20.6	12.6	3.5	0	11	9.0	6000	11

Food tables

		Portion weight g	Energy kcal	Energy kJ	Protein g	Fat g	Carbohydrate g	Fibre g	Minerals Calcium mg	Iron mg	Vitamin A mg	Vitamin C mg
Pasta												
Spaghetti, white, boiled	1 serving	150	156	663	5.4	1.1	33.3	2.7	11	0.8	0	0
wholemeal, boiled	1 serving	150	170	728	7.1	1.4	34.8	6.0	17	2.1	0	0
Poultry												
Chicken, roast, meat and skin	1 serving	85	184	767	19.2	11.9	0	0	8	0.7	0	0
Puddings												
Fruit crumble, made with white flour	1 serving	120	238	1002	2.4	8.3	40.8	2.6	59	0.7	96	4
made with wholemeal flour	1 serving	120	232	976	3.1	8.5	38.0	3.6	38	1.1	96	4
Fruit salad, fresh	1 serving	185	98	416	1.1	0.2	24.6	3.9	30	0.6	19	26
Ice cream, dairy, vanilla	1 serving	75	146	611	2.7	7.4	18.3	0	98	0.1	111	1
Pulse dishes												
Baked beans, in tomato sauce, canned	1 serving	200	128	540	10.2	1.0	20.6	13.2	90	2.8	N	0
Rice												
Brown rice, boiled	1 serving	165	233	985	4.3	1.8	53.0	2.5	7	0.8	0	0
White rice, boiled	1 serving	165	203	861	3.6	0.5	48.8	1.3	2	0.3	0	0
Vegetables												
Carrot, raw, grated	1 serving	35	8	34	0.2	Tr	1.9	0.9	17	0.2	700	2
Celery, sticks, raw	1 serving	40	3	14	0.4	Tr	0.5	0.6	21	0.2	Tr	3
Coleslaw	1 serving	85	68	282	1.6	4.7	5.2	1.9	36	0.4	N	27
Cucumber, slices	1 serving	30	3	13	0.2	0	0.5	0.1	7	0.1	Tr	2
Lettuce	1 serving	30	4	15	0.3	0.1	0.4	0.4	7	0.3	50	5
Potatoes, boiled	1 serving	150	120	514.5	2.1	0.15	29.55	1.5	6	0.45	Tr	6-21
Potatoes, chips	1 serving	150	379.5	1597.5	5.7	16.35	55.95	0	21	1.35	Tr	7.5-24
Potatoes, roast	1 serving	150	235.5	993	4.2	7.2	40.95	0	15	1.05	Tr	7.5-24
Potatoes, salad	1 serving	105	140	586	1.4	8.7	15.1	0.5	13	0.4	N	4
Tomatoes, raw	2 tomatoes	150	21	90	1.4	Tr	4.2	2.1	20	0.6	150	30
Vegetable salad, canned	1 serving	100	122	510	1.7	8.4	10.7	2.5	23	0.9	273	7
Sauces												
Brown sauce, bottled	1 serving	9	9	38	0.1	0	2.3	N	4	0.3	N	N
Mayonnaise	1 serving	20	138	569	0.2	15.1	0.3	0	2	0.1	21	N
reduced calorie	1 serving	20	58	238	0.2	5.6	1.6	0	N	N	N	N
Sugar												
Honey	1 tsp	7	20	86	0	0	5.3	N	0	0	0	0
Sugar, brown	1 tsp	5	20	84	0	0	5.2	0	3	0	N	0
white	1 tsp	5	20	84	Tr	0	5.3	0	0	Tr	0	0
Yoghurt												
Low-fat yoghurt, flavoured	1 small carton	150	135	576	5.7	1.4	26.9	Tr	225	0.2	15	2
Whole milk yoghurt, fruit	1 small carton	150	158	662	7.7	4.2	23.6	N	240	Tr	63	2

A trace value for a nutrient is represented by Tr. Where a nutrient is present in significant quantities, but there is no reliable information on the amount, the value is represented by N.

Chapter 10
Recipes

Breakfast dishes

Breakfast smoothie

Serves 2

Ingredients
2 bananas
8 strawberries, stalks removed
10 blueberries
Half a mango, peeled and chopped
200ml orange or apple juice

Equipment
Chopping board, sharp knife, jug, hand blender/liquidiser, 2 tall glasses, straws.

Method
1 Save 2 strawberries for decoration. **Blend** the remaining fruit and juice until smooth.
2 **Serve** in glasses, decorated with strawberries or orange slices.

Variations
- 200g frozen mixed berries may be used instead of fresh fruits.
- Four to five ice cubes may be added when blending ingredients.
- 75ml of natural or fruit yoghurt may be added to give a thick, creamy smoothie.

Porridge with dried fruit

Serves 2

Ingredients

50g porridge oats
450ml milk
25g ready-to-eat dried apricots, chopped
25g ready-to-eat dried prunes, chopped
2 tbsp seeds of your choice
    (sesame, pumpkin, linseed)

Equipment

Saucepan, measuring jug, tablespoon,
wooden spoon, serving bowls.

Method

1 **Place** oats, milk and fruit into
  a saucepan.
2 Bring to the boil and **simmer** for
  3–5 minutes until thick.
3 **Serve** in 2 bowls, sprinkled
  with seeds.

Breakfast muffins

Makes 12

Ingredients

125g chopped seeded dates (or dried
    cranberries, apricots or mixed fruit)
1 egg, beaten
125ml vegetable oil
375ml buttermilk
175g plain flour
1 tsp ground cinnamon
1 tsp bread soda
150g muesli
100g brown sugar
30g wheat bran

Equipment

Large mixing bowl, measuring jug,
chopping board, chopping knife,
tablespoon, teaspoon, wooden spoon,
dinner knife, fork, muffin paper cases,
12-hole muffin tin, wire tray, serving plate.

Method

1 **Preheat** oven to 200°C/180°C fan/gas
  mark 6. **Place** paper cases in muffin tin.
2 **Chop** dates (or apricots, if using).
3 **Mix** egg, oil and buttermilk in a jug
  with a fork.
4 **Sieve** flour, cinnamon and bread soda
  into mixing bowl, and **add** muesli,
  sugar, bran and fruit.
5 **Add** liquid ingredients to dry
  ingredients and **mix** gently. Do not
  over mix.
6 **Spoon** mixture into prepared tin.
7 **Bake** in preheated oven for about
  25 minutes. **Cool** on a wire tray.

American pancakes

Makes 8–10

Ingredients

225g plain flour
Pinch of salt
1 tbsp baking powder
1 tsp sugar
2 eggs, beaten
30g butter, melted
300ml milk
Oil for frying
Butter and maple syrup to serve

Equipment

Large mixing bowl, measuring jug, hand blender or whisk, frying/crêpe pan, fish slice, 2 small bowls, saucepan, 2 plates, serving plate.

Method

1 **Sieve** flour, salt, baking powder and sugar into mixing bowl.
2 Make a well in the centre and **beat** in the eggs, melted butter and milk until smooth.
3 **Transfer** batter to a jug, and **chill** for 20 minutes if possible.
4 **Heat** 1 tsp oil in pan and **pour** tablespoonfuls of the mixture onto the pan, spaced well apart.
5 **Cook** over a low to medium heat until little bubbles appear on the surface and the undersides are golden. **Turn** carefully with a fish slice and cook until golden. **Transfer** to a plate over a saucepan of simmering water, and cover with a second plate to keep warm.
6 **Repeat** steps 4 and 5 until batter is used up.
7 **Serve** pancakes topped with butter and maple syrup.

Variation

Sprinkle blueberries, raspberries or sliced strawberries onto the top (uncooked) side of the pancake after pouring the batter into the pan.

Brunch pasta

Serves 4

Ingredients

2 pork sausages
4 rashers
1 onion
6 tomatoes
100g mushrooms
100g wholemeal pasta
   (fusilli, penne or macaroni)
1 tbsp oil
2 eggs
50g garlic and herb cream cheese
50g grated cheddar cheese, to garnish
Fresh chopped parsley, to garnish

Equipment

2 large saucepans, colander, 2 chopping boards, sharp knife, small bowl, hand whisk or fork, grater, tablespoon, wooden spoon, serving plate.

Method

1 **Cut** sausages into 2cm chunks and **quarter** the rashers.
2 **Peel** and **slice** onion, and **cut** tomatoes and mushrooms into quarters.
3 **Boil** pasta in large saucepan as per instructions on packet.
4 **Heat** oil in second saucepan and **fry** onion, sausage and rashers for 5 minutes on a low heat.
5 **Add** the mushrooms and **fry** for another 5 minutes.
6 **Add** the tomatoes and continue to **fry** for 10 minutes. Keep the heat low.
7 **Beat** eggs and cream cheese until smooth. **Drain** pasta.
8 **Add** the pasta to the meat and tomato sauce and **stir. Add** the egg mixture and **stir** gently, allowing the heat of the pasta and meat to cook the eggs.
9 **Serve**, garnished with grated cheddar cheese and chopped parsley.

Light lunches and suppers

Cheese and onion tart

Serves 6

Ingredients

Pastry
500g plain flour
250g margarine
120–150ml cold water
Filling
6 rashers
3 onions
8 cherry tomatoes
140g Cheddar cheese
10g butter
200ml cream
1 egg, beaten

Equipment

1 34cm × 25cm baking tin, frying pan,
2 chopping boards, sharp knives, grater,
measuring jug, rolling pin, flour dredger,
wooden spoon, mixing bowl, pastry brush,
serving plate.

Method

1 **Preheat** oven to 220°C/200°C fan/
   gas mark 7.
2 **Make** pastry (see method on page 174)
   and **roll** out 2cm larger than baking tin.

Transfer to baking tin and **roll** edges up.
Press down with fingers to create a
raised border. **Bake** blind for
10 minutes.

3 **Chop** rashers into bite-sized pieces,
   thinly **slice** onions, and **halve** cherry
   tomatoes. **Grate** half the cheese and
   crumble the remainder.
4 **Heat** the butter in the frying pan and
   add rashers. **Cook** for 6 minutes on a
   medium heat. **Add** the onions and **cook**
   on a very low heat until soft and golden.
5 **Pour** in cream. Remove from heat and
   allow to cool in a mixing bowl.
6 **Add** grated cheese and the beaten egg
   (reserving a little). **Spread** mixture
   over the pastry and **scatter** the
   tomatoes and crumbled cheese over.
7 **Brush** pastry borders with remaining egg
   and **bake** for 20–30 minutes until golden.
8 **Serve** hot or cold with a selection
   of salads.

Cheese, leek and potato tortilla

Serves 4

Ingredients
1 leek
2 medium potatoes, cooked
75g Cheddar cheese
2 eggs
Salt and pepper
1 tbsp oil

25g cooked ham, shredded
1 tbsp fresh sage or parsley, chopped

Equipment
Chopping board, grater, measuring jug,
sharp knives, fork or hand whisk,
non-stick frying pan, fish slice/plastic
spatula, serving plate.

Method

1 **Wash** and thinly **slice** leek. **Peel, halve and cut** potatoes into slices ½ cm thick. **Grate** cheese.
2 **Beat** eggs, **add** seasoning, grated cheese and chopped herbs.
3 **Heat** oil in frying pan and **cook** leek on a medium heat for about 5 minutes until soft. Remove from pan.
4 **Add** a little extra oil to the pan if needed. **Add** in potatoes and **cook** for 2 minutes. **Add** the egg mixture and shredded ham. **Cook** on a low heat for 10 minutes until nearly set. **Place** under a hot grill and **cook** until the top is set and golden.
5 **Slice** into wedges and **serve** with a green salad.

Chilli chicken fajitas

Serves 2

Ingredients

2 chicken breasts
1 onion
1 red or green pepper
100g green beans
  (or use a small tin of chilli beans)
2 tbsp oil
2 tsp chilli powder
1 tin chopped tomatoes or 500g passata*
4 flour tortillas
4 tbsp soured cream or Greek yoghurt
Chopped coriander or flat leaf parsley,
  to garnish

* Passata is sieved tomatoes. It produces a smooth-textured sauce.

Equipment

Large frying pan, 2 chopping boards, sharp knives, tin opener, teaspoon, tablespoon, wooden spoon, plates, serving plate.

Method

1 **Cut** chicken breasts into strips. **Halve** and **slice** onion. **Deseed** and **slice** pepper into thin strips. **Top** and **tail** green beans.

2 **Heat** oil in frying pan and **add** chicken. **Cook** on a high heat until beginning to brown. **Add** chilli powder and cook for a minute.
3 **Remove** chicken from pan and **add** onion and pepper to pan. **Cook** on a low heat until softened.
4 **Add** the green beans, tomatoes and chicken and **simmer** for 15 minutes until sauce has reduced by half.
5 **Heat** the tortillas in the microwave for 20 seconds on high power or wrapped in foil in a preheated oven at 180°C/160°C fan/gas mark 4 for 10 minutes.
6 **Stir** chopped herbs into chicken mixture, **top** with a dollop of sour cream, and **roll** in warm tortillas. **Serve** with a green salad.

Methods of cooking rice

Serves 2

Method 1

1 **Boil** a large saucepan of water.
2 Gradually **add** 150g rice, bring to the boil and boil for 12 minutes.
3 **Drain** and fluff up.

Method 2

1 **Measure** a cupful of rice into a saucepan and add 2½ cupfuls of cold water.
2 **Bring to the boil** and cover. **Simmer** for 20 minutes without removing the lid.
3 **Remove from heat** and fluff up.

Plain omelette

Serves 1

Ingredients

2 eggs
Salt and pepper
15g butter or margarine,
   chopped into small cubes
Pinch of mixed herbs
1 tbsp water
1 dessertspoon oil to fry

Equipment

Small bowl or jug, fork or hand whisk, tablespoon, dessertspoon, small frying pan, egg slice/palette knife, serving plate.

Method

1 Lightly **whisk** together all ingredients except oil.
2 **Heat** oil in pan.
3 **Pour** egg mixture all at once into frying pan.
4 Using an egg slice or palette knife, **push** the mixture to the centre as the uncooked egg runs to the edges and sets.
5 While the centre is still soft, **flip** the sides over to the middle.
6 **Turn out** onto a plate and **serve** immediately.

Omelette fillings

- **Fines herbes:** Add 1 level tsp mixed herbs such as parsley, chives, chervil or tarragon before cooking.
- **Cheese:** Add 2 tbsp grated cheese before cooking.
- **Tomato:** Put chopped tomato in the centre of the omelette before folding.
- **Mushrooms:** Wash and slice 50g mushrooms and fry until soft. Put in the centre of the omelette before folding.
- **Ham:** Add 50g chopped ham and 1 tsp chopped parsley to the beaten egg before cooking.
- **Fish:** Flake cooked fish. Heat gently in a little cheese sauce. Put in the centre of the omelette before folding.
- **Shrimp:** Sauté 50g shrimps in melted butter with a squeeze of lemon juice. Put in the centre of the omelette before folding.

Sausage rolls

Makes 12

Ingredients

200g shortcrust pastry (see page 174)
8 sausages
1 egg, beaten (to glaze)

Equipment

Mixing bowl, sieve, palette knife, rolling pin, flour dredger, sharp knife, fork, jug, pastry brush, baking tray.

Method

1 **Preheat** oven to 200°C/180°C fan/ gas mark 6.
2 **Roll** pastry into oblong shape, approximately 30cm × 20cm.
3 **Remove** skins from sausages, if necessary and **roll** into two long 'sausages'.
4 **Cut** pastry in two lengthwise and place sausage meat in centre of each. **Dampen** edges of pastry.
5 **Roll** pastry around sausage meat towards cut edges. **Press** to seal. **Cut** to about 5cm long.
6 **Glaze** with beaten egg and **prick** with a fork.
7 **Place** on baking tray and bake for 15 minutes. **Reduce** temperature to 180°C/160°C fan/gas mark 4 and **bake** for a further 15 minutes.
8 **Serve** hot or cold.

Pizza

Serves 4

Ingredients

Scone base
250g plain flour
2 tsp baking powder
50g butter or margarine
2 eggs
3 tbsp milk
Topping
1 red, yellow or green pepper
4 rashers
5 spring onions
75g Cheddar cheese
1 tbsp olive oil
2 tbsp tomato purée mixed with
   2 tbsp tomato ketchup
8 cherry tomatoes

Equipment

Mixing bowl, 2 small bowls, sieve, wooden spoon, teaspoon, rolling pin, flour dredger, chopping board, sharp knives, pizza tin, frying pan, palette knife, serving plate

Method

1 **Deseed** and thinly **slice** pepper. **Chop** rashers. Thinly **slice** spring onions. **Grate** cheese.

2 **Preheat** oven to 220°C/200°C fan/ gas mark 7. **Sieve** flour and baking powder into a bowl and **rub** in butter until the mixture resembles breadcrumbs.

3 **Mix** eggs and milk together and **stir** into the dry ingredients to make a soft dough. **Knead** and **roll** into a large circle to fit tin.

4 **Heat** oil in a frying pan and **fry** pepper and bacon until pepper begins to soften. **Remove** from heat and **add** spring onion.

5 **Spread** tomato mixture over pizza base, followed by pepper and bacon mixture. **Scatter** over the tomatoes and grated cheese. **Bake** for 25–30 minutes until golden. **Serve** with a salad.

Cheese and onion potato bake

Serves 4

Ingredients

4 medium potatoes
4 rashers
1 red onion
5 mushrooms
2 garlic cloves
1 tbsp olive oil
200g soft cheese (e.g. Philadelphia)
100g grated cheese
    (Cheddar, Edam or Gouda)
Pinch of paprika

Equipment

Ovenproof dish, saucepan, frying pan,
2 chopping boards, wooden spoon,
aluminium foil.

Method

1 **Preheat** oven to 200°C/180°C fan/
   gas mark 6. **Peel** and **chop** the
   potatoes into large chunks and **boil**
   for 10 minutes. **Drain.**

2 **Chop** rashers into bite-size pieces.
   Dice onion. **Slice** mushrooms and
   crush garlic.

3 **Heat** oil in frying pan and **fry** onion on
   a medium heat for 5 minutes. **Add**
   rashers, mushrooms and garlic and
   cook for 5 minutes. **Remove** from heat.
   Add soft cheese and **mix** well.

4 **Add** mixture to potatoes, with half the
   grated cheese and paprika. **Stir** gently
   to avoid breaking up potatoes.

5 **Pour** into a greased ovenproof dish and
   cover with foil. **Bake** for 25 minutes.

6 **Remove** foil and **sprinkle** with
   remaining cheese. **Return** to oven for
   another 10 minutes until golden
   brown. **Serve** with steamed vegetables
   or a side salad.

Home baking

Tea scones

(Rubbing-in method)

Makes approximately 12–16

Ingredients

450g self-raising flour
100g margarine
50g caster sugar
1 egg, beaten
150ml milk

Equipment

Baking sheet, sieve, mixing bowl, wooden spoon, flour dredger, pastry brush, scone cutter, jug, wire tray, rolling pin, serving plate.

Method

1 **Preheat** oven to 220°C/200°C fan/ gas mark 7.
2 **Lightly** grease or flour a baking sheet.
3 **Sieve** flour into mixing bowl and **rub** in margarine. **Stir** in caster sugar.
4 **Beat** the eggs and milk together. **Make** a well in the centre of the flour and add almost all the egg and milk mixture (reserve some for glazing). Mix to a soft dough with a wooden spoon.
5 **Turn** onto a lightly floured board and **knead** lightly.
6 **Roll** to a thickness of 2cm and **cut** with a floured cutter.
7 **Place** on a baking sheet. **Brush** tops with beaten egg and milk.
8 **Bake** for 15 minutes until well risen and golden. **Cool** on a wire rack. **Serve.**

Variations

- **Sultana scones:** Add 50g sultanas with sugar at step 3.
- **Pear and almond scones:** Add 1 peeled and finely diced pear with sugar at step 3; add ½ tsp vanilla essence to egg and milk mixture at step 4; sprinkle scones with 25g flaked almonds at step 7.
- **Cinnamon scones:** Add 1 tsp cinnamon to flour at step 3; add 50g sultanas, raisins, dried cranberries or mixed fruit at step 4.
- **Cheese and herb scones:** Omit sugar and add 50g grated Cheddar cheese and 3 tbsp chopped fresh parsley or sage at step 3.

Wholemeal bread
(Rubbing-in method)

Ingredients
150g white flour
1 level tsp bread soda
150g wholemeal flour
50g margarine
25g bran
25g wheat germ
2 tsp caster sugar
1 egg, beaten
350ml buttermilk
1 tbsp porridge oats or mixed seeds

Equipment
½kg loaf tin, mixing bowl, sieve, jug, wooden spoon, spatula, palette knife, teaspoon, wire tray.

Method
1 **Preheat** oven to 190°C/170°C fan/ gas mark 5. **Grease** loaf tin.
2 **Sieve** white flour and bread soda into a bowl. **Mix** in wholemeal flour.
3 **Rub** in margarine until mixture resembles breadcrumbs.
4 **Stir** in bran, wheat germ and sugar.
5 **Beat** egg and buttermilk together. **Add** egg and buttermilk mixture to dry ingredients to form a soft, wet consistency. **Mix** well.
6 **Spread** mixture into tin, sprinkle with porridge oats or seeds and bake for 1 hour.
7 **Turn** onto a wire tray to cool.

Variations
● **Seed bread:** Add a dessertspoon each of sesame seeds, sunflower seeds and pumpkin seeds at step 4.
● **Wholemeal scones:** Follow the recipe above to step 4. Reduce buttermilk to 100ml and add to the dry ingredients with egg. Mix to form a soft dough. Knead, roll and cut out scones. Bake at 220°C/200°C fan/gas mark 7 for 15 minutes.

Corn bread

Serves 3–4

Ingredients

75g plain flour
½ tsp bread soda
1 tsp cream of tartar
175g cornmeal
Pinch of salt
1 tbsp caster sugar
1 egg
1 tbsp oil
300ml milk

Equipment

19cm square tin, greaseproof paper, mixing bowl, fork, wooden spoon, jug, sieve, teaspoon, palette knife, spatula, skewer, wire tray.

Method

1 **Preheat** oven to 200°C/180°C fan/ gas mark 5. **Grease** tin and **line** base.

2 **Sieve** flour, bread soda and cream of tartar into a bowl.
3 **Stir** in cornmeal, salt and caster sugar.
4 **Beat** the egg with the oil and milk and **add** to the dry ingredients. **Mix** well.
5 **Pour** into baking tin and **bake** for 25 minutes. **Test** centre with a skewer.
6 **Turn out. Serve** warm.

Muffins

Makes 18

Ingredients
300g self-raising flour
150g plain flour
1 tsp bread soda
200g brown sugar
2 eggs
375ml milk
180ml oil
Topping
50g brown sugar
35g plain flour
40g butter

Equipment
Muffin tin, 2 mixing bowls, muffin paper cases, sieve, fork or whisk, chopping board, sharp knife, corer, peeler, teaspoon, wooden spoon, small bowl, jug, spatula, tablespoon, dinner knife, wire tray.

Method
1. **Preheat** oven to 200°C/180°C fan/ gas mark 6. **Line** muffin tin with paper cases.
2. Make the **topping**: Mix flour and sugar in a small bowl and rub in butter.
3. **Sieve** flours, bread soda and sugar into mixing bowl.
4. **Combine** eggs, milk and oil and **stir gently** into dry ingredients.
5. **Add** ingredients for your chosen variation, following instructions below. **Spoon** into muffin cases, sprinkle with topping and bake for 20 minutes.

Variations
- **Apple and cinnamon:** Sieve **2 tsp cinnamon** with dry ingredients at step 3. Peel, core and grate **1 cooking apple** and stir half into the mixture at step 5. Sprinkle muffins with remaining apple and topping. Bake.
- **Blueberry:** Mix **200g fresh or frozen blueberries** into mixture at step 5.
- **Banana walnut:** Stir **1 ripe mashed banana** and **50g chopped walnuts** into mixture at step 5. Sprinkle muffins with **50g chopped walnuts** and topping.
- **Chocolate fudge:** Add **25g cocoa** to flour at step 3. Add **3 tbsp sour cream** to liquids at step 4. Add **150g chocolate chips** to mixture at step 5. Omit topping.

Never fail chocolate cake

(All-in-one method)

Ingredients

200g plain flour
1 tsp baking powder
1 tsp bread soda
2 tbsp cocoa
150g caster sugar
150ml sunflower oil
150ml milk
2 eggs, beaten
2 tbsp golden syrup
Icing
1 quantity chocolate butter icing
  (see page 173)

Equipment

2 × 16cm sandwich tins, greaseproof
paper, mixing bowl, 1 small bowl,
balloon whisk, wooden spoon or electric
mixer, measuring jug, spatula, palette
knife, tablespoon, wire tray.

Method

1 **Preheat** oven to 160°C/140°C fan/gas
  mark 3. **Grease** and **line** the base of two
  16cm sandwich tins.

2 **Sieve** dry ingredients into a large
  mixing bowl. **Combine** oil, milk, eggs
  and golden syrup in measuring jug.

3 **Make a well** in the dry ingredients
  and **add** liquid, **mixing** well with a
  balloon whisk.

4 **Pour** half of the mixture into each of
  the prepared tins. **Bake** for 30–35
  minutes until surface of cake springs
  back when lightly pressed.

5 Allow to **cool slightly** in the tins before
  turning out onto a wire rack. **Remove**
  paper and allow to cool fully.

6 **Sandwich** together and **ice** top of cake
  with chocolate butter icing. Decorate
  with sieved icing sugar, chocolate curls,
  fresh berries or walnuts.

Sponge cake

(Whisking method)

Ingredients

3 eggs
75g caster sugar
75g self-raising flour, sieved
Filling
3 tbsp jam
100ml whipped cream
Icing sugar, to dredge

Equipment

2 × 16cm sandwich tins, greaseproof paper, sieve, electric mixer, mixing bowl, tablespoon, spatula, wire tray, palette knife.

Method

1 **Preheat** oven to 190°C/170°C fan/ gas mark 5.
2 **Grease and line** the base of 2 sandwich tins.
3 **Whisk** eggs and caster sugar with an electric mixer until thick and creamy (this may take up to 10 minutes).
4 Gently **fold in** the sieved flour with a metal spoon.
5 **Pour** mixture into the tins and **bake** for 15–20 minutes.
6 **Cool** on a wire tray. When cold, **sandwich** cakes together with jam and cream.
7 **Dredge** sieved icing sugar over the top.

Variation

Chocolate sponge: Replace 1 tbsp of the flour with 1 tbsp cocoa.

Swiss roll

See page 131 for how to line a Swiss roll tin. Follow sponge recipe on page 169 as far as step 4, and then do the following:

5 **Pour** into prepared tin and **bake** at 220°C/200°C fan/gas mark 7 for 10–12 minutes.
6 **Sprinkle** a sheet of greaseproof paper with caster sugar.
7 Turn the cake onto the paper, **trim off** crusty edges and **roll up** with the greaseproof paper.
8 **Cool** on a wire rack.
9 **Unroll** when cold, **remove** paper and **spread** with filling of your choice. **Reroll.**

Note: If jam is used for filling, warm the jam first, spread it on cake while hot, then roll up.

Queen cakes

(Creaming method)

Makes 12

Ingredients

100g butter or margarine
100g caster sugar
2 eggs, beaten
Few drops vanilla essence
150g self-raising flour

Equipment

Patty/bun tin, paper cases, wooden spoon or electric mixer, tablespoon, jug, dessertspoon, knife, wire tray, spatula.

Method

1 **Preheat** oven to 190°C/170°C fan/ gas mark 5.
2 **Place** paper cases in patty/bun tin.
3 **Cream** butter/margarine and sugar together until light and fluffy.
4 **Add** egg a little at a time and **beat well**. Add vanilla essence.
5 **Fold** in flour gently until well mixed.
6 Using a dessertspoon and a knife, two-thirds **fill** the paper cases with the mixture.
7 **Bake** for 15–20 minutes.
8 **Cool** on a wire tray.

Variations

● **Sultana cakes:** Add 50g sultanas at step 5 and fold in gently.
● **Chocolate cakes:** Replace 1 tbsp flour with 1 tbsp cocoa and fold in at step 5.
● **Chocolate chip cakes:** Fold in 50g chocolate chips at step 5.
● **Cherry cakes:** Toss 50g halved glacé cherries into the flour and fold in at step 5.
● **Butterfly cakes:** When cakes are cold, cut a thick slice off the top of each slice, and cut this into 2 halves. Spread a little jam and 1 tsp of whipped cream (or butter icing, see page 173) on each cake. Arrange the two cut pieces on top to resemble wings. Dredge with sieved icing sugar.
● **Glacé icing:** When cakes are cold, spread glacé icing (see page 173) on top. Decorate as desired.

Parsnip and maple syrup cake

(Melting method)

Ingredients

1 medium parsnip
1 eating apple
75g pecans or walnuts
1 small orange
175g butter
175g demerara sugar
100ml maple syrup
3 eggs
250g self-raising flour
2 tsp baking powder
2 tsp mixed spice

Icing

250g tub mascarpone
3–4 tbsp maple syrup

Equipment

2 × 20cm sandwich tins, greaseproof paper, saucepan, balloon whisk, wooden spoon, teaspoon, peeler, corer, sharp knife, chopping board, grater, juicer, spatula, 2 mixing bowls, palette knife, sieve, wire rack.

Method

1 **Preheat** oven to 180°C/160°C fan/ gas mark 4. **Grease** and base **line** sandwich tins.

2 **Peel** and **grate** parsnip. **Peel, core** and **grate** apple. **Chop** pecans. **Squeeze** orange and **grate** zest.

3 **Melt** butter, sugar and maple syrup in a saucepan over a gentle heat. **Transfer** to a mixing bowl and cool slightly.

4 **Whisk** eggs into this mixture, then **sieve** in flour, baking powder and mixed spice.

5 **Stir in** grated parsnip, apple, orange zest and juice, and pecans (reserving some for decoration).

6 **Pour** into sandwich tins and bake for 45 minutes, until the tops spring back when pressed lightly.

7 **Cool** cakes slightly in tins, and turn onto a wire rack to cool completely.

8 **Mix** together the mascarpone and maple syrup. **Spread** half over one cake and sandwich the cakes together.

9 **Spread** other half of icing on top. **Scatter** pecans over icing.

Butter icing

Ingredients (sufficient to fill and ice one cake)
150g butter, softened
200g sieved icing sugar
1–2 tbsp hot water

Flavouring of choice:
- **Lemon or orange:** Zest of half a lemon/orange and 1 dessertsp juice.
- **Chocolate:** 3 tbsp cocoa sieved in with icing sugar.
- **Coffee:** 2 tbsp coffee powder dissolved in 1 tbsp hot water.
- **Vanilla:** 1 tsp vanilla essence.
- **Mocha:** 1 tbsp cocoa and 1 tbsp coffee powder dissolved in 1 tbsp hot water.

Method
1 **Cream** butter and icing sugar together until soft and creamy. Add hot water for a creamy consistency.
2 **Beat in** flavouring ingredients. Use to fill or decorate cakes.

Glacé icing

Ingredients (sufficient to ice 12 queen cakes)
200g icing sugar
1 tsp flavouring (see options above)
15–30ml boiling water
2–3 drops colouring (if required)

Method
1 **Sieve** icing sugar into a bowl.
2 **Add** flavouring and **gradually add** 15–30ml boiling water. The icing should be thick enough to coat the back of a spoon. If necessary, add more water or sugar.
3 **Add** colouring, if required.

Shortcrust pastry

Makes 200g

Ingredients
200g plain flour
Pinch of salt
100g block margarine
3–5 tbsp cold water

Equipment
Sieve, mixing bowl, tablespoon, palette knife or dinner knife, flour dredger, rolling pin, jug.

Method
1 **Sieve** flour and salt into mixing bowl.
2 **Cut** the margarine into small pieces and **rub** into the flour until the mixture resembles breadcrumbs.
3 Gradually **add** the water and blend with a palette knife to form a firm dough.
4 **Knead** lightly on a floured surface.
5 **Allow** to relax in a refrigerator before rolling to required shape.

Uses: Fruit tarts, mince pies, quiches, sausage rolls, Bakewell tart.

Rich shortcrust pastry

Makes 225g

Ingredients
225g plain flour
125g caster sugar
100g ground almonds
125g block margarine
1 egg, beaten
1 tbsp water (if necessary)

Equipment
Mixing bowl, flour dredger, rolling pin, jug.

Method
1 **Mix** flour, sugar and ground almonds in mixing bowl.
2 **Rub in** margarine until mixture resembles breadcrumbs.
3 **Add** egg (and water if required) and mix to a soft dough.
4 **Knead** lightly on a floured surface.
5 **Allow** to relax in a refrigerator before rolling to required shape.

Uses: Fruit tarts and flans, mince pies, Bakewell tart.

Mince pies

Makes 12–16

Ingredients

225g rich shortcrust pastry (see page 174)
450g/1 jar mincemeat
Icing sugar, to dredge

Equipment

Sieve, mixing bowl, tablespoon, teaspoon, palette knife or dinner knife, flour dredger, rolling pin, jug, bun tin, scone cutter, star cutter, cling film.

Method

1 **Preheat** oven to 200°C/180°C fan/gas mark 6. Lightly **grease** bun tin.
2 **Make** rich shortcrust pastry as above.
3 **Roll** pastry to a thickness of 3–4mm between two sheets of cling film (this makes it easier to handle).
4 **Cut** rounds with a cutter to fit bun tin. **Put** a teaspoon of mincemeat into each and **cut** a 'lid' with the star cutter from the remaining pastry to put on top.
5 **Bake** for 15 minutes until golden brown.
6 **Dredge** with icing sugar and serve hot or cold.

Cranberry and macadamia cookies

(Creaming method)

Makes 12–15

Ingredients
100g butter
100g brown sugar
1 egg, beaten
150g plain flour, sieved
½ tsp baking powder
75g porridge oats
50g macadamia nuts, chopped
50g white chocolate chips
50g dried cranberries

Equipment
2 large baking trays (18cm × 28cm), bowls, wooden spoon, whisk, sieve, teaspoon, chopping board, sharp knife, wire tray, palette knife.

Method
1 **Preheat** oven to 180°C/160°C fan/ gas mark 4.
2 **Cream** butter and sugar until soft.
3 **Beat** in egg.
4 **Stir** in sieved flour, baking powder, oats, nuts, chocolate chips and cranberries and mix well.
5 **Roll** the mixture into small balls and place on baking trays, leaving about 4cm between them. **Flatten** slightly.
6 **Bake** for 12–15 minutes until golden.
7 **Cool** on a wire tray.

Variations
- **Chocolate chip cookies:** Substitute 100g milk chocolate chips for the dried cranberries and macadamia nuts.
- **Chocolate cookies:** Omit cranberries, macadamia nuts and white chocolate chips. Substitute 50g cocoa for 50g plain flour at step 4.

Low-fat chocolate brownies

(Melting method)

Makes 16

Ingredients

85g dark chocolate, 70% cocoa solids
85g plain flour
25g cocoa powder
¼ tsp bread soda
100g golden caster sugar
50g light brown sugar
½ tsp instant coffee granules
1 tsp vanilla essence
2 tbsp buttermilk
1 tbsp warm water
1 egg
100g low-fat mayonnaise
Icing sugar to dredge

Equipment

Brownie tin (23cm square and 4cm deep), greaseproof paper, saucepan, 2 mixing bowls, sieve, tablespoon, wooden spoon, spatula, sharp knife, skewer, wire tray.

Method

1. **Preheat** oven to 180°C/fan 160°C/ gas mark 4
2. **Oil** and base **line** a brownie tin.
3. **Melt** chocolate in a bowl over a saucepan of simmering water, and allow to cool slightly.
4. **Sieve** flour, cocoa powder and bread soda into another bowl.
5. **Stir** both the sugars into the cooled chocolate with the coffee, vanilla and buttermilk.
6. **Stir** in 1 tbsp warm water. **Beat** in the egg, and then **stir** in the mayonnaise until smooth and glossy.
7. Gently **fold** in the flour and cocoa mixture with a spatula. Do not over-mix.
8. **Pour** the mixture into the tin and **bake** for 20–30 mins. When a skewer is inserted into the middle, it should come out with just a few moist crumbs sticking to it. Leave in the tin until completely cold. **Dredge** with icing sugar and **cut** into squares.

Whoopie pies
(Creaming method)

Makes 12

Ingredients
35g cocoa powder
300g plain flour
1 tsp baking powder
1 tsp bread soda
Pinch of salt
100g butter
175g dark brown sugar
1 egg
1 tsp vanilla essence ⎫
125ml milk   ⎭ *blended together*

Filling
100g butter
200g icing sugar
½ tsp vanilla essence
Icing sugar, to dredge

Equipment
2 baking sheets, sieve, teaspoon,
2 dessertspoons, electric mixer or wooden
spoon, fork, 2 large mixing bowls, jug,
spatula, wire tray, serving plate.

Method
1 **Preheat** oven to 170°C/150°C fan/gas
   mark 3. Lightly **grease** 2 baking sheets.
2 **Sieve** together the cocoa, flour, baking
   powder, bread soda and salt into a
   mixing bowl.
3 **Cream** the butter, sugar and egg in
   another mixing bowl.
4 **Add** the cocoa mixture to the butter
   mixture, alternating with the milk
   mixture, and **beat** until smooth.
5 **Dip** 2 dessertspoons in hot water and
   spoon the batter into 12 small mounds
   on each baking sheet, flattening lightly
   with the back of the spoon. Allow
   room for the mixture to spread.
6 **Bake** for 15 minutes until firm.
   Cool on a wire rack.
7 Filling: **Cream** butter, icing sugar
   and vanilla essence together until
   light and smooth.
8 **Spread** filling over the flat side of
   half of the whoopies and **sandwich**
   with the remaining cakes.
9 **Dredge** with icing sugar and **serve**.

Variation
Substitute ½ tsp peppermint essence
for vanilla essence in filling (step 7)
for a minty flavour.

Coconut crumble cookies

(Melting method)

Makes 18–20

Ingredients

85g porridge oats
85g desiccated coconut
100g plain flour
50g caster sugar
100g butter
1 tbsp golden syrup
1 tsp baking powder

Equipment

2 baking trays, mixing bowl, saucepan, small bowl, wooden spoon, tablespoon, teaspoon, spatula, wire rack.

Method

1. **Preheat** oven to 180°C/160°C fan/ gas mark 4. **Grease** baking trays.
2. **Mix** oats, coconut, flour and sugar together in a bowl.
3. **Melt** butter in a saucepan and **stir** in golden syrup.
4. **Add** baking powder to 2 tbsp boiling water and **stir** into the butter mixture.
5. Make a well in the centre of the dry ingredients, and **pour** in the liquids. **Stir** gently.
6. **Roll** the mixture into small balls and place on baking trays, allowing room to spread.
7. **Bake** for 8–10 minutes until golden.
8. **Cool** on a wire rack.

Desserts

Apple tart

Serves 6–8

Ingredients

200g shortcrust pastry (see page 174)
2 medium cooking apples
3–4 tsp sugar
4–5 cloves
1 egg, beaten (to glaze)

Equipment

Sieve, mixing bowl, teaspoon, palette knife, flour dredger, rolling pin, chopping board, sharp knife, apple corer, pastry brush, fork, ovenproof plate/dish.

Method

1 **Preheat** oven to 230°C/210°C fan/ gas mark 8.
2 **Make** pastry and chill in refrigerator.
3 **Divide** pastry in two. **Roll out** each half and place one half on plate. Return to refrigerator.
4 **Peel, core** and **slice** apples. **Place** on pastry. **Sprinkle** with sugar and cloves.
5 **Brush** edge of pastry with water and **cover** with second round of pastry, pressing well together.
6 **Trim** and **decorate. Prick** with a fork.
7 **Brush** with beaten egg and **bake** in a hot oven at 230°C/210°C fan/gas mark 8 for 10 minutes. **Reduce** to 190°C/ 170°C fan/gas mark 5 to finish cooking (approximately 30 minutes more).
8 **Serve** with whipped cream, ice cream or custard.

Strawberry flan

Serves 6–8

Ingredients

*175g shortcrust or rich shortcrust
   pastry (see page 174)*
*350g fresh strawberries, hulled
   and washed*
Pastry cream
25g plain flour
150ml milk
25g margarine
25g caster sugar
1 egg yolk
1 tbsp cream
Glaze
150g redcurrant jelly

Equipment

Mixing bowl, sieve, palette knife, rolling
pin, flour dredger, 20cm flan case,
greaseproof paper, baking beans, 2
saucepans, hand whisk, chopping board,
sharp knife, pastry brush, serving plate.

Method

1 **Preheat** oven to 180°C/160°C fan/
   gas mark 4.
2 **Line** a flan case with pastry and **bake**
   blind (see below).
3 Place flour, milk and margarine in a
   saucepan and bring to the **boil**,
   whisking continuously.
4 Reduce heat and **simmer** for 2–3
   minutes. Cool slightly.
5 **Whisk** in sugar, egg yolk and cream
   and fill flan case.
6 **Halve** strawberries and arrange on
   pastry cream, cut side down.

7 Spoon redcurrant jelly into a
   saucepan and **heat** gently, without
   stirring, until clear.
8 Brush over fruit, working from
   centre outwards.
9 Serve cold.

To bake blind

1 **Prick** base of pastry and place a round
   of greaseproof paper on it. **Cover** this
   with baking beans to prevent rising.
2 **Bake** at 180°C/160°C fan/gas 4 for
   15 minutes.
3 **Remove** paper and beans and **return** to
   oven for 10–15 minutes.
4 **Remove** from oven and allow to cool.

Variations

● When strawberries are not in
   season, use blackberries or halved
   seedless grapes.
● Alternatively, use tinned peaches
   or pears.

Berry Bakewell tart

Serves 8

Ingredients

150g ground almonds
150g butter
150g caster sugar
150g self-raising flour
3 eggs
1 tsp vanilla essence
250g raspberries (or blueberries,
    strawberries or blackberries)
2 tbsp flaked almonds
Icing sugar, to dredge

Equipment

20cm loose-bottomed cake tin, mixing
bowl, teaspoon, spatula, wooden
spoon/electric mixer, sieve, serving plate.

Method

1 **Preheat** oven to 180°C/160°C fan/gas
mark 4. **Grease** and base **line** cake tin.
2 **Cream** the ground almonds, butter,
sugar, flour, eggs and vanilla essence
until creamy and well mixed.
3 **Spread** half the mixture in the cake tin
and smooth the top. **Scatter** the
raspberries over, then spoon over the
remaining cake mixture. Roughly
spread with a spatula.
4 **Scatter** with flaked almonds and **bake**
for 50 minutes until golden.
5 **Cool**, remove from tin and **dredge** with
icing sugar. **Serve.**

Caramel apple crumble

Serves 6

Ingredients

3 medium cooking apples
1 tbsp golden syrup
Juice of 1 orange
Crumble
140g porridge oats
100g plain flour
1 tsp cinnamon
100g butter
100g light brown sugar
1 tbsp golden syrup

Equipment

Chopping board, sharp knife, peeler, corer,
tablespoon, teaspoon, ovenproof dish,
2 mixing bowls, knife.

Method

1 **Preheat** oven to 190°C/170°C fan/gas
mark 5. Lightly **grease** ovenproof dish.
2 **Peel, core** and thinly **slice** apples and
mix with golden syrup and orange juice.
Spread over the ovenproof dish.
3 **Mix** the oats, flour and cinnamon in a
large bowl. **Rub in** butter.
4 **Stir** in sugar. **Drizzle** over golden
syrup and **mix** with a knife to form
small clumps.
5 **Spread** crumble evenly over apples and
bake for 30–35 minutes.
6 **Serve** with custard sauce, ice cream or
Greek yoghurt.

Custard sauce

Ingredients
1 egg
2 tsp sugar
200ml milk
½ tsp vanilla essence

Equipment
Mixing bowl, balloon whisk or fork,
saucepan, sieve, teaspoon, wooden spoon.

Method
1 **Whisk** egg and sugar lightly.
2 **Heat** the milk in a saucepan until it
   steams – do not allow to boil.
3 **Pour** the milk onto the egg, stirring well.
   Strain back into the rinsed saucepan.
4 **Cook** over a gentle heat, stirring all the
   time, until the mixture thickens and
   coats the back of the spoon. Do not boil.
5 **Add** vanilla essence and **serve** hot
   or cold.

Baked berry cheesecake

Serves 8

Ingredients

8 digestive biscuits
50g melted butter
600g cream cheese
2 tbsp plain flour
175g caster sugar
½ tsp vanilla essence
2 eggs
1 egg yolk
140ml soured cream or crème fraîche
300g raspberries
1 tbsp icing sugar

Equipment

Plastic bag, rolling pin, 20cm springform tin, mixing bowl, saucepan, wooden spoon/electric mixer, tablespoon, teaspoon, fork.

Method

1 **Preheat** oven to 180°C/160°C fan/ gas mark 4.
2 Place biscuits in a plastic bag and **crush** with rolling pin. **Melt** butter in a saucepan and **mix** in biscuits. **Press** into tin and **bake** for 5 minutes. **Cool.**
3 **Beat** the cream cheese with the flour, sugar, vanilla essence, eggs, yolk and soured cream until light and creamy.
4 **Stir** in half the raspberries and **pour** into the tin. **Bake** for 40 minutes until set but slightly wobbly in the centre. **Leave** in tin to cool.
5 **Save** a few raspberries for the top and put the rest in a saucepan with the icing sugar. **Heat** until raspberries have softened. **Mash** with a fork and sieve.
6 **Scatter** raspberries over the top and **drizzle** over raspberry sauce. **Serve.**

Variations

● Use oatmeal or ginger biscuits instead of digestive biscuits.
● Use halved strawberries, blueberries, blackberries or blackcurrants instead of raspberries.

Starters and soups

Dips to serve with crudités

Crudités can consist of sticks of raw carrot, celery, cucumber, red pepper. Florets of broccoli and cauliflower and cherry tomatoes or radishes are also suitable.

Hummus

Serves 4

Ingredients

1 × 400g tin chickpeas
50ml olive oil
100ml lemon juice
1 tbsp light tahini
2–3 cloves of garlic, peeled
Pinch of salt and pepper
Pinch of ground cumin (optional)
Pinch of ground coriander (optional)
1 tsp olive oil for drizzling
Fresh herbs, to garnish
Pitta bread, crackers or crudités, to serve

Equipment

Small sharp knife, food processor, serving dish.

Method

1 **Blend** all the ingredients together in a food processor. If hummus is too thick, add a little water.
2 **Spoon** into a small bowl. **Drizzle** with a little olive oil.
3 **Garnish** with fresh herbs.
4 **Serve** with pitta bread, crackers or crudités.

Tomato dip

Serves 4–6

Ingredients

4 ripe tomatoes, finely chopped
1 tsp tomato purée
½ tsp brown sugar
1 dessertsp wine vinegar
1 dessertsp olive oil
Crudités, to serve

Equipment

Chopping board, chopping knife, mixing bowl, spoon, serving dish.

Method

1 **Mix** all ingredients in a bowl.
2 **Spoon** into a serving dish and **serve** with crudités.

Creamy herb and lime dip

Serves 4–6

Ingredients

150g low-fat natural yoghurt
2 tbsp mayonnaise
Pinch of salt and pepper
Rind and juice of half a lime
1 tbsp chopped herbs – coriander or basil
Crudités, to serve

Equipment

Chopping board, chopping knife, grater, juice extractor, mixing bowl, spoon, serving bowl.

Method

1 **Mix** all ingredients in a bowl.
2 **Spoon** into a serving dish and **serve** with crudités.

Carrot and orange soup

Serves 4

Ingredients

700g carrots, peeled and chopped
1 onion, peeled and chopped
25g butter or margarine
25g white flour
1 litre stock
½ tsp dried mixed herbs
Pinch of salt and pepper
Juice and grated rind of 1 orange
Fresh parsley or basil leaves, to garnish
Wholemeal bread, to serve

Equipment

Chopping board, chopping knife, large saucepan, juice extractor, measuring jug, large spoon, liquidiser.

Method

1 **Sauté** the carrot and onion in butter for 10 minutes.
2 **Add** flour and **cook** for 2 minutes.
3 **Add** the stock, herbs, salt and pepper. Bring to the **boil** and **simmer** for 20 minutes.
4 **Add** the orange juice and grated rind. **Simmer** for 2 minutes.
5 **Purée** the soup using a liquidiser.
6 **Serve** hot, garnished with parsley.

Tomato and lentil soup

Serves 6

Ingredients

1 tbsp vegetable oil
50g bacon, chopped
1 onion, finely chopped
2 cloves of garlic, peeled and crushed
1 potato, peeled and diced
1 carrot, peeled and diced
200g red lentils
2 × 400g cans chopped tomatoes
1½ litres vegetable stock or water
1 tbsp tomato purée
Pinch of sugar
Salt and black pepper
Fresh chopped herbs, to garnish

Equipment

Chopping board, chopping knife, large saucepan, colander, measuring jug, large spoon, liquidiser.

Method

1 **Fry** the bacon in the oil for 2 minutes.
2 **Add** the onion and garlic and sauté for 3 minutes. **Add** potato and carrot and cook for 3 minutes.
3 **Rinse** lentils in a colander under running water. **Drain**.
4 **Add** lentils, tomatoes, stock, tomato purée, sugar and seasoning to the potato mixture.
5 **Simmer** for 20 minutes with lid on. **Stir** and **remove** from heat.
6 **Taste** and adjust seasoning. **Liquidise** (optional) for a smooth soup.
7 Garnish with herbs and **serve** with crusty bread.

Main courses: meat

Cottage pie

Serves 4

Ingredients

1 tbsp oil
1 onion, peeled and finely chopped
1 tsp curry powder
1 tsp ground coriander
½ tsp paprika
500g minced beef
2 carrots, peeled and grated
4 tbsp tomato purée
200ml beef stock
1 tsp cornflour, mixed with 1 tbsp water
150g frozen peas
Topping
4 large potatoes, peeled and chopped
25g butter or margarine
75ml milk
Salt and pepper
50g Cheddar cheese, grated

Equipment

Large casserole dish, frying pan, chopping
board, chopping knife, pot stand, large
spoon, potato masher.

Method

1 **Preheat** the oven to 180°C/160°C fan/
   gas mark 4. **Fry** the onion in oil for
   5 minutes. **Add** the spices and cook for
   1 minute. **Add** the mince and fry until
   browned. **Mix** in the carrots, tomato
   purée and beef stock. **Cover** and
   simmer for 30 minutes.
2 **Add** the cornflour paste and peas to
   the mince, bring to the boil and
   simmer for 2 minutes. **Pour** the
   mixture into a casserole dish.
3 To make the topping, **boil** the potatoes
   until soft. **Drain** and **mash**. **Add** the
   butter and milk. **Season** to taste.
4 **Spread** the mash over the mince using a
   fork. **Sprinkle** the cheese evenly on top.
   Bake for 25 minutes.
5 **Serve** with steamed broccoli.

Mini meatballs

Serves 3

Ingredients

2 tsp olive oil
1 small onion, peeled and chopped
1 garlic clove, peeled and crushed
1 small carrot, peeled and finely grated
200g minced beef, lamb or pork
50g fresh white breadcrumbs
1 tbsp chopped parsley
1 tbsp tomato ketchup
1 large egg, beaten

Equipment

Chopping board, chopping knife, frying pan, mixing bowl, food tongs or fish slice, serving dish.

Method

1 **Preheat** the oven to 190°C/170°C fan/ gas mark 5. Gently **fry** the onion and garlic in oil for 3 minutes until softened.
2 **Mix** the carrot, mince, breadcrumbs, parsley and tomato ketchup. Then **add** the egg, onion and garlic and **bind** together.
3 **Divide** the mixture into 15 equal balls. **Place** on a lightly greased baking tray and **cook** in the preheated oven for 15 minutes or until cooked through, turning over halfway through cooking.
4 **Serve** with tomato sauce (see page 196).

Hamburgers

Serves 4

Ingredients

450g beef, lamb or pork mince
2 garlic cloves, crushed (optional)
1 tbsp Worcestershire Sauce
1 egg, lightly beaten
1 small onion, finely chopped
½ tsp mixed herbs
30g Parmesan cheese, grated
1 tbsp breadcrumbs
8 burger buns
4 lettuce leaves, washed and dried
4 slices Cheddar cheese
2 tomatoes, sliced

Equipment

Mixing bowl, chopping board, chopping knife, grater, salad spinner, serving dish, food tongs.

Method

1 In a large bowl, **mix** together the meat, garlic, Worcestershire Sauce, egg, onion, herbs, Parmesan cheese and breadcrumbs until well combined.

2 **Divide** the mixture into four balls and flatten each to a thickness of 2cm. **Drizzle** a little oil on each hamburger.

3 **Preheat** the grill and **grill** the burgers for 5 minutes on one side. **Turn** them once only, and cook for a further 5 minutes.

4 **Reduce** the heat and continue cooking for another 8–10 minutes until the juices run clear.

5 **Toast** the burger buns.

6 **Place** a burger on each bun. **Top** with lettuce, sliced cheddar cheese, sliced tomatoes and remaining bun halves and **serve**.

Chicken and chorizo stew

Serves 6

Ingredients

100g chorizo sausage,
* sliced 3mm thick*
2 onions, chopped
2 cloves garlic,
* peeled and chopped*
2 tbsp olive oil
75g plain flour
1 tbsp paprika
4 chicken fillets, each cut into 4 pieces
500ml chicken stock
½ tsp mixed herbs
1 × 400g tin chickpeas
1 × 400g tin chopped tomatoes
salt and pepper

Equipment

Chopping board, chopping knife, measuring jug, frying pan, large saucepan, casserole dish, plastic bag, large spoon. *Note:* A casserole dish which can be used on the hob is very useful for making this dish.

Method

1 **Preheat** the oven to 190°C/170°C fan/ gas mark 5.

2 **Heat** 1 tbsp oil in a frying pan and fry the chorizo, onions and garlic for 3 minutes. **Transfer** the mixture to the saucepan.

3 **Mix** the flour and paprika in the plastic bag. Put the chicken pieces in the bag and **toss** until the chicken is coated.

4 **Remove** the chicken pieces and discard the excess flour.

5 **Heat** 1 tbsp oil in the frying pan and **fry** the chicken pieces until golden brown. **Transfer** to the saucepan.

6 **Add** the chicken stock and herbs, tomatoes and chickpeas and a pinch of salt and pepper.

7 **Cover** and **simmer** for 45 minutes, **or** bring to the **boil, transfer** to the casserole dish, **cover** and **place** in the preheated oven for 45 minutes.

8 **Serve** with baked potatoes.

Chicken baked with plums

Serves 4

Ingredients

4 chicken breasts
4 tbsp vegetable oil
1 onion, peeled and chopped
1 dessertsp lemon juice
1 dessertsp soy sauce
½ tsp ground ginger
1 dessertsp tomato purée
1 tbsp brown sugar
Pinch of salt
3 tbsp plum jam
Pinch of dry mustard powder
1 dessertsp Worcestershire sauce
1 garlic clove, peeled and crushed
4 fresh plums, stoned and quartered

Equipment

Chopping board, chopping knife, large spoon, large frying pan, medium saucepan, casserole dish.

Method

1 **Preheat** the oven to 180°C/160°C fan/ gas mark 4.

2 **Fry** the chicken in 2 tbsp oil until brown. Remove from heat.

3 **Add** the remaining oil to a saucepan and **sauté** the onion over a low heat for 5 minutes.

4 **Add** all the remaining ingredients except the fresh plums and **simmer** for 3 minutes.

5 **Place** the chicken pieces in a casserole dish. **Pour** the sauce over the chicken and arrange the plums on top.

6 **Bake** in the oven for 45 minutes.

7 **Serve** with boiled rice or couscous.

Traditional chicken casserole

Serves 4

Ingredients

2 red onions, thinly sliced
2 sticks celery, chopped
2 carrots, thinly sliced
100g mushrooms, sliced
4 rashers, derinded and chopped
1 tbsp oil
25g butter
4 chicken breasts
25g flour
500ml chicken stock
Pinch mixed herbs
Fresh chopped parsley, to garnish

Equipment

Chopping board, scissors, chopping knife, measuring jug, casserole dish, frying pan, large spoon, plates.

Method

1 **Preheat** oven to 180°C/160°C fan/ gas mark 5.
2 **Chop** the chicken breasts into bite-sized pieces.
3 **Fry** onions, celery, carrots, mushrooms and rashers in oil and butter until golden brown. **Remove** from pan and place in a casserole dish.
4 **Fry** the chicken in the oil for 5 minutes until golden brown. **Remove** and place it in the casserole dish.
5 **Stir** the flour into the remaining fat in the pan and **cook** for 2 minutes.
6 **Stir** in the stock and bring to the boil. **Add** the mixed herbs, salt and pepper.
7 **Pour** over the chicken.
8 **Cover** and **cook** in the oven for 40 minutes.
9 **Garnish** with parsley and **serve** with baked potatoes.

Spiced chicken goujons

Serves 4

Ingredients

4–6 skinless chicken fillets
100g white flour
1 tbsp dried oregano
1 tbsp dried thyme
1 tbsp dried rosemary
Pinch of chilli flakes
Pinch of salt
Freshly ground black pepper
2 eggs
100ml milk
250ml sunflower oil

Equipment

Freezer bag, rolling pin, large plate or tray, chopping board, chopping knife, small mixing bowl, frying pan, baking sheet.

Method

1 **Preheat** oven to 200°C/180°C fan/gas mark 6.
2 **Put** the chicken fillets one at a time into a freezer bag. Bash with a rolling pin so that the fillet is quite thin. Remove from the freezer bag and cut each fillet into six strips (goujons).
3 **Mix** all the dry ingredients together and **spread** on a large plate or baking tray.

4 **Beat** the eggs and milk together and dip the chicken into the egg mixture. Then **toss** it around in the flour mixture so that it gets lightly coated, and **transfer** to a plate or baking tray.
5 **Heat** the oil in a large frying pan. When the oil is hot, fry the chicken pieces slowly in batches until golden brown.
6 **Transfer** the chicken to a clean baking tray and, when it has all been fried, bake it in the oven for another 15 minutes, **turning** the pieces over occasionally until they are dark golden brown.
7 **Serve** immediately with Romesco sauce (see page 195).

Romesco sauce

Serves 4–6

Ingredients

*2 red peppers, deseeded and
    roughly chopped*
8 cloves of garlic with skins on
2 tomatoes, sliced
4 tbsp olive oil
50g flaked almonds
Pinch of smoked paprika
30g breadcrumbs
3 tbsp sherry vinegar
Salt and pepper

Equipment

Chopping board, chopping knife, roasting
tin, liquidiser or food processor.

Method

1 **Preheat** oven to 220°C/200°C fan/
  gas mark 7.
2 **Arrange** the peppers, garlic and
  tomatoes in a roasting tin, **drizzle** with
  half the olive oil and season well with
  salt and pepper.
3 **Roast** in the oven for 20 minutes.
4 **Remove** the garlic cloves and allow to
  cool for a few minutes.
5 **Squeeze** out the garlic cloves and
  discard the skins.
6 **Combine** the cooked ingredients with
  all the other ingredients and **blend**
  using a liquidiser or food processor.
7 **Serve** as an accompaniment to meat,
  fish or vegetable dishes.

Pork schnitzel with tomato sauce

Serves 4

Ingredients

4 pork chops, with fat removed
100g breadcrumbs
50g Parmesan cheese, freshly grated
*1 tbsp freshly chopped sage or
    1 tsp dried sage*
1 egg, beaten
2 tbsp vegetable oil
Salt and pepper
Sage leaves and lemon wedges, to garnish

Equipment

Steak hammer/rolling pin, 2 large plates,
large frying pan, serving dish.

Method

1 **Place** chops between two layers of
  cling film and pound with a steak
  hammer or rolling pin to flatten.
2 **Mix** the breadcrumbs, cheese, sage,
  salt and pepper on a plate.
3 **Whisk** the egg and pour onto
  another plate.
4 **Dip** the chops first in the egg, then
  into the crumbs, pressing them down
  to coat evenly.
5 **Heat** the oil in a frying pan, **add** the
  pork and **fry** until browned. **Turn** and
  continue to cook on a low heat for
  15–20 minutes.
6 **Garnish** with sage leaves and
  lemon wedges.
7 **Serve** with tomato sauce (see page 196).

Tomato sauce

Makes 350ml

Ingredients

1 tbsp vegetable oil
1 onion, finely chopped
1 garlic clove, peeled and crushed
400g can chopped tomatoes
2 tsp red wine vinegar
1 tsp caster sugar
2 tsp tomato purée
Salt and freshly ground black pepper
Optional: 1 tbsp chopped capers or
   pitted black olives

Equipment

Chopping board, chopping knife, medium saucepan, large spoon.

Method

1 **Sauté** the onion and garlic for 5 minutes in 1 tbsp hot oil.

2 **Add** the tomatoes, vinegar, sugar, tomato purée and capers or olives (optional).

3 **Bring** to the **boil** and **simmer** uncovered for 15–20 minutes, until the sauce has thickened.

4 **Serve** warm or cold as an accompaniment.

Main courses: fish

Spicy grilled salmon

Serves 3

Ingredients

400g salmon fillets, skin removed
Marinade
4 tbsp light sesame oil
50ml soy sauce
4 cloves garlic, peeled and finely chopped
Pinch of chilli flakes
Freshly ground black pepper
1 tbsp sesame seeds
2 tbsp sweet chilli sauce

Equipment

Chopping board, sharp knife, large flat dish, large spoon, serving dish.

Method

1 The salmon fillets can be left **whole** or **cut** into big chunks.
2 **Mix** all the ingredients for the marinade together in a large flat dish. Put the salmon in the marinade and **toss** to ensure that it is thoroughly coated. **Marinate** for at least 20 minutes.
3 **Preheat** the grill and **grill** the salmon until the fish is charred and cooked through.
4 **Baste** the fish with extra marinade while it is cooking.
5 **Serve** with crisp salad.

Mackerel baked with cider and apple

Serves 2

Ingredients

2 large mackerel, gutted
4 bay leaves
1 small onion, chopped
1 small apple, cored and sliced
50g butter, diced
200ml cider
Salt and freshly ground black pepper
1 tbsp oil to brush tinfoil
Fresh chopped parsley and orange
   segments, to garnish

Equipment

2 sheets of tinfoil, each 20cm × 30cm,
chopping board, chopping knife, baking
tray, serving dish.

Method

1 **Preheat** oven to 190°C/170°C fan/gas
   mark 5. **Brush** the two sheets of tinfoil
   with oil.
2 **Season** the cavities of the fish and put
   two bay leaves inside each fish.
3 **Mix** the onion and apple together and
   divide them between the two sheets of
   oiled foil.
4 **Put** the mackerel on top of the onion
   and apple and **dot** the butter over
   the fish.
5 **Fold** up the sides and ends of the
   parcels and then **pour** half the cider
   over each. **Seal** the parcels.
6 **Put** the foil parcels on a baking tray
   and **bake** for 25 minutes.
7 **Garnish** with chopped parsley and
   orange segments and **serve** with boiled
   potatoes and crisp salad.

Baked stuffed trout

Serves 4

Ingredients

4 trout, cleaned, with heads and fins removed
200g can salmon, drained and flaked
1 tbsp chopped parsley
50ml soya cream alternative or soured cream (optional)
100g breadcrumbs
2 tbsp lemon juice
1 egg, beaten
Salt and pepper
4 bay leaves (optional)
1 dessertsp oil
Fresh chopped parsley, to garnish

Equipment

Fish slice, mixing bowl, shallow ovenproof dish, tablespoon, dessertspoon, small bowl, whisk or fork, can opener, measuring jug.

Method

1 **Preheat** oven to 180°C/160°C fan/ gas mark 5.
2 **Combine** the salmon, parsley, soya cream alternative or soured cream, breadcrumbs, lemon juice and seasoning in a mixing bowl. **Add** just enough egg to **bind** the mixture.
3 **Divide** the stuffing into four and **place** in the cavity of each fish.
4 **Place** the fish in a shallow ovenproof dish. **Brush** with oil. **Place** a bay leaf on top of each fish.
5 **Cover** the dish with tinfoil and **bake** for 40 minutes.
6 **Remove** the tinfoil and bay leaves.
7 **Garnish** with freshly chopped parsley. **Serve** with boiled or baked potatoes and green salad or steamed vegetables.

Main courses: vegetarian

Mushroom risotto

Serves 4

Ingredients

100g mushrooms
1 onion
2 tbsp cooking oil for frying
750ml chicken or vegetable stock
200g arborio rice, washed
25g grated Parmesan cheese
Salt and pepper
Fresh chopped parsley, to garnish
Grated Parmesan cheese, to garnish

Equipment

2 saucepans, measuring jug, chopping board, chopping knife, grater, wooden spoon, serving dish.

Method

1 **Slice** mushrooms and finely **chop** onion. **Heat** oil in saucepan and **fry** mushrooms and onion on a medium low heat for 10–15 minutes.
2 **Boil** stock in the other saucepan.
3 **Add** the rice to the mushrooms and onion and **cook** for 5 minutes, stirring continuously.
4 **Pour** in half of the stock and **simmer** for 15 minutes, stirring at intervals.
5 **Pour** in the rest of the stock and **cook** for 20 minutes until the rice is 'al dente'.
6 **Stir** in the Parmesan cheese.
7 **Garnish** with parsley and serve immediately with a small bowl of Parmesan cheese and a selection of salads.

Note: 'Al dente' means that the rice is soft but still has texture or bite.

Variation

50g dried wild mushrooms can be used instead of fresh mushrooms. Put the dried mushrooms in a bowl of hot water while the onions are frying. Drain the water and discard. Add the mushrooms at step 3.

Potato and leek gratin

Serves 4–6

Ingredients

*1.5kg potatoes, peeled and
    very thinly sliced
900ml milk
1 bay leaf
2 thyme sprigs or pinch of dried thyme
3 garlic cloves, peeled and crushed
2 large leeks, white parts only, thinly sliced
Salt
Pinch of grated nutmeg
150g grated cheese (Gruyère or Cheddar)
50g butter, diced*

Equipment

Large casserole dish, medium saucepan,
chopping board, chopping knife.

Method

1 **Preheat** the oven to 190°C/170°C fan/
  gas mark 5.
2 **Put** the potatoes in a saucepan with the
  milk, bay leaf, thyme, crushed garlic,
  leeks and a pinch of salt.
3 **Slowly** bring to a **boil**, then **simmer**
  until the potatoes are barely tender
  but not to the point of falling apart.
  Discard the bay leaf and thyme
  sprigs. **Drain**.

4 **Make** a single layer of potatoes and
  leeks in the casserole dish. **Sprinkle**
  with nutmeg and **add** a layer of
  cheese. **Repeat** until all of the
  potatoes, leeks and cheese are used up,
  finishing with a layer of cheese.
5 **Add** enough of the milk to reach the
  last layer of potatoes.
6 **Scatter** the diced butter over the top
  and **bake** for 50 minutes until
  golden brown.
7 **Serve** with a selection of salads.

Vegetarian loaf

Serves 4

Ingredients

50g Puy lentils
150g red lentils
1 tbsp oil
1 small onion, peeled and chopped
2 carrots, peeled and finely diced
1 red pepper, diced
2 celery sticks, finely diced
3 garlic cloves, peeled and crushed
½ fresh red chilli, deseeded and
  finely chopped
1 tsp ground cumin
3 eggs
25g roasted hazelnuts, chopped
25g roasted peanuts, chopped
50g breadcrumbs
100g Cheddar cheese, grated
Salt and freshly ground black pepper

Equipment

Chopping board, chopping knife,
medium-sized loaf tin, baking parchment,
2 saucepans, colander, mixing bowl.

Method

1 **Preheat** the oven to 170°C/150°C fan/
   gas mark 3.
2 **Line** the base and sides of a medium-
   sized loaf tin with baking parchment.

3 **Place** the Puy and red lentils in
   separate saucepans. **Cover** each with
   cold water and **cook** the Puy lentils
   for 15 minutes and the red lentils for
   8 minutes. **Drain** in a colander and
   place in a mixing bowl.
4 **Heat** the oil in a large saucepan and
   add all the diced vegetables, garlic,
   chilli and cumin. **Cook** over a low heat
   for about 5 minutes.
5 **Remove** from the heat and add to the
   lentils with the eggs, nuts, breadcrumbs,
   cheese, salt and pepper. **Mix** well.
6 **Place** in the lined loaf tin and bake for
   45 minutes, until firm to the touch.
7 **Turn** onto a serving dish and **serve** hot
   or cold with a selection of salads.

Vegetables

Aubergine stew with chickpeas

Serves 4

Ingredients

1 aubergine
4 tbsp olive oil
1 large red onion, chopped
1 red bell pepper, roughly chopped
2 tsp paprika
2 garlic cloves, peeled and thinly sliced
2 tbsp tomato paste
6 tomatoes, quartered
1 × 400g tin chickpeas, rinsed
150ml water
Salt and freshly ground pepper
Freshly chopped parsley and diced goat's
    cheese, to garnish

Equipment

Chopping board, chopping knife, large
saucepan, frying pan, fish slice, serving dish.

Method

1 **Cut** the aubergine into 3cm × 2cm sticks.
2 **Heat** 2 tbsp oil in a frying pan and fry
   the aubergine for about 10 minutes
   until golden brown.
3 **Heat** 2 tbsp oil in a large saucepan.
   Add the onion, pepper, paprika and
   garlic and sauté for 8–10 minutes.
4 **Stir** in the tomato paste, tomatoes,
   aubergine, chickpeas, 150ml water and
   a pinch of salt and pepper.
5 **Lower** the heat and simmer, covered,
   for 20 minutes, stirring occasionally.
6 **Garnish** with chopped parsley and
   diced goat's cheese and **serve.**

Roast vegetables

Serves 4

Ingredients

1 parsnip, peeled and cut into 2cm dice
1 carrot, peeled and cut into 2cm dice
1 red onion, peeled and chopped roughly
1 red pepper, deseeded and sliced
4 cloves of garlic, peeled and chopped
1 courgette, cut into 2cm dice
1 tbsp freshly chopped or 1 tsp dried
    mixed herbs
1 tbsp olive oil
Chopped fresh herbs, to garnish

Equipment

Large roasting tin, chopping knife,
chopping board, tablespoon.

Method

1 **Preheat** oven to 220°C/200°C fan/
   gas mark 7.
2 **Place** the vegetables in a single layer
   in a large roasting tin.
3 **Scatter** the herbs over the vegetables
   and **drizzle** with oil.
4 **Roast** for 40 minutes until the
   vegetables are golden brown.
5 **Garnish** with chopped fresh herbs
   and serve.

Salads

Quinoa salad

Serves 4–6

Ingredients

200g quinoa
500ml vegetable stock
1 tbsp curry powder
2 tsp turmeric
50g raisins
3 cloves garlic, crushed
Grated rind of 1 lemon
75ml olive oil
2 tbsp pine nuts
2 tbsp freshly chopped coriander,
  plus extra to garnish

Equipment

Chopping board, chopping knife, large saucepan, measuring jug, grater.

Method

1 **Put** the quinoa, stock, curry powder and turmeric in a saucepan. Bring to the boil and simmer for 15 minutes until most of the liquid has evaporated. **Remove** from the heat.
2 **Add** the raisins, garlic and lemon rind.
3 **Partially cover** with a lid and let the quinoa steam for another 5 to 10 minutes.
4 When cooled down slightly, **add** the olive oil, pine nuts and coriander.
5 **Serve** cold, garnished with coriander.

Chickpea salad

Serves 6

Ingredients

1 onion, finely chopped
2 tbsp olive oil
2 garlic cloves, peeled and crushed
1cm piece of root ginger,
  peeled and grated
1 tsp curry powder
½ tsp ground cumin
½ tsp ground coriander
Pinch of turmeric
½ red chilli, finely chopped
1 × 400g can of tomatoes
2 × 400g cans of chickpeas,
  rinsed and drained
1 tbsp chopped chives
1 tbsp freshly chopped parsley

Equipment

Chopping board, chopping knife, grater, large spoon, medium saucepan, serving dish.

Method

1 **Sauté** the onion in oil over a low heat for 15 minutes.
2 **Add** the garlic, ginger, spices and chilli and **cook** for a further 2 minutes.
3 **Add** the tomatoes and cook uncovered on a low heat for 20 minutes.
4 **Remove** from heat and **add** the herbs and chickpeas. Allow to cool.
5 **Serve** as an accompaniment.

Curried rice salad

Serves 4

Ingredients

*150g long grain or basmati rice,
    white or brown*
1 tbsp curry powder
150g frozen peas
2 spring onions, chopped
1 small carrot, grated
½ red pepper, diced
½ cucumber, diced (leave skin on)
1 apple, diced (leave skin on)
75g peanuts
50g sultanas (optional)
50g dried apricot, chopped (optional)
Dressing
4 tbsp vegetable oil
2 tbsp wine vinegar
1 tbsp lemon juice
1 tbsp brown sugar
1 tsp curry powder

Equipment

Chopping board, chopping knife, large
saucepan, colander, tray or large flat dish,
small saucepan, serving dish.

Method

1 Place curry powder in a large saucepan
   of water. Bring to the **boil** and **cook** the
   rice according to packet instructions.

2 **Drain** the rice and spread out on a
   tray to cool.
3 **Cook** the peas in a little boiling water
   for 3 minutes.
4 Once the rice has cooled, **combine** with
   all the other ingredients.
5 To make the **dressing**, place all the
   ingredients in a bowl and stir until
   well mixed.
6 **Pour** most of the dressing over the rice
   mixture and mix gently. Add more
   dressing if required.
7 **Serve** as an accompaniment.

Avocado and green leaf salad

Serves 4

Ingredients

100g mixed green leaves – e.g. lettuce, rocket, spinach, watercress

2 avocados

Dressing

1 tsp Dijon mustard

1 tsp wine vinegar (either red or white)

3 tbsp olive oil

1 tbsp water

Equipment

Small jug or jar with a lid, large mixing bowl, chopping board, chopping knife, colander or salad spinner, small serving dish.

Method

1. **Make** the dressing by **mixing** together the mustard, vinegar, oil and water in a jug or jar with a cover.
2. **Wash** the leaves and **dry** in a salad spinner or colander.
3. To **stone** the avocado, **cut** lengthwise around the stone and **twist** the halves apart. **Ease** out the stone with a spoon. **Ease** a spoon between the skin and the flesh to **peel** the avocado. **Cut** the avocado into chunks.
4. **Place** the salad leaves and avocado chunks in a large bowl. **Pour** the dressing over and gently toss the salad.
5. **Serve** immediately.

Chapter 11
The practical cookery exam

The practical cookery exam is worth 35 per cent of the Home Economics marks at higher level and 45 per cent at ordinary level.

The exam is held at the end of the second term or the beginning of the third term of the school year.

It is 1½ hours long, with half an hour preparation time beforehand.

The exam tasks are given out two weeks before the exam. This allows you time to do research and fill in the preparation sheets.

The exam task is presented as a **design brief**.

The stages in completing the design brief in the practical exam are:

1 **Statement of the task.**

2 **Analysis:** What are you being asked to do? Break down the task and write it in your own words.

3 **Factors to be considered:** Include four factors, two of which relate specifically to the task, and two general factors such as time and skills.

>
> **Keynote**
>
> A **factor** is an important issue to be thought about when making a decision.

4 **Research:** Look up cookery books for recipes and ideas for menus. Ask your teacher for advice.

5 **Possible solutions:** Suggest two possible solutions for each part of the task, e.g. main course **and** drink/accompaniment. Possible menus should be written in proper menu form (see page 51).

6 **Solution:** Choose one solution and give two reasons for your choice. Reasons could involve your skills, time, equipment, nutritive value, dietary requirements and appeal of the dishes.

7 **Name of the dish(es) you intend to prepare:** Include a list of ingredients and equipment to be used. Include costing if required in the brief.

8 **Preparation time:** Plan what you will do during the half-hour preparation time. Prepare yourself, your equipment and your work area. Make out a time plan for the exam.

9 **During the exam:** Work through your time plan efficiently and with confidence. Present dishes attractively and ensure your work area is clean and tidy at all times.

10 **Evaluate the whole task:** Include the appearance, taste and texture of the dish. **Make sure** you also evaluate your own skills, efficiency and timing. Look back on the analysis of the brief – did you do what you were asked to do? In other words, did you meet the brief? **Always say whether or not you met the brief, and why. This is very important.**

The following is a worked example of a design brief.

Practical cookery exam

Task No. _____   Exam No. _____

Design brief/investigation

Calcium forms an essential part of a balanced diet.
Investigate some calcium-rich main course dishes that could be served as the main meal of the day.
Prepare, cook and serve one of the dishes you have investigated.
Prepare and serve an attractive salad to complement the meal.

2009 Junior Certificate Food and Culinary Skills Tasks

Analysis – what am being I asked to do?

I am being asked to investigate some calcium-rich main course dishes for the main meal of the day. I must prepare, cook and serve one of the dishes and prepare and serve an attractive salad to go with it.

What factors must I consider when doing my investigation/brief?

1 I must choose dishes that are high in calcium and vitamin D (for absorption of calcium).
2 The salad must go well with the main course.
3 I must prepare, cook and serve the two dishes in 90 minutes.
4 I must consider my skills and available equipment.

Possible solutions/ideas/menus

1 Quiche Lorraine, baked potato, green salad.
2 Macaroni cheese with mushrooms, bean salad.

Solution

Choose one solution and give two reasons for your choice.

I chose to make macaroni cheese with mushrooms and bean salad. The macaroni cheese includes milk and cheese, which contain calcium and vitamin D. It is a tasty dish and I have the skills to make it. The bean salad is high in protein, and is a colourful salad to complement the macaroni cheese. I will be able to complete both dishes in the time available.

Name of dish(es) you intend to prepare

Macaroni cheese with mushrooms.
Bean salad.

List of Ingredients	Cost	List of Ingredients	Cost
Macaroni Cheese with Mushrooms:		**Bean Salad:**	
400g macaroni		200g can red kidney beans, drained	
200g mushrooms, sliced		200g can chickpeas, drained	
3 tbsp cooking oil (for frying)		100g French beans	
25g flour		½ red pepper, deseeded and chopped	
1 vegetable stock cube		½ green pepper, deseeded and chopped	
600ml milk		Small red onion, chopped	
175g grated Cheddar cheese		Dressing:	
Pinch of mixed herbs		1 tbsp white wine vinegar	
Pinch of salt		1 tbsp balsamic vinegar	
1 tsp Dijon mustard		Pinch of caster sugar	
25g grated Parmesan cheese		1 tsp honey	
Fresh basil		4–6 tbsp olive oil	
2 cherry tomatoes		1 tsp Dijon mustard	
		Salt and pepper	
		1 tbsp fresh chopped parsley	

List of equipment

2 large saucepans, chopping board, chopping knife, measuring jug, colander, wooden spoon, casserole dish, grater, tablespoon, teaspoon, pot stand, small saucepan, can opener, screw-top jar, fork, salad serving bowl.

Insert copies of your recipes here.

What will I do during preparation time?

I will:

- prepare myself – remove jewellery, wash hands, tie back hair, wear apron and cover any cuts
- collect equipment and utensils on list
- make sure all equipment is clean
- set up my table
- collect dishcloth, tea towel and oven gloves
- weigh and measure ingredients and lay them out on plates and in bowls
- wash vegetables (but not peel); boil kettle
- put preparation sheets in a plastic folder, with a pen for evaluation.

Time plan

Starting Time 10.00 a.m.   **Finishing Time 11.30 a.m.**
Time

10.00	• Boil French beans for salad for 5 mins.
	• Chop red and green peppers and onion for salad.
	• Drain and cool French beans.
	• Mix salad ingredients together, cover with cling film and place in the fridge.
	• Mix salad dressing ingredients together in jar and place in fridge.
10.30	• Wash up.
	• Place macaroni in pot of boiling water and boil for 8 mins.
	• Slice mushrooms.
	• Heat oil and fry mushrooms for 3 mins.
	• Drain macaroni.
	• Add flour and stock cube to mushrooms and cook for 1 min.
	• Remove from heat and add milk, stirring well. Add Cheddar cheese, herbs, salt and mustard, and bring to boil.
10.50	• Simmer for 3 mins. Preheat grill.
	• Add macaroni to sauce and mix well. Transfer to casserole dish. Sprinkle with Parmesan cheese.
	• Brown under the grill.
	• Mix dressing into bean salad and serve.
	• Garnish macaroni with basil leaves and cherry tomatoes and serve on pot stand.
11.10	• Call examiner to taste dishes.
	• Wash up.
11.20	• Write evaluation.
11.30	• Finish.

Note: It is not necessary to write down the exact time for every step, but it may help to keep you on track.

Evaluation

Evaluate the whole task under these headings:

Did you meet the brief set out in the task? Explain.

Yes, I met the brief. I prepared, cooked and served a calcium-rich main course dish and a salad to complement it.

Comment on the specific requirements of the task (e.g. costing, variety, garnish, starter, dessert, icing, table setting, drink, nutritive value).

I investigated some main course dishes that were high in calcium and also in vitamin D (for the absorption of calcium). I prepared and served a salad that was colourful and attractive and that suited the main course dish.

Presentation

The macaroni was served in the cooking dish. I forgot to wipe the rim of the dish before placing it under the grill, so it had some splashes of sauce around the edges. The presentation was improved when I added basil and cherry tomatoes. The bean salad was presented with a simple garnish of fresh parsley in a plain white serving bowl. It looked tasty.

Colour

The macaroni was an attractive golden brown colour. The garnish added contrasting colour. The bean salad was colourful and attractive. The white serving bowl highlighted the variety of colours.

Taste and texture

The macaroni tasted strongly of cheese and mushrooms. The pasta was slightly firm and the sauce was smooth and creamy. The bean salad was firm and crunchy, and the dressing was tangy.

Efficiency and skills

My timing was good. The dishes were served up on time, and the washing-up and evaluation were finished before the end. I was pleased with my skills of weighing and measuring, chopping and sauce-making. I was careful when straining the macaroni and using the grill.

Are there any changes you would make?

Yes. If I was doing it again, I would make sure that I had wiped any splashes of sauce off the dish before putting it under the grill. I would also add some red peppers to the macaroni for extra colour.

Section two
Consumer studies

Chapter 12
Consumers

Consumer studies develops knowledge and skills such as judgement and decision-making. These skills allow consumers to use resources such as time and money wisely.

What is a consumer?

A consumer is anyone who buys goods or uses services.

Every day, consumers buy **goods**, such as:

- food
- clothes
- cars
- CDs
- books
- mobile phones.

And **services**, such as:

- electricity
- telephone
- Internet.
- dry cleaning
- hairdressing
- public transport
- doctors and dentists

The following **state services** are paid for by taxation:

- health
- education
- Gardaí
- roads
- street lighting
- postal services.

Consumers buying goods and services

Columba College
Killucan

Case Study

Make a list of the goods and services that Jenny encounters in her day.

It's 7 a.m. and Jenny's alarm goes off. She hits the snooze button and dozes for another ten minutes. Off it goes again, and she gets out of bed with a groan. She can't miss her bus to school as today is the day of the outdoor education trip. One of her friends texts to warn her not to forget her camera. That reminds her, she must stop off at the shopping centre on the way home and get her photos printed off. She'll definitely spend some time tonight uploading some onto her Facebook page as well. Her friends in the other school will want to see them. She has a quick shower, and quickly dries and dresses herself. As she's combing her hair, her mum reminds her about her orthodontist appointment tomorrow.

'Okay, Mum,' she says, 'and don't forget to phone the hairdresser. My hair needs a trim.'

She grabs a slice of toast and her bag on the way out the door. She has a minute to spare before the bus arrives and she hops on. She'll grab a coffee in the shop next door to the school, and maybe an apple for later. Her teacher is waiting at the minibus when she arrives at the school. All her classmates are waving at her to hurry up . . .

As consumers, our decisions to buy goods and services are affected by our **needs** and **wants**.

Needs are **what we must have to survive**, e.g.:

- food
- clothing
- shelter.

Wants are **the extras that may make life more pleasant or comfortable**, e.g.:

- holidays
- DVDs
- jewellery
- televisions
- designer clothes
- CDs.

Needs and wants may vary depending on:

1 Age (child, teenager, adult, OAP).

2 Circumstances (married/single, working/student, unemployed/part-time worker, parent/no children, live alone/with others).

3 Values (what is important to us, our priorities).

It is important that needs are met before wants. For example, it is unwise to buy an expensive TV if an overdue electricity bill hasn't been paid.

Summary

- **A consumer is a person who buys goods and services.**
- **Goods** (things) include **food, clothes, cars** and **DVDs.**
- **Services** (jobs done for you) **include doctors, dentists, hairdressers** and **dry cleaners.**
- **Consumer decisions** are influenced by **needs** and **wants.**
- **Needs are essential goods and services**, e.g. food, clothes and shelter.
- **Wants are non-essentials**, e.g. designer clothes, jewellery, CDs.
- Needs and wants may vary depending on **age**, **circumstances** and **values.**

Activities

1 Separate the following words into goods and services:

- cakes
- drinking water
- Internet
- magazines
- business suit.
- doctor
- theatre
- motorbike
- bread
- dentist
- text messages
- medicines
- taxi
- yoga class
- evening classes
- DVD player
- iPod

Goods		Services	

2 Indicate which of the above are needs and which are wants for (a) a teenager and (b) a working mother.

Teenager		Working mother	
Needs	Wants	Needs	Wants

Check if your answers are similar to those of your classmates.

Revision Questions

1 List four state services paid for by taxation.

2 What is a consumer?

3 Explain the difference between needs and wants. Give examples in your answer.

4 Name two factors that influence a consumer's needs and wants.

5 Explain what is meant by a 'priority'.

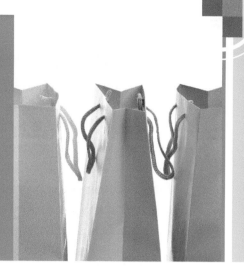

Chapter 13
Shopping

Window shopping

Shopping is an important part of our lives, something we must do in order to meet our basic needs and wants. Before going shopping, we must make **decisions** about what we are going to buy and where we are going to buy it.

The decision-making process

Define the decision to be made (what I must decide or choose).

Enquire about possible choices.

Consider the choices.

Investigate the results of different courses of action.

Decide on a plan and put it into action.

Evaluate the results. (Am I happy with the outcome?)

Remember: **D E C I D E !**

Our decisions are influenced by many **factors**.

- **Needs and wants:** What we must have and what we would like to have.
- **Resources:** The amount of money and time available.
- **Values/priorities:** What is important to us.
- **Other people:** Family and peer group may influence us.
- **Emotions:** We may feel very strongly about something.
- **Fashion:** Fashions in clothes, music and food.
- **Merchandising:** Easy payment options, discounts.
- **Advertising:** Can persuade us to buy things we may not need.
- **Culture:** We buy certain items at special times, e.g. Christmas, Hallowe'en.

When **shopping for goods and services**, consider the following.

- **Budget:** Can you afford it?
- **Quality:** Is it well made and designed to last?
- **Value:** Is it good value for money?
- **Design:** Is it well designed?
- **Comfort:** Does it fit well and is it comfortable?
- **Environment:** Is it environmentally friendly? Is it biodegradable?
- **Maintenance:** Is it easy to clean and look after?
- **Purpose:** Is it necessary and will it do the job it is designed to do?
- **Guarantee:** Does it have a guarantee, and if so, for how long?
- **Safety:** Is it safe to use? Are there any risks associated with it?

Keynote

Impulse buying (buying on the spur of the moment) can often lead to disappointment or 'buyer's remorse'.

Activities

1 What was the last major purchase you made? What factors influenced your decision to buy it?

2 Have you ever bought anything on impulse? Make a list of products which, because of their location in a shop or the manner in which they are promoted, could end up as impulse buys.

3 Discuss how the following may influence our buying decisions when buying food: fashion; other people; and advertising.

Shopping outlets

There are many different types of shopping outlet. Each offers different products and services to the consumer.

Department stores

Department stores stock a wide range of goods under one roof, e.g. footwear, clothing, furniture, food.

Most have facilities such as a restaurant and toilets, e.g. Marks & Spencer, Debenhams, Brown Thomas.

Supermarkets

These are self-service and sell food and general groceries. They stock a wide range of branded and 'own-brand' goods. Many have in-store bakeries and sell take-away hot and cold foods and drinks, e.g. Tesco, Superquinn.

A supermarket

A multiple chain store

An independent shop

Multiple chain stores

These are countrywide self-service shops with a distinctive appearance and layout. Many sell their own-branded goods, e.g. Dunnes Stores, Next, A-Wear, Penneys.

Voluntary chains

Voluntary chain stores are independently owned supermarket chains, e.g. Spar, Mace, Supervalu and Centra.

Independent shops

These are usually small and offer a personal service. They carry a smaller range of goods than larger supermarkets and their prices tend to be higher. Many stay open late.

A hypermarket or superstore

A boutique

Hypermarkets and superstores

These are huge shops that combine a supermarket and department store. They carry a vast range of goods, from garden furniture to fresh fish. They are usually built on the outskirts of towns.

Boutiques

Boutiques are specialist clothes shops that sometimes carry an exclusive range of stock. Prices are usually higher than in chain stores.

Discount stores

These offer a limited range of goods at a reduced price, e.g. Euro Two, Poundcity.

A specialist shop

A street market

Specialist shops

These shops specialise in particular products, such as jewellery, sports wear, fishing equipment or crafts.

Other outlets

Other outlets include street markets, mobile shops, vending machines, auctions, mail order, party plan selling, doorstep selling and online shopping.

Changes in shopping practices

Many changes have occurred in the way people shop and in the way shops operate.

- Increased competition has meant better prices for the consumer.
- Fewer shops give credit or provide a counter service.
- A wider range of goods is stocked in shops nowadays.
- More emphasis is placed on customer service.
- Facilities such as restaurants, crèches and toilets are provided.
- Many shops open late, on Sundays and even 24 hours.
- Home delivery services are available.
- There are more chain stores and out-of-town shopping centres.
- There is widespread use of customer loyalty schemes, e.g. Tesco Club Card, Dunnes Value Club Card.
- Free parking is provided by shops.
- There is greater flexibility in methods of payment for goods.
- Online and TV shopping facilities are available for a wide range of goods and services.
- Multicultural influences, e.g. Polish and African shops, are no longer confined to cities.

Multicultural influences are widespread

Self-service and counter service

Nowadays most shops offer self-service, i.e. the consumer picks up the items he/she needs and pays for them at the checkout. In the past, most shops operated a counter service, where the shopkeeper picked up the items and the consumer then paid for them.

Advantages of self-service:

Self-service

1 Quick and convenient.
2 Customer has more time to spend on selection.
3 Goods are well displayed and clearly priced.
4 Prices are lower due to bulk buying and lower staff costs.
5 Wide range of products available.
6 Quick turnover ensures that products are very fresh.
7 Own-brand goods are competitively priced.
8 Self-service checkouts may reduce queuing time.

Disadvantages of self-service:

1 Less personal contact.
2 More temptation to impulse buy.
3 Most foods are pre-packaged and may not suit a single person.
4 Credit is not usually available.
5 There can be long queues at checkouts.

Advantages of counter service:

1 Personal service.
2 Advice offered.
3 Credit sometimes offered.
4 Less effort for the shopper.

Disadvantages of counter service:

1 Higher prices.
2 More staff are needed, which leads to higher costs.
3 Smaller selection of goods.

Counter service

Buy, buy, buy!

Many **techniques** are used in supermarkets to **encourage the consumer to buy more.**

- Heavy goods are located at the entrance to encourage customers to use trolleys.
- Essentials like bread and milk are often at the furthest point from the entrance so that customers must walk right through the shop.
- Essential items are on low shelves, while luxuries are at eye level.
- Wide aisles allow customers to move around easily and spend time browsing.
- Items that can go together are often placed near each other, e.g. peanuts and crisps near the drinks, ice-cream sauces and wafers near the ice cream.
- Sweets and magazines or health and beauty items are often located near the checkout for last-minute impulse buys.
- Colourful fruit and vegetable displays give the impression of wholesome, healthy food.
- Background music is played to cover up the hustle and bustle.
- Special promotions are displayed away from their usual department, giving the impression of bargains.
- The aroma of freshly baked bread is circulated around the shop.
- The shop's own-brand products are displayed near those of the most expensive competitors to highlight the price difference.
- Use of money-off vouchers with customer loyalty cards to influence consumer decision-making.
- Food sampling encourages impulse buying.
- The presence of in-store ATMs guarantees a ready supply of cash.

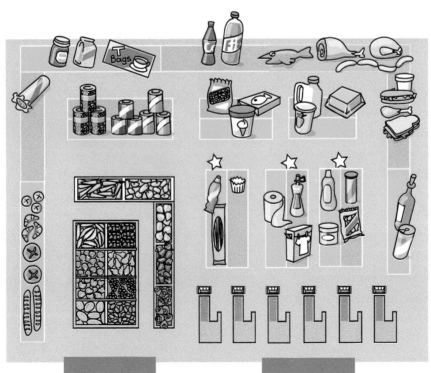

Entrance   Exit

Guidelines for shopping

- Always make a list and stick to it.
- Avoid going to the shop for just one item, as it wastes time and energy.
- Avoid impulse buying.
- Keep receipts for a while after purchase in case of a problem.
- Bulk buying non-perishables, e.g. toilet tissue, nappies, detergents, can be more economical.
- Shop around and compare prices and value for money.
- Look for quality and freshness.
- Check date stamping on perishable foods.
- Avail of special offers where genuine savings can be made.
- Avoid shopping when tired or hungry.
- Bring a shopping bag!

Packaging

The amount of packaging used for goods has increased in recent times. This is due to changes in consumer buying habits and the increasing number of convenience foods on the market.

Examples of over-packaging

Functions of packaging

- Advertises the product.
- Protects goods from damage.
- Carries bar codes.
- Keeps products (food) hygienic and fresh.
- Provides information.
- Makes it easier to store and sell products.

Characteristics of good packaging

Packaging should be:

- strong
- waterproof
- light
- non-toxic
- hygienic
- biodegradable
- easy to open
- easy to reseal, if desired.

Types of packaging

- **Glass:** Bottles and jars, plain or tinted glass.
- **Paper:** May be plain, waxed, cardboard or laminated, e.g. Tetrapak.
- **Metal:** Tin cans, aluminium cans, foil trays, aluminium foil.
- **Plastic:** Bottles, jars, bags, cartons, cling film, vacuum packing.

Product labelling

Labelling is important to:

- **identify** the product
- **advertise** the product
- **describe** what the goods are made of
- **warn** of the dangers of using or misusing the product
- **give advice** on how to use and care for the product, e.g. cooking and storage
- **tell** where the product was made
- carry **bar codes**.

Link...

Food labelling, page 143
Care labelling, page 370
Hazard symbols, page 316

Disadvantages of packaging/overpackaging

- Uses up valuable natural resources, e.g. paper and plastic.
- Adds to the price of the product.
- May be difficult to open and reseal.
- Can be deceptive, e.g. a large packet may contain a small item.
- Causes litter and pollution.
- Aerosols are dangerous if heated and some contain chemicals that harm the environment.

What can the consumer do?

- **Refuse** overpackaged goods and unnecessary plastic bags. Since the introduction of the levy on plastic bags in 2002, the number of plastic bags used in Ireland has dropped dramatically.
- **Reduce** the amount of pre-packaged items bought. Buy loose items if possible, e.g. apples.
- **Reuse** plastic bags and other containers. Refill printer cartridges.

Link...

Chapter 32 The Environment

- **Recycle** as much as you can. Recycling facilities are available in most towns and villages.

Technology

Technology has played an important part in changing the way we shop today. Computerised cash registers are used in most large shops. These 'read' the bar codes that are printed on each product.

Bar codes give details of products bought (size and brand) and they ensure that till receipts are more accurate. They help the retailer with stock control and ordering. However, with this system prices are not displayed on individual products. This makes it difficult for the consumer to compare prices and to remember how much an item costs unless the receipt is kept.

Marketing terms

Own brands

Some large shops use their own brands, e.g. St Bernard, Tesco. These products are usually packaged simply and are often cheaper than similar branded products. The quality of own brands is often equal to the more expensive branded products.

Unit pricing

This is where certain unpacked goods such as fruit, vegetables, meat and fish are priced according to a unit of measurement, such as 98c per kg. It is also used for other packaged foods, such as flour and soft drinks, to allow the consumer to compare prices where package sizes are different.

How much does 500g of Dover sole cost?

Bulk buying

This means buying large quantities of a product, usually because it is cheaper. It is useful for stocking up on goods such as detergents, kitchen paper and toilet rolls.

Loss leaders

These are products sold at a loss in order to attract customers to a shop. Once inside, they may buy other goods that are not reduced.

Methods of payment

Link...

Saving and buying on credit, page 243

Cash

Paying by cash is quick and easy

- Quick and easy.
- May be inconvenient for very expensive items.
- Cash can be lost or stolen.

Cheque

- Safer and more convenient than cash.
- Current account is required to write cheques.
- Easy to overspend.

Credit card, e.g. MasterCard, Visa

- Safe and convenient.
- Customer enters their PIN and a copy of the transaction is sent to the credit card company, e.g. Visa or MasterCard, which pays the seller. The customer then has up to 28 days to pay the credit card company.
- Credit may be interest free if the balance is cleared on time. If not, a high rate of interest is charged.
- Easy to overspend.

Credit card

3V voucher

- 3V Visa prepaid vouchers are disposable prepaid Visa numbers that can be used in the same way as a Visa credit card.
- They can be used for online, phone or mail order shopping.
- They can be topped up at selected shops and newsagents in the same way as prepaid mobile phone credit.

Weblink

See www.3V.ie for information about 3V vouchers

Debit card, e.g. Laser

- Money is taken from the customer's current account within one to two days of the transaction.
- Extra cash can be withdrawn when paying (cashback facility).
- Safe and convenient.
- Current account required.

Debit card

Weblink

See www.itsyourmoney.ie

Activities

1 Make a plan of your local supermarket. Indicate the location of different products. List the techniques used in this supermarket to encourage customers to buy more goods.

2 Compare prices for a number of similar items, such as sandwiches, mobile phones or football boots, in a range of shops to highlight the benefits of shopping around.

3 List the advantages and disadvantages of online shopping.

4 Make a list of goods and services that are available online. What shopping websites are popular among teenagers?

Summary

- **Decision-making process:** Define, enquire, consider, investigate, decide and act, evaluate.

- **Factors that influence decisions:** Resources, needs, priorities, advertising, people, fashion.

- **When choosing products,** consider budget, value, purpose, environment and guarantee.

- **Shopping outlets:** Multiple chain stores, department stores, supermarkets, voluntary chains and discount stores.

- **Techniques used by supermarkets** include promotions, placement of goods, music, sampling, etc.

- **Shopping tips:** Make a list, compare prices, avail of offers, keep receipts and check expiry dates.

- Packaging **functions: Protects, informs, advertises, is hygienic and carries bar codes**.

- **Types** of packaging: Glass, paper, metal, plastic.

- **Functions** of labels: **Identify, advertise, describe, warn, advise, inform** and **carry bar codes**.

- Disadvantages of packaging: **Wasteful, costly, difficult to use, deceptive, risky, litter**.

- Consumer should **refuse, reduce, reuse** and **recycle**.

- A **bar code** is a series of bars and spaces read by an electronic scanner.

- **Own brands:** A shop's own labels, e.g. SuperValu.

- **Unit price:** Goods priced according to a unit of measurement, e.g. a litre.

- **Bulk buying:** Buying goods in large quantities to save money.

- **Loss leader:** Goods sold at a loss.

- **Methods of payment:** Cash, cheque, credit card, 3V voucher and debit card.

Revision Questions

1 Consumers are required to make many decisions. List five factors that would influence the consumer when deciding on where to shop for groceries.

2 Give your views on how brand names influence a teenager's choice of clothing.

3 List two factors which should be considered when buying shoes for a teenager.

4 Describe each of the following types of shopping outlet: (a) supermarkets; (b) department stores; (c) specialist shops; (d) independent shops.

5 Give two advantages of mail-order shopping.

6 Give one advantage and one disadvantage of shopping on the Internet.

7 Suggest four modern-day changes which have influenced shopping patterns.

8 Suggest three ways in which shopping in supermarkets has changed in recent years.

9 (a) Describe three methods used in supermarkets to encourage customers to spend more money.

(b) Describe three marketing techniques used in supermarkets.

(c) Name the marketing technique you think is most effective and give a reason for your answer.

10 Why are essential items, such as bread and milk, often placed towards the back of supermarkets?

11 List the guidelines that should be followed when shopping for goods and services.

12 Outline ways to ensure *value for money* when shopping.

13 The cost of packaging adds to consumers' weekly shopping bills.

(a) Give four reasons why packaging of goods is necessary.

(b) What are the characteristics of good packaging?

(c) List three types of packaging and suggest a different use for each.

(d) List five items of information that you would expect to find on the label of packaged goods.

(e) What information would you expect to find on the packaging of a frozen chicken?

(f) Give four disadvantages of overpackaging.

14 Explain how consumers can dispose of the packaging on frozen foods in an *environmentally friendly* way.

15 A bar code is a series of lines and spaces which are read by a scanner. True or false?

16 Give two reasons why bar codes are used.

17 List three items of information that you would expect to find on a receipt.

18 Explain the terms 'loss leader', 'unit pricing', 'own brand', 'bulk buying' and 'impulse buying'.

19 Name three methods of payment that can be used when shopping. Give one advantage and one disadvantage of each method named.

20 Explain the *benefit* to the consumer of each of the following: (a) unit pricing; (b) keeping a receipt; (c) own-brand goods.

Section two
CONSUMER STUDIES

Chapter 14
Consumers' rights and responsibilities

A right is something to which you are entitled.

Consumers' rights protect us from dishonest sellers and manufacturers who may try to rip us off.

With rights come responsibilities.

A responsibility is something you must do and for which you are answerable. For example, it is the consumer's responsibility to know his/her consumer rights.

Consumers' rights

1 The right to choice

There is a wide range of goods and services available to consumers. This leads to competition among retailers. Consumers can choose which brand of goods or which service they wish to buy. If retailers want consumers to buy their goods and services, they must provide good quality and value for money.

Consumer choice

It is the consumer's **responsibility** to make good, informed choices before buying goods and services. In order to make informed choices, the consumer has to examine all details carefully.

A **monopoly** exists where only one manufacturer or supplier provides a service and there is no competition. An example is Iarnród Éireann.

2 The right to quality and value for money

Quality means that the item is of a high standard and fit for its purpose.

Often, the price paid for an item is in proportion to the quality of the item. For example, if you buy an expensive watch, you expect it to work well and last a long time.

It is the consumer's **responsibility** to examine products and services, and compare prices before buying.

Goods must be fit for sale and fit for their purpose.

3 The right to accurate information

Suppliers of goods and services must provide clear and accurate information about their products so that consumers can make informed decisions. It is illegal to give false or misleading information about a product, for example stating that a coat is waterproof when it isn't or that a scarf is 100 per cent silk when it isn't.

Accurate information

It is the consumer's **responsibility** to read labels and ask for information if in doubt.

Inaccurate food labelling could lead to serious health problems for people with allergies or an intolerance to peanuts or gluten, for example.

4 The right to safety

Consumers have the right to expect that goods and services will not be harmful or endanger their lives. Goods such as electrical appliances, upholstered furniture, children's clothes and toys must undergo strict tests before going on sale. Dangerous items such as bleach and oven cleaner must carry warning symbols.

It is the consumer's **responsibility** to heed warnings and to follow instructions carefully.

Goods are tested during manufacturing. This is called **quality control**.

5 The right to redress

This means that if a consumer pays for an item or service that later turns out to be faulty, he or she is entitled to complain and be compensated. This can take the form of one of the three Rs: a free *repair* (item is fixed), a full or partial *refund* (money back) or a *replacement* (a new item).

It is the consumer's **responsibility** to know his/her rights and complain if these rights have been refused.

Shops and suppliers are usually willing to compensate dissatisfied customers in order to keep their custom.

Consumers' responsibilities

The consumer has the responsibility to:

- be informed about goods, services, prices and consumer law
- examine goods and services before buying
- read labels, follow instructions and consider warnings
- complain if consumer rights have been refused or if consumer laws have been broken
- be environmentally aware when choosing and using resources.

Keynote

A **resource** is a means of doing something.

Consumers use personal resources, such as time, energy, money and skills. They also use the earth's natural resources, such as oil, gas, trees, water and metals. Many of these resources are becoming scarce and need to be conserved for future generations.

Link...

How to complain, page 236
Chapter 24 Management

Activities

1 Suggest ways of conserving the earth's resources.

2 Make a list of goods that must undergo thorough safety tests before being put on the market.

3 Have you ever complained about faulty goods? If so, what was the outcome?

4 Is there a service in your area that is unsatisfactory? If so, suggest ways in which consumers could go about improving it.

Summary

- The consumer has a **right** to: choice, value for money, accurate information, safety and redress.

- The consumer has a **responsibility** to: be informed, examine products, read labels and follow instructions, complain and use resources carefully.

Revision Questions

1 'Consumers have rights and responsibilities.' Explain this statement and include examples in your explanation.

2 Outline four consumer rights and four consumer responsibilities.

3 Choose the correct word from the following list to complete (a) and (b) below.

- redress
- wants
- quality control

(a) Goods are tested during manufacturing. This is called _____.

(b) A consumer has the right to _____ when an item is faulty.

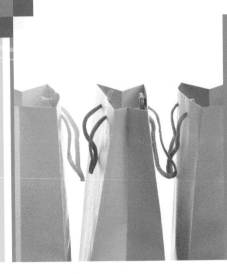

Chapter 15
Consumer protection

When you buy goods or services, a legal contract is set up between you (the buyer) and the seller. It does not have to be written, but it is legally binding. Under this contract, the seller has legal obligations to fulfil (duties or promises to keep).

Consumer protection is necessary to:

- protect the rights of consumers
- give consumers a way of redress if their rights are not granted
- guard against abuse by dishonest sellers and manufacturers.

The consumer is protected by:

- consumer laws
- statutory (government) agencies
- voluntary agencies.

Higher Level

Consumer laws

The two most important consumer laws are:

1 Sale of Goods and Supply of Services Act 1980.
2 Consumer Information Act 1978.

1 Sale of Goods and Supply of Services Act 1980

Under this Act, all **goods** should:

- be of merchantable quality – fit to be sold and in perfect condition
- be fit for their purpose – an electric kettle should boil water
- be as described – goods must match the description given on the label, advertisement or by the salesperson, e.g. 'waterproof'
- correspond with samples – if a sample is used to advertise or sell an item, the item must match the sample, e.g. a suite of furniture.

Services such as dry cleaning, hairdressing, car repairs, etc. are also covered by this Act.

The consumer is entitled to expect that:

● the supplier has the necessary skill to provide the service
● the supplier will provide the service with proper care and diligence
● materials used will be sound
● any goods supplied for the service will be of merchantable quality.

Guarantees

A guarantee is an extra bonus to the consumer. **It is a promise by the manufacturer that he/she will make good any faults in an item for a specific period of time after purchase.**

If a fault occurs in a purchased item, the consumer may claim under the Sale of Goods and Supply of Services Act 1980 or under the guarantee. Not only the buyer can claim, but also anyone who has possession of the goods during the period of the guarantee.

If goods or services are faulty, the consumer is entitled to compensation – a **refund**, **repair** or **replacement**. (Remember the 3Rs.)

However, *caveat emptor* (let the buyer beware).

Keynote

'To make good' means to compensate for any fault by way of a refund or repair.

Here are some points to consider.

● You are not covered if you misused the goods or ignored advice from the seller about how the goods should be used.
● You are not covered if you simply change your mind about the goods (although some shops will allow an exchange as a gesture of goodwill).
● You are not covered if the fault was pointed out to you before sale, e.g. goods marked as 'seconds' or 'slightly imperfect'.
● You are not obliged to accept a credit note in place of a refund, repair or replacement.
● While it is advisable to keep receipts and guarantees in a safe place, cheque stubs or credit card statements are acceptable proof of purchase.
● If you buy on credit or during a sale or you lease or rent goods, you are protected by the Sale of Goods and Supply of Services Act 1980.

Your 'statutory rights' are your rights under the law.

Link...

How to complain, page 236

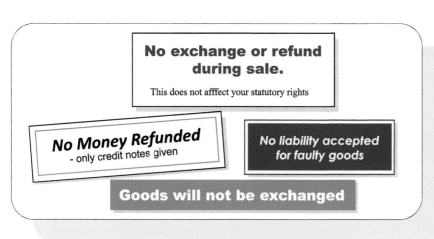

It is an offence to display notices such as these, as they attempt to take away a consumer's rights

2 Consumer Information Act 1978

The purpose of this Act is to **protect consumers against false or misleading claims about goods, services or prices.**

It is an offence for a seller to:

- make misleading claims about the price of goods
- advertise a misleading price reduction, e.g. in a sale
- publish an advertisement which is likely to mislead the public
- make false or misleading claims about goods and services.

Examples of claims about goods and services are shown in these illustrations:

Statutory (Government) Agencies

The **National Consumer Agency** was set up in 2007. Its functions are:

- to enforce the laws in relation to the sale of goods and services
- to represent the consumer
- to deal with complaints about false or misleading claims
- to educate and inform consumers about their rights.

The **Ombudsman** helps the consumer in complaints against government departments and state bodies, e.g. local authorities, the HSE, An Post. The Ombudsman **does not** get involved in disputes between retailers and the consumer.

The **Small Claims Registrar/Court** deals with claims relating to goods or services up to the value of €2,000. Consumer claims are handled quickly, cheaply and informally, without the need for a solicitor.

Voluntary agencies

Trade associations operate a code of practice for handling consumer complaints about their members, e.g. Irish Hotels Federation, Vintners' Federation of Ireland (drinks industry), SIMI (motor industry) and CIF (construction industry).

The **Consumers' Association of Ireland** is an independent, non-profit association of consumers. It publishes a monthly magazine, *Consumer Choice*, which gives advice and information on a range of goods and services.

Higher Level

Weblink

See www.consumerconnect.ie
and www.ombudsman.gov.ie

Consumer Choice magazine

Consumer information

Consumers need to be informed to:

● ensure they get value for money
● make informed decisions about goods and services
● understand consumer laws
● prepare them to take effective action if they seek redress.

Sources of consumer information

The consumer can get information from the following sources.

● **National Consumer Agency.**
● **Consumers' Association of Ireland (CAI):** To get *Consumer Choice* magazine, you must be a member of the CAI, as it is not sold through newsagents or bookshops.
● The **Office of the Ombudsman.**
● **Consumer programmes on TV and radio:** Compare different products and services and make recommendations.
● **Advertising:** Gives some honest information but is often biased, as it tries to show a product in a good light.
● **Manufacturers' leaflets and brochures:** Give detailed information on specifications and uses.
● **Shows, showrooms and exhibitions:** These offer an opportunity to collect a large amount of information, e.g. the Boat Show, Ideal Home Show, Off the Rails Roadshow.
● **Sales staff:** May be very well informed about products, but may put pressure on consumers.
● **Word of mouth:** Friends and contacts may have valuable experience and advice to offer.
● **Citizens Information Centres:** Provide information on consumer rights and government services.

The Boat Show

● **Libraries:** Have back issues of consumer magazines, e.g. *Consumer Choice, Which?*

Some sources of information are more **easily available** to the consumer than others, e.g. libraries, advertisements, word of mouth. Others, such as the National Consumer Agency, the CAI and the Ombudsman, are harder to reach, but are very **reliable** and worthwhile.

How to complain

If you buy something and then discover a problem with it, *you must complain.*

Complain as soon as possible.
Only complain to the seller or manager.
Make your case clear.
Persist and do not be fobbed off.
Let the seller know that you are aware of your rights.
Avoid losing your temper.
Indicate how you wish to be compensated and allow reasonable time.
Never play down your complaint.

There are a number of ways of making a complaint.

Complaining in person

1 As soon as a problem is discovered, go back to the seller with the item and receipt/proof of purchase.

2 Ask to see the manager. Be firm but polite.

3 Explain your complaint clearly and ask the manager what he/she intends to do about it.

4 If the manager is unhelpful, contact the head office or the trade association, if appropriate.

5 As a last resort, you may opt to get help from the National Consumer Agency, the CAI or the Small Claims Registrar.

Complaining by telephone

1 Stand up while you make your phone call. This improves assertiveness (confidence).

2 Ask for the customer services manager or someone who can deal with a complaint. Speak slowly and clearly and remain calm.

3 Ask for the name and title of the person to whom you are speaking. This can work well to focus their attention on your problem.

4 Record the date and time of your call.

5 Explain the problem clearly and ask what the company is prepared to do about it. Note the response.

6 If you hear nothing back from the company, don't give up. Write a letter of complaint.

Writing a letter of complaint

1 State the facts clearly and calmly. Avoid waffle.

2 Keep copies of letters sent.

3 Send letters by registered post or get a certificate of postage as proof that the letter has been sent and received.

4 Send copies of receipts, invoices or guarantees.

5 Never send originals.

6 If writing to a company's head office, address the letter to the Customer Services Manager.

7 Give a description of what you bought, including the make and model number.

8 State when and where you bought it and the price you paid.

9 Explain what is wrong and what steps you have taken so far to remedy the situation.

10 State what action you would like the company to take.

Sample letter of complaint

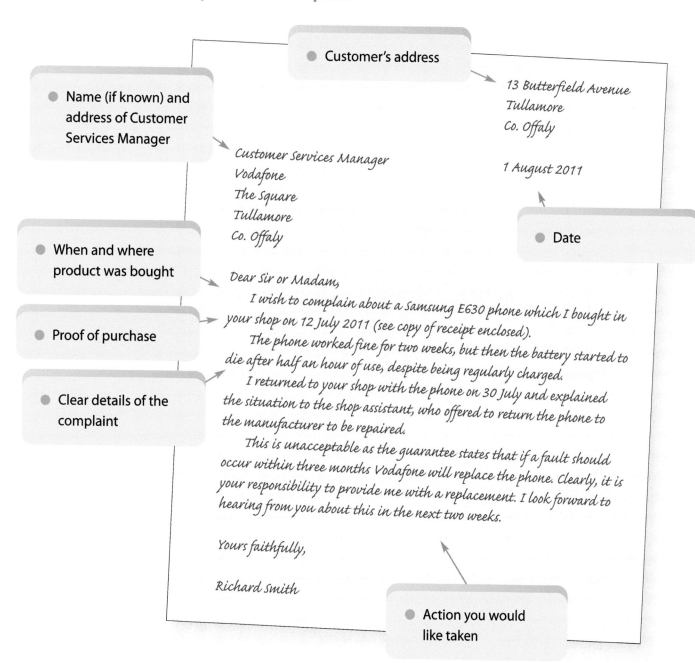

Customer's address

Name (if known) and address of Customer Services Manager

When and where product was bought

Proof of purchase

Clear details of the complaint

Date

Action you would like taken

13 Butterfield Avenue
Tullamore
Co. Offaly

1 August 2011

Customer Services Manager
Vodafone
The Square
Tullamore
Co. Offaly

Dear Sir or Madam,

I wish to complain about a Samsung E630 phone which I bought in your shop on 12 July 2011 (see copy of receipt enclosed).

The phone worked fine for two weeks, but then the battery started to die after half an hour of use, despite being regularly charged.

I returned to your shop with the phone on 30 July and explained the situation to the shop assistant, who offered to return the phone to the manufacturer to be repaired.

This is unacceptable as the guarantee states that if a fault should occur within three months Vodafone will replace the phone. Clearly, it is your responsibility to provide me with a replacement. I look forward to hearing from you about this in the next two weeks.

Yours faithfully,

Richard Smith

Activities

Here are some consumer problems. What advice and information would you offer?

1 I bought a pair of designer jeans which were reduced to half-price in the sales. One of the pockets fell off in the first wash. What should I do?

2 My hair straightener has stopped heating. It's still under guarantee, and the shopkeeper said I should contact the manufacturer directly. Is he right?

3 I recently bought a new pair of shoes to match a dress I had bought for an upcoming wedding. (I forgot to bring the dress to the shop when buying the shoes.) When I got home I found that the shoes didn't really match the dress. Can I get my money back?

Summary

- The **Sale of Goods and Supply of Services Act 1980** states that goods must be of **merchantable quality**, **fit** for their purpose, as **described** and conform with **samples**.

- Services must be carried out by a **skilled** provider, using **care** and **diligence** and **sound materials**.

- A **guarantee** is a promise by the manufacturer that he/she will make good any faults in an item for a specific time after purchase.

- The **Consumer Information Act 1978** protects against **false or misleading claims about goods, services or prices**.

- **Statutory** agencies include the **National Consumer Agency**, the **Ombudsman** and the **Small Claims Registrar**.

- **Voluntary** agencies include **trade associations** and the **Consumers' Association of Ireland**.

- **Other sources of information include advertising, sales staff, word of mouth, etc.**

- Remember: **C O M P L A I N !**

Revision Questions

1 What rights is a consumer entitled to when purchasing goods?

2 Explain the term 'merchantable quality'.

3 How does the Consumer Information Act protect the consumer?

4 Explain what a guarantee is. What is the benefit of a guarantee to the consumer?

5 When is a consumer not covered by the terms of a guarantee?

6 A guarantee is a contract between the manufacturer and the consumer. True or false?

7 Give two reasons why it is important to get a receipt when you buy an item.

8 List and explain four reasons why consumers need to be informed.

9 Name four sources of consumer information. Evaluate two of these sources with reference to reliability and availability.

10 Suggest three sources of information that would help you make a wise choice when buying an iPhone.

11 Give two functions of the Consumers' Association of Ireland.

12 Give two advantages of the Small Claims procedure.

13 What is the function of the Office of the Ombudsman?

14 (a) A mobile phone, still under guarantee, becomes faulty. List three forms of redress available to the consumer in this situation.

   (b) Write the consumer's letter of complaint to the shop where the mobile phone was bought.

15 Stephen bought a new pair of runners in the summer sale. After two weeks one shoe came apart. When he returned to the shoe shop where he had purchased the runners, he received no help from the shop assistant.

   (a) Write Stephen's letter of complaint to the manager of the shoe shop.

   (b) Give one possible reason why Stephen might not be entitled to redress in this situation.

16 List four items of information that should be included in a letter of complaint to a retailer.

17 Peter bought a new pair of black jeans. They shrank and faded in the first wash. Peter decided to return them to the shop and ask for his money back.

   (a) List four guidelines which Peter should follow when he returns to the shop to make his complaint.

   (b) If Peter does not get his money back, what should he do next?

Chapter 16
Money management

A **budget** is a **plan for spending money.** When you work out how much money you have and how you plan to spend it, you are planning a budget.

The purpose of a budget is to balance what you receive (**income**) with what you pay out (**expenditure**) so that you have enough money for what you want to buy, and you don't run short!

A good money manager uses a system when planning a budget.

1 **Goal:** To balance my income with my expenditure.

2 **Resources:** What I need in order to do something. In this case, my resources are money, time and energy.

3 **Plan:** To achieve my goal, I must make out a budget or spending plan.

4 **Action:** I must then put this plan into action.

5 **Evaluation:** I must evaluate my budget to check if my goal was reached – did my income balance with my expenditure?

Higher Level

Steps in planning your own budget

1 **Work out your weekly or monthly income in one column.** This might include pocket money, presents or earnings from a part-time job.

2 **Make a list of your weekly or monthly expenses and savings in a second column.** These could include bus fares, clothes, school items, entertainment, lunches/snacks, toiletries, magazines or savings.

3 **Add the totals in each column and balance your budget,** i.e. check that your expenditure is equal to your income.

4 **If expenditure is greater than income,** it means that you are overspending and may have to make changes in your expenses.

5 **If income is greater than expenditure,** extra savings may be made.

Activity

Plan a budget for yourself for (a) the month of July and (b) the month of October. Do you notice any differences in the budgets?

Planning a budget for a working person

A working person will have a regular income. He/she will pay tax on this income.

Income

Gross income is the total amount earned before deductions.
Deductions include:

1 **Income tax** – PAYE (Pay As You Earn): This is taken automatically by your employer from gross income. Tax is used to pay for state services.

2 **Pay Related Social Insurance** (PRSI): This pays for benefits if you become unemployed or unable to work due to illness or injury.

3 **Voluntary deductions (optional):** These include health insurance (e.g. VHI, Aviva), pension scheme and savings.

Net income is take-home pay after deductions have been made.

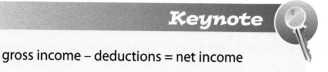

Keynote

gross income – deductions = net income

Tax credits

This is the part of a person's income that is not taxed by the government. Each week, the gross tax is calculated and then the tax credits are deducted from this to give the net tax, which must be paid.

gross tax – tax credits = net tax

Expenses and savings

A working person is likely to have the following expenses:

- rent or mortgage
- food
- travel
- fuel and electricity
- entertainment
- clothes
- toiletries/cosmetics
- savings towards holidays, car, etc.
- extras, e.g. presents, dentist, doctor, dry cleaning.

Case Study

Ciara is a 22-year-old secretary. She earns €400 per week. She rents an apartment with her friend and is currently saving to buy a car. She takes the bus to work, or walks if the weather is fine. She eats lunch every day at the office canteen as it is more convenient than going into town. Her hobbies include playing basketball, socialising and shopping! She would love to be able to afford to go on holidays this summer but finds it very hard to save extra money. Something always crops up! She often finds herself having to borrow from her flatmate. She wishes she knew how to budget . . .

Imagine you are Ciara's flatmate. Explain what it means to 'budget'. Work out a weekly budget for Ciara.

A household budget

The household budget for a family must take into account the basic needs of all the family members, e.g. food, clothes and shelter. Any leftover income can then be spent on other needs, and wants that the family considers important.

Link...

Needs and wants, page 215

The budget should be **flexible,** as the family situation may change from one year to the next. For example, unemployment, a child starting college or the arrival of a new baby could affect the budget.

The family income may consist of:

- net earnings
- state benefits, e.g. child benefit, unemployment benefit.

The family's expenses may include:

- housing (rent or mortgage)
- food
- clothes and shoes
- household bills (fuel, electricity, telephone, etc.)
- transport (car or fares)
- medical expenses
- insurance (house, contents, car, medical)
- education (books, uniforms, trips)
- child care.

The following guidelines suggest how income should be divided:

	% of income
Housing	25%
Food	25%
Household expenses	15%
Personal expenses	10%
Entertainment	10%
Education	5%
Emergencies	5%
Savings	5%

Advantages of budgeting

- Maximum use is made of income.
- Overspending is highlighted.
- More security is provided – fewer financial worries.
- Good example is set for children.
- Allowance is made for large bills and seasonal spending.
  (Seasonal spending is extra expense which occurs around
  Christmas, birthdays, back to school time, etc.)

Saving and buying on credit

When buying large, expensive items, consumers must decide whether to
save until they can afford to buy the item or buy it on credit.

Saving

Methods of saving

Before deciding where to save your money, consider:

- **interest rates** (how much
  will you earn on your
  savings?)
- **security** of your money
  (how safe is your money?)
- **ease of withdrawal** of
  your savings (how easy is
  it to withdraw money
  when you need it?)
- **incentives** (attractive
  offers such as free
  banking).

Where to save?

Options include:

- credit union
- bank
- post office.

Advantages of saving

1 Interest is earned.
2 It is often cheaper to pay for an item with money saved, rather than buying on credit.
3 There is no debt.

Buying on credit

Credit buying means 'buy now, pay later'. It is a way of borrowing money. Forms of credit include:

- credit card
- loan from bank, building society or credit union
- bank overdraft
- hire purchase.

Advantages of credit

1 Consumer has the use of the item before it is fully paid for.
2 Some large items could not be bought without credit, as it would take too long to save for them, e.g. houses, cars.

Disadvantages of credit

1 Credit costs more, as interest is charged.
2 Credit encourages consumers to buy more than they can afford, which can lead to serious debt.

Home filing

A home filing system is useful for storing important documents such as receipts, bills and guarantees. This helps family members find things easily.

Documents could be organised under headings such as Mortgage, Taxation, Insurance, Car (tax, insurance, service), Electricity, Fuel, Guarantees, Telephone, School Reports, Savings, Medical, Banking, etc. A folder, accordion file, filing cabinet or even a sturdy box could be used.

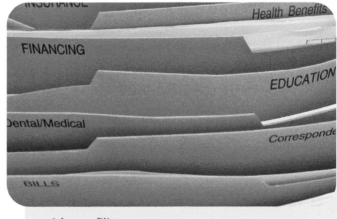

A home filing system

Advantages of home filing

1 Important documents are stored safely and can be found easily.

2 Unpaid bills are easily found and can be paid on time.

3 Spending patterns can be examined.

4 Receipts and guarantees are readily available if a problem should arise.

5 School progress can be monitored.

Activity

Design a filing system to suit your family's needs.

Summary

- **A budget is a plan for spending money.**
- **You should:**
  - ◆ **B**alance income and expenditure.
  - ◆ **U**se a management system.
  - ◆ **D**ecide on your needs and wants.
  - ◆ **G**ive priority to needs.
  - ◆ **E**valuate the outcome.
  - ◆ **T**ake note of changes to be made.
- **Gross income** is the total amount earned before deductions.
- **Net income** is take-home pay after deductions have been made.
- **Tax credit** is the part of income that is not taxed by the government.
- Review guidelines on how **income should be divided.**
- **Saving options** include An Post, credit unions, banks.
- **Credit means 'buy now, pay later'.**
- **A household filing system** is useful for organising, storing, checking and monitoring important documents.

Revision Questions

1 What is a plan for spending money called?

2 Give two advantages of household budgeting.

3 Ciara is about to start her first year at third-level college. She plans to live in rented accommodation with three other students and share living expenses.

(a) State the importance of budgeting for this group of students.

(b) Set out five guidelines the students should follow when planning their weekly budget.

4 Discuss five points that should be considered when planning a household budget.

5 List four essential expenses that should be considered when planning a household budget.

6 Plan a household budget based on an average weekly income.

7 Peter and Joan Murphy's daughter is going to attend post-primary school next year.

(a) List three major expenses that the Murphys may have as a result.

(b) Suggest two ways the Murphys might reduce these expenses.

8 Name two methods of saving which could be used to save for extra expenses.

9 John is planning to buy his sister her favourite team's jersey for her birthday, which is in three months. Suggest two methods of saving that John could use to save for the present. Give reasons for your suggestion in each case.

10 In relation to income, explain the difference between statutory deductions and voluntary deductions. Give one example of each type of deduction.

11 Explain the difference between gross income and net income.

12 Explain each of the following: (a) tax credit; (b) income tax – PAYE; (c) net income; (d) PRSI.

13 Net income is the total amount of money you earn. True or false?

14 Suggest two advantages of saving money.

15 Name two different places where a consumer can save money.

16 List the guidelines that should be followed when choosing a place to save.

17 Name two savings options you would use to save for a school trip.

18 Give two advantages of using a bank account.

19 List four types of credit buying.

20 List two advantages and two disadvantages of buying goods on credit.

21 State two disadvantages of borrowing money.

22 Buying on credit means 'buy now, pay later'. True or false?

23 List two types of credit available when buying a television.

24 Give two advantages of using a household filing system.

Chapter 17
Quality

Quality is a term used to indicate that **products or services are of a high standard.**

During manufacture, goods are put through strict tests to ensure that each product reaches a certain standard. This is called **quality control.** This is extremely important in the food and appliance industries, as any drop in standards could be dangerous for the consumer.

A good-quality product is:

- well designed and finished
- suitable for its purpose
- durable
- attractive.

Quality control

Quality and standard marks are awarded to goods and services that reach a high standard of quality. These marks may be on the goods themselves, on their label or on the box.

High standard of quality

Look out for the following symbols:

Guaranteed Irish

A product carrying this symbol has been manufactured in Ireland to a high degree of quality.

Q Mark

The Q Mark is awarded by EIQA (Excellent Irish Quality Association) to companies whose products or services have reached high standards of quality and excellence.

Kitemark

This is the symbol of the British Standards Institution (BSI). It means that the product has met high standards of quality, performance and safety.

Irish Standards Mark

This is the Irish equivalent of the Kitemark and is found on a wide range of electrical goods and appliances. It is awarded by the National Standards Authority of Ireland.

NSAI mark

An international quality standard awarded to companies with excellent quality management systems.

Pure New Wool

A product with the Woolmark symbol is made of pure new wool and is not blended or mixed with any other fibre.

Double insulated appliances

This indicates that an earth wire is not required, for example in electrical toasters and hairdryers.

Communauté Européenne

A safety mark awarded by the EU. It can be found on electrical equipment, machines, medical devices, toys, children's clothes, pushchairs and crayons.

Smoking kills

A government health warning found on cigarette packets and cigarette advertisements.

Link...

Hazard symbols, page 316
Care labelling, page 370
Chapter 33 Textiles in Use

Guarantees

A guarantee is a promise by the manufacturer that it will make good any faults in an item for a specific period of time after purchase.

Poor-quality goods seldom have a useful guarantee. By ensuring that good quality control is used during manufacture, a reliable company will be able to stand by its guarantees.

Services

To evaluate a service in terms of quality, consider the following:

✔ clean premises	✘ dirty premises
✔ well laid out	✘ untidy and disorganised
✔ wheelchair accessible	✘ no wheelchair access
✔ clean toilet facilities	✘ toilet facilities poor
✔ well managed	✘ disorganised staff
✔ friendly, competent staff	✘ dismissive, unhelpful staff
✔ good standard of personal hygiene	✘ careless personal hygiene
✔ appreciation of customer needs	✘ rudeness and unwillingness to help

The customer should:

- not feel ignored
- not have to queue for a long time
- not have to endure inadequate/unhygienic toilet facilities
- get what he/she pays for, e.g. a seat on public transport
- feel comfortable
- get value for money.

Remember that it is essential to complain about poor or inadequate services, otherwise standards will not improve.

Activities

1 Draw three quality and three safety symbols from page 248 into your copy and see if you can find items at home or in school which carry these symbols. Write them into your copy.

2 Write a paragraph about a day in the life of:
   (a) employees in a shop that was recently awarded the Q mark;
   (b) employees in a factory which does not give a guarantee with its products.

Summary

- **Quality is a term to indicate that products or services are of a high standard.**
- **Quality control** is a series of **tests** carried out to ensure that a product reaches a certain standard.
- **Quality symbols** include Guaranteed Irish, Q Mark, Kitemark, Irish Standards Mark and Pure New Wool.
- **Safety symbols** include double insulated, Communauté Européenne, BSI safety mark and government health warnings.
- A **guarantee** is also an indication of quality, as **it is a promise by the manufacturer to make good any fault for a specific time after purchase**.
- **Services** may be evaluated in terms of the **premises**, **staff** and **treatment of the customer**.

Revision Questions

1 What information do these symbols convey to the consumer?

(a)

(b)

(c)

Name one item on which each symbol is found.

2 What information does this symbol give to the consumer?

Name one item on which it is found.

3 Name a product that carries this symbol and give a reason why this symbol is used.

4 What information do these symbols convey to the consumer?

(a)

(b)

5 What information does this symbol give the consumer?

CE

Name one item on which it is found.

6 Sketch a safety symbol you might find attached to an item or product.

7 What is a guarantee?

8 Children's clothing, such as nightwear, must conform to certain safety regulations and standards. True or false?

9 Give two features of a good-quality service.

Chapter 18
Advertising

Billboard adverts

Hot-air balloon advert

Taxi advert

Advertising is any message designed to inform, persuade or influence consumers.

Some advertising is intended to make people change their behaviour or attitudes, for example an anti-smoking campaign.

Methods of advertising

We are all familiar with advertising. It is part of our lives and very difficult to avoid. We are exposed to numerous advertisements every day from the following **sources:**

- TV and radio
- newspapers and magazines
- cinema, video and DVD
- billboards
- carrier bags
- T-shirts
- taxis
- buses, trams and bus shelters
- packets
- ticket stubs
- receipts
- sponsorship
- hot-air balloons
- the Internet
- text messaging.

Sponsorship advertising

Carrier bag advert

Bus shelter advert

Functions of advertising

1 To introduce new products to the market.
2 To provide information on a product.
3 To promote brand names and present a good image of the company.
4 To increase sales of a product.

What makes an advertisement effective?

It should:

- capture the consumer's attention
- interest the consumer so that he/she will stop and listen to or read the advert
- create desire for the product
- persuade the consumer to buy the product.

In order to do all of this, the advertiser uses special techniques.

- **Language** and **slogans** are used to provide an image of the product; for example, 'the appliance of science' or 'the best a man can get'.
- Advertisers make **claims** about their products which may have no real meaning, but are just ways of persuading people, such as 'they're grrrreat!' or 'because I'm worth it' or 'finger-lickin' good'. These are **weasel words**.

> **Keynote**
>
> Weasel words are words that *suggest* something rather than giving real information.

Advertisers use various images and strategies.

- **Humour:** A funny situation, humorous logo or jingle.
- **Romance:** Often used to advertise perfumes, chocolates and cosmetics.
- **Glamour:** Attractive people and elegant surroundings are often used to advertise luxury goods.
- **Social acceptance:** Plays on people's desire to fit in and be popular.
- **Traditional images:** Views of the countryside, perfect families, spotless homes.
- **Hero worship:** Well-known celebrities promote or endorse products.

Humour in advertising

'Guerrilla' advertising is when a product or brand is inserted into entertainment or media, e.g. Aston Martin cars in the James Bond films, Cadillacs in *The Matrix Reloaded*.

Aston Martin car in the James Bond film, *Die Another Day*

Keynote

Advertising gives a selected amount of information – what the advertisers want you to know. The good points about the product are mentioned, but the drawbacks are not.

A large proportion of advertising money is spent on **classified ads.** These are non-commercial advertisements used to sell a wide range of goods and services.

CLASSIFIEDS

Jobs

GRAVEDIGGERS wanted. Night shifts only. Commencing 31 October. Bring your own shovel. Contact Burke & Hare Ltd. Ph: 034 394 9492.

OVERSEAS KAMIKAZE PILOTS required. Full training provided. Excellent rates. (No advance payments.) Ph: (+99) 008 117 294.

Lost and found

SEEKING black leather jacket with red trim. Left at the chip van, Main Street, Moate. Jacket contains winning lottery ticket for 1,000,000 euro. 50 euro reward. Ph: 032 660 9792.

REWARD OFFERED for return of two old urns. Sentimental value (contain remains of my ancestors). Contact Cecil: 034 508 7402.

Accommodation

BEAUTIFUL BEDSIT to let. Suit 12-14 students. No CH. Shared bathroom. Phone Joe on 033 149 3081.

HOUSE to let in Slasher Lane. Quiet neighbourhood. Louz E Lettings. Ph: 011 679 4944.

WANTED: Quiet house to let for single man and his elderly mother. Must have good working shower.
Contact N. Bates: 031 420 9401.

Family announcements

P. J. BURKE (UNDERTAKER) and Bridie Hannigan (Publican) are delighted to announce their engagement.

TINA AND THOMAS BREDWELL are delighted to announce the arrival of their beautiful triplets: Tom, Terence and Toby. Three new brothers for Tessa, Teresa, Tara, Ted and Tamara. Deo gratias.

Articles for sale

CHIP VAN for quick sale (owner emigrating). Excellent turnover. 350 euro. Also for sale: beautiful leather jacket, black with red trim. Good condition. 50 euro. Ph: 032 441 4472.

GOLD FILLINGS for sale. Also, two sets of false teeth. Good as new. Contact Burke & Hare Ltd. Ph: 034 394 9492.

PAIR OF COOKIE JARS for sale. Contact Grim's Antiques. Ph: 0301 650 9871.

Miscellaneous

MYSTIC MEGAN'S FORTUNE TELLING will be closed until further notice due to her unforeseen death.

DRIVING LESSONS available. Phone Blind Bill on 031 420 9401.

AUTUMN COOKERY COURSE (6 weeks). Contact Sal Monella. Ph: 033 149 3081.

DOCTOR CON'S MIRACLE PILLS. Students increase your brain power! Pass all exams without opening a book. See our website www.mymightyiq.org.

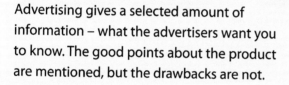

Classified ads

Advantages of advertising

1 It increases sales.
2 It provides employment to thousands of people.
3 It provides information on products, events and services.
4 It keeps down the cost of newspapers, magazines and TV programmes.

Disadvantages of advertising

1 It encourages materialism.
2 It makes exaggerated claims.
3 It encourages people to desire and buy things they can't afford.
4 Posters and billboards may spoil the landscape.
5 It increases prices of some products.
6 It emphasises gender stereotypes, e.g. a woman doing the laundry, a man driving a fast car.

A wise consumer will not allow himself/herself to be influenced by slick advertising, but will weigh up all the other factors before making a decision.

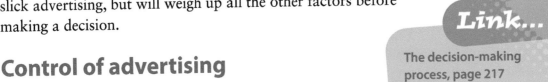

Link...

The decision-making process, page 217

Control of advertising

It is important that advertising standards are set and controlled so that the consumer is not taken advantage of. Advertising is controlled in two ways: legal control and voluntary control.

Legal control

The laws relating to advertising include:

- **EU Misleading Advertising Regulations:** Protect the public against the effects of misleading advertising.
- **Consumer Information Act 1978:** Makes it an offence to make false or misleading claims about goods or services.
- **Employment Equality Act 1998:** Makes it illegal for adverts to discriminate on the grounds of gender or marital status.

Voluntary control

Voluntary control is carried out by:

- **Advertising Standards Authority for Ireland:** Encourages advertisers to follow a code of standards that state that all advertisements must be legal, decent, honest and truthful.
- **Central Copy Clearance Ireland (CCCI):** Reviews all alcohol adverts in the Irish media.

Buy one, get one free

Sponsorship

Advertising

Attractive packaging

Marketing

Marketing is the process by which companies create customer interest in their products. It is used to identify the customer, satisfy the customer and keep the customer.

The **techniques** of marketing are:

- sales promotions, e.g. 'buy one, get one free'
- public relations activities, e.g. publicising the company to a wide audience
- sponsorship
- advertising
- attractive packaging and presentation.

Market research involves using surveys to find out the public's likes and dislikes. This research is important for manufacturers of products, package designers, retailers, shop designers and advertisers so that they can persuade the public to buy the product. They must supply the right **product**, at the right **price**, in the right **place**, using the most suitable **promotional** techniques. These are the **4Ps** of the **marketing mix**.

Activities

1 Make a list of (a) TV programmes, (b) sports personalities and (c) sports teams that are sponsored by various companies.

2 Describe three TV advertisements which you consider effective. Explain why you think they are effective. (Refer to language, slogans and images used.)

3 Examine a number of different types of magazine. Count the number of pages dedicated to advertisements. Comment on the types of goods and services being advertised.

Summary

- **Advertising is any message designed to inform, persuade or influence consumers**.

- **Methods** of advertising include **TV, leaflets, sponsorship, billboards, buses, text messages, etc**.

- **Functions** of advertising are to **introduce, inform, promote** and **increase sales**.

- An **effective** advertisement should **capture attention, interest, create desire** and **persuade**.

- **Images and strategies** used in advertising are **humour, traditional images, romance, glamour, hero worship** and **social acceptance**.

- **Advantages** of advertising: **Provides information, employment, decreases cost, increases sales**.

- **Disadvantages** of advertising: **Stereotypes, materialism, exaggeration, spoils landscape, increases prices**.

- **Legal control:** EU Misleading Advertising Regulations, Consumer Information Act 1978 and Employment Equality Act 1998.

- **Voluntary control:** Advertising Standards Authority, Central Copy Clearance Ireland.

- **Market research** is carried out to discover the **public's likes and dislikes**, in order to supply the **4Ps of the marketing mix**.

Revision Questions

1 Name four different methods/sources of advertising.

2 A good advertisement will make us want to buy the product. True or false?

3 List four functions of advertising.

4 What are the characteristics of an effective advertisement?

5 Describe two advertisements that you consider to be effective. Explain why you consider the advertisements to be effective.

6 Give three advantages and three disadvantages of advertising.

7 Name one organisation which controls advertising standards.

8 Outline the role of the Advertising Standards Authority for Ireland.

9 Describe three marketing techniques used in supermarkets.

10 Name the marketing technique you think is most effective and give a reason for your answer.

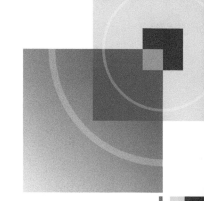

Section three

Social and health studies

Chapter 19
Family, roles and relationships

The family

A family is a group of people who are related by blood, marriage or adoption.

Types of family

- **Nuclear family:** Parents and their children living in the same house. Many nuclear families are one-parent families in modern society.
- **Extended family:** Parents and children together with other relations such as grandparents, aunts, uncles and cousins.
- **Blended family:** Created when two families are combined as a result of second relationships.
- **One-parent family:** One parent and his/her children.

Functions of the family

Our family provides for our needs.

- **Physical needs:** Food, clothing and shelter.
- **Emotional needs:** Family members give love and security to each other. They care for each other and allow good relationships to develop.
- **Economic needs:** Family members share money and other possessions.

Nuclear family

Extended family

Influences on family life

Cultural factors influence family life. In some cultures parents enforce harsh discipline on children and in other cultures they are more relaxed. Religion and race can have an important influence on family life. Some families encourage cultural traditions such as language and traditional music. Some families place great emphasis on certain sports or activities such as Gaelic football in Co. Kerry or hurling in Co. Kilkenny.

Social factors shape the lives of family members. The roles which males and females play at home, at school and at work are influenced by society. The development of technologies has influenced family life. The Internet is an important part of daily life in many families, for example in the areas of education and recreation.

Economic factors such as the amount of money available influence the lifestyle of the family. While many families can afford to provide for the needs of family members, some families lack the resources to provide adequate food, clothes and shelter. This is especially true in times of recession.

Activities

1 Cultural influences on family life include involvement in sports or activities. List some sports or activities which are strongly encouraged in the area in which you live.

2 Discuss the importance of the Internet in family life. Comment on both positive and negative aspects.

Rights and responsibilities of children

Children have the **right** to:

● love and understanding
● be cared for and to receive food, clothing and shelter
● receive an education
● be protected from cruelty, neglect and abuse.

Children have the **responsibility** to:

● respect their parents
● take care of personal space
● do homework and chores
● interact and play with siblings.

Roles

A role is the way we are expected to behave.

Each family member can have a different role. A woman might have the role of a doctor at work and at home she might have the role of a parent.

Children's role

Children spend a lot of time playing and learning. However, as children grow older, they should take responsibility for themselves and their possessions. It is good for children to have responsibilities.

Teenagers are sometimes confused about their role. They begin to take on the responsibilities of an adult but they may not be given the freedom they want. This can lead to **role confusion**.

Gender role

Gender means being male or female.

Gender role or **sex role** means **the way one is expected to behave because of one's gender.**

Gender roles are **learned** at home, at school and in the community. In the past males and females were treated unequally. They were under pressure to fit into a limited role. For example, boys were supposed to be 'tough' and girls were supposed to be 'caring'.

When this happens:

- Both boys and girls develop a limited role.
- Boys can have difficulty expressing their emotions and girls can be prevented from developing their talents.
- Boys and girls have greater difficulty developing relationships with each other as each acts out the role they are expected to adopt.
- It causes confusion and lack of confidence.

Parents' role

Parents have a very responsible role. They must ensure that the physical and emotional needs of their children are provided for. In family life, the roles of both men and women have changed in recent years. Men and women used to have more limited roles, and men were less involved in life within the home. In modern society men are more involved in child care, housework and food preparation. Women also have a broader role than in the past because nowadays many women work outside the home.

In modern society, men are more involved in child care

Stereotypes

A stereotype is a fixed image of how people should behave.
The old-fashioned image of boys being 'tough' and girls being 'caring' is an example of a gender stereotype. Males and females were associated with certain jobs in the past. For example, nurses were female and truck drivers were male. Today these gender role stereotypes are not as common. Stereotyping is damaging and hurtful. It causes discrimination against various groups in our society. 'Women are better at caring for children' and 'all teenagers cause trouble' are examples of stereotypes.

Gender equality and equity

Gender equality is the idea that males and females should have equal rights, responsibilities and opportunities. Both men and women should be free to develop their personal abilities without being limited by gender roles.

Gender equity means equal treatment of males and females.

Today, there is more equal treatment of men and women than there was in the past. In the workplace it is illegal to discriminate against men or women on grounds of their gender.

Relationships

There are different types of relationship within the family. The relationship between a father and mother is an adult relationship. It is usually a loving, trusting relationship in which each person respects the other. In a relationship between a father and a child or a mother and a child, the adult is the provider and he or she is responsible for discipline. It is also a caring and affectionate relationship. The relationship between siblings is based on sharing and caring for each other. They play together, co-operate and respect each other.

Children need to have a good relationship with their parents in order to feel secure and confident. Small children are highly dependent on their parents. As children get older they become more independent. However, the relationship between teenagers and parents is still very important. A good relationship between teenagers and parents can be maintained by having good communication. Teenagers should be given responsibilities and independence. Fair and consistent discipline is needed with reasonable sanctions.

Communication

Relationships are based on communication. Communication can be **verbal** (using words) or **non-verbal** (without words). Non-verbal communication is based on body language and facial expression.

Listening is the most important skill in communication. Good child–parent communication encourages emotional development in children (see page 269).

Conflict

Conflict arises because people see the same situation differently.

Parents and teenagers sometimes disagree over the rights and responsibilities of the teenager. This leads to **conflict**. Code of dress, homework, pocket money and time spent going out are examples of issues that lead to conflict between adults and teenagers. Peer pressure can also be a cause of conflict.

Conflict

Handling conflict

Conflict is part of our lives, so it is important that we learn how to manage it effectively.

- **Consider** the rights and responsibilities of both parents and teenagers.
- **Listen** to how the other person sees the problem.
- **Consider** possible solutions.
- **Choose** a solution that meets each person's needs.
- This choice may involve **compromise**.

Conflict can often cause anger, so it is important to calm down and take control over your feelings before saying something you might later regret.

The Irish Society for Prevention of Cruelty to Children (ISPCC) is an organisation which offers support to teenagers. This support is provided by a helpline called **Childline**. Children and teenagers can discuss their problems with a caring adult who will listen and offer advice.

Compromise

Weblink

ISPCC www.ispcc.ie

Link...

Peer pressure, page 270

Activities

1 Certain stereotypes are encouraged by the media. List three examples.

2 Discuss the effects of gender role stereotypes on boys and girls.

3 Make a list of three stereotypes that exist in our society. Discuss the effects you think each one has on the people involved.

4 Communicate a message using non-verbal communication.

5 Role play a conflict situation in which a teenager feels that he/she is being treated unfairly. Repeat the role play using the method for handling conflict outlined above.

Summary

● **A family is a group of people who are related by blood, marriage or adoption.**

● **Nuclear family:** Parents and their children.

● **Extended family:** Parents and children together with other relations.

● **Blended family:** Created when two families are combined as a result of second relationships.

● **One-parent family:** Consists of one parent and his/her children.

● Our family provides for our **physical needs, emotional needs and economic needs**.

● **Children have the right** to love, security, care, education and protection from neglect or abuse.

● **Children have the responsibility** to respect parents and to take care of their belongings.

● A **role** is the way we are expected to behave.

● **Gender** means being male or female.

● **Gender role** or sex role means the way one is expected to behave because of one's gender.

● Gender roles are **learned** at home, at school and in the community.

● A **stereotype** is a fixed image of how people should behave.

● Equal treatment of males and females is called **gender equity**.

● Relationships are based on communication.

● **Communication** can be **verbal** or **non-verbal**.

● **Listening** is the most important skill in communication.

● When **handling conflict**, consider the rights and responsibilities of everyone involved.

● The **ISPCC** is an organisation that offers support to teenagers.

Revision Questions

1. State three rights of a child.
2. Outline three responsibilities of children in the family.
3. Explain the term 'gender'.
4. Explain the term 'gender equality'.
5. 'Gender roles are learned.' Give your views on this statement.
6. List three reasons why men's roles in family life have changed in recent years.
7. What are the long-term effects of unequal treatment (a) on boys; (b) on girls?
8. Explain the term 'stereotype'.
9. List three things which cause conflict between teenagers and their parents.
10. Name an organisation which offers support to teenagers and outline how this support is provided.

Chapter 20
New life

It takes a man and a woman to make a new human life. An egg from the woman must join with a sperm from the man to make the first cell of a new baby.

Female sex organs

The female sex (reproductive) organs produce the eggs and provide a safe place for the baby to develop. The **ovaries** produce and store the eggs. The **Fallopian tubes** link the ovaries to the womb (uterus). The **uterus** is where the developing baby grows until birth. The neck of the uterus is called the **cervix**. The **vagina** (birth canal) is a tube that goes from the cervix to outside the body.

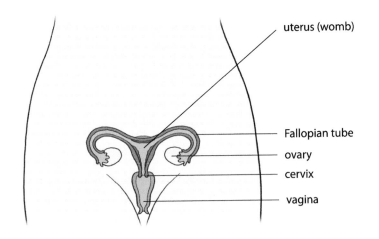

uterus (womb)

Fallopian tube

ovary

cervix

vagina

Ovulation

Every month a woman's body gets ready to make a new baby. An egg is released from one of the ovaries into the Fallopian tube. This is called **ovulation**. The egg travels along the Fallopian tube towards the uterus (womb). Ovulation usually occurs in the middle of the menstrual cycle.

Keynote

Female sex hormones control sexual development, ovulation and menstruation. These hormones are called **oestrogen** and **progesterone**.

Menstruation or menstrual cycle

After ovulation, the lining of the uterus becomes thick and soft. If the egg is fertilised, it will bury itself in this thick lining. If the egg is not fertilised, it dies. Then the unwanted lining of the womb and the egg flow out of the uterus, along the vagina and out of the body. This is called **menstruation,** or having a **period.** Periods begin at puberty. The menopause occurs at around age 45 to 55, when women stop having periods.

Male sex organs

The male sex organs produce **sperm** and place the sperm inside the woman's body. Sperm are made and stored in the **testes.** The testes are in a pouch of skin called the **scrotum,** which hangs outside the body. Sperm travel from the testes (testicles) through two **sperm ducts** to the **penis.** On the way to the **penis** the sperm mix with a liquid called **semen.** During sexual intercourse the semen and sperm spurt from the penis into the woman's body.

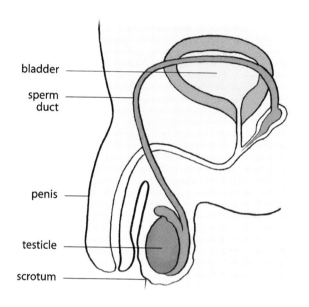

bladder

sperm duct

penis

testicle

scrotum

Sexual intercourse

During sexual intercourse, the blood vessels in the penis become filled with blood and it becomes stiff. This makes it possible for the penis to be inserted into the woman's vagina. Semen, which contains millions of sperm, is released into the vagina.

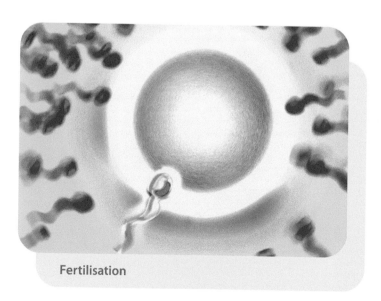

Fertilisation

Fertilisation

Sperm swim up through the vagina, into the womb and into the Fallopian tubes. **Fertilisation** occurs when a sperm unites with the female egg.

Reproduction and birth

Pregnancy

The fertilised egg travels along the Fallopian tube to the womb, where it implants (buries) itself in the lining of the womb. It is now called an **embryo**. The embryo grows in the womb for about 40 weeks. After about eight weeks it is called a **foetus**. The foetus is protected in the womb by a bag of fluid, called **amniotic fluid**, which surrounds it.

The umbilical cord attaches the foetus to the mother at the **placenta**. Oxygen and nutrients pass from the mother to the foetus at the placenta. Waste substances such as carbon dioxide and urea also pass from the foetus to the mother through the placenta.

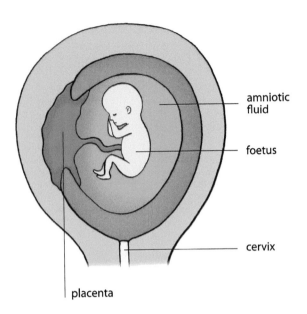

amniotic fluid

foetus

cervix

placenta

Healthy pregnancy

Harmful substances, such as cigarette smoke, alcohol and drugs, and viruses such as rubella can pass from the mother to the baby during pregnancy. Therefore, pregnant women should follow these guidelines to promote good health during pregnancy:

- avoid smoking
- avoid alcohol
- avoid all drugs except medicines prescribed by a doctor
- eat a healthy diet (see page 27).

Birth

A woman giving birth is said to be **in labour**. The bag of amniotic fluid bursts and the muscles of the womb begin to contract to push the baby out. The cervix must open so that the baby can go through into the vagina, usually head first. Once the baby comes out, the umbilical cord is clamped and cut. Then the placenta passes out of the mother's body. This is called the afterbirth.

A healthy pregnancy

Responsible sexual behaviour

A sexual relationship involves many emotions and must be treated responsibly. In most societies sexual activity occurs within the framework of marriage or in long-term, close relationships. Casual sex can cause the following serious problems:

- unwanted pregnancy
- low self-esteem and feeling used
- sexually transmitted infections (STIs). These infections can cause illness, infertility and death.

The Health Protection Centre states that the number of notified STI cases trebled between 1995 and 2006 (*The Voice of Young People: A Report on Attitudes to Sexual Health* 2006).

Weblink

www.healthpromotion.ie
www.irishhealth.com

Summary

- The **ovaries** produce and store the eggs.
- The **uterus** is where the developing baby grows until birth.
- **Ovulation** occurs when an egg is released from one of the ovaries.
- **Menstruation** occurs when the unwanted lining of the womb and the egg flow out of the body.
- The male sex organs produce **sperm**. Sperm are made and stored in the **testes**. During sexual intercourse, semen, which contains the sperm, is released into the vagina.
- **Fertilisation** occurs when a sperm joins with an egg.
- When the fertilised egg implants itself in the womb it is called an **embryo**.
- After about eight weeks it is called a **foetus**.
- The **foetus** is protected in the womb by a bag of fluid called **amniotic fluid**.
- The umbilical cord joins the foetus to the mother at the **placenta**.
- The **placenta** regulates the transfer of substances between mother and baby.
- A woman giving birth is said to be **in labour**.
- Casual sex can cause the following serious problems: unwanted pregnancy, low self-esteem and sexually transmitted infections (STIs).

Revision Questions

1 Explain each of the following terms: (a) ovaries; (b) menstrual cycle; (c) menopause.

2 Outline the function of each of the following: (a) testes; (b) sperm duct.

3 Explain each of the following terms: (a) ovulation; (b) fertilisation; (c) embryo/foetus.

4 Explain the function of each of the following: (a) umbilical cord; (b) placenta; (c) uterus (womb).

5 Give three guidelines which should be followed in order to promote good health during pregnancy.

6 Outline two problems associated with irresponsible sexual behaviour.

Basic human needs

We have basic human needs that enable us to grow and develop. We have **physical needs** such as food, clothing and shelter. We also have **emotional needs** such as love and understanding, comfort and security. Emotional needs also involve developing our personal relationships. As well as the physical and social aspects of our lives, we need intellectual or **mental stimulation** in order for the mind to grow and develop. This stimulation or encouragement comes from our environment.

Types of development

People grow and develop in several different ways throughout life. Each type of development can occur at a different rate.

Physical development

Children grow in weight and height as they get older. Both girls and boys grow rapidly during puberty and their bodies begin to change shape.

The reproductive or sexual organs begin to work. Hormones cause these changes. **Puberty** is the beginning of **adolescence**, the time when a child changes into an adult.

Changes in girls during puberty:

- increase in height and weight
- breasts begin to grow
- periods begin
- hair begins to grow at underarms and groin
- hips become wider.

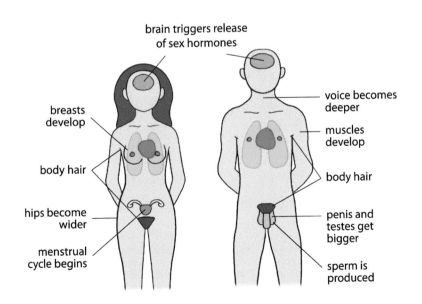

brain triggers release of sex hormones

voice becomes deeper

muscles develop

breasts develop

body hair

body hair

hips become wider

penis and testes get bigger

menstrual cycle begins

sperm is produced

Changes in boys during puberty:

- increase in height and weight
- penis becomes bigger
- erections and ejaculations occur (wet dreams)
- testes (testicles) produce sperm
- hair begins to grow on face, underarms and groin
- voice becomes deeper.

Adolescents feel awkward and self-conscious at first but gradually come to accept the changes.

Interesting toys stimulate the mind

Mental or intellectual development

Mental or intellectual development is the development of the mind.

Babies are curious and they have a natural tendency to learn. This interest in learning can be encouraged or discouraged by the child's environment. Interesting toys, activities, study and interaction with people all help to develop the mind.

Emotional development

Emotional development is learning to manage and deal with your feelings or emotions. Praise and encouragement from others help you to develop high **self-esteem**. Having high self-esteem means believing in yourself and having confidence. Being accepted by others and being treated fairly also help to develop high self-esteem.

Emotional maturity

Being emotionally mature allows us to handle feelings of **love**, **anger** and **fear**, e.g. we do not need to throw a tantrum or sulk to express anger. As a person becomes more emotionally mature, they are aware of how other people see them. Emotional maturity involves developing good relationships and making the most of one's talents.

Activity

Role play a situation where a person expresses anger in an immature way.
Repeat the role play to show how an emotionally mature person expresses anger.

When you have high self-esteem, you:

- feel **confident** and interested in trying new things
- feel **accepted** by others
- are more **assertive**, i.e. able to express what you want with confidence.

Personality development

Personality is part of our identity. One person might have an outgoing personality while another might be more reserved or quiet. Personality is determined (influenced) by heredity and environment.

- **Heredity:** You inherit personality traits from both your father and your mother.
- **Environment:** Your home lifestyle and the people around you influence your personality. Children learn by imitation.

Social development

Social development means learning how to get on with people in various situations and learning to fit into society. It involves having good manners and treating people with respect.

Norms

A norm is an acceptable way of behaving in our society.

We are expected to have good manners and behave in a responsible way. Examples of norms are attending school, having good manners and obeying the rules of the road.

Moral development

Moral development means knowing what is right and what is wrong.

Children accept their parents' morals or **values.** Teenagers, however, often question their parents' values. Although this may cause conflict, it is important for the young person to decide on their own personal values.

Peer groups

A peer group is a group of people of a similar age with similar interests.

When teenagers become more independent of their parents, the peer group becomes very important. Teenagers usually have close friendships with members of their peer group. They feel comfortable in the group, feel a sense of belonging to the group and feel accepted by the group.

Peer pressure

Peer pressure means being expected to copy others in the peer group, such as the way they dress. The peer group can have both **positive** and **negative** influences on its members.

Higher Level

Examples of **positive peer pressure:**

- helping to prevent bullying by encouraging respect
- encouragement to take part in team sports
- encouragement to study at school
- becoming involved in community work.

Examples of **negative peer pressure:**

- behaving in an anti-social manner
- becoming involved in bullying
- smoking and abusing alcohol and drugs.

Summary

- We have **physical needs**, **emotional needs** and the need for **intellectual stimulation**.
- **Puberty** is the beginning of adolescence.
- Changes in girls at puberty include breast development and menstruation.
- Changes in boys at puberty include wet dreams and growth of facial hair.
- **Mental or intellectual** development is the development of the mind.
- **Emotional** development includes learning to handle your emotions.
- When you have **high self-esteem**, you feel **confident**, **assertive** and **accepted** by others.
- **Assertiveness** means being able to express what you want with confidence.
- **Personality** development is influenced by **heredity** and **environment**.
- **Social** development is learning how to get on with people and fit into society.
- **Moral** development means learning to distinguish between what is right and what is wrong.
- A **peer group** is a group of people of the same age with similar interests.
- **Peer pressure** means being expected to copy others in the peer group.
- A **norm** is an acceptable way of behaviour.

Revision Questions

1. List three physical needs and three emotional needs provided by the family.
2. Explain each of the following in relation to human development: (a) emotional development; (b) social development; (c) moral development.
3. State two factors that promote educational development in children.
4. Explain the terms 'peer group' and 'peer pressure'.
5. Explain the term 'assertive'.
6. Outline three physical changes that occur in boys and three physical changes that occur in girls during puberty.
7. List two factors which contribute to the emotional well-being of teenagers.
8. List two factors which play an important part in the development of a child's personality.
9. Explain the term 'norms'.

Chapter 21
The body

Skin

The skin plays an important role in the body. It is an **excretory organ**, which means that it removes **waste**, such as **water** and **salts**, from the body.

Structure of the skin

The skin is made up of two layers:

- the **epidermis,** or outer layer
- the **dermis,** or inner layer.

Epidermis

The outer part of the epidermis is made up of **dead cells**. These dead cells are continuously replaced as they wear away. The **Malpighian layer** is inside. This contains **pigment** that protects the skin from the harmful rays of the sun.

Dermis

The dermis contains the following parts.

- **Sweat glands** remove water and salt (sweat) from the blood.
- The sweat goes out of the body through the **pores.**
- **Blood vessels** supply the skin with oxygen and nutrients.
- **Nerves** allow us to feel sensations, for example cold, heat and pain.
- **Oil glands** produce oil to moisten the skin.
- **Hairs** help to keep the body warm.
- **Fat cells** insulate the body.

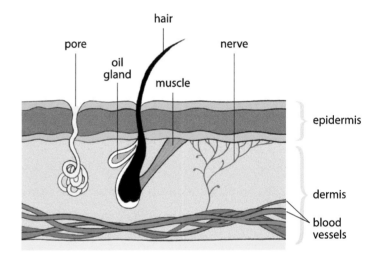

Keynote

Dead cells on the surface of the skin mix with oil from the oil glands. They can block the skin pores and cause blackheads if they are not removed.

Functions of the skin

- It **removes** excess water and salts in the form of **sweat**. Therefore it is an excretory organ.
- It controls body temperature and keeps the body at 37°C.
- It **protects** the body from disease by preventing micro-organisms from entering the body. The pigment also protects the body from harmful rays of the sun.
- It is an organ of touch which allows us to **feel** heat, cold and pain.
- **Vitamin D** is made by the skin in sunlight.

Sweating helps the body to stay cool during exercise

Guidelines for healthy skin

- Wash the body every day.
- Change underwear every day.
- Avoid touching spots.
- Wash hands regularly.
- Cleanse, tone (to close pores) and moisturise the face.
- Eat a healthy diet.
- Get enough sleep.
- Avoid over-exposure to the sun.
- Avoid skincare products which cause soreness or allergic reactions.
- Avoid cigarettes and alcohol.

Body odour

Body odour is produced when **bacteria** on the skin work on **sweat**.

An unpleasant odour is produced if the skin is not washed. This odour is strongest from under the arms, the groin area and the feet. Body odour should be removed by **washing** every day and **changing clothes**. Skincare products are used to help control body odour.

Deodorants help prevent body odour, while **antiperspirants** prevent perspiration (sweating).

Acne

Acne is a skin condition that occurs during adolescence. Extra oil produced in the skin blocks pores and bacteria on the skin cause infection. Hygiene is important, but there is no quick cure for acne.

The following guidelines help prevent acne from spreading:

- do not squeeze or pick spots
- clean skin thoroughly using antiseptic soap
- don't share face cloths or towels.
- avoid fatty foods
- drink lots of water.

Follow instructions on cleansing products carefully or consult your doctor if using medication.

Hair care

- Hair should be washed at least once a week using shampoo. Rinse thoroughly.
- Use conditioner if necessary.
- Keep brushes and combs clean.
- Have hair trimmed regularly.
- Do not overuse appliances such as hair dryers or straighteners because hair may be damaged by overheating.

Hand care

- Wash hands regularly.
- Dry hands well after washing to prevent chapping.
- Use hand cream to prevent dryness.
- Use protective gloves for dirty or dangerous jobs, such as handling chemicals.
- Keep nails short.
- Use a nailbrush to keep nails spotlessly clean.
- Avoid biting nails.

Foot care

- Wash feet daily with soap and warm water.
- Dry feet thoroughly, especially between the toes.
- Wear well-fitting shoes.
- Change socks or tights every day.
- Keep toenails clean and short.
- Cut toenails straight across.
- Consult your doctor if you notice colour changes in the nails because this may be caused by fungal infections.

Skincare in the sun

Over-exposure to the sun can damage a person's skin. It can cause skin cancer (melanoma), premature ageing and sunburn.

The risk of skin damage is high for many Irish people because of their pale skin.

When children are over-exposed to the sun, the risk of developing skin cancer in later life is higher.

Safe sunbathing

- Wear a wide-brimmed hat and a T-shirt.
- Avoid going out in the sun between 11.00 a.m. and 3.00 p.m.
- Use a high-protection sunscreen.
- Do not fall asleep in the sun.

Hair care

Skincare in the sun

Personal hygiene guidelines

- Wash hands properly after using the toilet and before eating.
- Wash all over your body every day, especially underarms, feet and groin area.
- Washing is very important after exercise.
- Brush your teeth every morning and night.
- Change underwear and socks every day.
- Change and wash outer clothes regularly.
- Wash hair at least once a week.
- Girls should change sanitary pads or tampons regularly during menstruation and wash hands afterwards.

Summary

- The skin is an **excretory organ** because it removes **water and salts** from the body.
- The skin contains the **epidermis** and the **dermis**.
- The epidermis contains **dead cells** and the **Malpighian layer**, which has a protective **pigment**.
- The **dermis** contains **sweat glands**, **blood vessels**, **nerves**, **fat cells** and **pores**.
- The functions of the skin include the **removal** of water and salts, **regulating body temperature**, **protection** of the body, ability to **feel** sensations and production of **vitamin D**.
- **Guidelines for healthy skin** include a skincare routine, a healthy diet, enough sleep and avoiding over-exposure to the sun.
- Body odour is produced when **bacteria** on the skin work on **sweat**. Body odour should be removed by **washing** every day and **changing clothes**.
- **Deodorants** help prevent body odour, whereas **antiperspirants** prevent perspiration.
- **Acne** is a skin condition that occurs during adolescence. Extra oil produced in the skin blocks pores and bacteria on the skin cause infection.
- **Over-exposure** to the sun is damaging to the skin.
- For **safe sunbathing**, wear a hat and a T-shirt, avoid the sun between 11.00 a.m. and 3.00 p.m. and use sunscreen.
- **Personal hygiene guidelines** should be followed to ensure clean and healthy skin.

Revision Questions

1 What causes body odour?

2 Outline four functions of the skin.

3 List four guidelines that an adolescent should follow in order to maintain good personal hygiene.

4 Suggest four guidelines that teenagers should follow to help prevent acne spreading.

5 What special guidelines should be followed by teenagers when caring for their feet and toenails?

6 Discuss the reasons why over-exposure to the sun is considered damaging to the skin.

7 List two ways of protecting the skin when sunbathing.

Teeth

Your teeth are your responsibility.

An attractive smile makes a wonderful first impression when you meet someone. **Healthy teeth** are important because they:

- help to digest food
- enable us to speak properly
- are attractive.

Unhealthy teeth can cause the following problems:

- bad breath
- infections in the mouth and gums
- stomach infections.

Healthy teeth

Types of teeth

A young child has 20 primary or 'milk' teeth. An adult has 32 permanent teeth. There are four different types of teeth, as shown in the diagram. Each type of tooth has its own function.

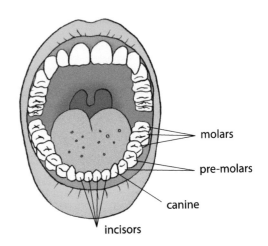

molars
pre-molars
canine
incisors

Type of tooth	Function
Incisors	Sharp teeth used to bite and cut food
Canines (eye teeth)	Pointed teeth used to tear food
Pre-molars	Double-pointed teeth used to chew and grind food
Molars	Large teeth used to chew and grind food

Structure of a tooth

The tooth consists of two main sections:

1 The **crown**, which is the visible part of the tooth.

2 The **root**, which is embedded in the gum.

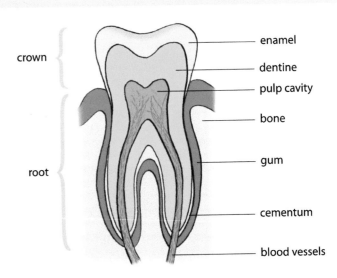

crown
root
enamel
dentine
pulp cavity
bone
gum
cementum
blood vessels

The tooth contains the following parts.

- **Enamel:** A hard substance that protects the tooth.
- **Dentine:** A bone-like substance (softer than enamel) that is under the enamel.
- **Pulp cavity:** A space at the centre of the tooth which contains blood vessels and nerves.
- **Cementum:** A layer around the root which holds the tooth in place in the jaw.
- **Periodontal fibres:** These hold the tooth in the bone.

Plaque

Plaque consists of food particles, saliva and bacteria. It is constantly forming on the teeth and builds up on the surfaces of the teeth, especially near the gums and between the teeth.

Tartar

Tartar is hardened plaque on the teeth. Tartar allows bacteria to grow and it causes teeth to become stained.

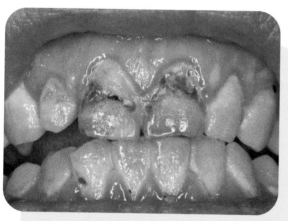

Tooth decay

Tooth decay

If plaque is not removed, **bacteria** present in the mouth act on food particles (especially sugar) to produce acids. The acids attack tooth enamel, wearing it away until it reaches the dentine underneath. This is tooth decay. The main cause of tooth decay is sugar consumption.

Brushing your teeth

Remember that teeth have five surfaces.

- Brush the outer surfaces of all the teeth.
- Brush the inner surfaces of all the teeth.
- Brush the chewing surfaces.
- Clean between the teeth using dental floss.

Dental health products

- **Dental floss:** A thin nylon cord that helps to remove food from between the teeth. This prevents plaque/tartar from building up.
- **Fluoride toothpaste:** Reduces tooth decay because fluoride strengthens the teeth. Toothpaste also freshens breath.
- **Antiseptic mouthwash:** Reduces infection and helps prevent gum disease.
- **Disclosing tablet:** Shows the plaque on teeth, which makes it easier to remove by brushing.
- **Interdental brush:** Removes plaque from between the teeth.

Guidelines for healthy teeth and gums

- Avoid sugary foods and drinks between meals.
- Brush teeth properly at least twice a day using fluoride toothpaste.
- Visit your dentist regularly.
- Replace your toothbrush every three months.
- Use dental floss to clean between teeth.
- Eat crunchy foods such as raw fruit and vegetables.
- Eat a healthy diet which includes calcium for strong teeth.

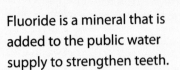

Keynote

Fluoride is a mineral that is added to the public water supply to strengthen teeth.

Activity

Examine the labels on a range of pre-packed food products to find out the sugar content. Compare them to see which has the highest and which has the lowest amount of sugar.

Summary

- Healthy teeth are **attractive**, enable us to **speak** properly and to **digest food**.
- A young child has 20 primary or 'milk' teeth. An adult has 32 permanent teeth.
- There are four different types of teeth: **incisors**, **canines**, **pre-molars** and **molars**.
- The tooth consists of two main sections: the **crown** and the **root**.
- The tooth contains **enamel**, **dentine**, **pulp cavity**, **cementum** and **periodontal fibres**.
- **Plaque** consists of food particles, saliva and bacteria.
- Plaque causes tooth decay.
- **Dental health products** include dental floss, fluoride toothpaste, antiseptic mouthwash and disclosing tablets.

Revision Questions

1 Explain the importance of healthy teeth.

2 Name four types of permanent teeth.

3 Outline the function of each of the following parts of the tooth: (a) enamel; (b) pulp cavity; (c) cementum.

4 What is plaque?

5 Explain how plaque affects the teeth.

6 Name the mineral that is added to the public water supply to strengthen teeth.

7 List three important guidelines to follow to ensure healthy teeth and gums.

8 Explain how diet affects the teeth.

9 Name two problems that are the result of poor dental hygiene.

10 What are the benefits of: (a) antiseptic mouthwash; (b) fluoride toothpaste; (c) dental floss?

Higher Level

Respiratory (breathing) system

Excretion

Excretion is the removal of waste from the body. The body has three **excretory organs**: the lungs, the skin and the kidneys. The lungs remove carbon dioxide and water vapour from the body. The skin removes water and salts (sweat). The kidneys remove waste in the form of urine.

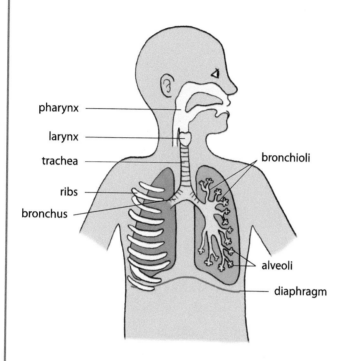

The breathing system

When we breathe in (inhale), we take in oxygen from the air. Oxygen combines with food to give us energy. This is called **oxidation**. Waste products (carbon dioxide and water) are formed as a result. We get rid of this waste when we breathe out (exhale).

Structure of the breathing system

- Air passes through a series of pipes as it goes from the nose and mouth to the lungs.
- Air passes through the **nose and mouth**. The air is **warmed** and hairs in the nose **filter** the air.
- The air then passes through the space at the back of the mouth called the **pharynx**.
- A flap of skin called the **epiglottis** covers the opening of the trachea to prevent food getting in.
- The air passes through the **larynx** (voice box), which contains the vocal cords.
- The air then travels into the **trachea** (windpipe).
- The trachea divides into two tubes called the **bronchi**. Each bronchus divides again to form narrow tubes called **bronchioli**. At the end of the bronchioli are the air **sacs**, or **alveoli** (singular: alveolus). This is where the oxygen reaches the blood and where carbon dioxide is removed.

Position of the lungs

The lungs are in the chest. They are like large pink sponges which expand as they are filled with air and shrink as the air is removed. They are surrounded by the rib cage, the breast bone and the back bone. The heart is between the lungs.

Functions of the lungs

The lungs have the following **functions:**

- take oxygen into the body
- remove carbon dioxide from the body
- remove water from the body.

Exchange of gases

The alveoli (air sacs) have very thin walls and are covered with capillaries (tiny blood vessels). Oxygen passes from the air sacs through the walls and into the blood in the capillaries. Carbon dioxide passes from the blood into the air sacs. This is called the **exchange of gases.**

nose
▼
pharynx
▼
larynx
▼
trachea
▼
bronchus
▼
bronchioles
▼
alveoli

Higher Level

Link...

Smoking, page 290

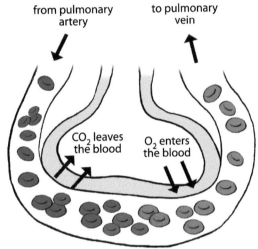

from pulmonary artery

to pulmonary vein

CO_2 leaves the blood

O_2 enters the blood

Exchange of gases in the alveolus

Summary

- **Excretion** is the removal of waste from the body.
- The body has three **excretory organs**: the lungs, the skin and the kidneys.
- Oxygen combines with food to give us energy. This is called **oxidation**.
- Air passes through the following organs as it goes from the **nose** and **mouth** to the **lungs**: **nose ⇒ pharynx ⇒ larynx ⇒ trachea ⇒ bronchi ⇒ bronchioli ⇒ alveoli**.
- The **functions** of the **lungs** are to take oxygen into the body, remove carbon dioxide from the body and remove water from the body.
- When oxygen passes from the air sacs into the blood and carbon dioxide passes from the blood into the air sacs, it is called the **exchange of gases**.

Revision Questions

1 Name two excretory organs in the body.

2 Give two functions of the lungs.

3 State the function of each of the following: (a) nose; (b) larynx; (c) epiglottis.

4 Explain the term 'oxidation'.

5 Explain the term 'exchange of gases'.

Higher Level

Circulatory system

The circulatory system consists of a network of blood vessels (pipes) which transport substances all over the body.

About five litres of blood are circulated several times every day by the heart. The heart is a pump which keeps the blood moving.

Blood

An adult has about five litres of blood, which consists of watery liquid called **plasma**. There are many substances dissolved in the plasma, such as digested foods, oxygen and carbon dioxide. There are three types of cell in the plasma: **red blood cells**, **white blood cells** and **blood platelets**.

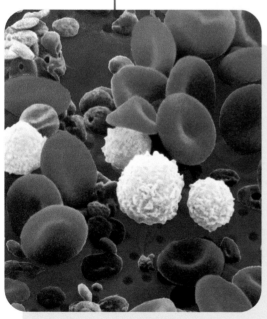
Red blood cells, white blood cells and blood platelets

Red blood cells

Red blood cells are red in colour because they contain a red pigment called **haemoglobin**. Haemoglobin combines with oxygen and carries it around the body in the blood. Iron is needed to make haemoglobin.

White blood cells

White blood cells are larger than red blood cells. White blood cells fight bacteria to protect the body from disease.

Blood platelets

Platelets are tiny cells that help to clot the blood to stop bleeding.

The clot hardens to form a scab, which keeps the wound clean until new skin grows.

Functions of the blood

- It **carries dissolved substances** such as oxygen, carbon dioxide and digested food around the body.
- It **protects the body** from disease – white blood cells fight infection and platelets help clot the blood and stop bleeding.
- It helps to **control body temperature** by carrying heat around the body and giving off heat when the body becomes too hot.
- It **transports** hormones and enzymes around the body.

Blood vessels

There are three types of blood vessel: **arteries, veins** and **capillaries.**

Arteries

Arteries carry blood **away** from the heart. The blood is rich in oxygen. The walls of the arteries are thick and elastic. This is because blood is forced under pressure from the heart into the arteries. Arteries do not have valves.

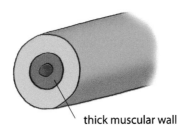

Artery

thick muscular wall

Veins

Veins carry blood **towards** the heart. The blood is rich in carbon dioxide. Veins have thinner walls than arteries. Blood flows more slowly in the veins, therefore veins have valves which prevent the blood from flowing backwards.

Vein

Capillaries

Capillaries are tiny blood vessels which link arteries and veins.

Capillary walls are only one cell thick. This allows for the passage of oxygen and carbon dioxide through the walls of the capillaries. This happens when oxygen and carbon dioxide are exchanged.

Capillary: walls are only one cell thick

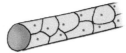

The heart

The heart is in the middle of the chest, between the lungs. It is about the size of a clenched fist. It is made of a special type of muscle called **cardiac** muscle. Cardiac muscle contracts without being instructed by the brain and it never gets tired.

Higher Level

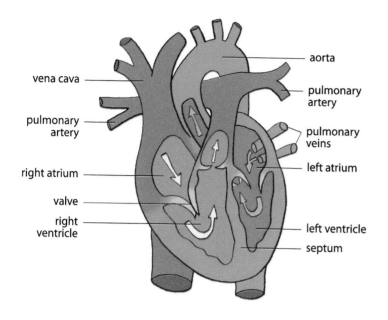

vena cava

pulmonary artery

right atrium

valve

right ventricle

aorta

pulmonary artery

pulmonary veins

left atrium

left ventricle

septum

Parts of the heart

- The heart is divided into two main areas, the **left** side and the **right** side. There is a muscular wall down the centre called the **septum**.
- Each side is divided into two chambers, a thin-walled **atrium** on top and a thick-walled **ventricle** below. Therefore, there are four chambers.
- Valves in the heart stop blood flowing backwards.
- The main artery leaving the heart is the **aorta**.
- The main veins entering the heart are called the **venae cavae** (singular: vena cava).

Blood flow through the heart

- Blood returns to the heart from around the body. This blood enters the **right atrium** through the vena cava. It then passes to the **right ventricle** before it is pumped to the lungs to pick up oxygen.
- Oxygen-rich blood from the lungs enters the **left atrium** by the pulmonary veins. This oxygen-rich blood then passes into the **left ventricle** before it is pumped out through the aorta to the rest of the body.

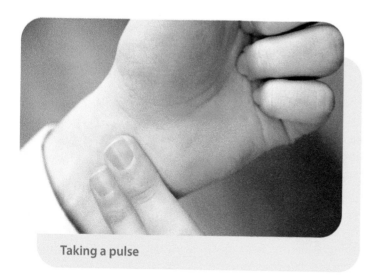

Taking a pulse

Pulse

When the blood is pumped along an artery, it can be felt at points where the artery is close to the skin. This is called a **pulse**, which is caused by the heartbeat. The average adult heart beats around 72 times per minute.

Press the tips of two fingers on the inside of the wrist, just below the thumb. Count the number of beats in 15 seconds. Multiply the number by four to find the number of heartbeats per minute.

Coronary heart disease

The heart is supplied with blood by the coronary arteries.

When cholesterol builds up as deposits on the walls of the arteries, they become narrower. This can cause high blood pressure, stroke or heart attack.

Factors that increase the risk of heart disease include:

- heredity (runs in one's family)
- high-fat diet
- overweight
- lack of exercise
- smoking
- stress
- too much alcohol.

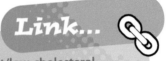

Link...

Low-fat/low-cholesterol diet, page 35

Guidelines for reducing the risk of coronary heart disease

- Reduce foods high in saturated fat/cholesterol.
- Increase intake of polyunsaturated fat, e.g. in olive oil and oily fish.
- Avoid overeating.
- Reduce alcohol consumption.
- Do not smoke.
- Exercise regularly.
- Avoid stress/worry.

Salad with oil-based dressing

Exercise reduces the risk of coronary heart disease

Summary

- Blood consists of **plasma**. There are three types of cell suspended in the plasma: **red blood cells**, **white blood cells** and **blood platelets**.
- **Haemoglobin** in red blood cells combines with **oxygen**.
- White blood cells fight bacteria to protect the body from disease.
- Platelets help to clot the blood to stop bleeding.
- **Functions of blood: carries dissolved substances** around the body; **protects the body** from disease; helps to **control body temperature**; and **transports** hormones and enzymes around the body.
- There are three types of blood vessel: **arteries**, **veins** and **capillaries**.
- The heart pumps blood around the body and is made of **cardiac muscle**.
- The heart is divided into four chambers: left and right **atria** and left and right **ventricles**.
- **Valves** in the heart stop blood from flowing backwards.
- The main artery leaving the heart is the **aorta**.
- The main veins entering the heart are called the **venae cavae**.
- Blood low in oxygen enters the heart at the **right atrium**. It then passes to the **right ventricle** before it is pumped to the lungs to pick up oxygen. Oxygen-rich blood from the lungs enters the **left atrium**. This blood then passes into the **left ventricle** before it is pumped out through the aorta to the rest of the body.
- The **pulse** is caused by the heartbeat.
- **Coronary heart disease** is the build-up of cholesterol on the walls of the arteries, which causes high blood pressure, stroke and heart attack.
- Factors that **increase the risk of heart disease** include heredity, a high-fat diet, being overweight, lack of exercise, smoking, stress and a high intake of alcohol.

Revision Questions

1 Give one function of each of the following: (a) platelets; (b) red blood cells; (c) white blood cells.
2 What is the function of haemoglobin in red blood cells?
3 Describe the position of the heart in the body.
4 List the functions of blood.
5 Name three blood vessels and explain the differences between any two of the blood vessels you have named.
6 Explain how a person's pulse is taken.
7 What is meant by coronary heart disease?
8 Outline five guidelines which should be followed to reduce the risk of coronary heart disease.

Chapter 22
Health

Health means well-being. It includes mental health and physical health.

Parents have responsibility for their children's health. Teenagers should take more responsibility for their health as they get older. We need to follow guidelines to ensure good health as well as taking precautions to prevent ill health.

Weblink

Mental Health Ireland –
www.mentalhealthireland.ie

Guidelines for good health

- Eat a balanced diet.
- Practise good personal hygiene.
- Take regular exercise.
- Get sufficient rest and sleep.
- Don't smoke or abuse drugs or alcohol.
- Develop a positive attitude.
- Visit the doctor regularly.
- Develop hobbies.

Mental health

Good mental health means having a healthy mind. It involves feeling content with life and having a positive attitude. It means having the ability to cope with everyday life and having high self-esteem.

Guidelines for good mental health

- Have a good balance between work and relaxation.
- Spend time with people whose company you enjoy, whether at home, in school or in a club.
- Take regular exercise.
- Talk about your worries with someone you trust.
- Make the most of your talents.
- Seek help for problems if necessary.

Precautions against disease

Some diseases or conditions can be prevented.

● Babies and children are checked at regular intervals by screening tests to identify problems concerning their development.
● Adults should have regular health checks.

Immunisation or **vaccination** against disease is given to people of all ages to **prevent** diseases such as mumps, measles and rubella. A small dose of the disease is given to the person, usually by injection.

The body reacts to this dose by producing antibodies which fight the disease. If the person comes into contact with the disease again, their body is ready to fight it and therefore they don't catch the disease. A **booster shot** is a **top-up** on the immunisation to ensure that it will last for a long time.

Women need breast examinations and cervical screening tests. Men need to be tested for testicular cancer. Both men and women need to have their cholesterol levels checked.

Weblink

Information on health check-ups:
Irish Heart Foundation –
www.irishheart.ie
Department of Health and Children –
www.doh.ie

Physical exercise

A person becomes physically fit by taking physical exercise. A person who is fit is:

● strong
● supple (can bend easily).
● has plenty of stamina (energy)

Aerobic exercise

Aerobic exercise is exercise that makes you breathe faster and makes your heart and lungs work harder. Examples include walking, running and swimming. Aerobic exercise helps prevent heart disease and high blood pressure.

Benefits of regular exercise

Regular physical exercise contributes to a healthy body and a healthy mind in the following ways:

● reduces the risk of heart disease and stroke
● reduces stress
● creates a 'feel good' factor
● is a way of socialising
● helps you to sleep better
● helps to maintain a healthy weight
● helps to control blood pressure.

Aerobic exercise

Guidelines for helping to maintain fitness and health

- Include at least 30 minutes of exercise every day as part of your normal daily activities (play, sport, transport and leisure).
- Engage in three or more 20-minute sessions of moderate to vigorous activity per week.
- Choose an activity you **like**.
- Exercise with friends if it is more fun.
- Stretch your muscles before and after exercising.

Stress

Stress is the emotional and physical strain caused by your response to real or imagined problems in your life. Stress is a normal part of life. It can be positive, keeping us alert. However, it becomes negative when it becomes excessive. You can experience stress from your thoughts, your body or your environment.

Stress may have physical or mental effects on the body. These include headache, upset stomach, problems sleeping and depression. Some people use unhealthy ways of dealing with stress such as using drugs to relax, overeating or undereating, smoking or spending hours in front of the television or computer.

Guidelines to reduce stress

- Become aware of the sources of stress in your life.
- Relax daily.
- Take regular exercise.
- Balance your diet.
- Only think about one day at a time.
- Express your feelings appropriately. (Use 'I' statements. See Communication, page 261.)

Stress may have physical or mental effects on the body

Rest and sleep

It is essential for the body to rest, otherwise we would 'burn out'. Sleep is the most effective type of rest. To ensure a good night's sleep, avoid drinking tea and coffee at night and try to relax before bedtime. **Insomnia** is the inability to sleep.

Adequate sleep has the following benefits:

- we **feel** better
- we **look** better
- we have better **concentration** levels
- it improves our **mood**.

The **Health Promotion Unit** is an organisation concerned with health promotion, run by the Health Service Executive. It provides information to the public on health matters and produces literature advising the public on various topics, such as diet and disease.

Importance of leisure

Leisure time is time to unwind after school or work. Leisure time is the time when you **choose** to do activities you **like**. Leisure has the following benefits:

- reduces stress
- allows you to learn new skills
- helps you make new friends
- reduces boredom
- keeps your brain active
- sports activities keep you fit.

Summary

- **Good mental health** means feeling positive and having the ability to cope with everyday life.
- A person who is physically **fit** is **strong**, **supple** and has plenty of **stamina**.
- **Aerobic exercise** is exercise that makes you breathe faster.
- To help maintain fitness, choose an **activity** you like and exercise for at least 30 minutes every day.
- **Insomnia** is the inability to sleep.
- Adequate sleep helps you to **work** better, **look** better, have better **concentration** levels and **feel better**.
- **Leisure** time is time when you **choose** to do activities you **like**.
- The **Health Promotion Unit** provides information to the public on health matters.

Revision Questions

1 List four guidelines that should be followed in order to promote good health in teenagers.
2 Explain what is meant by mental health and list three factors that contribute to good mental health.
3 Outline two benefits of regular exercise.
4 What is aerobic exercise?
5 State two examples of aerobic exercise that you would recommend for teenagers.
6 State two reasons why it is important to get enough sleep.
7 State three possible effects of stress on the body.
8 List two guidelines that can help to reduce stress.
9 Give three reasons why leisure is important in a teenager's lifestyle.
10 List four guidelines that can help maintain fitness and health.
11 Suggest a fitness programme suitable for a school-going teenager.
12 Explain the terms: (a) immunisation; (b) booster shot.
13 Name one organisation concerned with health promotion and briefly outline the work it carries out.

Chapter 23
Health hazards

Smoking

Tobacco is the second major cause of death in the world, according to international research.

Most teenagers who smoke start between the ages of 13 and 15.

Weblink

www.spunout.ie
www.thinkuknow.co.uk
http://kidshealth.org

Why do some young people smoke?

- **Peer pressure:** People smoke to fit in with their peer group.
- **Curiosity:** Young people want to experiment.
- **Image:** Many young people think that they are more glamorous and grown-up when they smoke.
- **Moving to second-level school:** The new environment and the desire to fit in influences teenagers to experiment with tobacco.
- **Alcohol:** Teenagers smoke more when they drink alcohol.

Harmful substances in cigarettes

Cigarettes contain harmful substances that damage the body:

- **nicotine** causes **addiction**
- **tar** from cigarettes **clings** to the lining of the lungs, making breathing difficult
- tobacco **smoke** contains a gas which **reduces** the blood's ability to carry **oxygen** around the body
- **irritants** cause **smoker's cough.**

Addiction is an uncontrollable craving for a drug. Nicotine is a drug found in cigarettes which causes addiction. People who are addicted to **nicotine** feel tension and discomfort if cigarettes are unavailable.

Harmful effects of smoking

Smoking contributes to many illnesses and diseases.

- **Lung cancer:** 90 per cent of people who get lung cancer are smokers.
- Smoking is linked with **cancer of the mouth, throat and bladder.**
- **Breathing difficulty:** This is caused by tar, which clings to the lining of the lungs.
- **Heart disease:** Smoking causes narrowing of the arteries.
- **High blood pressure:** This is linked to heart disease.
- **Emphysema:** This is a respiratory disease.
- **Damage to unborn babies:** During pregnancy, regular smoking damages the foetus. Babies born to regular smokers are **smaller** at birth than babies of non-smokers. Pregnant women who smoke also run a greater risk of **miscarriage** and **stillbirth.**

Passive smoking (second-hand smoke)

Passive smoking occurs when non-smokers inhale smoke from a nearby smoker. Passive smokers also suffer from smokers' diseases.

Steps taken to reduce smoking in Ireland

- It is illegal to sell cigarettes to people under 18 years old.
- It is illegal to smoke at work.
- Advertising, sponsorship and promotion have been banned.
- Ten-pack cigarettes are no longer sold.
- The Office of Tobacco Control was established.
- There are high taxes on cigarettes and tobacco.

Activity

Design an anti-smoking advertisement using these ideas:

- Smoking – how others see me.
- Smoking – affects my health.

Alcohol

Research has shown that increasing numbers of Irish children and adolescents are experimenting with alcohol. Many teenagers are developing patterns of alcohol use that could lead them into alcohol-related harm. They are starting to drink at an earlier age and there is increasing evidence of binge drinking and drunkenness.

Binge drinking and getting **drunk** are particular problems in Ireland today, among both teenagers and adults. Binge drinking is drinking heavily over a short period of time or drinking continuously over a number of days.

One unit of alcohol = half a pint of beer, a glass of wine or a pub measure of spirits. Men should not drink more than 21 units per week and women should not drink more than 14 units per week.

Why do young people abuse alcohol?

- Alcohol gives them more confidence.
- Family example encourages young people to take alcohol.
- Peer pressure forces people to fit in with their friends.
- Availability of alcohol encourages people to abuse it.
- Young people are curious about alcohol.
- Some people feel that it helps them to relax.

Short-term effects of drinking

- A person cannot think clearly and may take risks, such as driving while drunk, or sexual risks.
- Co-ordination and judgement are lost. A person can have difficulty walking and driving.
- People lose self-control and may get involved in arguments or fights.
- Very heavy drinking can cause unconsciousness and even death.

Teenage alcohol abuse

Effects of long-term alcohol abuse on the body

- A person can become addicted to alcohol.
- Brain cells are permanently damaged, which affects memory and judgement.
- Cancers may develop in the mouth, gullet, liver and bladder.
- A person may become depressed.
- Unborn babies are damaged if the mother drinks during pregnancy.

Effects of alcohol abuse on society

- Increase in the rate of crime.
- Increase in road accidents and deaths.
- Absenteeism from work.
- High costs to the state of treating alcohol-related illness.

Guidelines for sensible drinking

- Drink slowly.
- Drink in moderation and avoid getting drunk.
- Don't put pressure on others to drink.
- Don't drink on an empty stomach.
- Don't drink and drive.
- Avoid buying rounds.

Steps taken to reduce alcohol consumption in Ireland

- The Intoxicating Liquor Act 2008 restricts the sale and availability of alcohol.
- It is illegal for people aged under 18 years to buy alcohol.
- Off-licence hours have been reduced.
- Children are not allowed in pubs after 9.00 p.m.

Help available

- **Alcoholics Anonymous** is an organisation that helps people who suffer from alcoholism – www.alcoholicsanonymous.ie
- **Al-Anon** helps the families of alcoholics – www.al-anon-ireland.org
- **Alateen** helps children of alcoholics: www.al-anon-ireland.org

Activity

Discuss the risk-taking behaviour which is associated with abuse of alcohol.

Drugs

A **drug** is a chemical that changes how the body functions physically, mentally or emotionally.

Types of drug

Commonly used drugs include alcohol, caffeine and nicotine.

There are five main types of drug.

- **Depressants** (e.g. alcohol) cause sleepiness.
- **Sedatives** (e.g. sleeping tablets, Valium) have a calming effect.
- **Opiates** (e.g. heroin) cause a euphoric (happy) feeling.
- **Stimulants** (e.g. cocaine) change the body's natural levels of energy and alertness. Caffeine is a stimulant drug found in coffee and tea.
- **Hallucinogens** (e.g. LSD, magic mushrooms) cause strange visions.

Reasons why people take drugs

- Curiosity causes many young people to experiment with drugs.
- Peer pressure forces people to take drugs.
- People want to escape from boredom or worry.
- Some people think it is 'cool' or fashionable to take drugs.
- People enjoy the effect that the drug has on them.

Teenage drug abuse

Taking drugs

Drugs are taken in various ways, including eating, drinking, chewing, smoking, inhaling and injecting. The most dangerous way of taking drugs is by injection. The risk of overdose is high and disease is spread by sharing needles.

Controlled drugs

Controlled drugs are drugs that are available only with a doctor's prescription.

When you buy a prescribed drug you are sure that the medicine contains the right amount of the drug. However, when people buy illegal drugs, they do not know what they are buying and the risk of ill effects is high.

Drug abuse

Drug abuse is the use of a drug that damages some aspect of a person's life. This damage may be physical, mental or emotional. Relationships, work, school or family life may suffer.

Effects of drug abuse on the body:

- **Addiction** occurs, which means that the person suffers an uncontrollable desire for the drug.
- **Dependence** occurs when the person depends on the drug to make him/her feel good.
- **AIDS** is spread through sharing needles.
- **Death** can often result from an overdose. Suicide or accidental death may occur.

Effects of drug abuse on the family and society:

- **Family disruption** is caused when money is spent on drugs.
- Many drugs are **illegal**. Drug addicts sometimes resort to **crime** to get money for drugs.
- **Costs** of law enforcement and medical care are high.
- **Absenteeism** from work.

Activity

Make a list of advertisements that encourage the use of drugs for medical conditions. Discuss whether or not you think these advertisements are effective.

Summary

- **Addiction is an uncontrollable craving for a drug**.
- **Harmful substances** in cigarettes include **nicotine**, **tar**, **smoke** and **irritants**.
- **Passive smoking** occurs when non-smokers inhale smoke breathed out by smokers.
- **Government controls** include restrictions on the sale and use of cigarettes.
- **Short-term effects of drinking** include unclear thinking, impaired judgement, loss of self-control, unconsciousness and even death.
- **Effects of long-term alcohol abuse** include addiction, cancers, depression and damage to unborn babies.
- **Effects of alcohol abuse on society** include increases in the rate of crime, in road accidents, in absenteeism from work and in costs to the state.
- **Steps taken to reduce alcohol consumption in Ireland:** Intoxicating Liquor Act 2008; illegal for under-18s to buy alcohol; reduction in off-licence hours; children are not allowed in pubs after 9.00 p.m.
- **Alcoholics Anonymous**, **Al-Anon** and **Alateen** are organisations that help people affected by alcohol.
- A **drug** is a chemical that changes how the body functions physically, mentally or emotionally.
- Drugs that are available by prescription from a doctor are called **controlled drugs**.
- **Drug abuse** is the use of a drug that damages some aspect of a person's life.
- **Effects of drug abuse on the body:** Addiction, dependence, AIDS and death.
- **Effects of drug abuse on society:** Family disruption, crime, wasting money and work absenteeism.

Revision Questions

1 Why do some young people smoke?

2 Outline two harmful effects of smoking on the body.

3 Name one harmful substance found in cigarettes and state how this substance affects the body.

4 What is meant by passive smoking?

5 Suggest two ways in which the government has tried to control smoking.

6 What is meant by addiction?

7 List four effects of long-term alcohol abuse on the body.

8 Give two effects of alcohol abuse on society.

9 What steps have been taken to reduce alcohol consumption in Ireland?

10 Explain what is meant by controlled drugs.

11 What do you understand drug abuse to mean?

12 Give four effects of drug abuse on the individual.

Section four

Resource management and home studies

Chapter 24
Management

Management is the skilful use of time, energy and other resources.
A resource is something we can use to help us achieve our goals.

- **Human resources** include time, energy and skill.
- **Economic resources** include money and property.
- **Environmental resources** include trees, water, air and light.

A goal is what we want to achieve.

There are many types of manager – team managers, hotel managers, bank managers, school managers, etc.

Manager

- A school manager uses time, energy, money and the skills of teachers and other staff to provide a pleasant and well-run school.
- A team manager uses time, energy, money and the skills of players and staff to ensure that the team wins games.

Home management

Home management is the efficient running of the home.

The main aims of home management are healthy living and happy family members.

The tasks involved in running a home include:

- budgeting
- child care
- shopping
- laundry
- cooking
- gardening
- cleaning and maintenance.

Home management is the efficient running of the home

Many of these jobs are done by parents, but other family members may also help out in other areas, such as cleaning, laundry and shopping.

A **management system** can be used in the management of the home. It involves the following steps:

1 **Goals:** Set out what needs to be done, e.g. weekly shopping, cooking meals, spring cleaning, laundry.

2 **Resources:** These are what will help the manager achieve these goals. Resources include:
- time – enough for each task
- people to help with tasks
- energy to do the work
- equipment to perform tasks and save time and energy
- money to buy necessities and other resources.

3 **Plan:** Plan the steps to be followed and the resources to be used to achieve goals. Cookery time plans, work rotas and shopping lists are examples of simple plans.

4 **Action:** Put the plan into action.

5 **Evaluate:** Examine the outcome of the plan. Were there any changes that could have been made? Could the job have been done faster or made easier? Were all resources used efficiently?

Here is an example of how a management system might be used to organise the family laundry.

1 Goals:
- Organise the family laundry for a weekend, i.e. sort, wash, dry, iron and put away clothes.

2 Resources:
- Time (enough for each individual task).
- People (family members).
- Energy (to do the work).
- Equipment (laundry baskets, washing machine, detergent, clothes line, dryer, iron, ironing board).

3 Plan:
- Decide who is going to collect dirty laundry from all family members and when.
- Decide how the clothes are going to be washed (type of machine wash programme or hand wash) and dried (clothes line or tumble dryer).
- Plan how the clean clothes are going to be sorted, who is going to iron them and who is going to put them away.

4 Action:
- Friday evening – gather dirty laundry from each person. Sort into wash loads and machine or hand wash. Hang on clothes line to dry.
- Saturday afternoon – sort dry laundry into separate bundles to be folded (underwear, towels, sweaters) or ironed (shirts, trousers). Iron clothes and fold or store on hangers. Put away clothes.

5 Evaluate:
- Was the laundry done successfully?
- Were all the clothes properly washed and dried?
- Could the job have been done faster or made easier?
- Are there any improvements that could be made for next time?

Work plans

Routines and work plans are important when managing the home.

They ensure that jobs are done regularly and that all family members play a part.

Here are some guidelines for organising work plans:

- Make a list of all the jobs that need to be done daily, weekly and occasionally.
- Calculate the time it takes to do different jobs so that the workload is spread evenly.
- Don't spend too long on any one task.
- Include a couple of weekly tasks each day, e.g. vacuuming, and an occasional task each week, e.g. defrosting the fridge.
- Place the jobs in a logical order which will suit the family's lifestyle.
- If possible, include all family members in the work routine.
- Try out the work plan for a couple of weeks to check if it is working or needs to be changed.
- Work in an organised way to save time and effort. For example, when cleaning a room:
  - tidy
  - sweep (if not vacuuming)
  - dust
  - vacuum
  - wash
  - polish.

Effects of good management on family life

All family members benefit from good management. Everything runs more smoothly and stress is avoided.

Consider the following case study.

Case Study

Mrs Smith totally forgot to pay the phone bill! She had the bill in her handbag and intended to pay it at the post office . . . four weeks ago! Now the phone has been cut off and she can't ring her friend to arrange a lift to school for the children tomorrow morning. She has to drive Mr Smith to the station as he has to catch an early train to Dublin for a breakfast meeting. Paul is complaining that he can't go online to do research for his project, which is due in next week. Pauline wants to check her page on Facebook . . .

Paulette arrives in from college, tired and hungry, only to be met by a frazzled mother and whining siblings. Dinner will be late as the shopping hasn't been done and Mr Smith is picking up something to eat on the way home from work. The breakfast dishes are still on the table. It's Paul's turn to fill the dishwasher, but he has a project to do. Pauline is wondering if her football gear has been washed for her semi-final tomorrow. She searches, and finds it . . . lying at the bottom of the laundry basket, where she left it last Thursday!

Case Study

Mr Smith finally arrives home, with a cold take-away. 'I'd forgotten about the roadworks – it delayed me fifteen minutes,' he groans. Paulette starts to set the table, only to find that there is very little clean cutlery in the drawer. Most of it is in the dishwasher . . . unwashed.

Paul reminds his mother that his friend is staying over tomorrow night. Mrs Smith wonders if there are clean sheets for the spare bed in Paul's room . . .

Activities

1 List the effects of good management on family life. Consider stress, time, leisure, relaxation, satisfaction, happiness, efficiency and tasks.

2 Comment on the effects of poor home management on the Smith family.

3 What changes could they make to better manage their household?

4 Write a paragraph based on a day in the life of the Jones family, a well-managed household.

Summary

- **Management** is the skilful use of time, energy and resources.
- **Home management** is the efficient running of the home.
- A **goal** is what we want to achieve.
- A **resource** is something we use to help us achieve our goals.
- A **management system** includes a **goal**, **resources**, **plan**, **action** and **evaluation**.

Revision Questions

1 List three principal resources used in the management of the home.

2 What are human resources? Give two examples.

3 A work routine is essential when managing the home. List four guidelines for planning a work routine.

4 Plan a simple daily routine which would help a teenager with asthma maintain a high standard of hygiene in his/her bedroom.

Chapter 25
Home and community

Shelter is one of our basic needs. It is a place that provides **protection**, **covering** or **safety**.

For thousands of years, people have used houses of one kind or another to provide shelter for their families.

Types of shelter/housing

People choose to live in different types of shelter.

- **Houses:** Terraced, detached or semi-detached; bungalow, two- or three-storey.
- **Apartments or flats:** Purpose-built, or a large house divided into different apartments.
- **Bedsits:** One room divided into different areas for sleeping, cooking, etc.
- **Caravans, mobile homes, houseboats:** May be temporary or permanent.
- **Sheltered housing:** Small groups of houses purpose-built for elderly or disabled people; usually supervised.
- **Residential accommodation:** Old people's homes, convents, boarding schools.

Houses

Apartments or flats

Bedsit

Mobile homes

Sheltered housing

Residential accommodation

What makes a house a home?

When a house is newly built and not yet lived in, it is not considered a home. It doesn't feel warm or inviting. To make it a home, it needs to be filled with people, their belongings, sounds, warmth and light. A **home** provides for many of our basic human needs.

- **Physical needs:** Shelter, warmth and protection.
- **Emotional needs:** Safety, security, privacy and a caring and relaxing environment.
- **Social needs:** A place for entertaining and leisure.

Link...

Needs and wants, page 215

Factors to be considered when choosing a family home:

- Location – is it near school, work, shops and other amenities?
- Size – is it big enough for all the family?
- Cost – is it affordable?
- Personal preferences – terraced, detached, apartment or dormer style?
- Energy efficiency – is it insulated and will it be economical to heat?

Community services and amenities

When people live together in an area, they form a community.

All communities have a number of services and amenities. An **amenity** is a useful or pleasant facility, e.g. community centres, parks, beaches, shops, banks, playgrounds.

Community services are provided by state (statutory) and voluntary organisations.

Statutory services

- Gardaí.
- Postal service.
- Social welfare.
- Public libraries.
- Health (hospitals, health centres).
- Education (schools).
- Community information centres.
- Local authority housing.

Voluntary services

- Youth clubs.
- GAA clubs.
- ISPCC.
- St Vincent de Paul.
- Rehab.
- Neighbourhood Watch
- Meals on Wheels.
- ALONE.

Statutory service

Activities

1 Make a list of the voluntary services available in your area. Are you a member of any service? If so, give details.

2 Make a list of the amenities available in your area. Indicate which of these are man-made and which are natural.

3 Plan your ideal community. Use posters to illustrate your ideas.

Summary

- **Shelter** is a place that provides protection, covering or safety.
- **Housing options** include houses, apartments, bedsits, institutions, caravans and sheltered housing.
- **A home provides for our basic needs**: **physical** needs (shelter, warmth), **emotional** needs (safety, security) and **social** needs (entertainment, leisure).
- Factors to consider when choosing a house include: **location, size, cost, preferences, energy efficiency.**
- A **community** is formed when people live together in an area.
- An **amenity** is a useful or pleasant facility.
- **Community services** may be statutory, e.g. Gardaí, schools, hospitals; or voluntary, e.g. GAA, Rehab, ISPCC.

Revision Questions

1 Suggest two different types of accommodation suitable for a student living away from home.

2 Give two factors which should be considered when choosing a family home.

3 What do you understand by 'local amenities'? Give two examples of local amenities found in your community.

4 Name three services provided by the state, i.e. statutory services.

Chapter 26
Design

Interior design

Everything we wear, travel in, live in and use in our daily lives has been designed.

The best designers build their ideas around how the human body works in the home and workplace. When designing a home and everything in it, the following are all equally important.

- **Function:** Does it do its job well?
- **Appearance:** Does it look attractive?
- **Comfort and quality:** Is it well made and comfortable to use?

Features of design

Function

An item is designed to carry out a particular function, i.e. to do a job.

An electric kettle must be able to boil water safely; a chair must be comfortable to sit on.

If an item does not suit its function, it is badly designed.

Product design

Colour

Colour is often one of the first design features we notice in clothes, interiors, packaging and other items. When used wisely, it can create many different effects, and even change the atmosphere of a room.

The **colour wheel** shows how colours relate to each other and how they combine to make other colours.

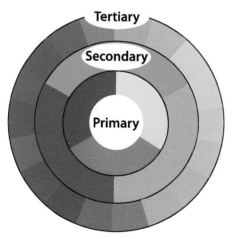

The colour wheel

Warm colours

Cool colours

Strong colours

Light colours

- **Primary** colours are red, yellow and blue.
- **Secondary** colours are made by mixing two primary colours; examples are green, orange and purple.
- **Tertiary** colours are made by mixing a primary and a secondary colour, e.g. red and purple = wine (see the colour wheel on the previous page). Tertiary colours are indigo, wine, turquoise, lime, etc.
- **Warm** colours are red, pink, orange and yellow. They make a room seem warm and cosy.
- **Cool** colours are blue, green, pale yellow and blue-violet. They create a cool, calm environment.
- **Strong** colours seem to move forward, making a room seem smaller.
- **Light** colours seem to draw back, making walls and ceilings appear further away.
- **Neutral** colours are black, white, grey, beige and cream. They are useful for combining with more definite colours, or can be used in an all-neutral colour scheme.
- **Pastel** colours are pale, delicate colours, e.g. baby blue, lemon yellow. They are sometimes called 'ice cream' colours and they blend easily to give a light, airy effect.

What basic shapes are used in house design?

Form (shape and line)

Shape is the outline of an object. The four basic shapes that are used in design are **square**, **circle**, **triangle** and **rectangle**.

Houses themselves and most objects in the home are based on these shapes.

Vertical lines

Horizontal lines

Diagonal lines

Curved lines

Line can be used in four ways to create different effects:

1 **Vertical** lines make an object seem taller.
2 **Horizontal** lines make an object seem wider.
3 **Diagonal** lines create a dramatic effect.
4 **Curved** lines are soft and graceful.

Texture

Texture is the 'feel' of an object – whether it is rough, smooth, soft or hard. Every room should have a variety of textures to add interest. Texture can influence the strength of a colour and can change the overall atmosphere of a room.

- **Rough textures,** such as brick, stone and tweed, absorb sound and light, making them quiet and cosy.
- **Smooth textures,** such as polished wood, marble and glass, reflect sound and light. They are easy to clean and create a cool effect, but may be noisy.

Rough textures

Smooth textures

Pattern

Pattern is a decorative design, e.g. print, floral, check. It is used to provide interest and contrast – a plain area can be boring.

Too many patterns can create a cluttered effect.

Generally, small patterns work best in small areas, while large patterns suit larger areas.

Design principles

The following principles or rules will help to create good results in home design.

- **Balance:** This means that there is an **equal spread** of colour, pattern and texture in the room.
- **Proportion:** The **link between the sizes** of different items in the room, e.g. a low armchair and a coffee table are in proportion to each other.
- **Rhythm:** This is where there is a **regular or repeated** colour or pattern in the design to connect each part of the room.
- **Emphasis:** A part of the design which **stands out** and draws the eye. Colour, pattern, texture or lighting may be used to create emphasis or to highlight a feature.

Pattern

Higher Level

Can you see which design principles are used in this room?

Activities

1 Give examples of how the four basic shapes are used in the home. Which shape is most commonly used in the home?

2 Describe how line can be used in the following situations:
(a) a large room with a high ceiling; (b) a short, broad person who wishes to appear taller.

3 Using the guidelines described above, make a list of items in your home that you think are well designed. Are there any items you think are badly designed? If so, explain why.

Summary

The following are **features** of design:

1 **Colour:** The colour wheel contains primary, secondary and tertiary colours. Colours may be warm, cool, strong, light or neutral.

2 **Form: Shape** is the outline of an object. **Line** can create different effects.

3 **Texture** is the feel of an object.

4 **Pattern** is a decorative design.

The following are design **principles**:

1 **Emphasis:** The part of the design that stands out.

2 **Balance:** Equal spread of colour, pattern and texture.

3 **Proportion:** The link between the sizes of objects.

4 **Rhythm:** Repeated colour or pattern, which draws the room together.

Revision Questions

1 Name two warm colours and two cool colours.

2 Name one colour that creates a cool, restful atmosphere.

3 Pattern is used to provide interest and contrast in interior design. Where is pattern used in most rooms in the home?

4 State one desirable property and one undesirable property of wood flooring.

5 Explain each of the following when used in relation to room planning: (a) emphasis; (b) balance; (c) proportion.

Chapter 27
Room planning

The aim of room planning in the home is to arrange furniture and fittings in a comfortable and practical way so that all members of the household are happy with it.

Here are some guidelines for planning the layout of a room.

- Consider the **function** of the room, e.g. is it a family living room or a study?

- Adequate **ventilation** is important in kitchens and bathrooms.

- Consider the **likes** and **dislikes** of the occupants, e.g. a child's bedroom.

- Consider **safety** and **hygiene**, especially in kitchens and bathrooms.

- Make good use of all the available space and plan for sufficient **storage** space in the room.

- The room should be **comfortable** and **attractive**, with a good balance of colour, pattern and texture.

- Consider the **aspect** of the room. This is the direction the room faces. If the room faces north, it gets little sunlight and so needs warm colours. If a room is south facing, cool colours may suit.

- Existing fixtures and fittings (doors, windows, fireplace and radiators) will influence the **layout** of furniture in the room.

- **Heating** and **lighting** systems should be well planned and flexible (allow for plenty of power points for extra lamps or portable heaters, etc.).

- **Traffic flow** is an important factor. This is the free movement in a room, with enough space allowed between pieces of furniture.

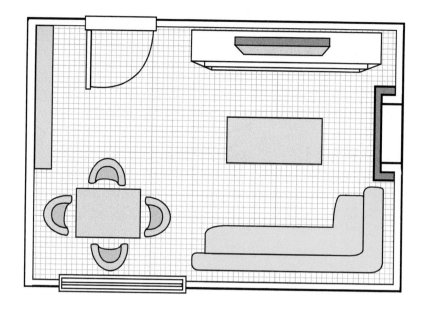

Floor plan

When planning a room, it is useful to make a floor plan of the room. This should be drawn to scale on graph paper and should show the position of fixtures and fittings, e.g. doors and windows. Furniture can also be drawn to scale, cut out and moved around on the floor plan. This will show how the room will look when the furniture is arranged in different ways.

Designing a bedroom

When planning and designing a bedroom, there are many options to choose from.

- **Colour scheme:** Consider the aspect of the room and the preferences of the occupant.
- **Floor:** Carpet, polished wood (hard or soft), laminated flooring.
- **Walls:** Paint or wallpaper.
- **Furniture:** Bed, wardrobe, chest of drawers, bookshelves, bedside locker, desk, chair.
- **Soft furnishings:** Curtains, blinds, duvet cover, cushions, lampshades, bedspread, throw.
- **Heating:** Central heating radiator, underfloor heating, portable electric heater, open fire.
- **Lighting:** Central fitting, bedside lamp, study lamp, novelty lights, e.g. lava lamp, fairy lights.
- **Ventilation:** Window.

Kitchens

The kitchen is one of the busiest rooms in the home and so demands very careful planning to ensure efficiency, comfort and safety. All the guidelines for planning the layout of a room apply.

The layout of a kitchen is a very good example of **ergonomics** in action.

Ergonomics is the study of the efficiency of people in their workplace. It involves designing equipment and room layouts to suit people so that time and energy will not be wasted.

Preparing food follows a set pattern or **sequence**. It involves four types of activity:

1. **Storage:** fridge and food cupboards.
2. **Preparation:** worktops and sink.
3. **Cooking:** cooker/oven and hob.
4. **Serving:** worktop and serving dish cupboard.

When designing kitchens, the **work sequence** and **work triangle** must be considered. Kitchen units and equipment should be arranged following the work sequence, regardless of whether the kitchen is laid out in a U-shape, L-shape, island or galley design.

Keynote

The work triangle is an imaginary triangle which links the three main pieces of equipment in the kitchen: the fridge, cooker and sink.

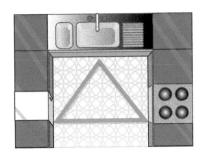
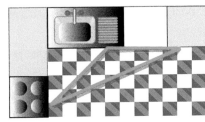
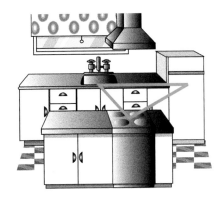

When preparing a meal, a person constantly walks between the fridge, cooker and sink. Their location will either: (a) make the work triangle very big and lead to unnecessary extra walking; or (b) make the work triangle very small and therefore cramped.

The idea of the work triangle should be applied to the design of every kitchen.

Remember that the efficiency of the kitchen depends not on how big it is, but on how it is laid out.

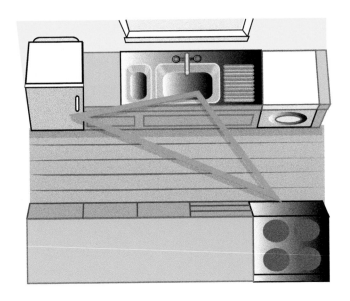

Activities

1 Plan the layout of a kitchen for a small apartment. Show the work triangle and describe the colour scheme you would use.

2 Draw a floor plan for a family living room with a southerly aspect. Show the position of furniture and fittings. Indicate the colour scheme.

3 Examine some interiors magazines and pick out a picture of a room which you like. Comment on: (a) the colour scheme; (b) balance; (c) proportion; and (d) emphasis in the room.

Summary

- When **planning a room**, consider: function, likes and dislikes, traffic flow, storage space, aspect, existing fixtures and fittings, heating, lighting and ventilation, comfort and appeal.

- **Ergonomics** is the study of the **efficiency of people in their workplace**.

- **A work sequence is a set pattern of work** that is normally followed when doing a job, e.g. preparing a meal.

- The **work triangle** is an imaginary triangle which links the three main pieces of equipment in the kitchen – the **cooker**, **sink** and **fridge**.

Revision Questions

1 Explain the following terms in relation to design in the home: (a) traffic flow; (b) aspect.

2 (a) List the factors which should be considered when planning a family living room.
(b) Draw a plan of the living room and indicate on the plan the position of:
(i) the window(s); (ii) the door(s); (iii) the furniture; (iv) suitable lighting.

(c) Suggest (i) a colour scheme, (ii) a floor covering and (iii) a heating system suitable for the living room and give a reason for your suggestion in each case.

3 You have been asked to plan the layout of a teenager's study-bedroom.

(a) Give four guidelines that you would follow when planning the layout of the room.

(b) Indicate two suitable positions for electrical sockets on the floor plan you have sketched and give two reasons why you think these positions are suitable.

(c) Suggest two soft furnishings which you would consider suitable for the study-bedroom.

4 List four guidelines to follow when planning the layout of a kitchen.

5 Explain the importance of the work triangle in kitchen design.

Chapter 28
Safety and first aid

Accidents

A home can be an extremely dangerous place, something which a lot of people don't believe until it's too late. More accidents occur in the home than anywhere else, so safety is a very important aim of the home manager.

What causes accidents?

There are three main causes of accidents:

1 **People:** May be careless, untidy, curious, or have slow reactions.
2 **Buildings:** May be badly designed and maintained, or have poor lighting.
3 **Objects:** Equipment may be faulty, or dangerous substances may be stored incorrectly.

Often, a combination of these reasons, or just bad luck, may lead to accidents.

Prevention of accidents

Electricity

- Electricity and water do not mix. Never handle anything electrical with wet hands.
- Never take anything electrical into the bathroom.
- Look for safety symbols on all appliances.

- Never overload sockets or repair frayed flexes.
- Avoid trailing flexes.
- Ensure appliances are wired correctly with the correct fuse.

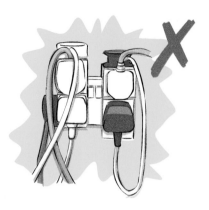

Fire

- Use a fireguard around open fires.
- Install smoke alarms and test them regularly.
- Keep a fire extinguisher and fire blanket in the house – most useful in the kitchen.
- Switch off and unplug electrical appliances at night.
- Ensure cigarettes are properly quenched after use.
- Never smoke in bed.
- Never leave matches or lighters where children can get at them.
- Never leave a chip pan or frying pan unattended.
- Ensure nightwear is fire resistant (especially for children).

Fire extinguisher

Falls

- Ensure that toys and other small items are not left lying around on the floor or stairs.
- Wipe up spills immediately.
- Do not over-polish floors and avoid frayed rugs and carpets.
- Ensure that stairs are well lit with a two-way switch.
- Install handgrips on showers and baths for elderly people.

Children

- Keep plastic bags, medicines, cleaning agents and other dangerous chemicals out of reach.
- Use short, coiled flexes on electrical appliances.
- Fit window locks and stair gates.
- Ensure that babies are strapped securely into high chairs and buggies.
- Never leave a young child unattended in a bath or anywhere near water.
- Keep hot drinks away from the edges of tables and turn saucepan handles inwards.

Fire drill

In the event of a fire:

- Keep calm. Call the fire brigade.
- Ensure that everyone leaves the house by the quickest route.
  Close doors on the way out to prevent the fire from spreading.
- Do not stop to collect valuables.
- Do not re-enter the house.

For small fires (e.g. frying pan or chip pan):

- Use a fire blanket or fire extinguisher to quench the fire.
- Never use water on electrical items or burning oil.

Hazard symbols

Cleaning agents and household chemicals carry hazard symbols and
safety warnings to protect users. Always follow instructions carefully.

| Highly flammable | Harmful; irritant | Environmentally damaging | Corrosive – can eat into body tissues | Explosive | Toxic |

First aid

First aid is the first treatment given to a person who has been injured or
suddenly taken ill before the arrival of an ambulance or doctor.

The aims (and benefits) of first aid are to:

- **preserve** life
- **prevent** the condition worsening
- **promote** recovery.

Basic rules of first aid

1 Act quickly and calmly.

2 Make sure the area is safe, e.g. turn off the engine or electric switch.

3 Do not place yourself in danger when trying to help the victim.

4 Check for consciousness.

5 Check for breathing.

6 Look for a pulse and check for bleeding.

7 Move the victim as little as possible to avoid worsening any injuries.

8 Avoid giving the victim anything to eat or drink, as he/she must be fasting if an anaesthetic is needed later in hospital.

9 Dial 999 or 112 for an ambulance if necessary.

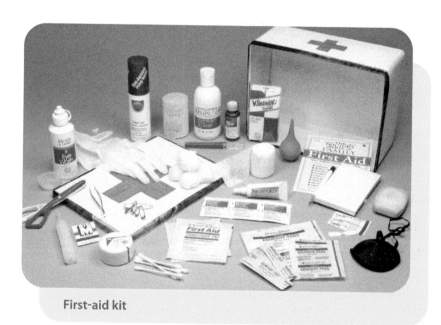

First-aid kit

First-aid kit

Every home should have a well-stocked first-aid kit. This should be kept in a convenient place, out of the reach of children. The photo shows some of the items to be included in a first-aid kit.

Medicines such as paracetamol, aspirin and prescribed medicines should be kept separately in a locked cabinet.

Simple first aid

Burns and scalds

Burns are caused by dry heat, e.g. fire, a hot appliance, the sun.
Scalds are burns caused by wet heat, e.g. steam or hot liquids.

Minor burns and scalds:

● Make the victim comfortable.
● Carefully remove any clothing or jewellery from the affected area before the injury starts to swell.
● Pour cold liquid on the injury for 10 minutes.
● Cover the burn and surrounding area with a sterile dressing or a clean piece of material.
● Do not break blisters or apply lotions, fat or ointments to the injury, or use adhesive dressings.

Severe burns and scalds:

- Lay the victim down and protect the burned area from contact with the ground, if possible.
- Gently remove any rings, watches, belts or shoes from the injured area before it starts to swell.
- Pour cold water over the burned area.
- Cover the injury with a sterile dressing to protect it from germs and infection.
- While waiting for help, reassure the victim and treat for shock.
- Do not burst blisters or apply lotions, ointments, fat or adhesive tape to the injury. Do not remove anything sticking to the burn.

Shock

This occurs when too little blood circulates to the brain. It can be caused by severe bleeding or burns, vomiting or diarrhoea, an allergic reaction, heart attack and some types of poisoning. The symptoms include rapid, shallow breathing; cold, clammy skin; rapid, weak pulse; dizziness; and fainting.

- Lay the victim down. Use a blanket to protect him/her from the cold ground.
- Raise the victim's legs as high as possible and support them.
- Treat any cause of shock, such as bleeding.
- Loosen tight clothing.
- Do not allow the victim to move, eat or drink.

Choking

Choking is caused by a blockage to the airway. It is important to remove this blockage as quickly as possible.

- Bend the victim over and slap him/her on the back.
- If this fails to work, try the abdominal thrust (Heimlich manoeuvre):
    - Stand behind the casualty. Put your hands around him/her and put one fist below the rib cage.
    - Link your hands and pull sharply inwards and upwards.
    - Continue abdominal thrusts until the blockage clears.
    - If the victim is a baby, lay him/her face down along your forearm and slap between the shoulder blades up to four times.

Cuts

- If the cut is dirty, clean it by rinsing lightly under running water.
- Pat dry and apply a plaster.
- If there is severe bleeding from a cut, cover with a sterile dressing and apply pressure over the wound with your fingers.
- Raise the wounded part above the level of the heart if possible.
- Lay the victim down.
- Apply a bandage firmly in place.
- Check the circulation around the bandage and loosen it if needed.
- Call an ambulance if bleeding continues.

Falls

A fall can cause a broken bone, strain or sprain. If the casualty is unable to move a limb, it is likely that a fracture or dislocation has occurred.

> A **strain** is a pulled or stretched muscle.
> A **sprain** is a torn or damaged ligament.

- Do not attempt to move the victim. Send for an ambulance.
- A strain or a sprain may be treated by the RICE procedure.
  - a) REST the injured part.
  - b) Apply ICE or a cold compress (ice pack or a cloth soaked in ice water).
  - c) COMPRESS the injury (apply gentle, even pressure).
  - d) ELEVATE or raise the injured part.

Poisoning

- If a person has swallowed a poisonous substance, take him/her immediately to the casualty department of a hospital.
- Bring the container of poison to the hospital to help identify the treatment required.
- Never try to make the victim vomit.
- If the victim is conscious and the lips are burned, give him/her frequent sips of cold water or milk.
- If the victim is unconscious, place him/her in the recovery position and send for an ambulance.

The **recovery position** prevents the tongue blocking the airway and allows liquids to drain from the mouth. This prevents the victim inhaling and choking on vomit.

The recovery position

Summary

- **Causes** of accidents include careless, untidy or curious **people**, badly designed or maintained **buildings**, faulty equipment or incorrect storage of dangerous **objects**.
- The following areas are high risk and require special attention to prevent accidents: **electricity**, **fire**, **children**, **floors**.
- **Fire drill**: Keep calm, dial 999/112, leave quickly, close doors, do not re-enter.
- **Aims and benefits of first aid**: **preserve** life, **prevent** condition from worsening, **promote** recovery.
- Revise simple **first aid procedures** for burns and scalds, shock, choking, cuts, falls and poisoning.
- The **recovery position** is the safest position for the victim, as it prevents choking if vomiting should occur.

Revision Questions

1. Give four of the main causes of accidents in the home. For each cause you have given, suggest one way in which it can be prevented.

2. Outline two safety precautions which should be taken when using electricity in the home.

3. Suggest four health and safety guidelines that should be followed in the kitchen.

4. Explain why water should not be used to extinguish a fire caused by an electrical fault.

5. List the safety guidelines which should be followed in order to prevent a fire in the home.

6. Give two examples of fire safety equipment that you would recommend for the home.

7. Outline the procedure that should be followed to ensure the safety of the occupants of the house in the event of a household fire. How would you extinguish a fire caused by a frying pan overheating?

8. What information do these symbols convey to the consumer?

   (a)    (b)

9. State two benefits of first aid.

10. List the items which should be included in a first-aid kit. Where should the first-aid kit be stored in the home?

11. Describe the first aid treatment for the following: (a) a major burn or scald; (b) a minor burn or scald; (c) a minor cut.

Chapter 29
Technology in the home

Technology is the practical use of science in our lives.

Because of technology, running a home today is very different from what it was 50 years ago. The amount of time and labour involved in doing household tasks has decreased greatly.

The invention of electricity, the small motor, the microchip and the mass production of goods have all contributed greatly towards changing and improving our quality of life and standard of living.

Technology and household tasks

Food preparation

Before modern food preparation equipment was available, much time and effort was given to preparing meals. Now, the job is much easier.

1 Refrigerators and freezers help keep food fresh for longer.

2 Kettles, blenders, juicers, coffee makers, food mixers and food processors help convert food quickly into meals.

3 Cordless and 'intelligent' electrical appliances improve safety and efficiency in the kitchen.

Cooking appliance

Cooking

- Modern cookers and microwave ovens enable us to cook food quickly and efficiently.
- Modern features such as induction hobs, multifunction ovens, fan-assisted ovens, dual-circuit rings, halogen hobs and timers have all made cooking easier and more energy efficient.
- Convenience foods save time and energy.

Link...
Cookers, page 325

Modern cooker

Home maintenance

- Easy-to-clean materials such as synthetics, plastic and stainless steel are used for many household goods and surfaces, e.g. saucepans, worktops, sinks, Corian and laminated work surfaces.
- Non-stick surfaces are used on saucepans and oven linings.
- Electric drills, saws, lawnmowers and paint and wallpaper strippers make home improvements easier.
- Built-in vacuum systems, remote-controlled vacuum cleaners, steam cleaners and multipurpose floor cleaners save time and energy.
- Household cleaning and laundry are made easier with the availability of easy-care products, e.g. stain resistant, crease resistant, drip-dry, etc.
- Cleaning agents are available for every purpose.
- 'Intelligent' washing machines, dryers and dishwashers use sensors to ensure that the correct programme is selected for the load.
- Sewing and knitting machines have become extremely versatile and sophisticated.

Electric lawnmower

Sewing machine

Link...
Guidelines for home hygiene, page 344

'Intelligent' washing machine

Flatscreen television

Games consoles

Home entertainment

- Televisions have become thinner and more sophisticated, with teletext, interactive features, and access to digital and satellite channels.
- Videos have been replaced by DVDs (digital versatile discs).
- MP3 players and iPods provide music and film.
- Games consoles provide hours of entertainment for all ages.
- Telephone, fax, mobile phones and e-mail allow people to stay in touch.
- Automatic systems and appliances, e.g. for household heating, lighting, security and auto-timer cooking, allow more free time for leisure.

Information and communication

- Most homes now have access to a computer.
- A PC, laptop or notebook may be used for word processing, doing household accounts, and operating security, heating and lighting systems.

Laptop

- The Internet can be used for gathering information, shopping, banking, booking holidays or concert tickets, accessing films or music, and e-mail.
- 'Wireless' technology has provided easier access to computers and all their functions.
- Mobile phones have become multi-purpose gadgets.
- GPS (global positioning system) is used widely by drivers to locate where they are and navigate to where they want to go.

GPS

Advantages of technology

1 Less time and energy spent on household tasks.
2 More time available to spend with family and friends.
3 Better standards of hygiene.
4 Greater access to the outside world through the telephone, Internet and e-mail.
5 More security in the home (alarm systems).
6 The home can be a self-sufficient entertainment centre.

Disadvantages of technology

1 The cost of buying, running and maintaining machines can be high.
2 Many machines are tricky to operate and difficult to assemble and clean.
3 Environmental problems may arise when disposing of old machines.
4 Some jobs can be done better or more efficiently by hand.
5 Many would argue that the skills of spelling and letter writing are being lost through overdependence on text messaging and e-mail. Do you agree?

Activities

1 List five pieces of food preparation equipment which you consider essential in the home. List five more which you consider to be luxuries. Give reasons for your answers.

2 Are there any jobs you would rather do by hand, even though there is a machine available? If so, list them and give reasons.

3 Find out the average cost of the following appliances: a microwave oven, dishwasher, washing machine, fridge, tumble dryer.

4 Conduct a survey among your classmates to find out (a) how many own games consoles and (b) the most popular brand of mobile phone.

Choosing household appliances

When choosing household appliances such as fridges, washing machines or TVs, consider the following.

- **Cost:** The initial cost, installation cost and running cost.
- **Energy efficiency:** Check the energy efficiency label on the appliance. An A or B rated appliance will cost less to run than a G or H rated appliance.
- **Reliability and quality:** Choose a reliable brand and look for quality symbols.

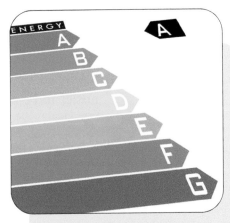

Energy efficiency label

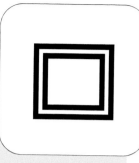

Double insulated symbol

CE symbol

Irish standards symbol

● **Safety:** Buy from a reliable dealer and look for safety symbols.
● **Needs:** The size of the family and the amount of use the appliance will get will decide the size and type of appliance selected.
● **Specifications:** The size of the appliance must suit the space and location for it in the home.
● **Design and ease of use:** It should be well designed and easy to use and clean.
● **Guarantee:** It is always wise to choose an appliance that comes with a guarantee, as this offers extra protection to the consumer.
● **After-sales service:** Check that servicing can be done locally.

Link...

Chapter 17 Quality Guarantees, page 233

There are three main types of household appliance.

1 Appliances with a motor (moving parts) – food mixer, food processor, electric carving knife, hand blender.

2 Appliances with a heating element (heat up) – kettle, contact grill, toaster, deep fat fryer.

3 Large appliances with both an element and a motor – washing machine, tumble dryer, cooker.

Cookers

Cookers may be fuelled by gas or electricity, or by a combination of both. Solid fuel and oil-fired ranges are also available.

All cookers consist of the following parts.

● **Hob.** Usually four **solid hotplates, coiled rings** or **ceramic plates** (heat-resistant surface). A gas hob has four **burners** of various sizes.
● **Grill.** Eye level or waist level. Some grills can also be used as a small oven.
● **Oven.** Heated by elements at the sides or back, or by a gas flame at the bottom. A **fan oven** heats quickly and cooks evenly.

Hob, grill and oven

Features of modern cookers

Hob

Electric

- Economy **dual rings** may be used for small saucepans.
- **Halogen rings** use halogen bulbs fitted under the ceramic hob. They heat up quickly and are very easy to control.
- **Induction hob** creates heat in the saucepan.
- **Split-level** cookers may be built into a kitchen. The hob is set into a worktop. The oven is separate and may be built into a unit at eye level or lower.

Gas

- Many gas cookers have a **surface combustion grill** (with small flames over the heating surface to give a larger grilling area).
- **Gas cookers** may have **push button ignition** or may be lit with a **pilot light**.

Grill

Electric and gas

- **Dual grill** allows one half of the grill to be used for small amounts of food.

Oven

Electric and gas

- **Glass-panelled external oven door**.
- May have a **removable drop-down door and oven roof** for easy cleaning.
- **Cool touch doors** for safety.
- **Stay-clean or self-cleaning oven linings**.

Electric

- **Multifunction ovens** may be adjusted to suit different cooking conditions, e.g. with or without fan assistance.
- Clock and **auto-timer**. Oven may be pre-set to switch itself on and off automatically.

Gas

- **Oven flame-failure device** (safety feature to stop gas flow if burner goes out).

Halogen rings

Split-level cooker

Auto-timer

A **thermostat** keeps the oven at the temperature set on the control dial. A light indicates whether the appliance is on or off. When preheating an oven, the light is always on to indicate that the oven has not yet reached the chosen temperature.

Methods of heat transfer in a cooker

- The hob heats saucepans by **conduction**.
- The liquid inside the saucepan heats by **convection**.
- The grill heats foods by **radiation**.
- The oven heats by **convection**.

Care and maintenance of cookers

1 Wipe up spills immediately.
2 Wipe out grill pan after use.
3 Never drag heavy saucepans across the hob (especially a ceramic hob), as they can scratch it.
4 Avoid using harsh abrasive cleaning agents on the surface, as they damage the enamel and chrome.
5 Use a special cleaner for ceramic hobs.
6 When cleaning the cooker:
   a) protect your hands, clothes and surroundings
   b) use a special caustic oven cleaner to dissolve burnt-on food in the oven
   c) wash out, rinse and dry the oven
   d) wash, dry and polish the remaining parts, not forgetting the spill tray under the hob.

Link...

Heating, page 338
Insulation, page 339

Choosing a cooker

1 The choice between a gas or electric cooker may depend on where you live and the availability of the fuel.
2 Gas cookers heat quickly and are easily controlled, but are not as clean as electric cookers.
3 Decide whether you want a freestanding cooker or a separate oven and hob.
4 If you opt for an electric cooker, decide on the type of hob you would prefer: ceramic, solid plate or coiled ring.

Positioning a cooker

- Position near a gas or electric connection.
- Ensure gas cookers are positioned away from draughts.
- Do not place cookers beside a refrigerator or at the end of a line of units.

Refrigerator

Fridge freezer

Larder refrigerator

Refrigerators

A refrigerator is a thermostatically controlled, insulated appliance.
It has a scratch-resistant worktop, interior light, magnetic door seal,
and moulded plastic-coated shelves.

A refrigerator keeps food cool by using a special liquid refrigerant,
which takes heat from the food and the air inside the refrigerator.
The temperature should be between 2°C and 5°C.

A refrigerator:

- keeps perishable foods fresh for a period of time
- reduces wastage of leftover foods
- limits shopping trips
- protects food from dust and flies
- helps reduce the risk of food poisoning
- stores frozen foods in the icebox and in fridge-freezers
- can freeze fresh food.

Features of modern refrigerators

Feature	Function
Integrated door panel	To match other kitchen fittings
Door which can be adjusted to open from the left or the right	To suit kitchen layout
Adjustable feet	To adjust height
Movable plastic-coated shelves	To fit large items
Cold drinks dispenser	For convenience
Split shelves	To store taller items
Wine rack	To chill wine bottles horizontally
Ice dispensers	For convenience
Zoned refrigeration	Different parts may have different temperatures
Automatic defrost	Prevents build-up of ice

How to use a refrigerator

- The refrigerator should be placed away from the cooker or other heat sources, as this will put extra pressure on the motor.
- Cover food before refrigerating to prevent it drying out.
- Wrap strong-smelling foods to avoid passing flavours to other foods.
- Never refrigerate apples, bananas or root vegetables.
- Never put hot food in the refrigerator, as this will raise the temperature.
- Do not pack the shelves with food, as this will prevent circulation of cold air.
- Do not open the door unnecessarily.
- Store food in the most suitable position. The part nearest the icebox is the coldest, while the door is the least cold.
- When not in use, unplug and leave the door open to allow air to circulate.

Care and maintenance of a refrigerator

1 Defrost regularly, as a build-up of ice in the icebox can affect the efficiency of the refrigerator.

2 The inside of the refrigerator should be cleaned with a solution of 1 tbsp bread soda to ½ litre warm water. Rinse and dry. Detergents may affect the flavour of the food.

3 Wash, dry and polish the outside.

Choosing and buying a refrigerator

1 Choose one large enough to suit the family.

2 Decide whether you want a refrigerator or fridge-freezer.

3 Ensure there is enough space for it.

4 Consider how it has to be defrosted.

5 Note the star rating on the frozen food compartment.

The **star rating** indicates how long frozen food can be stored in the icebox or fridge-freezer.

Link...

Food storage, page 45

Star rating	Temperature	Description
*	–6°C	Stores frozen food for one week
**	–12°C	Stores frozen food for one month
***	–18°C	Stores frozen food for three months
****	–18°C to –25°C	Freezes fresh food and stores frozen food (fridge-freezer) for up to one year

Disposing of an old refrigerator

Under the WEEE Directive (EU Directive on Waste Electrical and Electronic Equipment 2005) all old electrical appliances must be brought to special collection points where they will be recycled. The disposal charge is built into the cost of all new appliances. This charge varies depending on the size and type of appliance.

Microwave ovens

Microwave ovens cook food very differently from conventional ovens.

Microwaves are energy waves which are attracted to water and fat molecules in the food. **They enter the food and make the food molecules vibrate, causing friction. This friction produces heat in the food.** This heat is then conducted through the food and the food starts to cook.

Microwaves are **reflected** by metal, and **pass through** glass, plastic and paper. Therefore, they bounce off the metal walls of the oven, pass through the container, and enter the food.

Microwave oven

Uses of microwave ovens

- Cooking food quickly.
- Reheating foods.
- Defrosting frozen foods.
- Melting chocolate.
- Softening jam, jelly, butter, etc.

Cookware

- Glass, paper, plastic and china dishes are suitable for use in a microwave oven, as they allow microwaves to pass through.
- Metal containers, metal-trimmed dishes, aluminium foil or foil-lined covers should not be used in a microwave oven as they can produce sparks, which can damage the oven.

Suitable microwave cookware (left)

Advantages

- Quick and convenient.
- Healthy (little loss of nutrients).
- Saves washing up.
- Food keeps its colour (e.g. vegetables).

Disadvantages

- Unsuitable for large quantities of food.
- Does not brown foods.
- Does not tenderise tough cuts of meat.
- Foods may be overcooked or burned easily.

Using a microwave oven

1 Follow manufacturer's instructions.
2 The size, thickness and amount of food influence the cooking time.
3 Cover foods to prevent drying out or soiling the interior of the oven.
4 Pierce foods with a skin, such as potatoes, to prevent bursting.
5 Arrange food in a circle, to ensure even cooking.
6 Turn large food items and stir liquids during cooking.
7 Allow 'standing time' – leave the food to stand outside the oven for a few minutes before eating. The food continues to cook in this time.
8 Wipe up spills immediately.
9 Do not switch on when empty, as this can cause damage.

Buying a microwave oven

Consider all the points for choosing household appliances (see page 324), plus the following:

- some ovens have **turntables,** which ensure more even cooking
- the higher the **wattage,** the more powerful the oven and the faster it cooks (wattage ranges from 600W to 1,000W)
- ovens may have push-button and/or dial **controls.**

Push-button and dial controls

There are many special features available, such as:

- **automatic programming** facilities (user can programme in their own settings for a favourite food or recipe)
- **temperature probe** (to calculate cooking time)
- **auto-weight defrost** (automatically calculates power and time for defrosting)
- **a browning dish** (to brown foods that are normally grilled or fried)
- **a browning element** (like a grill)
- **a child lock.**

Summary

- **Technology** influences all aspects of the home – food preparation, cooking, maintenance, entertainment, computers.
- When choosing household appliances, consider **cost, energy efficiency, reliability, safety, needs, specifications, design, guarantee, service.**
- A **thermostat** keeps the appliance at the temperature set on the control dial. It works on the principle of the **bimetal strip.**
- Methods of **heat transfer** in a cooker include conduction and convection (hob), radiation (grill) and convection (oven).
- **Star ratings** indicate how long frozen food can be stored in the icebox or freezer.
- Follow guidelines on **using and choosing** specific household appliances.

Revision Questions

1 List four factors which should be considered when buying a new television.

2 Name a different electrical appliance under each of the following headings:

Appliance with a motor   **Appliance with a heating element**

3 (a) List four features of modern cookers and suggest one advantage of each feature.

   (b) Give three guidelines which should be followed when positioning a cooker in a kitchen.

4 List the methods of heat transfer. Name the methods of heat transfer that occur in (a) the grill and (b) the oven.

5 Which type of cooker (gas or electric) would you buy for your own home? Give two reasons for your choice.

6 Technology can influence many aspects of modern living. List four food preparation appliances used in the home.

7 Bearing in mind the need to protect the environment, write a note on refrigerators under each of the following headings: (a) choice; (b) use; (c) care and cleaning; (d) disposal.

8 Name and give the function of three modern refrigerator features.

9 Discuss the importance of temperature control in a refrigerator.

10 Using the letters A, B, C, D and E, indicate on the diagram where each of the following foodstuffs should be stored in the refrigerator: (a) milk; (b) butter; (c) lettuce; (d) raw meat; (e) yoghurt.

11 List four foods which are unsuitable for freezing.

12 A microwave oven is a popular resource in the modern kitchen.

   (a) Give three advantages of microwave cooking.

   (b) Suggest four different uses of the microwave oven in food preparation.

   (c) Name three materials suitable for microwave cookware/dishes.

   (d) List the rules that should be followed when (i) using and (ii) cleaning a microwave oven.

   (e) Explain what is meant by 'standing time' in microwave cooking.

   (f) Explain the purpose of a turntable in a microwave oven.

   (g) List four important points that should be considered when buying a microwave oven.

Chapter 30
Services to the home

The main services to the home are electricity, gas and water.

Electricity

Electricity is a form of energy rather than a fuel. You cannot see or smell it, but the effects of it can be felt as an electric shock. All electricity is generated, by water power, wind power, oil, gas, turf or coal. The main suppliers of electricity in Ireland are the Electricity Supply Board (ESB), Airtricity and Bord Gáis. In the home, electricity is used for space and water heating, lighting and to run all electrical appliances.

Advantages of electricity		Disadvantages of electricity
Clean	Relatively cheap	Affected by power cuts
Efficient	Safe	May be dangerous if used carelessly

Higher Level

Electricity is transmitted from power stations to homes through the **service cable**, which is attached to the supplier's **main fuse.**

The electricity is then passed through the **meter**, which measures the amount of electricity used in the house.

Sometimes there may be a second meter if off-peak **Nightsaver electricity** is being used. From the meter, wires pass into the **consumer unit or fuse box.** From there, wires carry electricity all around the house.

Service cable ···⟩ main fuse ···⟩ meter ···⟩ consumer unit

Electrical appliances need at least two wires – a **live wire** (**brown**) to carry electricity to the appliance, and a **neutral wire** (**blue**) to return it to the generator.

There may also be a third **earth wire** (**green and yellow**) as a safety device. Its function is to convey electric current to the earth if a fault occurs. Appliances without an earth wire are double insulated and carry this symbol:

Miniature circuit breaker

A **fuse** is a **safety device**. It is **a deliberate weak link in the electrical circuit.** It contains a wire that melts and breaks the circuit if there is an overloading of sockets, overheating of appliances or if a live and neutral wire touch (short circuit).

A **miniature circuit breaker** (**MCB**) fulfils the same function as a fuse. If the circuit is broken due to one of the above causes, the MCB switches off. When the problem is fixed, it can then be reset with a simple flick of the switch.

Wiring a plug

1 Unscrew central screw and remove plug top.
2 Remove fuse and loosen flex clamp screws.
3 Loosen screws of the three terminals – E (earth), L (live) and N (neutral).
4 Carefully push wire through the flex clamp. Fasten in place.
5 Carefully strip enough insulation from the inner sheaths to expose about 6mm of wire and insert wiring under the screw at the correct terminal.
6 Tighten screws.
7 Fit fuse. Replace cover.

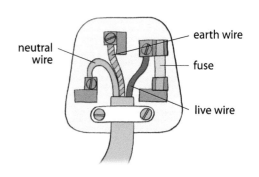

Using electricity safely

● Use good-quality plugs and appliances.
● Replace frayed flexes. Do not attempt to repair them.
● Do not overload sockets or adapters.
● Never take portable electrical appliances into the bathroom.
● Never let water come into contact with an electrical appliance.
● Lights and fixed heating appliances in the bathroom should be operated by pull-cord switches.

Gas

The two types of domestic gas available in Ireland are **natural gas** and **bottled gas.**

Higher Level

Natural gas is piped ashore from under the seabed off the coast. A smaller branch of the main gas **pipeline** enters the house, where the supply is controlled by a **meter control valve.** The **gas meter** records the amount used in **cubic metres.**

> **Pipeline** ···⟫ **meter control valve** ···⟫ **gas meter**

Bottled gas is available in areas that do not receive piped gas.

Advantages of gas	Disadvantages of gas
● Clean	● Flammable
● Efficient	● Produces carbon monoxide (which must be removed)
● Not affected by power cuts	● Requires good ventilation

Gas is used in the home in cookers, heaters and central heating boilers. It has many advantages.

However, there are some **safety precautions** that must be followed when using gas:

1 All gas appliances should be installed by a qualified person.

2 Gas cookers, boilers and heaters should be serviced regularly.

3 A good ventilation system is essential, as gas uses oxygen when it is burning. This produces fumes, which can be toxic if allowed to build up.

4 Never block wall vents.

5 Gas has a distinctive smell so that leaks can be recognised quickly.

6 Never look for gas leaks with a naked flame, as gas is flammable and explosive.

If you suspect a gas leak:

1 Open doors and windows.

2 Check gas appliances to see if the flame has gone out and if the gas is still on.

3 If no appliances have accidentally been left on, turn off the gas at the meter control valve.

4 Telephone the gas company emergency number.

5 Never ignore the smell.

6 Don't smoke or use any naked flames.

7 Don't touch light switches or thermostats, as they give off a tiny spark if turned on or off.

8 Don't use any electrical appliances.

Water

Water is one of the most important services to the home. It is used for washing, cooking, heating and sanitation. Fresh water is provided to homes by the local authority (city or county council) or by a private group water scheme. Before entering the mains into our homes, it must first be treated to ensure that it is free from impurities.

Water treatment

● Large objects such as stones and grit are removed by **filtering** the water through layers of gravel and sand.

● **Chlorine** is added to destroy harmful bacteria.

● **Fluoride** is added to prevent tooth decay.

Higher Level

The water leaves the **reservoir** through a **mains** pipe. A **service pipe** leads from the mains to each house. This supplies water directly to the cold tap in the kitchen sink.

A separate pipe fills the storage tank in the attic, and from there, cold water flows to toilets, baths, other sinks in the house, the boiler and hot water cylinder.

Reservoir ┄┄▸ mains pipe ┄┄▸ service pipe ┄┄▸ storage tank in attic ┄┄▸ toilets, baths, etc.
┄┄▸ kitchen sink

Water heating

Water may be heated using one or more of the following methods:

- central heating system
- instantaneous water heater or electric shower
- solar panels
- immersion heater (fitted into hot water cylinder)
- back boiler (behind open fire).

Solar panels

The kitchen sink

The kitchen sink is usually situated near a window, for:

- good light
- ventilation
- ease of plumbing.

Beneath the sink is an **S-trap** or a **U-bend**. This **holds water and prevents unpleasant odours and germs entering the kitchen from the drain.**

Sometimes a sink becomes **blocked** and water is slow to drain away. If this happens, take the following steps:

1 Remove any pieces of food that may be blocking the sink outlet.

2 Block the overflow with a cloth and use a plunger vigorously over the outlet.

3 If this fails, put some washing soda crystals down the drain, followed by boiling water.

4 If this still doesn't work, place a basin under the U-bend and unscrew the nut. Use a piece of wire to loosen the blockage, flush with hot water and replace the nut.

Burst pipes

In the winter, water pipes may freeze and eventually burst, as water expands when it freezes. If this happens:

1 Turn off water at the mains.

2 Run all cold taps to drain the system.

3 Turn off the central heating system and avoid lighting a fire if there is a back boiler installed.

4 Call a plumber.

5 If pipes have frozen, wrap in hot rags or thaw using a low setting on a hairdryer. Work backwards from the part of the pipe nearest the tap.

Heating

Heat is transferred from a heat source in three ways:

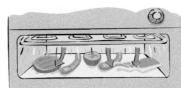

1. **Conduction:** Heat is transferred along a solid object, e.g. a poker in the fire.
2. **Convection:** Air (or liquid) is heated and rises from the heat source, and cool air (or liquid) replaces it. This sets up convection currents, e.g. convector heaters, fan heaters.
3. **Radiation:** Heat rays travel in straight lines and heat the first object they hit, e.g. radiant heaters and grill.

A home can be heated by:

1. **Central heating:** Water is heated by a boiler and passes around the house through radiators, which heat the rooms in the house. Central heating boilers may be powered by solid fuel, oil or gas. This system may be **fully automatic** and has the advantage of **heating water** as well. 'Dry' central heating is another option. This system uses under-floor heating and warm-air heating.

2. **Background heating:** Storage heaters, which use off-peak (cheaper) electricity, may be used to give off low levels of background heat.

3. **Individual heaters:** Heaters may be fixed (on a wall) or portable. Examples include electric fan heaters, radiant and convector heaters and gas 'Super Ser' heaters, open fires and stoves.

Open fire

Home heating systems can be controlled by timers and thermostats.

- **Timers** can be set to turn the heating on or off at different times.
- **Thermostats** can be set to control the temperature on the central heating boiler, at radiators or in individual rooms. Once the required temperature is reached, the thermostat switches off the heating system.

Timer

Room thermostat

Fuels for home heating

Fuel	Advantages	Disadvantages
• Gas	• Clean • Efficient • Not affected by power cuts • Can also be used for cooking	• Dangerous if not handled properly • Natural gas not widely available • Storage space needed for gas cylinders and tanks
• Oil	• Convenient • Easy to use • Automatic • Energy efficient	• Storage tank required • May be expensive
• Solid fuel, e.g. coal, turf, wood	• Creates cosy atmosphere • Reasonably cheap, or may be freely available • Helps ventilation in an open fire or stove	• Dirty • Constant cleaning required • Storage space required

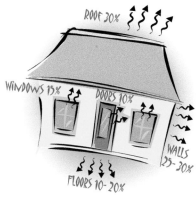

ROOF 30%
WINDOWS 15%
DOORS 10%
WALLS 25-30%
FLOORS 10-20%

Insulation

A house can lose 75 per cent of its heat if there is no insulation.

Insulation means **trapping heat in the house by using insulating materials.** Good insulating materials are poor conductors of heat.

Forms of insulation

- **Polystyrene** sheets are used in cavity walls.
- **Fabrics** are used on floors (carpets and underlay).
- **Fibreglass, foam pellets and sheep's wool** are used in attics.
- **Still air** is used in cavity walls and double-glazed windows.
- **Lagging jackets and factory-insulated sprayed-on coatings** are used on hot water cylinders.
- **Heavy fabric curtains** and **draught excluders** are used on windows and doors.

Polystyrene sheets

Fibreglass

Lagging jacket

Ventilation

A good ventilation system removes stale air and allows in fresh air without creating a draught.

Ventilation is necessary to:

- remove stale air
- provide fresh air
- control humidity levels
- control air temperature
- prevent condensation.

Methods of ventilation

- Doors.
- Windows.
- Room vents.
- Fireplace.
- Extractor fans (in kitchens and bathrooms).
- Cooker hoods (in kitchens).

Cooker hood

Condensation occurs when warm air comes into contact with a cool surface.

This may cause dampness, rusting of metals, decay of wood and growth of mould.

Condensation can be controlled by:

- good ventilation
- insulation
- an efficient heating system
- efficient removal of moisture (steam) by the use of vents, windows or extractor fans
- venting of tumble dryers to outside the house.

Condensation

Lighting

Good lighting is essential in the home to:

- prevent eye strain
- prevent accidents
- create atmosphere in a room
- provide sufficient light for activities.

Natural light is provided by sunlight entering a house through windows, doors and skylights.

Artificial light can be provided by tungsten filament lamps, tungsten halogen lamps, fluorescent tubes, light-emitting diodes (LEDs) and compact fluorescent lights (CFLs).

Tungsten filament lamp

1 **Tungsten filament lamps (incandescent)** last for approximately 1,000 hours and are available in clear, pearl, white or coloured glass. Strength is measured in watts, e.g. 40W is less bright than 60W. These have become less popular as they are not very energy efficient. They are being phased out by the European Union.

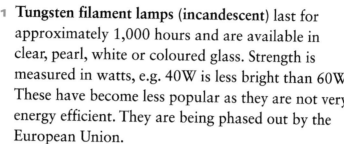

Fluorescent tubes

2 **Fluorescent tubes** give off more light than filament lamps. They last for approximately 3,000 hours and are available in lengths from 30cm to 2.5m.

3 **Compact fluorescent lights** (CFLs) give the same light as an ordinary filament lamp, yet use only 20 per cent of the electricity. They last for 8,000 hours. Because their running costs are low, they work out cheaper in the long run.

Compact fluorescent light

4 **Tungsten halogen lamps** contain a tungsten filament and halogen gas, which improves their efficiency. They produce a crisp white light and are ideal for spotlighting, display and decorative lighting. They last from 2,000 to 6,000 hours, depending on type.

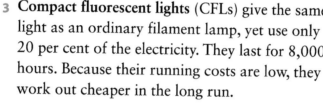

Tungsten halogen lamp

5 **Light-emitting diodes (LEDs)** are small energy-saving bulbs which can be used in place of any other lamps. They are available in different colours and produce a light that is very close to natural daylight, which is thought to be easier on the eyes. They last about 100,000 hours.

Light-emitting diodes (LED)

Building Energy Rating

This is similar to the energy labels found on electrical appliances such as fridges. The rating has a scale of A to G. A-rated homes are the most efficient, and G-rated the least efficient. Building Energy Ratings are carried out by specially trained BER assessors. The BER is calculated using details of house construction, insulation, ventilation, heat systems, lighting, pumps and fans. All houses for sale or rent require a BER certificate.

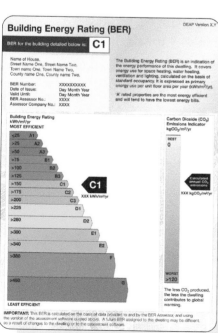

Building Energy Rating

Weblink

www.sei.ie/ber

Energy efficiency tips

- Turn down the thermostat on central heating boilers.
- Take showers instead of baths.
- Unplug or switch off TVs and stereos – leaving them on in stand-by mode uses electricity.
- Choose energy-saving appliances. Look for the energy label.
- Avoid washing under a running tap.
- Switch off radiators in rooms that are not being used.
- Use a jug kettle to boil water, as it is more economical.
- Use dishwashers and washing machines with a full load only, or use economy/half-load options.
- Ensure that all chimneys and heating appliances are checked and cleaned regularly so that they work more efficiently.
- Use energy-saving light bulbs such as CFLs.
- Install a timer on the immersion heater.
- Switch off lights when not needed.
- Use low-temperature programmes on washing machines and dishwashers.
- Whenever possible, dry clothes outdoors.
- Use a lagging jacket on the hot water cylinder.
- Draught-proof your home.

Summary

- **Electricity: Service cable ⋯▷ main fuse ⋯▷ meter ⋯▷ consumer unit.**
- Electrical appliances may have three wires – **live (brown), neutral (blue) and earth (green/yellow).**
- **A fuse is a deliberate weak link in a circuit.**
- **Gas: Pipeline ⋯▷ meter control valve ⋯▷ gas meter.**
- Review **advantages and disadvantages of gas.**
- **Water: Reservoir ⋯▷ mains pipe ⋯▷ service pipe ⋯▷ storage tank ⋯▷ toilets, baths, etc.** ⋯▷ **kitchen sink**
- Water treatment involves **filtering and the addition of chlorine and fluoride.**
- The **S-trap** or **U-bend** in a sink holds water and prevents odours and germs entering the kitchen.
- Methods of heat transfer are **conduction, convection** and **radiation.**
- Learn the difference between **timers** and **thermostats.**
- Review **advantages** and **disadvantages** of fuels for home heating.
- **Insulation** means trapping heat by the use of insulating materials.
- **Ventilation** removes stale air and introduces fresh air without causing a draught.
- **Condensation** occurs when warm air comes into contact with a cool surface.
- Lighting may be **natural** or **artificial.**
- **Building Energy Rating** rates the energy efficiency of the home.

Revision Questions

1 Outline two safety precautions which should be taken when using electricity in the home.

2 Name any two wires in an electrical plug and state the colour(s) of each wire named.

3 What device records the amount of gas/electricity used in the home?

4 What is the purpose of a fuse in an electrical circuit?

5 What actions should be taken in the event of a gas leak in the home?

6 A supply of pure, fresh water is one of the most important services to the home.

   (a) List three uses of water in the home.

   (b) State four ways of conserving water in the home.

   (c) Give two other examples of services to the home.

   (d) Give one cause of water pollution.

7 Why are chlorine and fluoride added to the domestic water supply?

8 Give two reasons why kitchen sinks are usually placed under a window.

9 Heating and insulation are two important factors to consider in a modern home.

   (a) Name two methods of heat transfer used in home heating and give one example of each.

   (b) Name three fuels used for home heating.

   (c) Give two advantages and two disadvantages of one of the fuels named.

   (d) Outline the benefits of using a central heating system in the home.

   (e) List four ways of saving energy when using a central heating system.

10 What is the function of a thermostat? Briefly outline how a thermostat works.

11 Explain what is meant by insulation.

12 Give two reasons why houses should be insulated.

13 Suggest three areas in the home where good insulation is important.

14 Suggest one suitable method of insulating the following areas in the home:
   (a) attic; (b) windows; (c) doors; (d) hot water cylinder; (e) walls.

15 Suggest two reasons why good ventilation is necessary in a kitchen.

16 List two ways of ventilating a bathroom.

17 (a) Give two reasons why good lighting is important in the home.

   (b) What is meant by compact fluorescent lights (CFLs)?

   (c) Why are CFL bulbs used in the home?

   (d) Give two advantages of good lighting in the home.

18 Making your home more energy efficient saves money and helps to protect the environment. Identify two ways of saving energy in the following areas:
   (a) lighting; (b) water heating; (c) the use of appliances.

Chapter 31
Home hygiene

Hygiene relates to cleanliness and the protection of health.

A hygienic home plays a part in good health and well-being. As well as ensuring that the home is a clean and pleasant place to be, there is less risk that anyone in the home will catch or spread disease.

Bacteria need **food, moisture, warmth, air** and **time** to grow and multiply.

Where bacteria are allowed to grow, e.g. in damp and dirty conditions, the risk of disease is high. High standards of hygiene will ensure that these conditions are not available.

The **kitchen** and the **bathroom** are two areas of the home where high standards of hygiene are essential. Low standards may lead to food poisoning or the spread of diseases, e.g. skin infections.

Guidelines for home hygiene

1 Remove unnecessary clutter from surfaces.

2 Ensure that the house is well ventilated.

3 Wipe up spills immediately.

4 Keep the house warm and dry to prevent dampness.

5 Ensure that the house is well lit so that areas that need cleaning can be seen.

6 Keep the drains clean and free from blockages.

Kitchens

- Surfaces should be smooth and easy to clean.
- Change the dishcloth and tea towels every day.
- Keep sink and draining board clean and tidy.
- Use a bin with a lid. Wash and disinfect weekly.
- Wipe down surfaces before and after preparing food.
- Sweep and wash kitchen floors regularly.
- Banish pets!

A clean kitchen

Bathrooms

- Keep a set of cloths and rubber gloves especially for cleaning the bathroom.
- Change hand towels, sponges and face cloths daily.
- Keep toilet bowl, seat and flush handle spotlessly clean. Disinfect regularly.
- Avoid toilet seat covers and mats, as these hide germs.

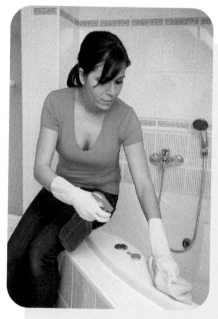

A clean bathroom

Equipment

The following are useful in the 'fight against grime':

- rubber or latex gloves
- dusters and rags
- dishcloths
- sweeping brush
- mop and bucket
- vacuum cleaner
- old toothbrush (for difficult-to-reach spots).

Cleaning agents and equipment

Keep cleaning equipment and cleaning agents together in one cupboard, away from food and cooking utensils. Polishes and bleaches should be kept out of reach of young children, as many household chemicals are poisonous if swallowed.

Cleaning agents

The following cleaning agents are commonly used.

Cleaning agent	Uses
Bicarbonate of soda	Used as an abrasive, it is used to clean fridges, toilets and hard floors. Used dry, it will absorb unpleasant odours from kitchen bins and from the fridge.
Borax	Can be used as an alternative to bleach. Removes odours, stops mould growth, disinfects, and freshens laundry.
White vinegar	Removes limescale. Good for cleaning windows, mirrors and removing rust from stainless steel sinks.
Essential oils such as eucalyptus, tea tree and lavender	Good for cutting through grease, as well as being anti-fungal, anti-bacterial and anti-viral.
Lemon juice	Can be used to remove stains such as blood, grass and mildew. It will bleach wooden chopping boards, and clean copper and brass when combined with salt.
Soda water	Removes red wine and coffee stains.
Cola and denture-cleaning tablets	When left (separately) overnight in the toilet bowl, they will remove stains.

Water is an all-purpose solvent. Cold water will soften dirt and stains.
Hot water will melt grease.

There are also many commercial cleaning agents available.

Commercial cleaning agent	Uses
Abrasives, e.g. Brillo	Stubborn stains on scratch-resistant surfaces
Bleaches, e.g. Parazone	Stain removal
Cream cleaners, e.g. Cif	Sinks, cookers, smooth surfaces
Detergents, e.g. washing-up liquid, etc.	Washing dishes, clothes, etc.
Disinfectants, e.g. Dettol	Killing germs in sinks, bins, floors
Multi-purpose cleaners, e.g. Dettox	Cleaning work surfaces and floors
Oven cleaners, e.g. Mr Muscle	Stubborn stains on oven surfaces and glass doors
Polishes	Metals, furniture, windows, floors

When **choosing** and **buying** cleaning agents, examine products carefully and consider the following.

- The cost of the product and the quantity in the container.
- Can it be used for different cleaning jobs?
- Can it harm or scratch surfaces?
- Are there any health risks in using the product?
- Does it have clear instructions for use?
- Is it environmentally friendly?

Link...

Hazard symbols, page 316

Activities

1 Name some smooth, easy-to-clean surfaces which would be suitable for kitchens and bathrooms.

2 (a) Find out the cost of the cleaning agents mentioned on page 346. (b) Design a test to compare the efficiency of one commercial cleaning agent with an alternative, e.g. window cleaner versus white vinegar.

When **using** cleaning agents:

- Protect yourself and your surroundings.
- Use in a well-ventilated area.
- Follow instructions carefully.
- Always rinse away all traces of cleaning agent.
- Store away from foods and out of reach of children.

Summary

- **Home hygiene** is essential for good health and to prevent disease and infections.
- Kitchens and bathrooms are two areas of the home where **hygiene is a priority**.
- There are many **cleaning agents** on the market. Some are job-specific; others are multipurpose. **Choose wisely and use carefully.**

Revision Questions

1 List three conditions which promote the growth of bacteria in the kitchen.

2 List four general guidelines which should be followed in order to ensure a high standard of hygiene in the kitchen.

3 A clean, hygienic home contributes to healthy living.

(a) Give four guidelines necessary to ensure a high standard of hygiene in the home.

(b) List four factors which should be considered when selecting and using household cleaning agents.

(c) Give four rules to be followed when storing cleaning agents in the home.

(d) Sketch one hazard symbol to convey that a product is either: (i) highly flammable **or** (ii) toxic **or** (iii) harmful and an irritant.

Chapter 32
The environment

> 'The earth does not belong to man – man belongs to the earth.'
>
> *Chief Seattle, 1854*

The earth provides many resources, such as oil, coal, gas, water, metals and trees. Each year, huge amounts of these resources are taken from the earth to be changed into fuel, energy and consumer goods. In using the earth's resources, all consumers contribute to pollution of the environment.

Remember: one of our responsibilities as consumers is to use environmental resources carefully.

Link...

See Consumers' responsibilities, page 231

Pollution

Water pollution

Air pollution

Noise pollution

Litter

Type	Causes	Effects	What you can do
Water	Human sewage, animal slurry, oil spills	Dead fish, bad smells, illness	Choose phosphate-free detergents; Use safe garden chemicals; Use the correct quantity of fertiliser needed
Air	Sulphur dioxide, carbon monoxide and smoke from coal and oil, carbon dioxide from breathing	Respiratory diseases, eye irritation, acid rain, climate change	Use natural gas and smokeless coal; Choose energy-efficient appliances; Use pump-action sprays instead of aerosols
Noise	Factories, transport (planes, trains, cars), loud music	Depression, anxiety, irritation, insomnia	Choose products with lower noise emissions, e.g. dishwashers, lawnmowers, motorbikes
Litter	Careless disposal of waste (plastics, chewing gum, old appliances, cigarette butts)	Damage to towns, cities and countryside, negative effect on tourism	Dispose of waste carefully; Recycle; Avoid unnecessary packaging; Don't litter and don't tolerate those who do

Acid rain is formed when air pollutants such as sulphur dioxide, carbon dioxide and carbon monoxide mix with moisture in the atmosphere. The resulting acid rain damages fish, trees, limestone and metals in buildings.

Greenhouse gases are released into the atmosphere when we burn oil, petrol and gas. These gases add to the layer of insulation around the earth and this results in a rise in the earth's temperature (known as the 'greenhouse effect' or 'global warming').This contributes to climate change. In Ireland, **climate change** will bring more unpredictable and unstable weather conditions. It will affect the crops we can grow and cause a rise in sea levels.

Waste

Each year we throw away millions of tonnes of waste. Much of our household waste is disposed of by local authorities or private companies.

Waste may be:
- **organic** (can be broken down), e.g. food waste, paper, sewage; or
- **inorganic** (cannot be broken down easily), e.g. plastic, metal and glass.

Biodegradable waste can be broken down and made harmless by bacteria or other natural means. All organic waste is biodegradable.

Landfill (burying waste) and incinerator (burning waste) options for disposing of waste can be hazardous to humans and to the environment. Therefore, we need to find ways of dealing with waste in an **environmentally friendly** way.

The **hierarchy of waste management** refers to the 3Rs – **reduce, reuse** and **recycle**. It classifies methods of waste disposal according to their appeal, in order of importance. The aim of the hierarchy is to get the maximum practical benefits from products and to produce the minimum amount of waste.

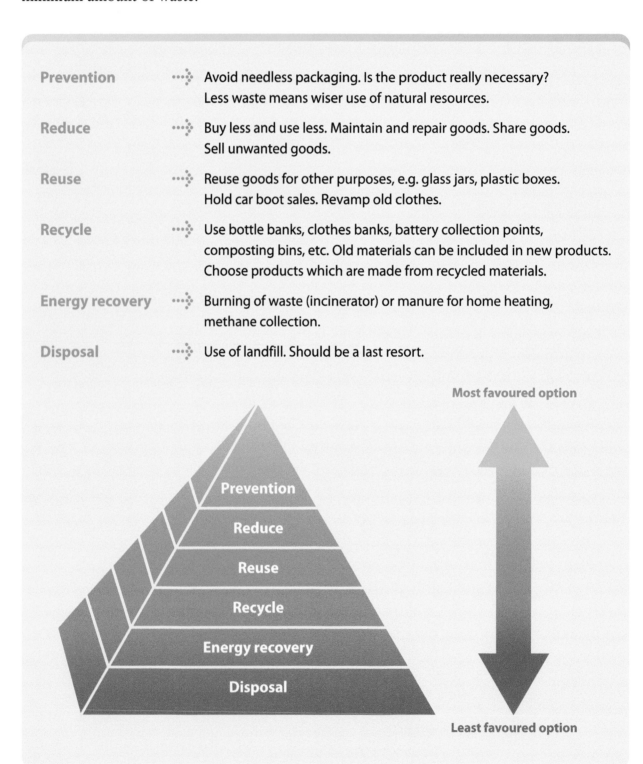

Prevention	Avoid needless packaging. Is the product really necessary? Less waste means wiser use of natural resources.
Reduce	Buy less and use less. Maintain and repair goods. Share goods. Sell unwanted goods.
Reuse	Reuse goods for other purposes, e.g. glass jars, plastic boxes. Hold car boot sales. Revamp old clothes.
Recycle	Use bottle banks, clothes banks, battery collection points, composting bins, etc. Old materials can be included in new products. Choose products which are made from recycled materials.
Energy recovery	Burning of waste (incinerator) or manure for home heating, methane collection.
Disposal	Use of landfill. Should be a last resort.

Most favoured option

Prevention
Reduce
Reuse
Recycle
Energy recovery
Disposal

Least favoured option

Recycling

What can be recycled?

- **Metals:** Old metal appliances and aluminium cans
- **Glass:** Bottle banks are available for all types of glass
- **Paper:** Magazines, newspapers, cardboard, office waste
- **Oil:** Used engine and lubricating oils
- **Plastics:** Farmyard plastics, e.g. silage coverings
- **Clothes and rags:** Collected by charity organisations and used in upholstery stuffing
- **Batteries and mobile phones**

Recycle symbol

Benefits

It saves on:
- waste disposal costs
- the need for landfill sites
- raw materials
- import bills
- energy
- trees

It also:
- reduces litter
- creates jobs

Composting

What can be composted?

- Grass clippings
- Eggshells
- Fruit and vegetable waste
- Dead leaves
- Coffee grounds
- Tea bags
- Uncooked food scraps (but not meat/fish)
- General garden waste

Food waste

Benefits

- Saves landfill space
- Reduces greenhouse gas emissions from landfills
- Cuts down on burning waste in the garden
- Enriches the soil
- Saves money

Environmentally friendly shopping guidelines

1 Bring a reusable shopping bag.

2 Do not buy overpackaged goods.

3 Buy products which use recycled material in their packaging.

4 Buy concentrated products (e.g. detergents, fabric conditioners) – they use less packaging.

5 Choose products which come in refillable containers, e.g. cosmetics.

6 Buy loose goods when possible.

7 Buy in bulk where possible.

8 Buy products which are CFC-free.

9 Look for the EU Ecolabel on products.

10 Choose energy-saving appliances.

11 Walk to the shop!

The EU Ecolabel indicates that products and services are environmentally friendly. This voluntary scheme covers 26 types of product and service, including cleaning products, electronic equipment, paper products, textiles, home and garden products, and services such as tourist accommodation.

Ecolabel

The ozone layer

Higher
Level

The ozone (O_3) layer is located high in the atmosphere. Its function is to absorb the sun's harmful ultraviolet (UV) rays and prevent serious damage to life on earth. These rays can have serious effects, such as:

● skin cancers
● cataracts and eye disorders
● reduction in the harvest of certain plants
● damage to marine life and building materials.

Ozone is destroyed by:

● CFCs, which are found in old refrigerators, air-conditioning systems, aerosols and foam packaging
● halons, which are found in fire extinguishers.

Higher Level

In the 1970s scientists discovered a hole in the ozone layer which may have been caused by CFCs and halons. Today, there is a ban on CFCs in most countries.

Play your part in saving the ozone layer:
- Choose only ozone-friendly aerosol sprays.
- Use non-aerosol products such as pump-action sprays or roll-on deodorants.
- Choose products, e.g. meat, eggs, fast foods, which are packaged in cardboard or other CFC-free containers.
- When replacing old refrigerators or air conditioners, look into arrangements for recycling CFCs in the old equipment.

> Greenpeace, ENFO, the Environmental Protection Agency, Green Schools, An Taisce and the Green Party are all organisations concerned with environmental issues.

Activities

1 Find out what the following symbol means:

2 Make a list of the ways in which your local environment is being polluted. Suggest possible solutions.

3 What use can you suggest for recycling: (a) old clothes; (b) old mobile phones; (c) tin cans? What other waste can your family recycle? What method/s would you suggest?

Summary

- The environment can be **polluted** in many ways, e.g. air, water and noise pollution, litter.
- **Biodegradable waste can be broken down and made harmless by nature**.
- All **organic** waste is biodegradable.
- **Inorganic** waste cannot be broken down easily.
- The **hierarchy of waste management** suggests environmentally friendly ways of disposing of waste.
- Many household waste items can be **recycled**.
- Home **composting** has many advantages.
- How we **shop** can play a part in **protecting the environment**.
- The function of the **ozone layer** is to absorb harmful UV rays and prevent damage to life on earth.

Revision Questions

1 Give two causes and two effects of (a) air pollution and (b) water pollution.

2 Suggest four ways in which consumers can reduce the pollution of the environment.

3 Explain (a) organic waste and (b) inorganic waste. Give two examples of each.

4 Explain the term 'biodegradable waste'. Give one example of biodegradable waste.

5 Give two benefits of recycling household waste.

6 Suggest an environmentally friendly method of disposing of each of the following:
(a) vegetable peelings; (b) clothes; (c) coloured glass; (d) paper; (e) plastic ice-cream cartons.

7 What is the function of the ozone layer?

8 Suggest two ways in which the ozone layer can be protected.

Section five
Textile studies

Chapter 33
Textiles in use

Household textiles

Textiles are all around us in the home. Towels, tablecloths, bed linen and carpets are all examples of textiles in use.

Activity

Look at the illustration of the room and list the uses of textiles.

Uses of textiles in the home

- **Soft furnishings:** These are items other than furniture which are used to decorate a room. They reflect our personality and lifestyle. Examples include curtains, blinds, rugs, cushions, chair covers, lampshades and table centres.
- **Carpets:** Various types of carpet are available. Some are very hardwearing; others are not as durable.
- **Upholstery:** Upholstery means the covering fabric and fillings used in furniture such as sofas, armchairs and mattresses.
- **Bed linen:** Sheets, pillowcases, duvets and duvet covers, blankets, bedspreads and throws.
- **Table linen** and **towels:** Tablecloths, place mats, table runners (narrow tablecloths which run the length of the table), napkins, tea towels and bathroom towels.

Higher Level

Properties of textiles

A property is a characteristic or quality. For example, **hardwearing** textiles are used in carpets and **absorbent** textiles are used in towels; **warm** textiles are used in blankets and **fire-resistant** textiles are used on sofas.

The most **desirable properties** are the ones that are the most important for a particular use. For example, it is essential that towels are **absorbent**. By law, certain household items such as upholstered furniture must be fire resistant.

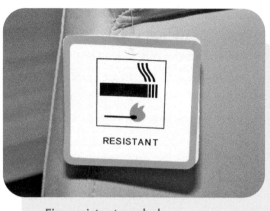

Fire-resistant symbol

Activity

Write the following list of household items in your copy. Suggest a property that you think the fabric should have to perform successfully in each case:

- bed sheets
- towels
- cushion covers
- curtains.

Use these examples of properties to help you:

- flame resistant
- absorbent
- stain resistant
- hardwearing
- waterproof
- stretchy.

- resilient
- crease resistant
- insulating
- shrink resistant
- stain repellent

Soft furnishings

Functions of soft furnishings

Soft furnishings:

- make a room look attractive
- make a house more comfortable
- allow us to express our taste and style.

Choosing soft furnishings

- Consider the **function** of the item. For example, blinds may be used to give privacy but let light through at the same time, and cushions should be comfortable. No matter how attractive an item is, it is useless if it does not serve its purpose.
- Soft furnishings should look **attractive**. Consider the colour, pattern and texture (feel) of the item. Colour can make a room warm or cool. Pattern can make a room more interesting. Texture can make a room feel cosy.
- Soft furnishings should be **easy to clean**. Some decorative features, such as appliqué or decorative fringes, can be difficult to clean. They may have to be washed, dry cleaned or vacuumed.
- Soft furnishings should be **durable**. Choose fabrics that are hardwearing and will therefore last a long time.
- Consider the **cost** of the item. A more expensive hardwearing item might be better value for money than a cheaper lightweight item which might not last.

Soft furnishings

Link...

Chapter 26 Design

Curtains

Curtains have been used for hundreds of years. Styles have changed and have become less fussy in recent years. When choosing curtains, consider the type of window and the style of the room. Curtains can be full length or short. The fabric width should be 2–2.5 times the width of the window to allow for gathering.

Higher Level

Functions of curtains

- Curtains keep out light, especially if they are lined.
- They keep out sound.
- Curtains keep in heat. This is called insulation. Heavy lined curtains provide a lot of insulation.
- They reduce draughts, especially if they are lined.
- They give privacy.
- Curtains make a room look attractive. They can provide colour, pattern and texture.

Desirable properties in curtain fabric

Curtains should:

- hang/drape well
- be resistant to fading
- be closely woven (so that they will keep out light)
- be washable or dry cleanable
- be pre-shrunk (so that they will not shrink when washed)
- be fire resistant.

Textiles used in curtains

Curtains can be made of cotton, Dralon, polyester, linen or wool.

Carpets

Many carpets are handmade today, but some are manufactured by machines. Manufactured carpets are made by weaving or fixing tufts of yarn into a backing. The **pile** (surface fibres or hairs) may be short, long, twisted or have raised designs (embossed).

Higher Level

Grades of carpet

Carpets are graded according to how hardwearing they are.

- **Light domestic:** Used in bedrooms.
- **General domestic:** Used in living rooms.
- **Heavy domestic:** Used in halls, stairs and living rooms.

Desirable properties in carpets

Carpets should be:

- hardwearing
- fire resistant
- resilient
- mothproof
- warm.

Textiles used in carpets

- **Wool** is used because it is **warm** and **resilient**.
- **Nylon** and **acrylic** are used because they are **hardwearing**.
- Warm, hardwearing carpets are made by **mixing** 80 per cent wool and 20 per cent nylon.

Upholstery

Desirable properties in upholstery fabric

- Fabric should be hardwearing.
- It should be easy to clean.
- It should be stain resistant.
- Outer fabric should be closely woven.
- It should comply with fire safety regulations. In the past, fillings used in upholstery produced toxic fumes when burned. New upholstery must contain combustion-modified high-resilience foam (CMHR).

Textiles used in upholstery

Upholstery fabrics include:

- heavy cotton
- linen
- wool
- velvet
- leather
- Dralon.

Bed linen

Desirable properties in bed linen

Sheets and **pillowcases** should be:

- absorbent
- washable
- smooth
- crease resistant.

Duvets and **blankets** should be:

- easy to clean
- lightweight
- warm.

The warmth of a duvet is measured by tog rating. The least warm is a tog value of 4.5 and the warmest is a tog value of 15.

Soft furnishings

Higher Level

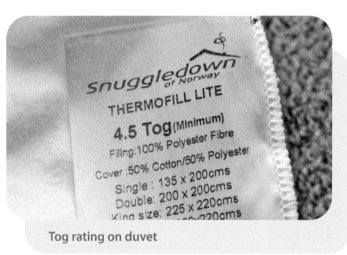

Tog rating on duvet

Textiles used in bed linen

Sheets, pillowcases and duvet covers

Cotton is used because it is absorbent, comfortable and washable.

Blends of cotton and polyester are comfortable, crease resistant and easily washed and dried. Flannelette (brushed cotton) is soft and warm and is popular for children's bed linen.

Duvet fillings

Fillings are made from down feathers or polyester wadding.

Blankets

Wool is used because it is warm. Wool and nylon blends are warm and hardwearing. Acrylic is cheaper than wool and easier to wash, but not as warm.

Summary

- Textiles are used in soft furnishings, carpets, upholstery, bed linen, table linen and towels.
- A **property** is a characteristic or quality of a textile.
- **Soft furnishings:** Comfortable, attractive, allow us to express our taste.
- **Choosing soft furnishings:** Consider function, attractiveness, ease of cleaning, durability and cost.
- **Curtains** provide shade, privacy, decoration, comfort and insulation and reduce noise and draughts.
- **Desirable properties** in **soft furnishings** are durability, ease of cleaning, fade resistance and fire resistance.
- Desirable properties in **carpets** are warmth, resilience and durability.
- Warm, hardwearing carpets are made from 80 per cent wool and 20 per cent nylon.
- New upholstery must contain **combustion-modified high-resilience foam**.
- **Cotton** is a very useful household fabric because it is hardwearing, absorbent and washable.

Revision Questions

1 Suggest four uses of household textiles.

2 Outline the properties that should be considered when choosing fabric for household textiles.

3 List two soft furnishings, other than curtains, suitable for a living room.

4 List two reasons why soft furnishings are used in the home.

5 Discuss the factors to be considered when choosing soft furnishings for the home.

6 Explain 'texture' in relation to fabric.

7 Explain the term 'upholstery'.

8 List four functions of curtains.

9 List two desirable properties of carpet.

10 List two desirable properties of cotton as a household textile.

11 List two desirable properties of textiles suitable for upholstery.

Chapter 34
Clothes

We wear clothes for many reasons. They keep us warm, but they also allow people to express their personalities.

Functions of clothes

- **Express personality:** We can express ourselves by the clothes we choose to wear. Some people are casual and others are more formal.
- **Protection from weather:** Clothes keep us warm in cold weather and protect us from the sun in very hot weather. Windproof and waterproof garments protect us from wind and rain.
- **Modesty:** We are expected to wear clothes to cover our bodies. On the beach we are expected to wear at least swimwear.
- **Identification:** Uniforms are used to identify people. Uniforms are used in schools, at work and in sports.
- **To flatter:** Clothes can make the body look good. Certain styles of clothes suit different body shapes and sizes.
- **Safety:** Clothing provides safety for various activities. Protective gear is worn by workers such as fire fighters, chefs, soldiers and builders. Clothes provide protection for sports.

Protection from weather

Modesty

Identification

To flatter

Safety

Guidelines for buying clothes

- **Function:** Consider the function (purpose) of the garment. When and where do you intend to wear it? What properties are needed in the fabric? Do you need it to be stretchy, windproof, waterproof, warm, etc.?
- **Care:** Choose clothes that are easily washed. Dry cleaning can be expensive. Special care is needed when washing and drying fabrics such as wool. Check the care label.
- **Fit:** Consider the fit of the garment. Measurements are written on clothes labels to help us choose well-fitting garments. Jeans, for example, have various leg and waist measurements to suit different figures.
- **Cost:** Decide whether the clothes are good value for money. Some clothes are expensive because they have designer labels. It is possible to buy cheaper clothes that look just as good.
- **Style:** Consider whether the garment is flattering to your figure.
- **Durability:** Consider the quality of the item. Will it last a long time? Denim is a very durable fabric, as are most synthetic fabrics.

Link...

Care labelling, page 370

Buying clothes

Accessories

Accessories are extra items worn to complete a look or change the look of what we wear. Accessories include shoes, ties, hats, belts, bags and gloves. Accessories are worn because they:

- complete an outfit
- create an interesting look
- change the look of an outfit
- express our taste and style
- can be functional, for example a bag or rucksack.

Accessories can be functional

Activity

List two accessories which are currently fashionable (a) for girls and (b) for boys.

Properties of clothing fabrics

Modern lifestyles and activities require clothes with a range of desirable properties. For example, children's wear needs to be durable and washable. Rainwear needs to be waterproof. Sports activities such as running require fabric which is comfortable and lightweight.

Children's wear

Fashion

Fashion can be applied to almost anything we do. Fashion means wearing the latest style of clothes or hair style. However, fashion is also associated with areas such as music, food, cars, technology, hobbies and architecture.

Fashion trends

Fashion is constantly changing. These fashion changes are called **fashion trends**. Trends can last for a very long time or they can change quickly. A **fashion fad** is a very short-lived fashion, lasting just a few weeks or months. A fad is usually not expensive and may be a simple idea, such as wearing a trendy accessory.

Higher Level

Influences on fashion trends

The following factors influence fashion trends:

● famous people
● historical events
● the media
● the fashion industry
● street fashion.

Famous people such as film stars, pop stars, sports stars and fashion designers are sometimes known as trendsetters or fashion leaders.

Historical events such as wars have caused great changes in fashion. During the world wars, women's clothes became more suitable for working in factories and new fibres such as nylon were developed.

The media promote particular styles in magazines and on TV, which then become popular.

The fashion industry promotes new colours and styles every season. This means that the clothes from the previous season are no longer in fashion.

Therefore, people buy more clothes that are fashionable.

Street fashion is an influence on fashion when everyday clothes become fashionable, such as dancewear, denim clothes and sportswear.

Trendsetters

Historical influences

Fashion magazines

Couturier

Haute couture

Prêt-à-porter

The fashion industry

The fashion industry involves the design, production, distribution and sale of clothes and accessories.

- **Couturier:** Fashion designer. Twice a year, designers show their collections in the fashion capitals of London, Milan, New York and Paris. These designs set the trends for the next season.
- **Haute couture** (high fashion): Original and very expensive clothes made by fashion designers for individual people.
- **Prêt-à-porter:** A designer's 'ready-to-wear' collection. They are good-quality, well-made clothes that are more readily available and cheaper than haute couture.
- **Off-the-peg clothing:** The clothes you see in most shops. It is affordable fashion for the general population. The clothes are made using cheaper fabrics and faster production methods.

Activity

Look for the names of two famous Irish fashion designers and describe some of the clothes they have designed.

Designing an outfit

Consider the following points when designing an outfit:

- occasion (formal or casual)
- comfort
- cost of outfit
- fashion
- colour
- size
- design.

Fashion designer

Link...

Chapter 36 Fibres and Fabrics

Line

By changing the line, a person can be made to look taller or shorter, thinner or broader.

- Vertical lines add height and make a person look slimmer.
- Horizontal lines make a person look broader.
- Curved lines, such as uneven hems, give a soft look to clothes.
- Diagonal lines are dramatic and striking.

Vertical lines

Horizontal lines

Curved lines

Diagonal lines

Sketching an outfit

Fashion drawing allows you to show your ideas. Sketches are used to present ideas for outfits and accessories. **Diagrams must be fully labelled.** You do not need to draw the person wearing the garment.

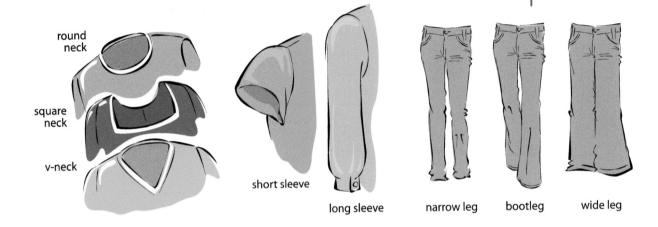

round neck

square neck

v-neck

short sleeve

long sleeve

narrow leg

bootleg

wide leg

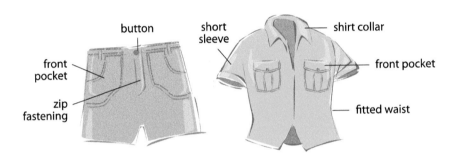

button

front pocket

zip fastening

short sleeve

shirt collar

front pocket

fitted waist

Activities

1 Sketch the outfit described below.

● **Jeans**

Features/ style:
Fit: loose fitting
Leg style: straight
Fastening: zip
Waist style: low waist
Pockets: front
Colour: blue denim.

● **Top**

Features/ style:
Fit: tight fitting
Neck: round
Length: waist length
Sleeves: short
Colour: white.

2 a) Sketch and label an outfit of your choice.

b) Describe the feature/style and colour of each garment in the outfit. Include details of the following: collar, neckline, pockets, fastenings, sleeve, leg, fit.

Summary

- The **functions of clothes** include **protection from weather**, **identification**, **safety**, **expression** and **modesty**.
- Guidelines for **buying** clothes include **function**, **fit**, **care**, **durability**, **cost** and **style**.
- The following factors **influence** fashion trends: **famous people**, **the media**, **historical events**, **the fashion industry** and **street fashion**.
- **Accessories** are **extra** items worn to complete a look.
- Fashion applies to many areas of life, such as clothes, architecture, music and food.
- Fashion changes are called **fashion trends**.
- A **fashion fad** is a very short-lived fashion.
- **Haute couture** (high fashion): Original and very expensive clothes.
- **Prêt-à-porter**: A designer's 'ready-to-wear' collection.
- When designing an outfit, consider **cost**, **fashion**, **occasion**, **comfort**, **colour**, **size** and **design**.

Revision Questions

1 List four functions of clothing.

2 (a) List three reasons why it is necessary for some people to wear protective clothing.

  (b) Name two occupations where protective clothing is worn.

  (c) Describe the types of clothes worn in these situations.

3 List four guidelines which should be followed by teenagers when buying clothes.

4 (a) State the advantages of using fashion accessories.

  (b) Name one fashion accessory.

5 List two properties of textiles suitable for rainwear.

6 List four desirable properties of textiles suitable for children's clothing.

7 List four factors that influence fashion trends.

8 Explain the following fashion terms: (a) haute couture; (b) prêt-à-porter.

9 Explain how each of the following can change the appearance of a garment: (a) vertical lines; (b) horizontal lines.

10 (a) List the points you would consider when designing an outfit.

  (b) Sketch and describe the outfit you would design.

  (c) Suggest suitable fabric(s) for the outfit and give three reasons for your choice.

  (d) Suggest two suitable accessories for the outfit you have designed.

Chapter 35
Fabric care

Our clothes provide us with comfort and a sense of style. We need to care for them so that we will look good and our clothes will last longer.

Taking care of clothes

- Remove stains and wash or dry clean.
- Mend clothes before storing.
- Use shaped or padded hangers to hang clothes.
- Fold knitwear and store it flat.
- Polish shoes and leather accessories regularly.

Care labelling

There are five basic symbols on care labels attached to clothes and household items.

- Washing instructions:
- Drying instructions:
- Ironing instructions:

- Bleaching instructions:
- Dry-cleaning instructions:

An X through a symbol means that the treatment should **not** be carried out.

Washing instructions

Washing instructions include details on:

- **temperature**
- **action** (movement of clothes during the wash)
- **length of spin** (full spin or short spin).

Tables like the one below are found on detergent packets. They give instructions for washing.

Textile / machine code	Machine wash	Hand wash	Fabric
95°	*Maximum* wash in cotton cycle.	Hand hot (50°C) or boil. Spin or wring.	White cotton and linen articles without special finishes.
60°	*Maximum* wash in cotton cycle.	Hand hot (50°C). Spin or wring.	Cotton, linen or viscose articles without special finishes where colours are fast at 60°C.
50°	*Medium* wash in synthetic cycle.	Hand hot. Cold rinse. Short spin or damp dry.	Polyester/cotton mixtures. Nylon polyester. Cotton and viscose articles with special finishes. Cotton/acrylic mixtures.
40°	*Maximum* wash in cotton cycle.	Warm. Spin or wring.	Cotton, linen or viscose where colours are fast at 40°C but not at 60°C.
40°	*Medium* wash in synthetic cycle.	Warm. Cold rinse. Short spin. Do not hand wring.	Acrylics, acetate and triacetate, including mixtures with wool. Polyester/wool blends.
40°	*Minimum* wash in wool cycle.	Warm. Do not rub. Spin. Do not hand wring.	Wool. Wool mixed with other fibres, silk.
⊠	Do not wash.	Do not wash.	Fabrics which cannot be washed. See care label.

Bar symbol

The bar symbol shows the washing action and the type of spin to be used.

- **No bar:** Maximum washing action and spin. [40°]

- **Single bar:** Medium washing action and short spin. [40°]

- **Broken bar:** Minimum washing action. This is the cycle used for wool. [30°]

Drying instructions

- Dry flat:
- Tumble dry:
- Line dry:
- Do not tumble dry:
- Drip dry:

Ironing instructions

- Hot iron:
- Cool iron:
- Warm iron:
- Do not iron:

Dry-cleaning instructions

- Dry clean: Ⓐ Ⓟ Ⓕ
- Do not dry clean:

Bleaching instructions

- Bleach may be used: △cl
- Do not use bleach:

Activity

Using the care label shown, outline the guidelines which should be followed when (a) washing and (b) drying this garment.

Machine wash

Preparing laundry

- Empty pockets.
- Mend clothes if necessary.
- Remove stains that are unlikely to come out in the wash.
- Close zips and buttons.
- Sort the clothes according to the colour and washing care labels
  The colour in **colour-fast** fabrics does not run in the wash.
  Non-colour-fast fabrics must be washed separately because the colour will run in the wash.
- Follow special instructions, such as 'do not use biological detergent'.

Activities

1 Design a care label for (a) a white cotton shirt; (b) a wool sweater.
2 Look at the care label on your favourite garment. Copy the label and explain what it means.

Washing delicate fabrics

Some fabrics such as wool and silk need special care.

- Use a low temperature and a mild detergent.
- Squeeze the garment instead of rubbing it.
- Rinse several times, gently squeezing out water.
- Do not wring.
- Roll in a towel and dry flat or drip dry.
- Use a cool iron.

Fabric care products

Detergents

A detergent is a substance which removes dirt. Washing detergents are made from a mixture of chemicals. Detergents are available in various forms, such as powder, tablets, liquid and gel.

Types of detergent

- Biological detergents: Biological detergents contain chemicals called enzymes which break down protein stains such as blood and gravy.
- Non-biological detergents.
- Low-foaming detergents for automatic washing machines.
- Hand washing detergents.
- Detergents for delicate fabrics.
- Eco-friendly detergents.

Which of these laundry products is the most environmentally friendly?

Fabric conditioners

A fabric conditioner is a substance that makes fabric softer. Fabric conditioner also reduces creasing and static cling. Some products contain both detergent and conditioner.

Fabric conditioners are available in various forms. Liquid conditioner is placed in the washing machine, whereas conditioning sheets are placed in the tumble dryer.

Colour run removers and colour catchers

Colour run removers remove the unwanted colour when colours run in the wash. Colour catchers trap colours which run in the wash. This prevents the colour seeping into other fabrics.

Colour catchers

Stain removal

- Act quickly before the stain dries into the fabric.
- Scrape or blot off as much as you can, but do not rub in the stain.
- Start with a mild treatment, such as soaking in cold water.
- If using a commercial stain remover, first test it on a hidden part of the garment, such as the hem.

Stain	Method of removal
Chewing gum	Freeze and scrape off. It may be necessary to remove grease stain, in which case use a grease solvent, e.g. benzene.
Perspiration, tea or coffee	Soak in warm water with a biological detergent. Wash as usual.
Blood, gravy and egg (protein stains)	Soak in cold water immediately. If the stain has set, soak in warm water with a biological detergent.
Grass, ink	Soak stained area in methylated spirits. Wash as usual.
Chocolate	Wash in hot water. If stain remains, dab with glycerine. Wash as usual.
Grease	Wash in hot water and detergent. If stain remains, dab with a grease solvent, e.g. benzene. Wash as usual.

Commercial stain removers

Commercial stain removers are available in various forms, such as liquids, bars, sprays and powders. Some are for general use and others are for use on specific stains.

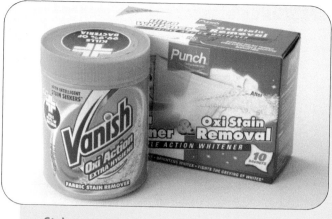

Stain removers

Guidelines for using commercial stain removers

- Follow the instructions on the product label.
- Test the product on a hidden part of the garment.
- Use in a well-ventilated area.
- Do not use near flames.
- Keep away from children.
- Use rubber gloves and wash hands after use.

Washing machines

Guidelines for use

- Wait until you have a full load if possible before using the washing machine.
- Use low-foaming detergent.
- Choose the correct washing programme.
- Use the economy programme where possible.

Drying clothes

- **Line drying** does not cost money and makes clothes smell fresh.
- **Clothes horse:** These can be used indoors, but drying causes condensation. Rooms should be well ventilated.
- **Tumble drying:** Tumble drying is convenient but it is not environmentally friendly because it uses a lot of electricity. Some fabrics, such as wool, shrink when tumble dried.

Ironing

There are two types of iron: dry irons and steam irons. Steam irons are more common nowadays. A steam iron contains a sole plate, a water tank which stores water and a thermostat which controls the temperature of the iron.

Guidelines for using a steam iron

- Follow manufacturer's instructions.
- Unplug iron to fill the water tank.
- Set the iron to the correct temperature according to care labels.
- Iron fabrics on the wrong side unless a shiny finish is wanted, for example on linen.
- Store iron in an upright position.

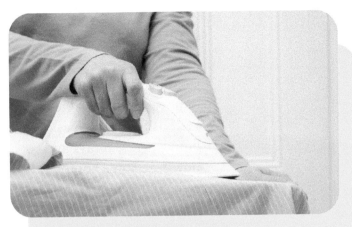

Using a steam iron

Summary

- **Care labels** include instructions for washing, drying, ironing, dry cleaning and bleaching. An X through a symbol means that that treatment should not be carried out.
- The **bar symbol** shows the **washing action** to be used.
- **Colour-fast:** Colour does not run in the wash.
- **Non-colour-fast:** Colour runs in the wash.
- A **detergent** is a substance that removes dirt.
- **Biological detergent** contains **enzymes** which break down protein stains.
- A **fabric conditioner** softens fabric; reduces static cling; reduces creasing.
- **Colour run remover** removes the unwanted colour when colours run.
- **Colour catchers** trap colours which run in the wash.

Revision Questions

1. Design a care label for a household item. Include at least four items of information.
2. Sketch and describe a suitable care label for a sports top.
3. What guidelines should be followed when (a) washing and (b) drying a cotton garment?
4. List two precautions which should be taken when using a commercial stain remover.
5. Explain what each of the following fabric care symbols indicates.

   (a)   (b) [Ⅲ] (c) [40°] (d) [—]

6. Explain the term 'colour-fast fabric'.
7. Outline the function of biological detergent.
8. List four guidelines which should be followed when washing a delicate item of clothing.
9. Describe how you would remove the following stains: (a) ink (biro); (b) chewing gum; (c) grass; (d) blood.
10. Outline the function of fabric conditioner.
11. List three guidelines that should be followed when using a steam iron.

Chapter 36
Fibres and fabrics

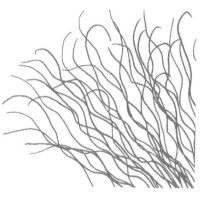

Fibres

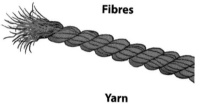

Yarn

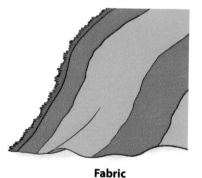

Fabric

Fibres

Fibres are fine, hair-like structures. They form the basic part of any fabric. **Continuous filaments** are very long fibres and **staple fibres** are short fibres.

Fibres are used to make yarn and **yarn is used to make fabric.** The properties or characteristics of a fabric depend on the fibres from which it is made. Ideally, fibres should be strong and flexible.

Classifying fibres

Fibres come from many different sources. They are produced from plants, animal hairs, worms, wood, minerals, coal and oil. Fibres are grouped according to their origin. **Natural fibres** come from nature and **manufactured fibres** are created from a mixture of raw materials.

Natural fibres include **plant sources** and **animal sources.** Plant sources include cotton, which comes from cotton plants, and linen, which comes from flax plants. Animal sources include wool from sheep and silk from silkworms.

Cotton plants

Flax plants

Wool from sheep

Manufactured fibres include **synthetic fibres** and **regenerated fibres**. Synthetic fibres are made from crude oil. Examples are nylon and polyester. Regenerated fibres are made from a mixture of natural substances such as wood. Examples are viscose and acetate.

Crude oil production

Natural fibres	Manufactured fibres
● Plant: cotton, linen ● Animal: wool, silk	● Regenerated: viscose, acetate ● Synthetic: polyester, acrylic

Stages in the production of fibres

Natural (plant) fibres

Cotton

Cotton grows in hot, moist climates. The largest producers of cotton in the world are China, the United States of America and India. It is the most common natural fibre.

PURE
COTTON

Production of cotton:

Higher Level

- Cotton fibres come from the part of the **cotton plant** called the **boll** or seed head. The fibres are 2–3cm long and are white and fluffy.
- The bolls are **picked** by hand or machine.
- The fibres are separated from the seeds (**ginning**).
- The fibres are pressed into bales.
- The cotton is **graded** according to the length of the fibres.
- Fibres are **combed** and **spun** into yarn.

Harvesting cotton

Teenagers wearing cotton clothes

Cotton bed linen

Higher Level

Properties of cotton		Fabrics and uses	
Desirable	**Undesirable**	**Fabrics**	**Uses**
• Absorbent	• Creases	• Flannelette	• *Clothes*
• Does not cling	• Not very	• Towelling	Jeans, sweatshirts,
• Cool	stretchy	• Poplin	shirts, T-shirts,
• Strong	• Burns easily	• Lawn	underwear, jackets,
• Easy to wash	• Damaged by	• Cotton	trousers, dresses, baby
and dry	mildew	• Gingham	clothes, nightwear
• Easy to dye	• Shrinks	• Muslin	• *Household*
and bleach		• Denim	Towels, sheets, duvet
			covers, curtains

Towelling

Gingham

Linen

Linen comes from the **flax plant**. Flax grows in cool, damp climates, for example in Ireland, Belgium, Russia and France.

Production of linen:

- Flax grows to about a metre in height and the stems are pulled up by their roots.
- The stems are left to soak for several weeks to rot (**retting**).
- The fibres are separated from the woody parts.
- The fibres are **combed** and spun into yarn.
- Long fibres produce fine yarn. Short fibres produce coarse yarn.

Irish linen fabrics are recognised worldwide.

Harvesting flax

Higher Level

Weaving linen

Higher Level

Properties of linen		Fabrics and uses	
Desirable	**Undesirable**	**Fabrics**	**Uses**
● Absorbent	● Creases easily	● Damask	● *Clothes*
● Cool	● Shrinks	● Canvas	Suits, dresses, shirts
● Strong	● Burns easily	● Cambric	● *Household*
● Hardwearing	● Damaged by		Tablecloths and
● Easily washed	mildew		napkins (damask),
● Does not	● Difficult to dye		sheets,
attract dirt			tea towels,
easily			curtains

Animal fibres

Wool

Wool is the most common animal fibre used. It is the soft hair of sheep.

Wool is produced in many countries, such as the UK, New Zealand, the USA and Ireland.

Spinning is a stage in wool production

Production of wool:

- The **fleece** (hair) is removed from the **sheep**.
- It is **graded** according to the colour, fineness and the length of the fibres.
- It is cleaned and combed (**carding**).
- It is then spun into yarn.

Properties of wool		Fabrics and uses	
Desirable	**Undesirable**	**Fabrics**	**Uses**
• Warm	• Shrinks if washed or dried carelessly	• Flannel	• *Clothes* Jumpers, coats, suits, dresses, underwear
• Soft		• Tweed	
• Absorbent	• Feels itchy beside the skin	• Velour	
• Stretchy		• Gabardine	
• Resilient	• Pills	• Jersey	• *Household* Blankets, carpets, upholstery, rugs
• Does not burn easily	• Easily scorched, damaged by moths	• Crêpe	
	• Does not dry easily	• Serge	
	• Can stretch out of shape when wet		

®

CERTIFICATION TRADE MARK

WOOLMARK

Woollen coat

Silk

Silk is soft, smooth and strong. It has been produced since ancient times. China and Japan produce most of the world's silk.

Silkworms in a mulberry tree

Production of silk:

- Silk is produced from the **silkworm.**
- The silk moth lays eggs and the new worms feed on the leaves of the **mulberry tree.**
- The worms spin **cocoons** of silk.
- The cocoons are heated and soaked and the threads are removed.
- The threads are then wound onto **reels.**
- The threads are spun into thicker yarn.

Formation of cocoons

Silk fabrics

Properties of silk		Fabrics and uses	
Desirable	**Undesirable**	**Fabrics**	**Uses**
• Absorbent	• Damaged by	• Wild silk	• *Clothes*
• Lightweight	careless handling	• Slub silk	Shirts, scarves,
yet warm	• Flammable	• Chiffon	evening wear, ties
• Crease resistant	• Damaged by	• Satin	• *Household*
• Strong	moths	• Taffeta	Curtains, cushions,
• Smooth	• Damaged by	• Organza	throws
• Drapes well	chemicals		

Manufactured fibres

The production of all manufactured fibres follows the same basic method. Manufactured fibres are either **regenerated** or **synthetic**.

Regenerated cellulose fibres

Regenerated fibres contain cellulose because they come from plants. Wood, seaweed and cotton waste are crushed and used to make fibres.

Production of regenerated fibres:

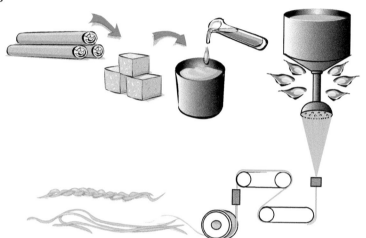

- **Cellulose** from trees and cotton waste is **pulped** and mixed with chemicals.
- It is made into a thick **liquid.**
- The liquid is forced through tiny holes in a **spinneret** (like a shower head) to make yarn.
- Yarn is twisted and cut.

Properties of regenerated fabrics		Fabrics and uses	
Desirable	**Undesirable**	**Fabrics**	**Uses**
• Absorbent	• Some fabrics, such as	• Viscose	• Lightweight
• Easy to dye	viscose, crease easily	• Acetate	clothes, tablecloths,
• Cool	and are not very durable	• Tencel	napkins, curtains

Regenerated fabrics

Synthetic fibres

Production of synthetic fibres:

- Various **chemicals** from petroleum are mixed to produce a thick liquid.
- The liquid is forced through tiny holes in a **spinneret**.
- Long uniform fibres (**continuous filaments**) are twisted together to make smooth yarn.
- Fibres can be **cut** into short (**staple**) fibres.

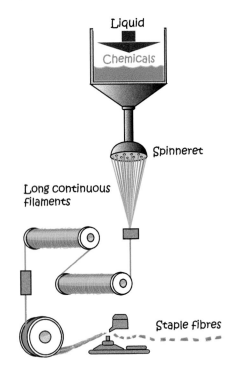

Liquid

Chemicals

Spinneret

Long continuous filaments

Staple fibres

Properties of synthetic fabrics		Fabrics and uses	
Desirable	**Undesirable**	**Fabrics**	**Uses**
● Strong ● Elastic ● Durable ● Stretchy ● Crease resistant ● Acrylic is warm	● Do not absorb moisture ● Clingy ● Cause static ● Flammable	● Nylon ● Polyester ● Acrylic (Dralon) ● PVC ● Elastane (Lycra)	● *Nylon*: tights, linings, underwear, waterproof clothes, carpets ● *Polyester*: shirts, trousers, sheets, fillings for cushions and duvets ● *Acrylic* (Dralon): jumpers, blankets, carpets ● *PVC* (polyvinylchloride): handbags, shower curtains, tablecloths ● *Elastane* (Lycra): swimwear, leggings, tights

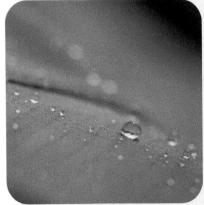

Waterproof fabric

Acrylic

PVC

Denier is used to describe the thickness of manufactured fibres. The lower the number, the finer the yarn.

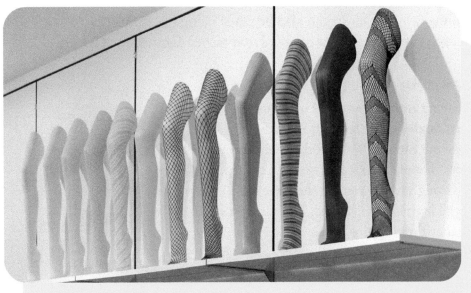

Lightweight tights have a low denier

Blended fabrics

Various fibres can be combined to create fabrics with many desirable properties. When cotton and polyester are mixed together polycotton is created. Polycotton is absorbent and it does not crease. Modern recycled fibres are used in blended fabrics to create environmentally friendly fabrics.

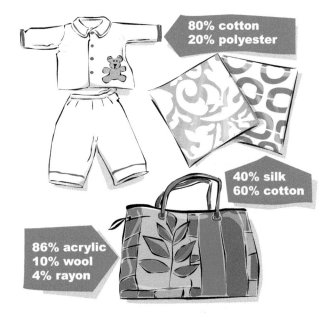

80% cotton
20% polyester

40% silk
60% cotton

86% acrylic
10% wool
4% rayon

Higher
Level

Fabric construction

Spinning yarn

Spinning is the process of twisting fibres into yarn. This gives strength to the fibres. Different amounts of twist can be applied to the yarn. A loose twist produces soft, bulky yarn, whereas a tight twist produces a finer, stronger yarn.

Making fabrics

Weaving yarn to make fabric is one method of making fabric. Tweed and denim are examples of woven fabric. **Knitting** is another method of making fabric. Fabrics can also be made using fibres directly without making yarn first. They are called **non-woven fabrics,** such as felt.

Weaving

Weaving is the interlacing of yarns at right angles to each other. Weaving is done on a **loom.** Woven fabric has two types of yarn: warp and weft. The **warp,** or strong thread, runs in the direction of the length of the fabric. The **weft,** or weaker thread, runs in the direction of the width of the fabric.

   The side of the fabric running in the direction of the warp threads is called the **selvage.** The selvage stops the sides fraying. Woven fabrics are used in clothes and soft furnishings.

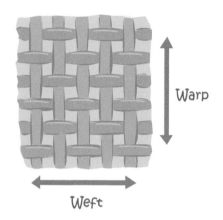

Warp

Weft

Straight grain

Straight grain means the direction of the warp threads in a fabric. The straight grain should run down the length of an item, such as trousers, tops or curtains. This makes them hang better.

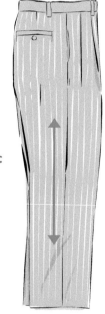

Straight grain

Bias

Bias is the diagonal line of a fabric. The fabric stretches when it is pulled along this line. Clothes cut on the bias drape well.

   Strips of fabric cut on the bias are called bias strips. They are joined together to make bias binding, which is used to neaten edges of fabric and to make piping for cushions and household items.

Bias

Link...

Cutting out fabric, page 402

Knitting

Knitting means linking together loops of yarn into knots called stitches. Knitting can be done by hand or machine. Knitted fabrics are stretchy. Some machine-knit fabrics can be cut and sewn just like woven fabrics. Jumpers, tracksuits, socks, tights and underwear are made from knitted fabric.

Advantages of knitted fabric:

- stretchy
- comfortable
- warm
- crease resistant.

Knitted fabric

Non-woven fabrics

Non-woven or bonded fabrics are made directly from fibres without being made into yarn. The fibres are held together using adhesive, heat, pressure or stitching. Felt and interfacing are examples of bonded fabric. Bonded fabrics are used in disposable clothes (hospital gowns), disposable cloths, masks, J-cloths, snooker tables, tennis balls, nappies, blankets, carpet underlays, fancy dress costumes and slippers.

Advantages of non-woven fabrics:

- do not fray
- are cheap to produce
- keep their shape well
- economical to use because there is no straight grain.

Non-woven fabric

Disadvantages:

- do not wear well
- felt is damaged by water
- non-woven blankets don't trap air and therefore are not as warm as wool.

Applying pattern to fabric

Dyeing

A dye is a substance added to fabric to give it colour. Natural dyes found in berries and leaves can be used. Synthetic dyes produce an endless variety of colours. Dyeing can take place at the fibre stage, the yarn stage or the fabric stage of textile production. Dyeing can be used to apply pattern, such as in **batik** and **tie-dye**.

Dylon dye for use in washing machine

Printing

Printing means applying colour and pattern to one side of the fabric only. There are various types of printing, such as **block printing** and **screen printing**. **Fabric pens**, transfer crayons and **fabric paints** can also be used to apply pattern to fabric.

Weaving, knitting and bonding

In woven and knitted fabrics, the yarns are arranged to form certain patterns. In non-woven or bonded fabrics, the fibres are arranged in various ways to produce patterns.

Applying texture to fabric

- Natural and manufactured yarns can be woven together (one hairy and one smooth). When the fabric is heat pressed the result is a crinkled, highly textured fabric.
- Soft fibres such as mohair produce a textured fabric.
- Shiny and metallic effects are produced by using synthetic fibres.
- Textured yarns can be used to give a textured fabric.

Pattern created by weaving

Identifying fibres

The burn test

You will need a metal tray, metal tongs, matches, a long taper and pen and paper.

Procedure

1 Using the tongs, hold a sample of the fibre or fabric over the metal tray.

2 Light the taper and move it slowly towards the fibres. Once the fibres start to burn, remove the taper.

3 Observe the way the fibres burn, the smell and the residue.

4 Write a report after each test using the headings given below.

Fabric	As it gets near the flame	When it touches the flame	After it has touched the flame	Smell	Residue (what is left after the test)
Protein fibres: Wool, silk	Fibres stick together and curl away from the flame	Burns very slowly	Stops burning	Like burning hair, feathers or nail clippings	Dark, soft ash, easy to crush
Cellulose fibres: Cotton, linen, viscose	Ignites as the flame draws near	Burns quickly	Goes on burning	Like burning paper	Grey ash, like a sheet of paper when burned
Nylon	Fibres melt and shrink away from the flame; may drip	Melts and burns slowly	Usually goes out	Like celery	Hard beads – light grey or beige

Fabric finishes

A fabric finish is a chemical treatment applied to a fabric to improve its appearance or performance. For example, fabric can be made crease resistant or waterproof.

Waterproof clothing

Finish	Purpose	Uses
Brushing	Makes fabric feel softer and warmer, e.g. brushed nylon or cotton (flannelette).	Children's nightwear and bed clothes.
Flameproof	Makes fabric less flammable.	Children's nightwear, furnishing fabrics.
Permanent pleating	Pleats don't fall out, no need to iron.	Skirts, trousers.
Waterproof	Prevents any water getting through.	Raincoats, outdoor sportswear.
Stain repellent	Prevents stains from penetrating.	Carpets, upholstery, clothing fabrics.
Shrink resistant	Prevents shrinking.	Furnishing fabrics and clothing.
Crease resistant	Creases fall out more easily, less ironing required.	Shirts, dresses, trousers, tablecloths, curtains.

SHELL FABRIC: 76%NYLON/24%PU
LINING: 100%POLYESTER

HAND WASH IN WARM WATER
USING A NON BIO POWDER
DO NOT BLEACH
DO NOT TUMBLE DRY
DO NOT DRY CLEAN
DO NOT IRON

Biological detergents damage waterproof and flame-resistant finishes

Summary

- **Fibres** form the basic part of any fabric.
- Natural fibres include fibres from **plant sources** and **animal sources**.
- Manufactured fibres include **synthetic fibres** and **regenerated fibres**.
- **Continuous filaments** are very long fibres and **staple fibres** are short fibres.
- Cotton fibres come from the **cotton plant**.
- Linen comes from the **flax plant**.
- Wool is the soft hair of **sheep**.
- Silk is produced from the **silkworm**.
- **Manufactured fibres** are produced when various liquids are forced through tiny holes in a **spinneret**.
- **Denier** is used to describe the thickness of manufactured fibres.
- **Weaving** and **knitting** are methods of making fabric from yarn. **Non-woven fabrics** are made using fibres without making yarn.
- Woven fabric has two types of yarn: **warp** and **weft**.
- **Selvage** is the side of fabric parallel to warp threads.
- **Straight grain** means the direction of the warp threads in a woven fabric.
- The **bias** is the diagonal line of a fabric.
- Dyeing and printing are methods of applying **pattern** to fabric.
- The **burn test** is used to identify fabrics.
- A **fabric finish** is a chemical treatment applied to a fabric to improve its appearance or performance.

Revision Questions

1 Give four examples of natural fibres and give one use for each.

2 Explain the term 'absorbent fabric'.

3 (a) Choose a natural fabric and outline the stages involved in its production.

  (b) State four desirable properties of the fabric you have chosen.

4 State one desirable property and one undesirable property of linen as a clothing fabric.

5 List three examples of cotton fabric.

6 List one desirable and one undesirable property of denim.

7 Sketch the symbol that indicates that fabric is pure cotton.

8 List two desirable and two undesirable properties of wool as a clothing fabric.

9 State three different uses of wool in the home.

10 List two examples of regenerated fibres.

11 Give two examples of synthetic fibres and suggest a different use for each.

12 State two ways in which yarn can be made into fabric.

13 Give two examples of woven fabric.

14 List two advantages of non-woven fabric.

15 Explain the terms: (a) denier; (b) selvage.

16 List two ways in which pattern can be applied to fabric.

17 Explain texture in relation to fabric.

18 Suggest two ways of introducing texture when making fabric.

19 List two uses for each of the following: (a) nylon; (b) polyester; (c) acrylic; (d) Lycra.

20 Explain the term 'fabric finish'.

21 Suggest two fabric finishes which could be applied to textiles for use in soft furnishings.

22 Name two suitable finishes that could be applied to fabric for a school jacket.

23 Describe a fabric test that could be carried out in order to identify wool.

Chapter 37
Needlework skills

Essential items of sewing equipment

Good-quality sewing equipment gives a professional finish to your work. Some items of equipment are essential, such as:

- needles
- thread
- pins
- thimble
- scissors.

- pinking shears
- stitch ripper
- measuring tape
- tailor's chalk

Sewing equipment

Selecting fabric for home sewing

Successful sewing largely depends on the right choice of fabric.

- Consider the **cost** of the fabric.
- Consider the **colour** and **pattern** of the fabric.
- Fabric should **not fray too much** and should not have flaws.
- Fabric should be **easy to sew** and therefore should be non-slip and **not too stretchy.**
- Check the **weight** of the fabric.
- Work out the **amount** of fabric you need and check whether this amount is available in the shop.
- Avoid fabric with a **nap** or **one-way design**.
- Check the **width.** Fabric is sold in the following widths: 90cm, 115cm, 120cm, 140cm and 150cm.

Good-quality scissors

Nap and one-way designs

Nap means that the fabric has a raised surface and the fibres lie in one direction. It feels smooth if you rub it one way and rough if you rub it the other way.

One-way designs are patterns on fabric that all face the same direction.

Cutting out fabric, page 402

One-way design on fabric

Guidelines for hand sewing

- Use a single thread which is not too long.
- Pin seams and hems before tacking (see tacking stitch, page 395).
- Begin and finish sewing with secure stitching to prevent ripping.
- Protect your finger with a thimble when sewing thick fabrics.
- If you are right-handed, work from right to left; if you are left-handed, work from left to right.

Hand stitches

Tacking (basting)

Tacking is a temporary stitch used to hold fabric together while permanent stitching (machining) is being done. It is used:

- to hold two pieces of fabric (a hem or seam) in position while being stitched
- to hold a garment together for fitting
- as a guide for machining.

To make a tacking stitch:

- Pin fabric in position.
- Use a single thread in a contrasting colour, which will show up easily.
- Begin with a knot or double backstitch. (To form a backstitch, make a stitch and then go back into the same stitch again.)
- Make equal-sized stitches 1cm in length.
- Stitches and spaces should be of equal size.
- Do not pull tightly or fabric will pucker.
- Make a double backstitch to finish.

Running

This is basically the same as tacking but smaller. It is used for seams or for gathering fabric by hand.

Gathering

This stitch is used to make a wide piece of fabric fit a narrow piece, for example to fit a gathered frill into a cushion.

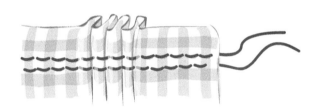

- Two parallel rows of running (or machining) stitches are worked along the line to be gathered.
- Use a looser machine tension than for normal machining.
- Threads are pulled to gather the fabric until it fits.
- The gathering stitch is removed afterwards.

Backstitching

A backstitch is a strong stitch that can be used instead of machining to sew seams.

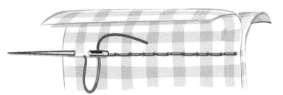

- Begin with a small double stitch, bringing the needle out 2–3mm beyond the first stitch.
- Put the needle back into the end of the stitch and bring it out 2–3mm beyond.
- Continue in this way and finish with a double stitch.
- Pass the needle through the fabric and cut the thread.

Hemming

Hemming is used to hold down facings, bindings, waistbands and collars.

This stitch shows on the right side and therefore it is not suitable for sewing hems of clothes.

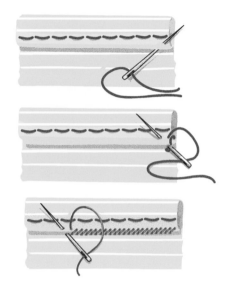

- Put the needle through the fold from left to right, leaving a small tail of thread. This tail is left in the fold.
- Work in small slanted stitches from right to left, picking up a thread of the single fabric and a thread of the fold before pulling the needle through.
- Continue to the end and make a V-shaped stitch to finish by sewing into the last stitch twice. Pull the needle through the fold and cut the thread.

Slip hemming

This is used on the hems of clothes because it is almost invisible on the right side. It can be made more secure by sewing a backstitch every now and then along the fold.

- Pass the needle through the fold from left to right and secure with a small backstitch.
- Pick up only one or two threads from the single fabric.
- Pass the needle through the fold for 5–10mm, depending on the thickness of the fabric and the depth of the hem.
- Keep the stitches quite loose as you continue in the same way.
- Make a double backstitch in the fold to finish.

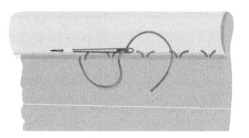

Top sewing

This small, secure stitch is worked on the right side of the fabric. It is used to join finished edges together.

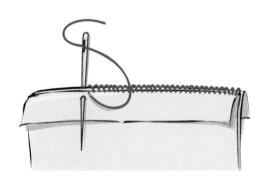

- Insert the needle through a single fold.
- Pull the needle through, leaving 1cm of thread lying along the top edge.
- Put the needle through the top of both folds and sew a row of small slanted stitches very close together, working from right to left.
- To finish, work three stitches from left to right so that they form three crosses.

Tailor tacking

Tailor tacks are used to transfer pattern markings from a pattern onto doubled fabric.

- Use a fairly long double thread without a knot.
- Make a small stitch through the pattern mark and both layers of fabric.
- Repeat the stitch, leaving a loop.
- Cut the thread, leaving a long tail.
- Remove the pattern carefully.
- Separate both layers of fabric and cut the threads between them.

Embroidery

Embroidery can be done by hand or machine. It is used to decorate fabric. Embroidery thread is sold in skeins. Each thread is made up of six strands. These are usually divided into two parts with three strands each unless you are using very thick fabric.

Use a crewel (embroidery) needle, which has a large eye. This makes it easy to pull the embroidery thread through.

Hand embroidery

- To begin, make a few running stitches along the line to be stitched.
- These will be covered with embroidery stitches as you work.
- Finish by weaving the thread through the wrong side of the stitches. Pull the thread through and cut it.

Stem stitch

A stem stitch is used for outlines.

- Start with a backstitch.
- Make even, slightly slanted stitches along a line, working from right to left.
- The thread must always be kept at the right of the needle.
- The thread should come out above the previous stitch.

Chain stitch

A chain stitch is used for outlines.

- Begin with a backstitch at the top of the outline.
- Work downwards, holding the thread with your free thumb to form a loop.
- Insert the needle inside the loop, beside where the thread emerged.
- Finish with a secure stitch, bringing the needle through to the back of the fabric. Weave the thread through a few stitches on the wrong side of the fabric. Cut the thread.

Satin stitch

A satin stitch is used to fill in shapes.

- Insert the needle through one side of the shape and out through the other.
- Stitches may be straight or slanted but must be very close together.
- To give extra thickness, work a running stitch around the edge or throughout the design before beginning the satin stitch.
- Stitches which are too long drag the fabric. Long and short stitch is more suitable for wide shapes.

Satin stitch

Long and short stitch

This is used to fill in shapes and give a shaded effect.

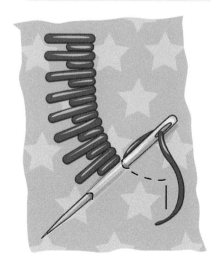

- First row: Make a long stitch and then a short stitch.
- Second row: Make a short stitch and then a long stitch so that the rows fit into each other.

The sewing machine

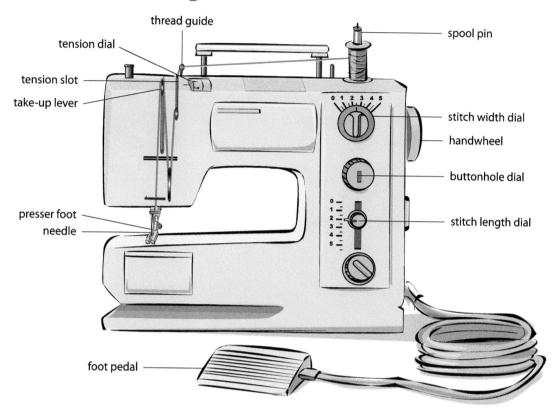

How a machine stitches

Two threads twist around one another, one from the top and the other from the bobbin. The stitching must have the correct tightness or tension. When tension is too loose it causes a loopy stitch. When tension is too tight it causes the fabric to pucker. Tension can be adjusted by changing the setting on the tension control.

Threading the sewing machine

The system of threading varies according to the machine.

1 Bring the thread from the spool pin to the thread guide on the top of the machine.

2 Put the thread through the tension slot and under the next thread guide.

3 Put the thread through the take-up lever.

4 Put the thread through the thread guides.

5 Thread the needle from front to back.

6 Insert the filled bobbin (see instructions in the booklet).

7 Turn the wheel until the needle thread catches the bobbin thread.

8 Pull both threads towards the back of the machine.

Machine stitches

Common machine stitches are:

Straight stitch

- **Straight stitch:** Used for most sewing, e.g. seams, to apply waistbands and to sew hems on non-stretch fabrics. The stitch length can be adjusted. Long stitches are used for thick fabric.

- **Zig-zag stitch:** Used for finishing seams, sewing stretchy fabric and appliqué.

- **Blind stitch:** Used for hems and decorative work.

- **Buttonhole stitch:** Used for making buttonholes.

- **Embroidery stitch:** Used for decorative work.

Buttonhole stitch

Using a sewing machine

1 Thread the machine properly.
2 Adjust the stitch length and tension to suit the fabric.
3 Test the stitch on a scrap of fabric.
4 Begin machining by pressing lightly on the foot pedal.
5 If you need to stop in the middle of a line or to turn a corner, leave the needle in the fabric.
6 At the end of a line, reverse for a few stitches to secure the stitching.
7 Raise the needle and lift the presser foot to remove the fabric.

Embroidery stitch

Choosing a sewing machine

Consider the following factors.

- The cost of the machine.
- Is the machine easy to use?
- What stitches and special features will you need?
- What attachments or extras are included with the machine?
- Does it have a reliable brand name?
- The after-sales service and guarantee.

Care of a sewing machine

- Follow the instructions for use and cleaning.
- Do not run a threaded machine without fabric.
- Cover when not in use to avoid dust.
- Oil moving parts occasionally.
- Have the machine serviced regularly.

Machine faults and possible causes

Machine fault	Possible cause
Needle breaks	• Pulling fabric before raising needle • Top tension too tight • Needle too fine or inserted incorrectly • Loose presser foot
Thread breaks	• Top tension too tight • Incorrect threading of machine • Poor-quality thread • Needle inserted incorrectly
Uneven stitches	• Incorrect threading • Needle set too high or too low • Pulling or pushing fabric while machining • Needle blunt or inserted incorrectly
Looped stitches	• Top tension too loose • Incorrect threading of machine • Bobbin threaded incorrectly
Slipped stitches	• Wrong size of needle • Needle set too high or too low • Needle inserted incorrectly
Puckered seam	• Tension set incorrectly • Needle too thin or too thick

Looped stitches

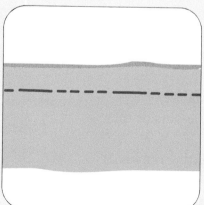

Slipped stitches

Puckered seam

Seams

Flat seam

Seams are made when two pieces of fabric are joined by a line of sewing. A flat seam is the basic method used to join fabrics.

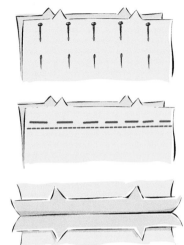

1   Place the two pieces of fabric together with the right sides facing and edges exactly on top of each other. Match notches.

2   Pin and tack on the fitting line.

3   Remove pins and machine. Remove the tacking and press the seam open.

4   Neaten the edges with a suitable seam finish.

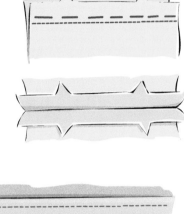

Seam finishes

A flat seam is usually finished using straight stitching (edge machining) or zig-zag stitching.

Edge machining is suitable for light and medium-weight fabrics.

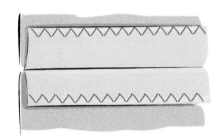

● Turn under a fold to the back of each seam allowance.
● Tack and machine close to the edge.
● Remove the tacking.

Zig-zag machining:

● Select a suitable size zig-zag stitch and test it on a scrap of fabric.
● Stitch each edge of the seam separately or stitch both together.
● Trim the fabric outside the stitching.

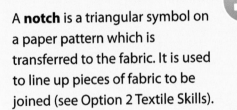

Pinking shears are sometimes used to trim the edges of closely woven fabric.

Cutting out fabric

● Place the pattern pieces flat on the fabric and pin in position.
● Use sharp scissors to cut the fabric.
● Leave a 1.5cm seam allowance outside the sewing line.
● Cut along the cutting line, cutting outwards around **notches**.
● Hold the fabric flat on the table while cutting.
● Transfer pattern markings, such as **construction marks**, onto the fabric.

A **notch** is a triangular symbol on a paper pattern which is transferred to the fabric. It is used to line up pieces of fabric to be joined (see Option 2 Textile Skills).

Construction marks include darts, pleats and pockets. A **dart** is a pointed, wedge-shaped fold of fabric. It is used to give shape to a garment, for example at the bust or hips (see Option 2 Textile Skills).

Transferring pattern markings

Pattern markings are transferred using:

- tailor tacking (see page 397)
- tailor's chalk
- tracing wheel and carbon paper.

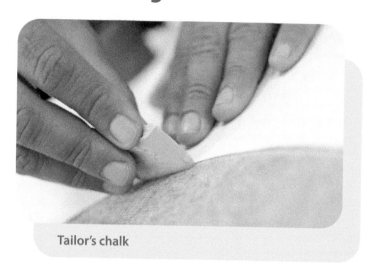

Tailor's chalk

Sewing project 1: a vest top

This top can be adapted to make it into a **fancy dress** garment or a **sports vest**.

Link...

Embroidery, page 397
Sketching an outfit, page 368

You will need:

- a pattern (see diagram 1)
- fabric
- thread
- four 20cm lengths of fabric tape (to tie the vest at the sides)
- for a fancy dress garment: materials to decorate the item, for example fabric pens.

How to make the vest top

1 Make the pattern.

2 Cut out the fabric.

3 Personalise the item. Decorate the fabric using fabric pens or fabric paint, embroidery, appliqué or tie-dyeing.

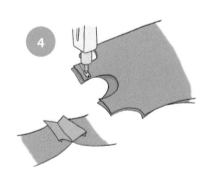

4 Pin, tack and stitch front to back at the shoulder seams. Iron flat and finish the seams using zig-zag or edge machining.

5 Along the sides and bottom, turn under the raw edges twice. Iron, tack and machine stitch.

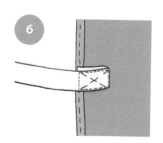

6 Stitch the four pieces of tape in place at the sides of the top, 10cm up from the bottom edge.

Sewing project 2: a drawstring duffel bag

You will need:

- a pattern
- cotton fabric
- 8cm length of fabric tape
- thick cotton cord (1 metre)
- sewing thread.

Duffel bag

How to make the bag

1 Make the pattern, which includes a circular base, a side panel and a pocket (seam allowance is included in the pattern).

2 Cut out the fabric.

3 Decorate the pocket using appliqué, embroidery, tie-dyeing or fabric crayons/paint.

4 Pin, tack and machine stitch a 1cm double hem along the top of the pocket.

5 Turn in a 1cm fold along the other three edges. Iron and tack.

6 Finish the edges of the side panel using zig-zag stitch.

7 Stitch the pocket to the right side of the side panel, 10cm up from the bottom edge. Use extra stitches at the top corners to reinforce the sewing.

8 Mark a point 10cm from the top edge of the side panel to indicate where the stitching will stop.

9 Turn in the raw edge (1cm) along the top of the side panel. Pin and tack. Then turn in a 5cm fold along the top edge of the side panel and iron to mark the fold. Unfold the 5cm turning.

10 Pin, tack and sew the side edges together, 1.5cm in from the edge. Sew from the bottom to the point you marked.

11 Pin and tack the 5cm fold in place along the top of the side panel to make the drawstring casing. Stitch close to the fold.

12 Fold the fabric tape in half and stitch both ends to the bottom of the seam on the right side of the side panel.

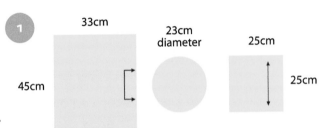

33cm

45cm

23cm diameter

25cm

25cm

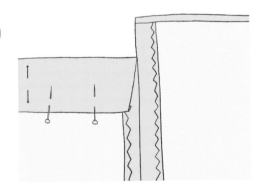

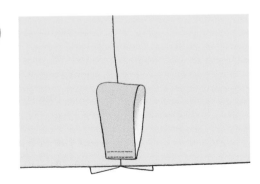

13 Cut a few 6mm notches along the edge of the circular base. Pin and tack the base to the side panel with right sides facing, 1.5cm in from the edge.

14 Stitch a double line and finish the edge with zig-zag stitch. Turn right side out.

15 Thread the cord through the casing using a safety pin fastened to one end of the cord. Put the cord through the tape loop and stitch or knot the ends of the cord securely together.

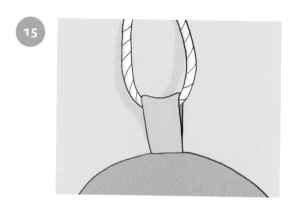

Summary

- **Fabric for home sewing** should not fray, not have flaws, be non-slip, not be too stretchy and have the correct colour. Avoid fabric with a nap or one-way design.
- **Nap** means that the fabric has a raised surface and the fibres lie in one direction.
- **Temporary stitches** include tacking, tailor tacking and gathering.
- **Tailor tacks** are used to transfer pattern markings from a pattern onto doubled fabric.
- **Permanent stitches** include running, backstitching, hemming, slip hemming, top sewing and machine stitching.
- **Embroidery stitches** include stem stitches, chain stitches, satin stitches and long and short stitches.
- **Machine stitches** include straight stitches, zig-zag stitches, blind stitch, buttonhole stitch and embroidery stitches.
- **To finish a flat seam**, use edge machining or zig-zag machining.
- **Transferring pattern markings:** Use tailor tacks; tailor's chalk; tracing wheel and carbon paper.

Revision Questions

1 Name the stitch shown in the diagram and state one use for it.

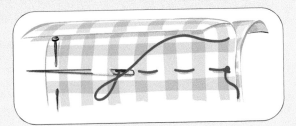

2 Name the stitch shown in the diagram and state one use for it.

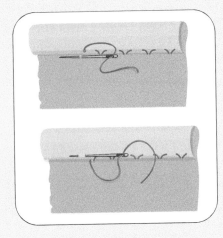

3 Name the stitch you would use to: (a) hold a hem in position; (b) embroider a design on a garment.

4 Name two machine stitches and state a different use for each.

5 Give one reason for each of the following sewing machine faults: (a) thread breaking; (b) looped stitches; (c) needle breaking.

6 Name two methods of neatening a flat seam.

7 Suggest two methods of transferring pattern markings to fabric.

8 Explain the term 'bias'.

9 List four factors the consumer should consider when choosing a sewing machine.

10 List five guidelines which should be followed when using a sewing machine.

11 List four guidelines which should be followed when caring for a sewing machine.

12 Name two machine stitches and suggest a use for each stitch.

13 (a) Sketch and describe an attractive household item you could make.

(b) State the fabric(s) you would use and give reasons for your choice.

(c) Outline the stages you would follow when making the household item. Use diagrams to illustrate your answer.

(d) Describe one method you could use to personalise the item.

14 (a) Sketch and describe a sports top you could make.

(b) Suggest two methods of personalising your sports top.

15 Explain each of the following sewing terms: (a) notch; (b) dart.

Option one
Child care

Chapter 38
Child development

From conception to birth

Before beginning this section, revise Section 3, Chapter 20.

Link...

Chapter 20 New Life

Conception occurs when a sperm from a male joins with an egg from a female. The fertilised egg attaches itself to the lining of the womb and develops into an **embryo**.

Stage	Development
4 weeks	The embryo is the width of a thumbnail and weighs less than 25g. Facial features are beginning to form. Tiny buds are appearing that will develop into arms and legs.
8 weeks	The embryo is now known as a **foetus** and starts to resemble a human baby. The beginnings of the eyes, ears and mouth can be seen. The eyelids are fused and fingernails appear.
16 weeks	The foetus makes small movements, which may be felt by the mother. This is the **quickening period**. The sex of the baby can now be seen by an ultrasound scan.
24 weeks	The foetus is 32cm long and weighs about 650g. Its skin is covered with fine, downy hair and a waxy coating. It moves around vigorously inside the uterus.
36 weeks	The lungs of the foetus have developed. Its fingernails have grown to reach the ends of its fingertips.
38–40 weeks	The pregnancy is now at full term and the baby is ready to be born. Its eyes are open and its head is covered with a variable amount of hair. It weighs around 3kg and is curled up in a head-down position. (Around 4 per cent of babies are in a bottom-down position, which is called the breech position.)

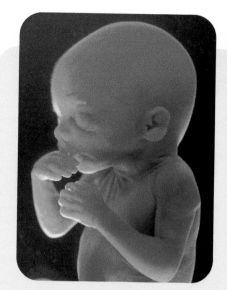

Foetus at 24 weeks

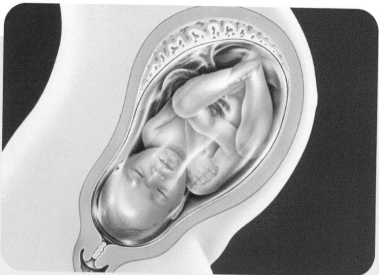

Foetus at 36–40 weeks

A healthy pregnancy

During pregnancy, an expectant mother must eat a well-balanced diet. This is necessary both to maintain her own health and to provide the foetus with the nutrients it needs to grow and develop.

A pregnant woman does not need to 'eat for two', as eating too much may lead to excessive weight gain. Pregnant women should avoid alcohol and cigarettes, spicy or rich foods, strong tea and coffee and too much fatty food. Cook-chill foods and soft, unpasteurised cheeses should also be avoided because of the risk of contamination by listeria (see page 43).

How a child grows and develops

The first year of a baby's life is a period of rapid growth and development – by the end of this year, the baby's birth weight will have **trebled**. In this first year, a baby learns many skills, such as smiling, crawling, talking and walking.

Developmental screening checks are carried out by a family doctor or public health nurse at regular intervals on all children from birth to five years. These checks are used to tell if a child is learning basic skills when they should, or if they are having any problems.

A child develops **physically**, **mentally** and **emotionally**.

Developmental milestones are skills or tasks that most children are able to do at a certain age. However, not all children who are developing normally reach these milestones at exactly the same time. Every child is unique.

Link...

Chapter 42 Health and Child Care Facilities

Age	Physical development	Mental development	Emotional development
Birth	<li> Head flops when lifted.<li> Hands close in a grasp reflex.<li> Waves arms and legs aimlessly.	<li> Is startled by loud noises.	<li> Is comforted by close physical contact.<li> Enjoys sucking and likes to feel warm and secure.
6 weeks	<li> Raises head slightly when lying on abdomen.<li> Turns head and eyes towards light.	<li> Watches parents' faces and tries to respond to speech.	<li> Quietens at the sound of parents' voices.<li> Smiles.
3 months	<li> Reaches, grasps and puts objects into mouth.<li> Kicks vigorously.<li> Eyes will follow moving objects.	<li> Watches and plays with own fingers.<li> Becomes excited when he/she sees food coming.	<li> Smiles instinctively on hearing a friendly voice or seeing a friendly face.<li> Enjoys being cuddled.
6 months	<li> Weighs twice his/her birth weight.<li> Can sit up with support.<li> Can roll from front to back.<li> First teeth appear.<li> Starts to chew.<li> Can feed with fingers.	<li> Shows interest in everything around him/her.<li> Makes two-syllable sounds such as 'googoo' or 'gaga'.	<li> Separates easily from parents and is friendly to strangers.<li> Can show pleasure or displeasure by laughing or crying.
9 months	<li> Crawls or attempts to crawl.<li> Pulls him/herself to a stand.<li> Can eat a biscuit and chew lumpy food.<li> Dribbles less.	<li> Can clap hands and play peek-a-boo.<li> Starts to understand simple words like 'no' and 'stop'.<li> Can say 'mama' and 'dada'.	<li> Has a strong fear of strangers. Starts to raise chin as a sign of protest.
12 months	<li> Can crawl and take a few steps alone.<li> Can pick up small objects using index finger and thumb.<li> Can hold and drink from a cup.	<li> Understands several words.<li> Responds to simple requests like giving a toy when asked.	<li> Responds to own name.<li> Starts to use single-syllable words.
18 months	<li> Can walk alone, forwards and backwards.<li> Can push, pull and carry toys around.<li> Can use a spoon to feed him/herself.	<li> Puts words together to form short sentences.<li> Tries to copy parents' actions.	<li> Shows anger by kicking and screaming, but can be easily distracted.
2–3 years	<li> Can walk on tiptoe and kick a ball forward.<li> Makes a good attempt at dressing and undressing.<li> Has a full set of milk teeth (20).	<li> Can draw a circle and paint with wrist action, making dots and lines.<li> Can build a tower of blocks.<li> Begins to ask simple questions.	<li> May show strong feelings of jealousy.

6 weeks

3 months

6 months

12 months

18 months

2–3 years

What affects a child's development?

- **Physical development:** Growth, use of the senses, development of skills and co-ordination. Influenced by heredity (traits or features inherited from parents), play, nutrition and health.
- **Social development:** Learning to form relationships with others, communication skills, discipline and a sense of independence. Influenced by communication, discipline and parental example.

Physical development

Social development

- **Mental development:** Learning to talk, play, read, solve problems, etc. Influenced by intelligence, encouragement, play and communication.
- **Emotional development:** Learning to deal with feelings, to give and receive love and to develop confidence and self-esteem. Influenced by affection, attention, encouragement and discipline.

Emotional development

'Mol an óige agus tiocfaidh sí.'

Good parents will provide an environment that encourages and promotes their child's development. To do this, parents must be aware of their child's **needs**, which include:

- **Physical care:** Protection, food, hygiene, rest and shelter.
- **Affection:** Physical contact, tenderness, approval, patience and understanding.
- **Security:** A stable family life, regular routines and a predictable home environment.
- **Stimulation:** Providing opportunities for play and education, praise, attention and encouragement.
- **Guidance and control:** Helping the child to learn acceptable behaviour and discipline.
- **Responsibility:** For looking after him/herself and his/her toys or clothes, and later on, for making decisions.
- **Independence:** With protection, but not overprotection. Overprotection may put pressure on a child and can lead to difficulties.

www.rollercoaster.ie
www.pbs.org/wholechild/
abc/index.html

Activities

1 Discuss (a) the type of play and (b) the type of toys which would help a child's physical and mental development.

2 Discuss how children learn social skills.

3 Make a list of the important nutrients which should be included in a child's diet to help physical development.

Option one
CHILD CARE

Chapter 39
Food and nutrition

For the first three months of life, milk is all the baby needs, as it provides all the necessary nutrients for the baby's growth and development. Babies may be breastfed or bottle fed.

Weblink
www.kidsandnutrition.co.uk

Babies being breast or bottle fed

Breastfeeding

Breastfeeding has many **advantages**:

1 Nutrients are present in the correct proportion for the baby's needs.
2 The baby is less likely to overfeed and become overweight, both as a baby and later in life.
3 Develops close bonding between mother and baby.
4 Gives pleasure to mother and baby.
5 Breastfed babies have better mental development, better mouth formation and straighter teeth.
6 The mother passes on resistance to infection.
7 Reduces the risk of developing eczema, asthma and skin rashes.
8 Reduces the risk of stomach upsets, coughs, colds and ear infections.

9 For the mother, there is less risk of breast and ovarian cancer and osteoporosis.

10 Helps the mother's uterus return to its normal size so she regains her figure more quickly.

11 Breast milk costs nothing and is available at all times.

12 There is no need to prepare bottles or sterilise equipment.

> Breast milk can be expressed and stored in the fridge.

Disadvantages:

1 The mother may feel embarrassed when feeding in public places.

2 May cause soreness to the breasts.

3 The father is excluded from feeding the baby unless the mother expresses milk.

4 The baby may have to be given vitamin drops to supplement breast milk.

Bottle feeding

Advantages:

1 Allows the mother more freedom.

2 The father and others may feed the baby and become more closely involved.

Disadvantages:

1 Does not provide protection against infection.

2 More expensive than breastfeeding.

3 Time-consuming to prepare feeds and sterilise equipment.

> **Infant formula milk** is made from cow's milk which is changed to make it as close as possible to breast milk. Soy milk formula is available for vegan babies and those who are allergic to cow's milk.

Prepared feeds may be stored in the refrigerator. To heat a feed, stand the bottle in a jug of hot water. Test the temperature on the inside of your wrist – it should feel comfortably warm. If using a microwave, shake bottle well after heating to avoid 'hot spots'. Check temperature as before.

Winding

All babies swallow some air with their feeds and may suffer from wind in the stomach. To help bring up the wind, hold the baby upright against your shoulder and gently rub or pat the baby's back until the wind is released.

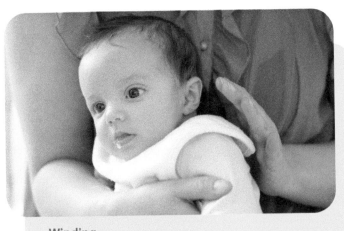

Winding

Weaning

Weaning is the process of introducing solid foods into the baby's diet with their usual milk feeds. The best time to start weaning is usually between four and six months. Signals that the baby is ready for weaning include:

- unsatisfied after a full milk feed
- attempting to put things in his/her mouth
- waking in the night with hunger
- sucking his/her fists vigorously.

> Introducing solids earlier than four months is not recommended, as the baby may not be able to digest the food properly.

Suitable foods include:

- baby rice or gluten-free cereal mixed with breast or formula milk
- puréed vegetables, e.g. broccoli, carrot, cauliflower, turnip, peas, beans, parsnip
- puréed fruit, e.g. apple, pear, banana
- mashed potato
- puréed meat, chicken or white fish
- melted cheese.

There is a wide variety of commercial baby foods available on the market, including jars, tins, packets and cartons. These are useful when travelling, for emergencies or when family food is not suitable, e.g. if it is too spicy. However, they can be expensive.

Gluten-free symbol

Foods to **avoid** include:

- low-fat or high-fibre foods
- wheat-based cereals (containing gluten) until the baby is six months old, as there may be the risk of coeliac disease
- foods with added sugar or salt: salt can put pressure on a baby's immature kidneys; and sugar can lead to the development of a 'sweet tooth'.

Commercial baby foods

Introducing a varied diet

From about eight months, the baby should be eating a varied diet which contains all the essential nutrients.

Link...

Chapter 3 A Balanced Diet

Include the following in a varied diet:

- fingers of toast
- raw vegetables, e.g. carrots and celery
- pasta shapes and rice
- fresh fruit pieces
- rusks
- boiled or scrambled eggs
- yoghurt
- diluted fruit juices.

Avoid highly spiced, fatty or fried foods.

Feeding toddlers

A plastic plate with a suction base and a two-handled feeder cup are useful when a child is learning to feed him/herself. Serve small portions of food that are colourful and attractive and with varied textures. Avoid giving sweets, chocolate and crisps between meals. Offer fresh fruit, dried fruit, popcorn, yoghurt, smoothies or crackers instead.

Research shows that nourishing food not only makes a child healthier, it makes him/her emotionally more stable and it improves concentration.

Activity

1 Examine a variety of commercial baby foods. Collect information from the containers and record your findings in a table like the one below.

Brand	Pack type	Meals per pack	Recommended age	Storage instructions	Price

2 Suggest interesting and exciting ways of encouraging a five-year-old to eat vegetables.

Chapter 40
Hygiene and safety

A baby is helpless and must rely on his/her parents to provide hygienic surroundings.

Food hygiene

A breastfed baby will receive a certain amount of immunity from his/her mother. However, all babies are at risk of infection if proper hygiene guidelines are not followed.

1   Wash hands before handling the baby's food or beginning feeding.

2   Use freshly boiled, cooled water for mixing feeds in sterilised bottles.

3   Store made-up feeds in the fridge for up to 24 hours.

4   Never keep milk warm for long periods and discard unfinished feeds.

5   After use, rinse bottle and teats in cold water. Then wash in hot, soapy water using a bottle brush and a teat brush.

6   Rinse and sterilise using one of the following methods:

   a) **Boiling** (for 20 minutes).

   b) **Steaming** in a steam steriliser. This takes approximately 10 minutes.

   c) **Chemical sterilisation.** Washed bottles and teats are placed in a sterilising solution, e.g. Milton, for 30 minutes.

Small plastic toys and some teething rings can also be sterilised using any of these methods.

Bottle brush   Steam steriliser

Bathing

A small baby should be bathed every day. If this is not possible, he/she should be 'topped and tailed'. This means washing the face and hands and washing and drying the nappy area. Use two separate washing bowls to avoid spreading infection from one area to another.

Toilet training

Children often show signs of being ready for toilet training between 18 and 24 months, but some children may not be ready until 30 months or older. A child is ready when he/she is able to walk without help, is aware when he/she is about to empty the bladder or bowels and has a fair understanding of language.

It is important that the child is toilet trained in a relaxed, happy atmosphere, as stress can slow down the process. Encouragement and praise will help a child to gain confidence. Other aids such as training pants, a trainer seat on the toilet and a step-stool will help to make the changeover easier for the toddler.

Aids for toilet training

Teeth

A baby's teeth are already formed at birth and usually start to come through at between five and seven months. To keep a baby's teeth healthy, limit sugary foods and avoid sweet drinks. Never put a baby to bed with a bottle of milk or fruit juice. Allow only plain water.

Teeth cleaning should start as soon as teeth appear. A soft cloth with a little toothpaste may be used at first, and later a special baby toothbrush.

There are 20 teeth in a baby's first set, known as **milk teeth**.

By 2½ years all the milk teeth will have come through.

Link...

Teeth, page 276

Safety

Accidents in and around the home are the most common causes of death or injury of young children. However, many of these accidents can be prevented if proper care is taken to make the danger areas in the home safe.

Link...

Chapter 28 Safety and First Aid

In the kitchen

Keep a fire extinguisher in the kitchen

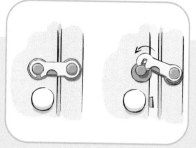

Doorknob covers and door locks keep children out of hazardous areas

Door stops and door holders prevent small fingers being crushed

Use corner and edge bumpers to prevent injuries from falls against sharp edges

Don't let tablecloths drag

Keep toys out of the kitchen

Put a child-resistant catch on drawers with knives

Check labels to make sure toys are safe for child's age, e.g. 'Warning: Choking hazard 0–3 years'

Buy short, coiled flexes for appliances

All household cleaners should be in a cupboard with a child-resistant lock

Fit a child-proof lock on the fridge

Put away appliances after use

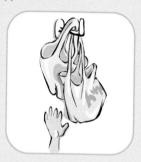

Keep polythene bags out of reach

Fit a guard around the hob

Use back rings

Turn saucepan handles back

In the living room

Houseplants should be placed out of children's reach

Ensure windows are closed and locked when children are around

Keep chairs and other furniture away from windows

Use a heater guard

Use safety covers on sockets

Fit an extending fire guard

In the bathroom

Use a cordless phone to ensure constant supervision of children in the bath

Keep medicines out of reach

Never use an electric heater or other electrical appliances in the bathroom

Put a bathmat in the baby's bath to prevent slips and to give extra security

On the stairs or at doorways

Use safety gates

Activity

List four ways you could prevent accidents to children in:
(a) the garden; (b) the bathroom; (c) the kitchen; (d) the car.

Chapter 41
Clothing

A **layette** is a complete set of clothes required for a newborn baby.

It may include the following:

- two baby blankets
- seven bodysuits or vests
- seven all-in-one stretchsuits/babygros
- three cardigans
- two hats
- one or two all-in-one suits (for outdoors)
- one or two pairs of mittens
- seven bibs
- one or two pairs of bootees.

This may seem like a lot of clothes, but young babies often bring up a little milk after a feed and nappies can leak. A household's wash load can increase significantly with the arrival of a new baby!

Guidelines for buying clothes

1 Buy a size that will last for at least two months.
2 Choose machine-washable items that don't require ironing.
3 Choose clothes that are easy to put on and take off.
4 Stretch garments with enclosed feet and mittens are useful for day and nightwear, as they are comfortable and keep out draughts.
5 Fabrics should be soft and comfortable, with no hard seams or rough stitching.
6 Nightwear should be flame resistant.
7 Avoid loose, lacy knitwear, as a baby's fingers can get caught in the holes.
8 Hand-knit garments should have a loose neck and wrist edges, with no ridges or bobbles.
9 Buttons should be firmly attached.
10 Choose garments without ribbons around the wrists, ankles or neck.

Suitable fabrics for baby clothes include:

- cotton jersey
- stretch terry towelling
- nylon
- knitted fabrics
- cotton/nylon mixtures
- acrylic.

Nappies

For modern parents, the choice is between cloth (bamboo or cotton) or disposable nappies. The choice may depend on cost, availability, convenience, lifestyle and environmental concerns.

- Cloth nappies are used with liners and nappy covers.
- Disposable nappies are available in a range of sizes.

Weblink

www.littlecomfort.com

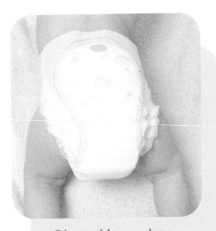

Disposable nappies

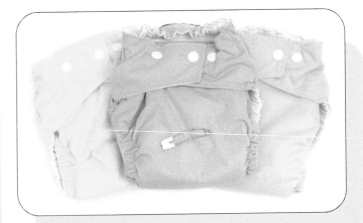

Cloth nappies

Chapter 42
Health and child care facilities

All babies are entitled to free health care, which is provided by baby clinics at local health centres and by home visits from the public health nurse.

Baby clinics are run by health centres. They provide health and developmental checks (sight, hearing and physical development) to ensure that there are no health problems.

The **public health nurse** visits mother and baby in their home to check on the baby's progress and to advise the mother on care and feeding of the baby. The nurse provides information on baby clinics and immunisations.

Immunisation

Babies are immunised/vaccinated against certain diseases such as tuberculosis, polio, whooping cough, tetanus and meningitis. Later, they receive vaccinations against measles, mumps and rubella.

The timetable on the next page gives details of the immunisations a child requires.

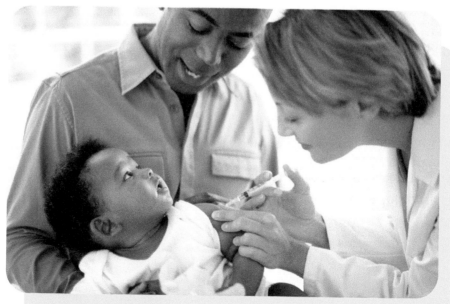

Baby being vaccinated

Immunisation schedule

Age to vaccinate	Type of vaccination
At birth	● BCG tuberculosis vaccine
2 months	● 6 in 1 (diphtheria, tetanus, whooping cough, Hib (haemophilus influenza B), polio, hepatitis B) ● PCV (pneumococcal conjugate vaccine)
4 months	● 6 in 1 ● Men C (meningococcal C)
6 months	● 6 in 1 ● Men C ● PCV
12 months	● MMR (measles, mumps, rubella) ● PCV
13 months	● Men C ● Hib
4–5 years	● 4 in 1 (diphtheria, tetanus, whooping cough, polio) ● MMR
11–14 years	● Td (tetanus, diphtheria)
12 years	● HPV (human papillomavirus)

Voluntary organisations for parents and children

Weblink

www.immunisation.ie

There is a wide variety of voluntary organisations in Ireland which provide services for parents and children. The following is just a small sample of what is available.

● **La Leche League:** A support group for breastfeeding mothers. www.lalecheleagueireland.com
● **Irish Society for the Prevention of Cruelty to Children (ISPCC):** A support service for parents and children. It operates Childline, a free phone-in service for children in distress. www.ispcc.ie
● **Irish Pre-School Playgroups Association:** Promotes quality play-based early childhood education and care. www.ippa.ie
● **Irish Society for Autism:** Provides support and services for autistic children. www.autism.ie

See also:

● www.asthmasociety.ie
● www.cura.ie
● www.downsyndrome.ie

Community services

The local health offices of the HSE (Health Service Executive) provide:

- **Family Support Services,** which include:
  - parenting skills
  - confidence and personal development
  - home care management
  - diet, nutrition and health care
  - budgeting and family finance.

- **Child Protection Social Workers** provide care, assessment and follow-up for children at risk of harm through abuse, and their families, through the Fostering and Child Protection Teams.

- **Foster Care** offers alternative family care to children whose parents cannot provide this for them in their own families, for a variety of reasons.

- **Child and Adolescent Mental Health Services** provide support for those experiencing difficulties with relationships, anxiety or depression.

- **Child Development and Education Services** such as:
  - crèches
  - nurseries
  - playgroups
  - pre-schools
  - homework clubs
  - after-school clubs.

Child care facilities

Child care facilities have increased significantly in recent years due to increasing demand from parents. The options for child care include the following:

- **Relatives** may be willing to look after a child.
- A **nanny** or **au pair** minds a child in the child's home.
- **Childminders** care for children in their own home.
- **Nurseries** provide full day care for a number of children.
- **Crèches** offer short-term care for children.
- **Community facilities,** as described above.
- **Private playgroups** are fee paying.
- **Kindergarten** and **Montessori pre-schools** are run in a child-friendly learning environment.
- **Private homework clubs** for older school-going children.

Guidelines for choosing child care facilities

- The premises should be spacious, safe and clean, with access to outside play space.
- There should be a good variety of activities and toys to stimulate a child's development.
- Safety equipment should be used where appropriate.
- Toilet and changing areas should be adequate.
- The carers should be well trained, caring and interested in children.
- The ratio of carers to children should be 1:3 for children under one year, 1:5 for children aged one to two and 1:8 for children aged three to eight.
- A fire drill procedure should be in place.
- There should be easy access for parents with buggies.
- Check insurance cover.
- Check that the facility is notified to the HSE.

Children at playschool

Activity

1 Find out what community services are available for parents and children in your own area.

2 Survey your classmates to find out what type of child care (if any) their parents use.

Chapter 43
Children with special needs

Some children have special needs due to a disability. A disability is a weakness or failure of some part of the body or brain. Greater effort is needed to do essential things like seeing, walking, talking, learning, eating and breathing.

There are four types of disability:

- **physical**, e.g. not able to walk properly
- **intellectual**, e.g. not able to learn or understand at a normal rate
- **sensory**, e.g. blind, deaf or unable to speak
- **emotional**, e.g. having difficulty in relating to others.

A **congenital** disability is one which is present at birth. Other disabilities may occur as a result of an accident or illness.

The following disabilities can affect children:

- ADD/ADHD (attention deficit disorder/attention deficit hyperactivity disorder)
- Asperger's syndrome
- asthma
- autism
- blindness
- brain damage
- cerebral palsy
- cystic fibrosis
- deafness
- Down's syndrome
- epilepsy
- hydrocephalus
- muscular dystrophy
- OCD (obsessive-compulsive disorder)
- spina bifida.

Here is some information on a few common disabilities.

- **Cystic fibrosis:** Overproduction of a sticky mucus by the glands of the body, leading to respiratory infections, breathing difficulties and failure to gain weight.
- **Down's syndrome:** Caused by a defect in part of the cell before birth. It is indicated by physical appearance and intellectual disabilities.
- **Cerebral palsy:** Caused by brain damage at or before birth. The symptoms are paralysis and/or jerky movements.
- **Autism:** A developmental disability caused by a disorder of the brain. The symptoms are an inability to communicate and interact with others and an insensitivity to pain.

Weblink

www.disability.ie
www.snapireland.net

Children with physical disabilities may have problems in mastering certain skills, but these problems can be overcome with praise, encouragement and support. These children are usually bright and eager to learn and should be treated as such.

Special needs

Children with disabilities need special help to achieve their full potential. This help includes:

- Extra care and attention.
- Special clothes, footwear, equipment, e.g. for those with spina bifida.
- Special transport for physically disabled children, e.g. adapted cars or wheelchairs.
- Special accommodation for physically disabled children, e.g. ramps, wide doorways, stair lift, toilet rails.
- Special medication, diet or hospital treatment.
- Special education for children who are blind, deaf or have learning difficulties.
- Physiotherapy or speech therapy for children with physical disabilities.

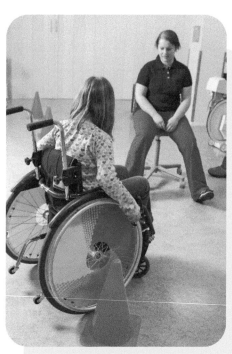

A child with special needs

Help and support is available from a number of organisations, such as:

- Special Olympics Ireland – www.specialolympics.ie
- Make a Wish Foundation – www.makeawish.ie
- National Council of the Blind of Ireland – www.ncbi.ie
- Enable Ireland Disability Service – www.enableireland.ie
- Down Syndrome Ireland – www.downsyndrome.ie
- Irish Association for Spina Bifida and Hydrocephalus – www.sbhi.ie

Activity

1 Which of the disabilities in the list on page 427 are (a) physical; (b) intellectual; (c) sensory; (d) emotional?

Chapter 44
The family and the law

> '...where the parents, for physical or moral reasons, fail in their duty towards their children, the state ... shall endeavour to supply the place of the parents...'
>
> Bunreacht na hÉireann, Article 42.5

Parents are legally responsible for providing food, clothing, medical care, shelter and education for their children. If they are unable to provide for their children, they must seek help from state or voluntary bodies.

The following are examples of laws which apply to the family.

- **Family Home Protection Act 1976** prevents one parent selling the family home without the consent of the other. This ensures that children are provided with shelter and accommodation.
- **Family Law (Maintenance of Spouses and Children) Act 1976** may be applied where a couple are separated or divorced. The partner who is working must provide financial support for any children.
- **Status of Children Act 1987** gives equal rights to maintenance and inheritance to children born within or outside of marriage.
- **Domestic Violence Act 1996** is used to protect a spouse, partner or anyone in the household by imposing a safety order, a protection order or a barring order against any member of the household who threatens or uses violence.
- **Family Law (Divorce) Act 1996** sets out the conditions for divorce.
- **Children Act 1997** makes it possible for an unmarried father to become joint guardian of his child without applying to the courts.
- **Child Care Act 1997** allows the HSE to take a child into care if he/she is at risk.

Help and advice

There are many organisations and institutions involved in providing help and advice to families who may need it.

- **Clanwilliam Institute:** Provides family therapy and mediation – www.clanwilliam.ie
- **One Family:** Provides services such as child care and parenting courses to one-parent families in Ireland – http://onefamily.ie
- **Adapt:** Provides shelter and support to women experiencing domestic violence and their children – www.safeireland.ie
- **Parent Line:** Offers a confidential helpline to parents who may need help and advice – www.parentline.ie
- **Alcoholics Anonymous, Al-Anon, Alateen:** Fellowships of adults and children whose lives have been affected by alcohol abuse – www.alcoholicsanonymous.ie
- **Barnardos:** Provides a wide range of family support services, including counselling, court representation and tracing services – www.barnardos.ie
- **Teen Between:** A specialised support service for teenagers whose parents are going through a divorce or separation. It can also help young adults who have experienced their parents' separation during their teenage years – www.teenbetween.ie
- **Families Anonymous, Narcotics Anonymous** and **Nar-Anon:** Fellowships of individuals and families affected by drug abuse – www.na-ireland.org
- **Rainbows** supports children, youth and adults after bereavement, divorce or separation – www.rainbowsireland.com

Activity

Find out about organisations in your area that are involved with the family.

Chapter 45
Child care project

As part of the Child Care Option you are required to do a project on a topic related to child development. This represents 15 per cent of the total mark for Junior Certificate Home Economics. The emphasis is on **child development from 0 to 12 years**, so the chosen topic must relate to this.

Choose the topic with your class teacher. Ensure that you pick a topic that interests you and one that you are capable of completing to an acceptable standard. It should be original and should show your creativity.

Suggested topics include:

- the importance of play
- childhood immunisations
- a child development case study
- infant nutrition
- child safety in the home
- toy safety
- a babysitter's manual
- the effect of a disability on child development
- dental development
- meningitis in children
- childhood asthma
- the influence of pre-school on child development
- breastfeeding versus bottle feeding.

Methods of research

- Library **books:** but do not copy directly from books.
- **Internet:** do not copy directly or use full printouts.
- **Letters:** to voluntary organisations and companies.
- **Visits** and **observations:** shops, pre-schools, clinics, dental surgeries.
- **Questionnaires** and **interviews:** parents, children, doctor, dentist, teacher.
- **Practical work:** tests, examinations.
- Information **leaflets:** available from clinics and surgeries.
- **Discussion:** with classmates, teachers, parents, children.

Presentation of the project

Your project should include:

- **Table of contents:** Include page numbers here and number each page.
- **Aims** of the project: Should be well developed and **relevant** to child development.
- **Methods of research:** Give details of how you investigated your topic and the techniques you used to gather information. At least **two** forms of research should be used.
- **Main content:** This should be relevant to your aim and show in-depth investigation of the topic. The information must be accurate and well organised. Results of questionnaires, tests, etc. must be presented here. Include plenty of pictures/graphics to break up text.
- **Conclusions:** Refer back to the results of the investigation and give **two** well-developed points relating to the aims and content of the project.
- **Acknowledgements:** Thank those who helped you with your project and those who supplied information.
- **Bibliography/sources of information:** List books (titles and authors), leaflets, websites, etc. from which you got information.
- **Appendix:** Include copies of letters sent and received, interviews and questionnaires, etc.
- Finally, the project should not exceed **1,500** words.

A craft item (presented with a design folder) may be used **if it relates to some aspect of child development,** e.g. a soft toy or mobile. The craft item on its own would not be viewed as a full project without evidence of research, development of solutions and evaluation.

Marking scheme

Part of exam	Graded on		Marks
Aim of project	● Clear statement ● Relevance		10
Research methodology/ problem	● Analysis ● Information-gathering techniques used and/or investigation of task		20
Content	● Relevance to aim ● Depth of treatment ● Testing information	● Practical work, e.g. models, etc. ● Accurate information ● Organisation of materials	40
Conclusion	● Conclusion drawn from results of investigation, to include a critical evaluation of any product produced against stated aims		10
Originality	● Indication of original input by way of analysis, interpretation and/or development of topic by the candidate		10
Presentation	● Layout ● Spelling/writing skills	● Quality of graphics, etc. ● Finish of product	10

Option two
Textile skills

Chapter 46
Textile skills

The Textiles Option is worth 15 per cent of the total mark for Junior Certificate Home Economics. This option is assessed by project only. It is **not** assessed on the written paper. For your project you must produce:

- **one or two items of clothing (80 marks)**
- **a support study folder (20 marks).**

Making the garment(s) (80 marks)

Self-made clothes are unique. They allow you to express your style. Modern patterns can be viewed online, and the wide range of fabrics available today allows you to be very creative.

Commercial patterns

Paper patterns for garments are made by various manufacturers, such as Simplicity, Style and Burda. Patterns are chosen from **pattern catalogues** and they are sold in **pattern envelopes**. The envelope contains the **tissue pattern** and an **instruction sheet**. A number of variations (views) of the garment are offered which have different features.

You should take approximately the same size in a pattern as in a ready-to-wear garment. Most patterns contain a range of sizes. The measurements for each size are given on a size chart.

Personal measurements

- Measurements should be taken before you buy a pattern.
- Get a friend to measure you, as it is easier than trying to measure yourself.
- Remove outer garments such as jacket and jumper.
- Use a tape measure that does not stretch.
- Stand straight, holding your shoulders back.
- Pull the tape measure so that it is snug, but not too tight.
- Recheck all measurements.
- Write down the measurements carefully.

Taking measurements

- **Height:** Remove shoes and measure height from top of head to toe.
- **Chest/bust:** Measure around the fullest part of the chest/bust. Raise the tape slightly at the back for bust measurement.
- **Waist:** Measure snugly around the waistline.
- **Hips:** Measure around the fullest part of the hips, usually 18–23cm below the waistline.
- **Back length:** Measure from the nape of the neck in a straight line to the waist.
- **Sleeve length:** Measure from shoulder to slightly bent elbow and from elbow to wrist.
- **Neck width:** Measure around the neck and add 12mm to this measurement.
- **Outside leg:** Measure from the side waistline to the required height from the floor.
- **Inside leg:** Measure from the crotch to the required length from floor.

Buying a pattern

- Choose a pattern that is easy to make.
- For Junior Certificate, you must include two processes such as sleeve, pocket, collar, zip or buttonhole.
- Choose a pattern that can be made using easy-to-sew fabric.
- The pattern should suit the wearer's figure.
- Consider the cost of the pattern.

Choosing fabric

- Consider the **cost** of the fabric.
- Check the **width.** Fabric is sold in 90cm, 115cm, 120cm, 140cm and 150cm widths.
- Consider the **colour** and **pattern** of the fabric.
- Fabric should **not fray too much** and should not have flaws.
- Fabric should be **easy to sew** and therefore should be non-slip and **not be too stretchy.**
- Check the **weight** of the fabric.
- Work out the **amount** of fabric you need and check whether this amount is available in the shop.
- Avoid fabric with a **nap** or **one-way design** (see page 394).

Understanding the pattern envelope

The envelope front shows:

- a front view of each garment
- the manufacturer's name
- the pattern reference number
- a letter or number for each style
- the range of sizes included in the pattern
- a back view of each garment.

The instruction sheet

The instruction sheet, which is found in the pattern envelope, includes:

- information on preparing the pattern
- diagrams of all the pattern pieces included
- lists of the pattern pieces needed for each view
- instructions for altering the pattern
- instructions for laying out the pattern on fabric of various widths
- cutting instructions
- a step-by-step guide to making the garment.

Pattern envelope: Learn to Sew

Pattern envelope: junior sportswear

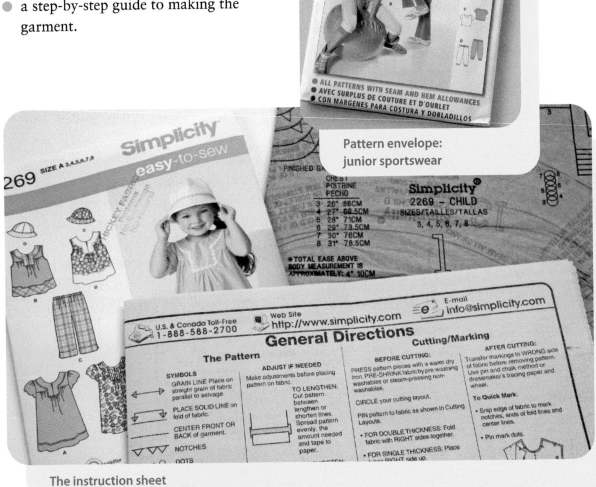

The instruction sheet

The tissue pattern

Pattern pieces are printed on large sheets of tissue. You must cut out the pieces that you need for your chosen garment. This information will be shown on the instruction sheet. Each piece of the pattern includes:

- number, name and size of pattern
- number and name of the pattern piece
- a variety of symbols which must be transferred onto the fabric: these are called **pattern symbols**.

Pattern symbols

Straight grain	⟶	Pattern pieces should be placed on the fabric so that the arrow is running along the warp, i.e. parallel to the selvage.
Fold line	↓ ↓	The arrows should be placed on the fold of the fabric.
Notches	▶	These are used to match one piece of fabric to another. Cut notches outwards.
Cutting line	—	This heavy line on the outer edge of the pattern piece is where you cut the fabric. If your pattern does not have a cutting line, allow a 1.5cm seam allowance.
Stitching line	- - - - - - -	Machine on this line in the direction of the arrows.
Balance marks	●	These mark important points on the garment, such as the end of an opening. They are also used for matching.
Button position	✕	These show where the button should be placed.
Buttonhole	⊢—⊣	These show where the buttonhole should be made.
Alteration lines	═	Cut pattern between these lines to lengthen or shorten.

Altering the pattern

Check all the measurements on the pattern pieces against your personal ones, measuring from inside the seam allowance. You may need to alter the length or width. Small alterations can be done while sewing by letting a seam allowance in or out. Larger alterations must be done on the pattern pieces before laying them on the fabric. The pattern pieces are marked with a lengthening/shortening line.

Lengthening

Example: Adding 2cm to the length of a pair of shorts.

1. Draw two parallel lines 2cm apart on a sheet of paper.
2. Cut the pattern between the alteration lines.
3. Lay the pattern pieces on the sheet of paper with one pattern piece along each of the parallel lines.
4. Pin or glue in place.
5. Redraw the cutting line.

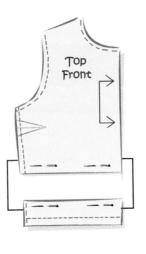
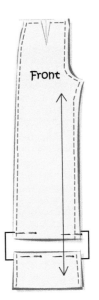

Shortening

Example: Shortening a sleeve by 2cm.

1. Make a fold at the alteration lines.
2. The fold should measure half the amount to be reduced, therefore 1cm in this example.
3. Pin or glue the fold in place.
4. Redraw the cutting line.

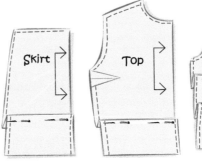
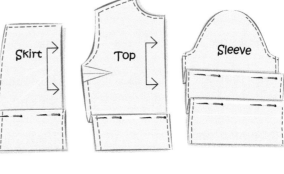

Increasing width

Example: Adding 2cm to the width of a pattern piece.

1. Draw two parallel lines 2cm apart on a sheet of paper.
2. Draw a vertical line on the pattern piece and cut on the line.
3. Lay the pattern pieces on the sheet of paper, with one pattern piece along each of the parallel lines.
4. Pin or glue in place.
5. Redraw the cutting line.

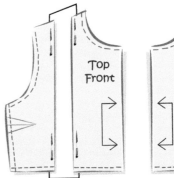
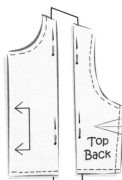

Note: When you increase the width of a pattern piece, all other pieces attached to it must also be widened.

Reducing width

Example: Reducing the width of a pattern piece by 3cm.

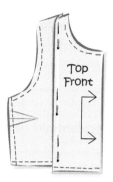

1 Draw a vertical line on the pattern piece.
2 Make a fold at the line.
3 The fold should measure half the amount to be reduced, therefore 1.5cm in this example.
4 Pin or glue the fold in place.
5 Redraw the cutting and sewing lines.

Preparing the pattern

1 Identify the pattern pieces which you need for the style you have chosen. (A list of pieces for each style is on the instruction sheet.)
2 Cut out the pieces from the tissue pattern.
3 Alter the pattern if necessary.

Preparing the fabric

1 Press the fabric.
2 Straighten the cut edges of the fabric by cutting along a thread line.
3 Fold the fabric as shown on the instruction sheet.
4 Highlight any flaws on the fabric using chalk so that they can be avoided when laying out the pattern.

Laying out the pattern

1 Place the pattern on the fabric according to the diagram on your instruction sheet.
2 Put large pieces in place first and then fit in the smaller pieces.
3 Make sure that the straight grain symbol is exactly on the grain line. Use a tape measure to check it.
4 Make sure that the fold line symbol is placed exactly on the fold.
5 Some pattern pieces may need to be cut out more than once. Cut 1, Cut 2, etc. will be written on each piece.
6 Pin each pattern piece in place.
7 Some patterns do not include a seam allowance. In this case use tailor's chalk to draw the cutting line on the fabric.

Cutting out the garment

1 Keep the fabric flat on the table.
2 Place one hand flat on the pattern.
3 Open the scissors wide and, using large strokes, cut on the cutting line.
4 Cut outwards around notches.

Transferring pattern markings

Pattern marks such as balance marks and button positions must be transferred onto the fabric before removing the pattern. You can transfer pattern marks using any of the following methods.

Tracing paper and wheel

1 Remove the pattern from the fabric and turn the fabric right side out.
2 Fold the carbon paper right side out and place it between the two layers of fabric.
3 Pin the pattern in position again.
4 Run the tracing wheel along the fitting lines, etc.
5 Mark X to indicate dots.

Tracing paper and wheel

Tailor's chalk

1 If seam allowance is not included in the pattern, draw around the pattern pieces to indicate the fitting line. Draw another line 1.5cm outside the fitting line to indicate the cutting line.
2 Use a ruler to draw straight lines.
3 Marks using tailor's chalk can be removed by brushing.

Tailor tacks

This is an excellent method of marking exact points on double fabric. See page 397 for guidelines.

Tailor's chalk

Making the garment

Your instruction sheet will show you the correct sequence for making your garment. In general, the following steps are followed:

1 Tack the main seams and darts by hand and make any fitting alteration before machine stitching.
2 Each section, e.g. the collar, is made first and then joined to the others.
3 Test the stitch length and tension on a scrap of fabric before stitching the garment.
4 Finish each seam, then press each seam and dart as soon as it is complete.

Making a garment

Fitting

- Once the main seams are tacked, pin the other seams together.
- Try on the garment right side out and pin any openings together.
- The garment should be comfortable when you move and stretch.
- If alterations are needed, remove the tacking and pin the new fitting line.
- Tack the fitting lines and follow the checklist below before stitching.

Fitting checklist

1 The garment should hang straight.
2 The shoulder seam should lie on top of the shoulder and not slope to the front or back.
3 Darts should taper towards the fullest part of the area which they shape.
4 Sleeves should hang straight.
5 Side, back and front seams should be straight and vertical.
6 Hem should be even and parallel to the ground.
7 The waistline should be on the waist.

Common alterations

Sloping shoulders

When a person has sloping shoulders, the shoulder seam is too loose at the armhole and generally too tight at the neck. The seam is generally taken in near the armhole and tapered towards the neck.

Tightness or looseness at waist and hips

The width can be increased by letting out the side seams. Garments can also be taken in, i.e. width reduced, at the side seams. Make equal alterations on both sides of the garment.

Fitting trousers

Tightness or looseness at the crotch of trousers can be corrected by lowering or raising the waistline. The zip position may need to be altered as a result.

Pressing

Pressing fabric means applying heat and pressure with the iron.

- Use a damp pressing cloth between the iron and the fabric if pressing on the right side of the fabric.
- Press the fabric along the grain to avoid stretching it.
- Press on the wrong side of the fabric to prevent shine.

Support study folder (20 marks)

Your support study folder must include **five** areas of information.

These two areas **must** be included:

- **factors** influencing choice of garment
- **evaluation.**

Three other areas should be described, such as:

- **pattern**
- **fabric**
- **sewing accessories**
- **equipment used.**

How to present your folder

1 Factors influencing choice of garment

Describe at least **three** of the following:

- my own skills
- availability of fabric
- my body shape
- fashion
- my budget.

2 Pattern

Describe:

- details of the pattern
- any modifications made.

3 Fabric

Describe:

- amount of fabric used
- cost
- composition (fabric test may be included).

4 Sewing accessories

Describe the notions, e.g. zips, buttons and fasteners, which you used.

5 Evaluation

In your evaluation, include reference to:

- the **finish** of the garment(s). Evaluate the seams and seam finishes, hems, pockets, zips, buttonholes, etc.
- the **fit** of the garment(s).

What would you change if you were to do it again?

The textile industry

The textile industry in Ireland employs people in a variety of areas, such as:

- fibre production, e.g. invention of new fibres such as microfibres
- yarn production, e.g. spinning
- fabric production, e.g. weaving or knitting, dyeing fabrics and fabric finishes
- production of fabric-based products, e.g. clothes, household textile items and soft furnishings
- design and manufacture of clothes and textile products
- retail.

Designers linked with the fashion industry in Ireland include:

- Joanne Hynes
- Philip Treacy
- Orla Kiely
- John Rocha
- Marc O'Neill
- Quinn and Donnelly
- Paul Costelloe
- Louise Kennedy.

Weblink

www.google.ie/images
Search for Joanne Hynes

Clothes designed by Joanne Hynes

Clothes designed by Paul Costelloe

Option three

Design and craftwork

Chapter 47
Design and craftwork

The Design and Craftwork Option makes up 15 per cent of the total mark for Junior Certificate Home Economics. This option is assessed by project only. It is **not** assessed on the written paper. For your project you must produce a **textile craft item** (70 marks) and a **design folder** (30 marks). The folder should contain a step-by-step account of the work you did as you produced the craft item.

Irish craftwork

Craft

Craft means using skill to create objects using various materials.

The craftsperson works on a material such as wood or clay to produce a craft item. Craft workers usually take great pride in their work. Examples of craft items are pottery tableware, glass, ceramics, metal jewellery and wood carvings.

Textile craft items are made using yarns or fabrics. Examples of textile crafts are appliqué, cross stitch, patchwork and toy making. Some crafts are **traditional** because they have been practised for hundreds of years. Knitting and weaving are examples of traditional crafts.

Contemporary crafts are modern crafts such as machine embroidery, which uses modern materials and designs.

Traditional Irish textile crafts

Contemporary Irish textile crafts

Craft industry in Ireland

At present the most important crafts in the Irish craft industry are pottery, glass, jewellery, textiles (especially knitwear), furniture and giftware. Many manufacturers use traditional, labour-intensive methods that require excellent skill. Therefore, many craft items are unique and special, unlike the many items that are mass produced in large factories.

The **Crafts Council of Ireland** is the national agency responsible for the development of craftwork in Ireland. It is an excellent source of information on the craftwork industry. It runs some training courses and helps to market craftwork both at home and abroad.

Weblink
www.ccoi.ie

Craftwork project

You must choose a craftwork item for your project. Consider the following **important** guidelines:

- Choose only a craftwork item which can be made using **textiles**.
- The item must include **enough craftwork** to show craft skills.
- If you choose embroidery, at least two stitch types must be shown.
- You must make an **item** with the craftwork, for example a cushion using patchwork or a table centre using embroidery.
- The craftwork item must fulfil the **brief** (the task given by your teacher).
- The craft and the materials chosen must suit the **function** (purpose) of the item. Therefore, items for babies should not have loose stitching.
- You must show a high level of **skill** when making the item. This is a **most important** aspect.
- The item should have an **attractive** design.
- You must show **creativity** in the design. Therefore, if you are using **commercial patterns,** modify the pattern by changing **two design features.** For copied designs, **investigate a range of stitches** and select your choice.
- The item must be properly **finished**. This means that all threads must be finished and the item should be pressed and clean.

Possible crafts

- appliqué
- embroidery
- knitting
- crochet
- lacework
- cross stitch
- toy making
- patchwork
- rug making
- weaving
- quilting
- macramé.

Possible craft items

- pet pillow
- storage systems, e.g. for toys, games consoles
- wall hanging
- quilt
- rug
- picture
- tableware, e.g. table runner, place mat
- clothes
- cushion cover
- play mat
- toy
- Christmas crafts.

The following crafts do not meet the requirements on their own:
- fabric painting
- batik
- tie-dye
- fabric printing.

Another needlework craft, e.g. embroidery, should also be included in the craft item.

Assessment of craft item

Marks are allocated as follows for the craft item:

- **Fulfilling the brief/suitability** of craft and materials used (brief must be stated) – 10 marks.
- **Application of skills** – 40 marks.
- **Design features** (aesthetic appeal and creativity) – 10 marks.
- **Quality or finish** of the item (item should be clean and pressed with all threads finished) – 10 marks.

Selection of textile crafts

The design folder

The design folder should contain **three** main sections.

1 **Statement and investigation of the brief (10 marks)**

   a) Statement of what you have been asked to do.

   b) Analysis – a list of the things that you must consider.

   c) At least two possible solutions must be suggested. Give evidence that you have investigated them.

2 **Solution (10 marks)**

   a) Choice and reasons for choice.

   b) Design, drawings, diagrams and pattern of chosen craft item. If you use a commercial pattern, **two modifications** (changes) must be made to it. If you use a **traditional craft,** a **history** of the craft must be presented **unless you modify the pattern.**

   c) List of materials and equipment and description of techniques. Samples of craftwork can be included to illustrate techniques.

   d) Work plan, showing what you intend to do during the various stages of your project.

3 **Evaluation (10 marks)**

   a) Does the item meet the brief? Why?

   b) Is the craft well done? How do you know?

   c) Is the design attractive? Why?

   d) Cost.

   e) Modification. What would you change if you were to do it again? Why? If a commercial pattern is used, modifications must be suggested in the evaluation.

Index

3V vouchers 226

accessories 364, 369
accidents 314–16, 320
    causes 314
    prevention 314–16
accompaniments, for food 75, 76
acid rain 349
acne 273, 275
acrylic 384
Adapt 430
ADD 427
addiction 290, 295, 296
additives, food 141–2, 146
    functions 141
    types 142
ADHD 427
adolescence 268
adolescents, diet for 25–6, 30
adults, diet for 26–27, 30
advertising 235, 251–6
    control 254, 256
    effective 252
    functions 252, 256
    methods 251, 256
Advertising Standards Authority
    254, 256
Aids 295
air pollution 349
Airtricity 333
Al-Anon 293, 296, 430
Alateen 293, 296, 430
alcohol 292–3, 294
    abuse 292, 296; effects of 292–3
    drinking, sensible 293
    unit 292
Alcoholics Anonymous 293, 296, 430
alveoli 279, 280
amenities 303, 304
American Pancakes 156
amino acids 4, 18, 19, 20, 21

amniotic fluid 266
anaemia 10, 12, 26
An Taisce 353
antiperspirants 273
aorta 283, 285
Apple Tart 180
appliances, household 324–31
    choosing 324–5, 331
    electrical 334
arteries 35, 282, 285
ascorbic acid see vitamin C
Asperger's syndrome 427
assertiveness 270, 271
asthma 427
atrium 283, 285
attention deficit disorder 427
attention deficit hyperactivity
    disorder 427
Aubergine Stew with Chickpeas 203
autism 427, 428
Avocado and Green Leaf Salad 206

babies
    bathing 418
    clothing for 421–2
    diet for 24, 30
    food hygiene for 417
baby clinics 423
backstitch 395, 405
bacteria 40, 41, 42–3, 46, 105, 108
    pathogenic 43, 46
Baked Berry Cheesecake 184
Baked Stuffed Trout 199
baking 73, 127–32, 133
    recipes 164–79
baking powder 129
bar codes 224, 227
barley 124
Barnardos 430
bar symbol, on care labels 371, 376
basting stitch 394–5

bathroom hygiene 345
batik 388
bed linen 356, 360
bedroom design 311
BER 341, 342
beri-beri 9
Berry Bakewell Tart 182
best before date 45, 46, 143, 146
bias (fabric) 386, 391
bile 19
bimetal strip 327, 331
binge drinking 292
birth 266
bleaching instructions 372
blindness 427
blind stitch 400, 405
blood 20, 281–5
    flow 283
    functions 282
    vessels 272, 276, 281, 282, 285
body odour 273, 275
boiling 71
Bord Bia Egg Quality Assurance
    Scheme 99, 101
Bord Gáis 333
bottle feeding 24, 414
brain damage 427
bread 126
    freezing 139
Bread, Corn 166
bread soda 129
Bread, Wholemeal 165
breakfast 49, 77–9
    dishes, recipes 154–7
    menus 51, 78
    trays 79
Breakfast Muffins 155
Breakfast Smoothie 154
breastfeeding 24, 413–14
    and diet 27–8, 30
breathing system 279–80

bronchi 279–80
bronchioli 279–80
Brunch Pasta 157
budgets 240
    advantages of 243
    household 242–3
    planning 240–3
Building Energy Rating 341, 342
bulk buying 225, 227
burns, treating 317–18
burn test (for fibres) 389
burst pipes 337
butter 105–6, 110
    types 105, 110
Butter Icing 173
buttonhole stitch 400, 405

caffeine 294
cake(s)
    fillings 173
    freezing 139
    icings 173
    making: 127–31; faults in 127;
        methods 130, 133
    mixes 131
    tins, preparing 131
calcium 11, 16
    deficiency diseases 11
    RDA 11
    sources 11
cambric 380
cancer 291, 293 *see also* lung cancer,
    skin cancer
canines (eye teeth) 276
canvas 380
capillaries 280, 282, 285
Caramel Apple Crumble 182
carbohydrates 4, 7–8, 16, 18–19, 21
    classification 8
    composition 7
    functions 8
    sources 8
cardiac muscle 282, 285
care labels 370–2, 376
carpets 356, 359
Carrot and Orange Soup 186
cash 225
caveat emptor 233
CCCI 254, 256
cellulose fibres 383
cementum 276, 277
Central Copy Clearance Ireland
    254, 256
central heating 338
cereal(s) 77, 122–6, 133
    cooking 125

fortified 123
grain, structure 122
nutritive value 122, 133
processing 123
products 123–5
refined 9, 16, 123
whole 9, 123
cerebral palsy 427, 428
cervix 264
CFCs 352–3
CFLs 341
chain stitch 398, 405
chain stores 219
cheese 107–9, 110
    composition 107
    cooking 109, 110
    nutritive value 107, 110
    production 108, 110
    types 108, 110
    uses 108–9, 110
Cheesecake, Baked Berry 184
Cheese, Leek and Potato Tortilla 158
Cheese and Onion Potato Bake 163
Cheese and Onion Tart 158
chemical change, in digestion
    18–19, 21
cheques 226
Chicken Baked with Plums 192
Chicken Casserole, Traditional 193
Chicken and Chorizo Stew 191
Chicken Goujons, Spiced 194
Chickpea Salad 204
chiffon 382
child
    development 408–12
    health 423–4
    protection 425
    safety 315, 418–20
Child and Adolescent Mental Health
    Services 425
Child Care Act 1997 429
child care facilities 425–6
Childline 262
children
    community services for 425
    diet for 25, 30, 413–16
    rights and responsibilities
        of 259, 263
    role of 260
    with special needs 427–8
Children Act 1997 429
Chilli Chicken Fajitas 159
Chocolate Brownies, Low-Fat 177
Chocolate Cake, Never Fail 168
choking, treating 318
cholesterol 284

chyme 19
cigarettes 290
circuit breaker, miniature 334
circulatory system 281–5
Citizen Information Centres 235
Clanwilliam Institute 430
classified ads 253
cleaning
    agents 322, 346–7
    equipment 345
climate change 349
clothes 362–9
    care of 370
    buying 363, 369
    functions 362, 369
Coconut Crumble Cookies 179
coeliac disease 37, 39
colour 305–6, 309
colour catchers 374, 376
colour run removers 374, 376
colour wheel 305
combustion-modified high-resilience
    foam 359, 361
Communauté Européenne symbol
    248, 325
communication 261, 263
compact fluorescent lights 341
composting 351, 354
conception 408
condensation 340, 342
conduction 70, 76, 327, 331, 338, 342
conflict 262
consumer(s) 214–16
    complaints 236–7
    information 235
    laws 232–4, 238
    programmes 235
    protection 232–8
    responsibilities 229, 231
    rights 229–30
Consumer Choice 234, 235
Consumer Information Act 1978 232,
    234, 238, 254, 256
Consumers' Association of Ireland 234,
    235, 238
consumer studies 214
continuous filaments 377, 391
convalescents, diet for 29, 30
convection 70, 76, 327, 331, 338, 342
convenience foods 144–5
cook-chill foods 145, 146
cookers 325–7
    care and maintenance 327
    choosing 327
    positioning 327
cookery exam 207–11

cooking
  effects of 69–70, 76
  methods 71–5, 76
  preparation 57–8, 67
  reasons for 69, 76
  terms 148–9
  utensils 64–5
Corn Bread 166
coronary heart disease 32, 35–6, 284, 285
Cottage Pie 188
cotton 378–9, 389, 391
cotton plant 378
counter service 221
couturiers 366
craft 446
  industry, in Ireland 447
Crafts Council of Ireland 447
Cranberry and Macadamia Cookies 176
cream 104–5, 110
  types 104–5, 110
credit 244
credit cards 226
crêpe 381
cross-contamination 42, 46, 92, 100
crown (teeth) 276
Curried Rice Salad 205
curtains 358, 361
Custard Sauce 183
cuts, treating 318
cystic fibrosis 427, 428

dairy products 102–10
damask 380
darts 402
deafness 427
debit cards 226
decision-making process 217–18, 227
decorations, food 53–4, 55
deficiency disease 3
dehydration 13
denier 385, 391
denim 379
dental floss 277
dental health products 277
dentine 276, 277
deodorants 273, 275
department stores 218
depressants 294
dermis 272, 275
design 305–9
  brief 207, 449
  features 305–8, 309
  folder 449
  principles 308, 309

dessert recipes 180–4
detergents 373, 376
development
  emotional 269, 271, 412
  mental 269, 412
  moral 270, 271
  physical 268–9, 411
  social 270, 271, 411
developmental milestones 409–10
developmental screening checks 409
diabetes 34, 35, 38, 39
diet
  balanced 22–30
  high-fibre 33–4
  low-cholesterol 35–6
  low-fat 35–6
  low-salt 32–3
  low-sugar 32
digestive system 18–21
  functions 18
  healthy 20
  parts of 19
dinner 49
  menus 52
Dips 185
Directive on Waste Electrical and Electronic Equipment (EU) 2005 330
disabilities 427–8
disclosing tablets 277
discount stores 219
disease, precautions against 287–8
Domestic Violence Act 1996 429
double insulated symbol 248, 325
Down's syndrome 427, 428
Down Syndrome Ireland 428
Dralon 384
drug(s) 294–6
  abuse 295, 296
  controlled 295, 296
dry-cleaning instructions 372
drying clothes 375
  instructions 372

Ecolabel 352
E. coli 43
edge machining 402
eggs 97–101
  buying 99
  composition 97
  cooking 100, 101
  nutritive value 97, 101
  storing 100, 101
  structure 97
  uses 98, 101
elastane 384

elderly people, diet for 28, 30
electricity 333–4, 342
  safe use of 334
electricity meter 333
Electricity Supply Board 333
embroidery 397–8, 405
embroidery stitch 400
embryo 266, 408
emphysema 291
Employment Equality Act 1998 254, 256
Enable Ireland 428
enamel (teeth) 276, 277
energy 14–15
  balance 15, 16
  efficiency 324
  measuring 14
  RDA 15
  requirements 14
ENFO 353
E numbers 141, 142
environment 348–54
enzymes 40, 46
  digestive 18, 21
epidermis 272, 275
epiglottis 279, 280
epilepsy 427
ergonomics 311, 313
ESB 333
excretion 279
excretory organs 272, 279
exercise 287
  aerobic 287, 289
expenses 241
  family 242

fabrics
  applying pattern to 388
  applying texture to 388
  blended 385
  bonded 388
  care 370–6
  clothing: 364; choosing 435
  colour-fast 372, 376
  conditioners 374
  construction 385–7
  cutting out 402
  delicate, washing 373
  dyeing 388, 391
  finishes 390, 391
  non-colour-fast 372, 376
  non-woven 386, 387, 391
  printing 388, 391
  widths 393
Fallopian tubes 264

falls
preventing 315
treating 319
Families Anonymous 430
family 258–63
functions 258
law 429–30
life, influences on 259
relationships 261
types 258
Family Home Protection Act 1976 429
Family Law (Divorce) Act 1996 429
Family Law (Maintenance of Spouses
and Children) Act 1976 429
Family Support Services 425
fashion 364–6, 369
fads 364, 369
industry 366
trends: 364, 369; influences on 365
fats 4, 6–7, 16, 18, 21
classification 6
composition 6
functions 7
saturated 6
unsaturated 6
fatty acids 6, 16, 18–19, 20, 21
fertilisation 265
fibre, dietary 8, 9, 16, 20
increasing intake 34
RDA 9
fibres 377–85, 391
animal 378, 381–2
identifying 389
manufactured 377, 378, 383–5, 391
natural 377, 378
production of 378–85
regenerated 378, 383, 391
synthetic 378, 384, 391
filing, home 244–5
fire
drill 316, 320
safety 315
first aid 316–20
kit 317
procedures 317–19
rules 317
fish 93–6
buying 94, 96
classification 93
composition 94
cooking 95, 96
filleting 95
frozen 96
nutritive value 93, 96
oily 93
preparing 94–5

processed 96
recipes, main courses 197–9
storing 94, 96
white 93
flannel 381
flannelette 379
flax 380
floor plans 311
flour 125–6
types 126, 133
fluorescent tubes 341
fluoride 278
fluorine 11, 12
foetus 266, 408
food
absorption 20
canned 140, 141, 146
choices 2, 16
dried 140, 141, 146
freezing 137–40, 146
frozen: 45, 46, 141; buying 139,
146; thawing 139
functions 2, 16
groups 22, 23, 30
hygiene 42, 44
irradiated 140, 146
labelling 143–4, 146
non-perishable 45
packaging 46
perishable 45, 46
preparation: equipment 64–7;
skills 68; technology 321–2
presentation 53
preservation: 135–42, 146;
methods 136–42, 146
processing 135–46
semi-perishable 45, 46
spoilage 40–41
staple 2, 16
storage 45, 46
tables 150–3
food poisoning 43, 46
food pyramid 23
foot care 274
form, in design 307, 309
fortified foods 141
foster care 425
freezers 140
fruit 78, 112–15
buying 117
classification 113, 120
cooking 114
EU regulations 117
freezing 139
nutritive value 113, 120
organic 117

preparation 114
processed 114–15, 120
seasonal 114, 120
storing 117
uses 114, 120
frying 74
function, in design 305
fuse 334, 342
fuse box 333

gabardine 381
gall bladder 19
garnishes, food 53, 55
gas 335–6, 342
bottled 335
leaks 336
natural 335
safety precautions 335–6
gas exchange 280
gathering stitch 395, 405
gender 260
equality 261
equity 261, 263
roles 260, 263
gingham 379
Glacé Icing 173
global positioning system 323
global warming 349
glucose 7, 16, 18, 21
absorption 20
gluten 37, 122, 126, 415
glycerol 6, 16, 18–19, 20, 21
goals 298, 299, 301
goods 214, 216
GPS 323
greenhouse gases 349
Green Party 353
Greenpeace 353
Green Schools 353
grilling 73
Guaranteed Irish symbol 248
guarantees 233, 238, 249, 250
gum (teeth) 276, 277

haemoglobin 12, 281, 285
hair care 274
hallucinogens 294
halons 352–3
Hamburgers 190
hand care 274
haute couture 366, 369
hazard symbols 316
health 286–9
guidelines for 286
hazards 290–6
Health Promotion Unit 288, 289

Health Protection Centre 267
healthy eating guidelines 23
heart 281, 282–4
heating, home 338–9
    fuels 339
heat transfer 70, 76, 327, 331,
    338, 342
hemming 396, 405
Herb and Lime Dip, Creamy 186
high blood pressure 32, 34, 291
home 303
    entertainment 323
    maintenance 322
    management 298–301
hormones, sex 264
housing 302, 304
    types 302, 304
Hummus 185
hydrocephalus 427, 428
hygiene
    home 344–7
    personal 275
hypermarkets 219
hypervitaminosis 11, 16

immunisation 287, 423–4
impulse buying 218
incisors 276
income 241
    family 242
income tax 241
infant formula milk 414
ingredients, weighing and
    measuring 60
insomnia 288, 289
insulation 339, 342
insulin 38, 39
interdental brushes 277
Internet 323
intestinal juice 19
intestine
    large 20
    small 19
Intoxicating Liquor Act 2008 293
iodine 11
Irish Association for Spina Bifida and
    Hydrocephalus 428
Irish Heart Foundation 33
Irish Pre-School Playgroups
    Association 424
Irish Society for Autism 424
Irish Society for Prevention of Cruelty
    to Children see ISPCC
Irish Standards Mark 248, 325
iron 11, 12, 16, 281
    absorption 12

deficiency diseases 12
    functions 12
    RDA 12
    sources 12
ironing 375–6
    instructions 372
irritants, in cigarettes 290, 296
ISPCC 262, 263, 424

jersey 381

kidney damage 32
kilocalories 14
    empty 15, 16
kitchen
    design 311–12
    hygiene 44, 344
    sink 337
Kitemark 248
knitting 386, 387, 388, 391

labelling 224, 227 see also care labels,
    food labelling
labour 266
lactovegetarians 36
La Leche League 424
landfill 350
larynx 279, 280
laundry, preparing 372
lawn (fabric) 379
layette 421
LEDs 341
leisure 289
light-emitting diodes 341
lighting 340–1, 342
linen 380, 389, 391
listeria 43
litter 349
liver 19
long and short stitch 398, 405
loss leaders 225, 227
lunch 49
    menus 52
    recipes 158–63
lung cancer 291
lungs 279, 280
Lycra 384

machine washing 372–3
Mackerel Baked with Cider and
    Apple 198
macronutrients 4, 16
main fuse 333
mains pipe (water) 336
maize 124
Make a Wish Foundation 428

Malpighian layer 272, 275
management 298–301
    systems 299, 301
manual workers 26, 27
margarine 106
marketing 255
    mix 255, 256
market research 255, 256
maturity, emotional 269
meal planning 48–52, 55
measurements, for making clothes
    434–5
meat 78, 86–90, 92
    buying 88, 92
    composition 86
    cooking 88, 89
    cuts 88
    freezing 139
    nutritive value 86, 92
    products 89
    recipes, main course 188–96
    structure 86
    substitutes 90, 92
    tenderising 87, 92
    toughness 87, 92
Meatballs, Mini 189
melanoma 274
menstruation 265, 267
mental health 286, 289
menus 50–2, 55
    à la carte 50, 55
    table d'hôte 50, 55
    writing 51
micronutrients 4, 16
micro-organisms 40, 46, 105
    growth of 41, 135
microwave
    cooking 75, 76
    ovens: 330–1; buying 331;
        cookware 330; using 331
microwaves 330
milk 78, 102–4, 110
    composition 102
    nutritive value 102, 110
    pasteurisation 103
    products 104–10
    types 103, 110
    uses 104, 110
milk teeth 276, 418
Mince Pies 175
minerals 4, 11
Mini Meatballs 189
Misleading Advertising Regulations
    (EU) 254
mobile phones 323
molars 276

money management 240–5
monopoly 229
moulds 40, 46
Muffins 167
muscular dystrophy 427
Mushroom Risotto 200
muslin 379

nap (fabric) 393, 394, 405
nappies 422
Nar-Anon 430
Narcotics Anonymous 430
National Consumer Agency 234,
    235, 238
National Council of the Blind of
    Ireland 428
needlework 393–405
needs 215, 216
    emotional 268, 271
    mental 268, 271
    physical 268, 271
nerves 272
neural tube defects 9
nicotine 290, 294
Nightsaver electricity 333
noise pollution 349
norms 270, 271
notches 402
NSAI mark 248
nutrients 3, 16
nutrition 3
nylon 384, 389

oats 124
obesity 32, 34, 35
OCD (obsessive-compulsive
    disorder) 427
oesophagus 19
oestrogen 264
Office of Tobacco Control 291
off-the-peg clothing 366
oil glands 272
Ombudsman 234, 235, 238
Omelette, Plain 160
    fillings 160
One Family 430
one-way designs 393, 394
opiates 294
organza 382
osteomalacia 10, 11
osteoporosis 10, 11
outfits
    designing 367
    sketching 368
ovaries 264, 267

ovens 61, 67
    conventional 61
    electric 61
    fan 61
    temperatures 61
overcooking 70
ovulation 264, 267
own brands 225, 227
oxidation 14, 16, 279
ozone layer 352–3, 354

packaging 223–4 *see also* food
    packaging
    characteristics 223
    functions 223, 227
    types 223, 227
packed meals 79–81
    planning 80
pancreas 19
pancreatic juice 19
Parent Line 430
parents, role of 260
Parsnip and Maple Syrup Cake 172
passive smoking 291, 296
pasta 124, 133
pastry 132, 133
    making 132, 133
    recipes 174
    types 132, 133
pattern 308, 309
patterns, garment 434, 435, 436–40
    markings 402, 403
    symbols 437
payment methods 225–6, 227
Pay Related Social Insurance 241
Peanut Butter Cookies 59
peer
    groups 271
    pressure 262, 270–1, 290
pellagra 9
penis 265
pepsin 19
periodontal fibres 277
periods 265
peristalsis 19, 20
pharynx 279, 280
phosphorous 11, 12
physical change, in digestion 18, 21
pinking shears 402
Pizza 162
placenta 266, 267
plaque 277
plasma 281, 285
platelets 281, 285
plug, wiring a 334
poaching 71

poisoning 319
pollution 348–9, 354
polyester 384
poplin 379
pores, in skin 272
Pork Schnitzel 195
Porridge with Dried Fruit 155
portion size 24
Potato and Leek Gratin 201
poultry 91, 92
    buying 91
    cooking 91
    nutritive value 91
    storing 91
pregnancy 266
    diet in 27–8, 30
    healthy 266, 409
    smoking during 291
pre-molars 276
pressure cooking 73
prêt-à-porter 366, 369
progesterone 264
protein 4–5, 16, 18, 21
    classification 4
    composition 4
    functions 5
    high biological value 4–5
    low biological value 4–5
    RDA 5
PRSI 241
puberty 268–9, 271
pulmonary artery 283
pulp cavity 276, 277
pulse 283, 285
Pure New Wool symbol 248
PVC 384

Q mark 248
quality 230, 247–50
    control 247, 250
    symbols 248, 250
Queen Cakes 171
quickening period 408
Quinoa Salad 204
Quorn 90, 92

radiation 70, 76, 327, 331, 338, 342
Rainbows 430
raising agents 128–9, 133
RDA 3, 5
recipes 59, 67
    costing 62
    modification 63–4, 67
recommended dietary allowance 3, 5
recovery position 319, 320
recycling 351, 354

red blood cells 12, 281, 285
reduce, reuse, recycle 224, 350
refrigerators 328–30
rennet 108
reproduction 266
research methods 431
resources 298, 301, 348
    economic 298
    environmental 298, 348
    human 298
respiratory system 279–80
rest 288
rice 123, 125, 133
    cooking methods 160
    types 125
RICE procedure 319
Rice Salad, Curried 205
Rich Shortcrust Pastry 174
rickets 10, 11
Risotto, Mushroom 200
roasting 74
Roast Vegetables 203
Romesco Sauce 195
room planning 310–13
root (teeth) 276
roux 84, 85
running stitch 395, 405
rye 124

safety symbols 248, 250
salads 120
    preparing 120
    recipes, 204–6
Sale of Goods and Supply of Services
    Act 1980 232–3, 238
saliva 19
salivary amylase 19
Salmon, Spicy Grilled 197
salmonella 43, 91
salt
    intake, reducing 33
    RDA 13, 32
sandwiches 81
satin stitch 398, 405
sauces 84–5
Sausage Rolls 161
saving 241
    methods 243–4
scalds, treating 317–18
Scones, Tea 164
scrotum 265
scurvy 9, 10
seams 402
    flat 402, 405
sedatives 294
sedentary workers 26, 27

self-esteem 269, 271
self-service 221
selvage 386, 391
semen 265
septum 283
serge 381
service cable (electricity) 333
service pipe (water) 336
services 214, 216, 249, 250
    community 303–4
    statutory 304
    voluntary 304
sewing
    fabric for 393, 405
    hand 394–8
sewing machine 399–401
    care of 401
    choosing 400
    faults 401
    threading 399
    using 400
sex organs
    female 264
    male 265
sexual
    behaviour, responsible 267
    intercourse 265
sexually transmitted infections 267
shelf life 45, 46
shellfish 93
shelter 302, 304
shock, treating 318
shopping 217–27
    decisions 217–18, 227
    environmentally friendly 352, 354
    guidelines 218, 223, 227
    outlets 218–20, 227
    practices 220
    technology 224
shops
    independent 219
    specialist 220
Shortcrust Pastry 174
silk 382, 389, 391
    slub 382
    wild 382
skin 272–5
    cancer 274, 352
    care 274–5
    functions 273
    healthy 273, 275
    pigment 272, 275
    structure 272
sleep 288
slip hemming 396, 405
Small Claims Court/Registrar 234, 238

smoker's cough 290
smoking 290–1 see also cigarettes
Smoking Kills symbol 248
snacks 49
sodium 11, 12, 13

soft furnishings 356, 361
    choosing 358
    functions 357
soup 82–3
    recipes 186–7
Special Olympics Ireland 428
sperm 265, 267
sperm ducts 265
Spiced Chicken Goujons 194
Spicy Grilled Salmon 197
spina bifida 9, 427, 428
Sponge Cake 169
sprain 319
stain removal 374–5
staphylococcus 43
staple fibres 377, 391
starch 7, 8, 16
star markings, on frozen food and
    freezers 45, 46, 329, 331
starters, recipes for 185–6
state services 214, 241
Status of Children Act 1987 429
statutory
    agencies 234, 238
    rights 233
steaming 72
stem stitch 397, 405
stereotypes 261, 263
sterilising babies' bottles 417
stewing 72
stimulants 294
stitches
    hand 394–8
    machine 400
    temporary 394, 405
stock 82
stomach 19
straight grain 386, 391
straight stitch 400, 405
strain 319
S-trap 337, 342
Strawberry Flan 181
stress 288
stroke 32, 34
sugars 8
    simple 7, 16, 18–19, 21
sunbathing 274, 275
sunburn 274
supermarkets 218
    layout 222

superstores 219
supper 49
    menus 52
    recipes 158–63
sweat glands 272
Swiss Roll 170

table linen 356
table setting 54–5
tacking 394–5, 405
taffeta 382
tailor's chalk 403, 405
tailor tacking 397, 403, 405
tar, in cigarettes 290, 296
tartar 277
tastes 3, 16
tax credits 241
Tea Scones 164
technology, home 321–31
Teen Between 430
teeth 10, 18, 19, 276–8
    babies' 276, 418
    care of 277–8
    structure of 276–7, 278
    types 276, 278
testes 265, 267
textiles, household 356–61
    properties 357
texture 308, 309
textured vegetable protein 90, 92
thermostat 327, 331, 338, 342
tie-dye 388
timers, heating 338, 342
tobacco smoke 290
toddlers, feeding 416
tofu 90, 92
toilet training 418
Tomato Dip 185
Tomato and Lentil Soup 187
Tomato Sauce 196
tooth decay 32, 277
toothpaste 277
top sewing 396, 405
towelling 379
towels 356
trachea 279, 280
tracing wheel 403, 405
trade associations 234, 238
Traditional Chicken Casserole 193

Trout, Baked Stuffed 199
tungsten lamps 341
TVP 90, 92
tweed 381

U-bend 337, 342
ultraviolet rays 352
umbilical cord 266, 267
unit pricing 144, 146, 225, 227
upholstery 356, 359
use by date 45, 46, 143, 146
uterus 264, 267

vaccination 287, 423–4
vagina 264
vegans 36
vegetables 78, 115–20
    buying 117, 120
    classification 115, 120
    composition 116
    cooking 118–19, 121
    EU regulations 117
    freezing 138
    nutritive value 116, 120
    organic 117, 120
    preparing 118, 121
    recipes 203
    seasonal 114
    storing 117, 120
    uses 116
Vegetables, Roast 203
vegetarian
    diet 26, 36–7
    dishes: 37; recipes 200–2
Vegetarian Loaf 202
veins 282, 285
velour 381
venae cavae 283, 285
ventilation 340, 342
ventricle 283, 285
villi 20
viscose 389
vitamins 4, 9–11, 16
    deficiency diseases 9, 10
    fat-soluble 10, 16
    functions 9, 10
    vitamin A 7, 10
    vitamin B group 9, 20
    vitamin C: 9; RDA 10

vitamin D 7, 10, 273
vitamin E 7, 10
vitamin K 7, 10, 20
water-soluble 9, 16

wants 215, 216
warp 386, 391
washing instructions 370–1
washing machines 375
waste 349–51, 354
    biodegradable 349, 354
    inorganic 349
    management, hierarchy of
        350, 354
    organic 349
water 13
    functions 13
    heating 337
    pollution 349
    sources 13
    supply 336–7, 342
    treatment 336
weaning 415
weasel words 252
weaving 386, 388, 391
WEEE Directive 330
weft 386, 391
wheat 123
Which? 235
white blood cells 281, 285
Wholemeal Bread 165
Whoopie Pies 178
winding babies 414
wireless technology 323
women, diet for 27
wool 381, 391
Woolmark 248
work
    plans 300
    sequence 312, 313
    triangle 312, 313

yarn 377
    spinning 385
yeasts 40, 46, 129
yoghurt 106–7, 110

zig-zag stitch 400, 402, 405